W9-AOB-498

CRIMINAL EVIDENCE

An Introduction

John L. Worrall
California State University, San Bernardino

Craig Hemmens
Boise State University

Foreword by
Rolando V. del Carmen
Sam Houston State University

Instructor's Manual/Testing Program
and Student Study Guide Available

Roxbury Publishing Company
Los Angeles, California

Library of Congress Cataloging-in-Publication Data

Criminal evidence: an introduction / John Worrall, Craig Hemmens.
p. cm.
Includes bibliographical references.
ISBN 1-931719-29-2
1. Evidence, Criminal—United States. I. Hemmens, Craig II. Title.
KF9660.W67 2005
345.73'06—dc22   2003022469
         CIP

Criminal Evidence: An Introduction

Publisher: Claude Teweles
Managing Editor: Dawn VanDercreek
Production Editor: Monica K. Gomez
Production Assistant: Kate Kaplan
Copy Editor: Jackie Estrada
Photos: Mark Ide
Cover Design: Marnie Kenney
Typography: SDS Design, info@sds-design.com

Printed on acid-free paper in the United States of America. This paper meets the standards for recycling of the Environmental Protection Agency.

ISBN 1-931719-29-2

**Instructor's Manual/Testing Program
and Student Study Guide Available**

ROXBURY PUBLISHING COMPANY
P.O. Box 491044
Los Angeles, California 90049-9044
Voice: (310) 473-3312 • Fax: (310) 473-4490
Email: roxbury@roxbury.net
Website: www.roxbury.net

To Don W. Worrall who was taken from his family far too early.

—John L. Worrall

To T. Mdodana Ringer, who introduced me to the rules of evidence, and to Rolando del Carmen, who introduced me to academic writing.

—Craig Hemmens

Acknowledgements

John Worrall would like to thank Craig Hemmens and all the folks at Roxbury.

Craig Hemmens would like to thank Mary Stohr and Emily Stohr-Gillmore for their love and support, and John Worrall for his patience. Thanks also to Claude Teweles and the people at Roxbury. It was Claude's idea that we write this book, and his staff helped assure that we followed through on our promise to do so.

Craig and John would also like to thank Professor Rolando del Carmen for his support and kind words, and the following reviewers for their useful comments and suggestions: Gayle Carper (Western Illinois University), Charles Chastain (University of Arkansas), Donald V. Hayley (Tidewater Community College), Patricia A. Parke (East Carolina University), Alisa Smith (Ramapo College of New Jersey), Mark Stevens (North Carolina Wesleyan College), and Robert C. Wadman (Weber State University). ✦

Contents

Section I
Preliminary Matters:
Setting the Stage

Section II
Arrest and Search Procedure

Section III
Criminal Evidence

Foreword

Rolando V. del Carmen

Evidence is defined in *Black's Law Dictionary* as "all the means by which any alleged matter of fact, the truth of which is submitted to investigation, is established or disproved." It is an integral part of the legal process and central to criminal justice. Without evidence, the process of justice cannot proceed—or, if it does, its ultimate result is suspect or null and void.This book discusses criminal evidence, so the use of evidence in civil cases officially falls outside its purvue. As all lawyers know, however, most of the concepts and doctrines discussed here apply in both criminal and civil proceedings. Written by experienced and productive professors in criminal justice, the book presents the complex subject of evidence to criminal justice students in a fashion and format that facilitate understanding and comprehension. Criminal justice programs in the United States offer criminal evidence and criminal procedure courses either separately or combined. All programs offer criminal procedure under various labels, but not all programs offer an evidence course. Consequently, criminal procedure textbooks abound, but there is a dearth of criminal justice textbooks for criminal evidence. Fewer still are textbooks that combine criminal evidence and criminal procedure. This book helps fill that gap. It is written primarily for use in courses that adopt the combined criminal evidence/criminal procedure approach, but the book may also be used in two separate courses. There is enough content and length here to justify its use as a text for separate courses in criminal evidence and criminal procedure. As the Table of Contents shows, the chapters may be grouped into three categories: general introductory materials (Chapters 1, 2, 3 and 4); primarily evidence topics (Chapters 5, 10, 11, 12, and 13), and primarily criminal procedure topics (Chapter 6, 7, 8, and 9). In reality, however, these chapters and topics dovetail and defy easy categorization. The topics covered are basic to and essential for a non-law student's understanding of evidence and court procedure. The reader will gain a good working knowledge of how the legal system proves or disproves guilt in the American system of justice. It should be learned well by those interested in justice and how it works inside the courtroom and in the world of lawyers and judges. Law can be abstract and puzzling to criminal justice students and practitioners. That is no surprise; it can be confusing to lawyers and law students as well. A challenge for authors of law textbooks written for undergraduates is conveying legal materials to readers who have only a meager background in law and who, understandably, might have minimal interest in the subject. The key is to present law concepts in understandable language without compromising precision. The authors of this book have done that well. They are accurate without being wordy, conceptual without being unduly abstract, and comprehensive without wasting space on peripherals. The essential and the basic are what the authors offer. Textbook writers aspire for student acceptance of their work. Although instructors determine the choice of a textbook, students acceptance is what ultimately matters. This is as it should be in an educational system in which success is often measured in terms of user satisfaction. The standard, however, should not be whether the book is easy to understand or simple to digest. The real test is whether the book informs, challenges, and demystifies. This criminal evidence text does that. Students and instructors using this book are encouraged to give feedback to the authors. I am sure they will welcome it. Good as this book is now, it will get even better in future editions as the authors hear from the audience they seek to serve.The difficult universe of criminal evidence is made easier for students because of this book. I commend the authors for making a significant contribution to the ever-expanding field of law textbooks for non-law students. The authors have fashioned another printed tool that enriches the criminal justice discipline.

—Rolando V. del Carmen
Distinguished Professor of Criminal Justice Law
Sam Houston State University

About the Authors

John L. Worrall is an Assistant Professor in the Department of Criminal Justice at California State University, San Bernardino. He received his Ph.D. in Political Science from Washington State University in 1999. His research interests are legal issues in policing and crime control policy. Dr. Worrall is the author of numerous journal articles and five books, including *Criminal Procedure: From First Contact to Appeal* (Allyn and Bacon 2004) and *Police Administration* (McGraw-Hill 2003). He is a Fellow with the California Institute for County Government in Sacramento, and recently has worked on projects with the Rand Corporation and the American Prosecutors Research Institute.

Craig Hemmens holds a J.D. from North Carolina Central University School of Law and a Ph.D. in Criminal Justice from Sam Houston State University. He is chair and professor in the Department of Criminal Justice Administration, where he has taught since 1996. Dr. Hemmens has published seven books and more than one hundred articles on a variety of criminal justice-related topics. He has been nominated for several teaching awards and is currently serving as the editor of the *Journal of Criminal Justice Education.* ✦

Section I

Preliminary Matters:
Setting the Stage

Chapter One

Introduction

A Brief History of Evidence Law

Key Terms

• Administrative regulations	• Individual rights
• Bills of attainder	• Judicial review
• Code of Hammurabi	• Legislation
• Common law	• Precedent
• Competent evidence	• Probable cause
• Constitution	• Rational basis test
• Dual sovereignty doctrine	• Relevant evidence
• Due process	• Selective incorporation
• Equal protection	• Stare decisis
• Evidence law	• Statute
• Ex post facto laws	• Strict scrutiny test
• Fundamental rights	• Suspect classifications
• Habeas corpus	• Total incorporation
• Incorporation	• Total incorporation plus

The law exists in large part because people need a mechanism for enforcing order and resolving disputes peacefully. All societies have developed methods of resolving disputes. Laws provide rules to guide conduct, as well as a means of resolving disputes and maintaining order. The court system of today is simply one form of conflict resolution. Laws are created by legislatures; the courts are the mechanism whereby laws are enforced.

In this text we focus on evidence law. **Evidence law** is the set of rules that govern how trials are conducted. Evidence law applies to both civil and criminal trials, although some significant and important differences exist between the civil and criminal law. This book focuses on the application of evidence law to criminal trials. Evidence law is (or at least should be) an exciting subject of study, as it governs the conduct of trials and plays a major role in the criminal justice process. Although much of evidence law may seem peculiar at first, there are very good reasons for (virtually) every rule of evidence. It is our hope that this book will help you, the student, understand the significance of this important subject.

In this chapter we discuss the historical development of the law, focusing on the Anglo-American concepts of the common law, precedent, and *stare decisis*. We also examine the sources of law, as well as the sources of evidence law in particular.

What is the statue of justice meant to represent?

The Development of the Law

The earliest examples of conflict resolution can be found in pre-industrial societies, which had informal rules for how individuals were to act and relate to each other. Disputes arose and were settled by the tribal leadership, which usually consisted of a king/chief and his deputies, or councilors. The tribal leader was expected to act on behalf of the entire tribe and not be an advocate for one side against the other.

The Western legal tradition may be traced to the **Code of Hammurabi:** the first known written legal code, which expressed a retributivist, "eye for an eye" philosophy. Roman law, the next major codified set of legal principles, was heavily influenced by Babylonian legal principles. The Twelve Tables (450 B.C.) was the first entirely secular written legal code. Around this time, crimes came to be seen as offenses against not just the victim but society as well. However, trials as we understand them today still did not exist.

The spread of the Roman Empire brought Roman law to Western Europe. The Norman Conquest (1066) brought feudal law to the British Isles. During the following several hundred years, England developed what came to be known as the common law system.

Common Law

After the Norman Conquest, the new rulers established new forms of government, including courts of law. By the reign of Henry II (1154–1189), a body of law had been developed that was applied not just in local courts, but nationally. Decisions began to be written down, circulated, and summarized. The result was a more unified body of law, which came to be known as the **common law,** because it was in force throughout the country; it was literally the law in common throughout England. The common law system was well developed in England by the thirteenth century.

The common law was judge-made law. That is, it was law created by judges as they heard cases and settled disputes. Judges wrote down their decisions and in doing so attempted to justify their decision by reference to custom, tradition, history, and prior judicial decisions. As judges began to rely on previous judgments, they developed the concepts of *stare decisis* and *precedent*. Of course, for there to be precedent there must be prior decisions. At first, judges made decisions without referring to other cases or courts. They simply heard a case and decided the appropriate outcome, based on their understanding of the law as they had learned it through the reading of legal treatises and encyclopedias. But as time went by, judges came to rely on prior decisions as a means of justifying their decision in a particular case. From this came the reliance on precedent and the concept of stare decisis.

Precedent and Stare Decisis

Under the common law system, every final decision by a court creates a **precedent.** This precedent governs the court issuing the decision as well as any lower, or inferior, courts. The common law system was brought to America by the early colonists. Many of the principles of the common law, including precedent and belief in *stare decisis*, remain in force today in American courts. Thus, all courts in a state are bound to follow the decisions of the highest court in the state, usually known as the state supreme court. All courts in the federal court system are bound to follow the decisions of the United States Supreme Court. This is the notion of precedent.

Precedent is binding only on those courts within the jurisdiction of the court issuing the opinion. Thus a decision of the Idaho Supreme Court is not binding on any court in Wyoming. Wyoming courts are not subject to the jurisdiction or control of Idaho courts, and thus are free to interpret the law differently from Idaho courts if they see fit to do so. Decisions from courts in other jurisdictions, while not binding, may be persuasive, however. This simply means that another court may give consideration and weight to the opinion of other courts. Thus a Wyoming court may, if it chooses, consider the judgment of an Idaho court.

Courts may do so when faced with an issue they have not dealt with before but that other courts have examined.

Stare decisis *means "let the decision stand." Under the principle of stare decisis,* if a prior decision on a legal issue applies to a current case, the court will be guided by that prior decision and apply the same legal principles in the current case. *Stare decisis* is thus a means of establishing the value of prior decisions, or precedent. In other words, if an issue has been decided one way, it will continue to be decided that way in future cases. Through a reliance on precedent and the principle of *stare decisis,* common law courts are able to provide litigants with some degree of predictability regarding the courts' decisions.

Precedent is not necessarily unchangeable. Judge-made law may be set aside, or overruled, by a legislative act if the constitution permits the legislature to do so. Additionally, the court that issued the precedent may overrule it, or a higher court may reverse the decision of a lower court. If an intermediate-level appeals court decides an issue one way and the losing party appeals to a higher appeals court (such as the state supreme court), that higher court may reverse the decision of the lower court.

How does the Constitution limit the types of evidence that can be admitted at trial?

Higher-level appeals courts are not bound by the judgments of lower courts; they are bound only by the decisions of courts above them. *Stare decisis* then involves a respect for, and belief in, the validity of precedent. Precedent is simply the influence of prior cases on current cases.

Courts are understandably reluctant to reverse decisions they made previously, as doing so is a tacit admission of error. Courts do make reversals, however, when presented with a compelling justification. Thus, *stare decisis* is not an inflexible doctrine but rather the general rule—there are always exceptions, as with most areas of the law! Alternatively, rather than expressly overrule a prior decision, a court may instead seek to distinguish the prior case from the present case on the ground that the facts are slightly different. By doing so, the court can avoid overruling a prior decision while coming to what it considers the proper result in the present case. Until a decision is expressly overruled, it stands as an accurate statement of legal principles, or "good law."

Sources of Law

There are several primary sources of law. The two main sources are judge-made law (the common law), and legislative law (which includes the Constitution, statutes, ordinances, and administrative regulations). There are others, but these are the most common. In addition, it should be remembered that there are other sources for what constitutes appropriate conduct, such as religion and ethics.

Legislation may be enacted by the legislature under the authority granted it by a constitution. A **constitution** creates a government; it literally constitutes the government. Legislatures are given the authority to act in certain areas. Legislative enactments, or bills, are often referred to as **statutes,** and statutes are collected in *codes.* Statutory law includes civil and criminal law. The criminal law is sometimes referred to as the *penal code.*

Legislators are sometimes referred to as lawmakers because they quite literally make law. Acts of the legislature are not, however, per se lawful. In other words, just because a legislature passes a bill does not mean the bill is a lawful exercise of the legislature's authority. Acts of the legislature may not limit the constitution under which the legislature was created. Thus, the United States Congress may not lawfully pass legislation that abolishes the First Amendment. The Constitution may be changed only by a constitutional amendment, which can be passed only by following certain procedures set forth in the Constitution itself.

Who decides when the legislature has acted beyond the scope of its authority? In the United States, it is the Supreme Court that has the final say as to the legality of statutes passed by either state or federal legislatures. This concept, known as the power of **judicial review,** is discussed in greater detail later in this chapter.

Administrative regulations are another form of legislation that may, under certain circumstances, have the force of law. This means they will be enforced by the courts just like statutes. Administrative regulations are issued either by agencies of the executive branch, which derive their authority from a delegation of power by the executive, or by independent agencies created through a delegation of power from the legislature. Examples include regulations affecting food and drugs and occupational safety requirements. Both the federal and state governments have administrative regulations.

Statutes are frequently written broadly, leaving administrative agencies with the task of filling in the blanks. Agencies are empowered to do so through the delegation of authority to them by the executive or legislative branch. Common examples include the Department of Health and Human Services, and the Department of Veterans Affairs. Violation of an administrative regulation is generally treated not as a crime but as a civil violation.

Just as statutes are often written broadly, leaving much room for interpretation, so too is the U.S. Constitution. For example, the Fourth Amendment prohibits "unreasonable searches and seizures." So what is unreasonable? For that matter, what constitutes a search or a seizure? There are no easy answers to these questions, and the U.S. Supreme Court has struggled to define the terms.

Why, then, are statutes ambiguous? Why don't the legislatures write more clearly and explain exactly what they mean? There are several reasons. First is the difficulty in defining, in a few sentences, something involving human conduct—there is an almost infinite range of possible actions by individuals. Second, legislators are politicians, and politics involves compromise. Thus, a statute may be written so that it appeals to the greatest possible number of legislators, but in doing this the language of the statute may be watered down and made less precise rather than more precise. This is particularly likely to happen when dealing with controversial issues. Politicians may simply decide to leave it to the courts to more clearly define the terms of a statute. While judges in some jurisdictions hold office for

Why was the Bill of Rights added to the Constitution?

life and cannot be removed simply for declaring legislation void, in many states judges are elected and thus are subject to removal if the electorate does not approve of their interpretation of legislation.

Sources of Individual Rights

There are several sources of *individual rights* in the United States. These sources, federal and state constitutions, case law, court rules, and legislation. **Individual rights** are those rights that are possessed by the individual and that protect him or her from others as well as the government. Examples include the freedom of speech, freedom of religion, and the right to counsel. The Constitution, particularly the Bill of Rights, is the primary source of individual rights. Although states are free to provide more individual rights than the Constitution does, neither Congress nor a state may enact a law that abridges a federal constitutional right. This is because the Constitution is paramount—it is the supreme law of the United States.

Table 1-1	Sources of Individual Rights
	Federal Constitution
	State constitution
	Case law
	Court rules
	Legislation

The Constitution

In 1787 delegates from 12 of the 13 original states met in Philadelphia, at the request of the Continental Congress, to write a new Constitution. The Continental Congress was hampered by lack of power vis-à-vis the states, so the delegates realized a new nation would need a strong central government. Supporters of a strong centralized government were called Federalists. Supporters of a weak central government, with power left almost entirely in the hands of the states, were what today are called states rights supporters.

The Continental Congress was formed through the adoption of the Articles of Confederation in 1781. This first attempt at creating a unified United States was a failure, in large part because the federal government created by the articles was virtually without power. It lacked the authority to tax, to raise an army, and to force the states to comply with any mandates.

The result of the convention in Philadelphia was the creation of the *United States Constitution.* The Constitution is different from ordinary legislation in that it is primarily concerned with establishing the powers and limitations of the government, both between the branches of government and between the government and the individual citizen. The Constitution itself contains few protections of individual rights. The only individual rights mentioned in the Constitution proper are the right to seek a writ of **habeas corpus,** the prohibition on **bills of attainder** (legislation imposing punishment without trial), and the prohibition on **ex post facto laws** (legislation making prior conduct criminal).

When the Constitution was submitted to the states for ratification, several states were reluctant to ratify it without more clear-cut protections of individual rights. In response to these concerns, the Bill of Rights was added. These provisions were initially drawn up by James Madison as additions to the original Constitution. Madison's proposals were condensed into ten amendments, commonly referred to as the *Bill of Rights.* With the addition of these amendments, the Constitution was ratified in 1788.

The Bill of Rights

There are twenty-three individual rights included in the first eight amendments. These rights include protections against government action of all kinds. It should be noted, however, that these rights were originally intended to apply only to actions by the federal government. The Bill of Rights was added to reduce the fears of states rights supporters who thought a strong central government would infringe on the rights of citizens of the states (Anastaplo 1995). It was not until the twentieth century that the provisions of the Bill of Rights were applied to actions of state governments, through a process referred to as *incorporation*. We will discuss incorporation later, after reviewing the most significant provisions of the Bill of Rights.

First Amendment. The First Amendment covers the freedom of religion, the freedom of speech, freedom of the press, and freedom of assembly. It is not surprising that the very first provision of the Bill of Rights deals with these topics because religion was a primary force in the settling of America. Religion held a central position in people's lives in England in the 1500s and 1600s, and many bloody conflicts had occurred over which should be the official religion of England. Colonists sought to avoid such conflicts and to avoid further persecution for their religious beliefs. Freedom of speech and of the press and the freedom to assemble peacefully were also issues of great concern for the colonists prior to the American Revolution.

With respect to religion, there are two guarantees in the First Amendment: The government shall not establish an official, state-supported religion, nor shall it interfere with individual's religious practices. The essence of these two clauses is that the government is not to be in the business of either promoting or destroying religion. Whereas the state was heavily involved in religion in England, the founding fathers wanted government to stay out of the business of religion entirely.

The first guarantee is often referred to as the *establishment clause*. It creates what the U.S. Supreme Court has referred to as a "wall of separation between church and state" (*Everson v. Board of Education*, 1947). This doctrine does not mean the government cannot be to some degree involved in religion, but the Supreme Court has stated that any statute affecting religion is valid only if three condition are met: The statute must have a secular (nonreligious) purpose, the primary purpose of the statute must be neither pro- nor anti-religion, and the statute must not foster "excessive" government entanglement with religion (*Lemon v. Kurtzman*, 1971).

This guarantee does not mean the freedom to worship is absolute. Otherwise valid government regulations that incidentally restrict religious practices are permitted. Thus a state may ban polygamy under its authority to enact health and safety regulations, even though this legislation at one time imposed a restriction on the religious practices of some Mormon sects.

The freedom of speech is one of the most treasured rights possessed by Americans. This right has been accorded great, but not total, weight by the Supreme Court. The Supreme Court has held that the freedom of speech includes the right to say things that may anger others, including so-called hate speech or speech directed at minority groups. The Court has also held that the freedom of speech includes not just verbal statements but written statements and some physical acts. These physical acts, when intended to make a point, are referred to as "symbolic speech" or "expressive conduct." Examples include signs, picketing, and even the burning of the American flag (*Texas v. Johnson*, 1989).

The freedom of speech is not absolute, however. The Supreme Court has held that the government can regulate obscenity (*Miller v. California*, 1973), as well as speech that is likely to provoke a violent response, or "fighting words" (*Chaplinsky v. New Hampshire*, 1942). Commercial speech may be regulated to a greater degree than so-called "political" speech (*Virginia State Board of Pharmacy v. Virginia Citizens Consumers Council, Inc.*, 1976). In general, however, the Supreme Court looks with disfavor on attempts to curb speech. Instead, the Court has repeatedly endorsed the view of Justice Oliver Wendell Holmes that society is improved by permitting a "free marketplace of ideas."

Second Amendment. The Second Amendment provides citizens with the right to "keep and bear arms," and states that this right shall not be "infringed." Opponents of gun control legislation seize upon this wording as support for their claim that the state may not limit the use and possession of firearms. The history of the amendment suggests this interpretation may not be completely accurate, however, and the Supreme Court has repeatedly held that states may regulate firearms, upholding legislation that prohibits the possession of certain weapons and that requires firearm registration.

The history behind the Second Amendment suggests it was intended, at least in part, not to allow individuals to possess any weapons they wanted as protection against other individuals, but rather to allow the states and groups of citizens (a militia) to have weapons to protect themselves against oppression by the federal government. There was a great concern at the time of the passage of the Bill of Rights that the federal government might become oppressive, and allowing states to form militias would not be of much use if the federal government had previously outlawed weapons. At this time there were no public stores of weapons, so if the federal government were to prohibit private ownership, states would be unable to fight back because their citizens would all be unarmed.

Third Amendment. The Third Amendment is another amendment that was a product of its times. Prior to the Revolution, English troops were sometimes housed in the homes of private citizens, against the wishes of the owner. The Third Amendment makes such a practice unconstitutional, by expressly forbidding the quartering of soldiers in private homes against the wishes of the owner at any time.

Fourth Amendment. The Fourth Amendment is the provision of the Constitution that stands most directly between the individual citizen and the police. This amendment forbids "unreasonable" searches and seizures and requires the existence of probable cause before warrants may be issued or a search or seizure may take place. Additionally, warrants are required to describe their subject with "particularity."

The particularity requirement is a response to the British practice in colonial times of issuing general warrants. General warrants allowed British customs inspectors to search for virtually anything, anywhere, at any time. The colonists found this practice most distressing, and it was one of the prime precipitating factors in the Revolution.

Requiring probable cause to search or seize was the founding fathers' attempt to limit the ability of the police to interfere at will in the lives of individual citizens. Instead, they must have some amount of evidence that the person is a criminal. This degree of proof is probable cause. **Probable cause** indicates a greater probability than not that a crime has occurred. It is less than proof beyond a reasonable doubt, but more than a hunch.

The Fourth Amendment does not forbid all searches and seizures but rather requires that they not be unreasonable. The obvious question, then, is what is reasonable? Courts have struggled mightily to define this phrase. Much of criminal procedure law is devoted to an explication of this phrase.

Fifth Amendment. The Fifth Amendment provides a number of protections for individual citizens. They include the right to an indictment by a grand jury, freedom from double jeopardy, the right to due process and just compensation, and the privilege against self-incrimination. These rights are all associated with criminal trials. Many of the provisions of the Fifth Amendment were born out of reaction to practices in Europe during the Middle Ages. The Star Chamber and the Spanish Inquisition are examples of the sort of intrusive activities by governments during this time, when arrested individuals had few rights and torture and forced confessions were common. Such practices made their way to American shores, as evidenced by the Salem witch trials.

The Fifth Amendment requires that a person be indicted by a grand jury before he or she may be tried on a criminal charge. The purpose of the grand jury is to ensure the government does not prosecute individuals without some proof of guilt. Thus the grand jury is meant to serve as a check on the power of the government, as a barrier standing between the individual citizen and the government.

It should be noted that the requirement of an indictment before a criminal prosecution is one of a handful of provisions of the Bill of Rights that have not been incorporated into the Fourteenth Amendment and applied to the states. In *Hurtado v. California* (1884) the Supreme Court expressly held that the right does not apply to state criminal trials, and this decision has never been overruled. Nonetheless, a number of states either require indictment by statute or state constitutional provision or provide prosecutors with the choice of seeking an indictment or proceeding via an information. An *information* is a substitute for an indictment and is filed directly with the court by the prosecutor.

The Fifth Amendment also prohibits placing someone in *double jeopardy*. This means a jurisdiction may not (1) prosecute someone again for the same crime after he or she has been acquitted, (2) prosecute someone again for the same crime after he or she has been convicted, and (3) punish someone twice for the same offense.

This provision does not mean a state may not try someone again if their first trial ends in a mistrial—in this situation there has been neither an acquittal nor a conviction. Additionally, if a conviction is overturned on appeal, the state may retry the person, as the reversal on appeal is not an acquittal.

While the double jeopardy clause bars multiple punishments for the same offense, there are exceptions. Under the **dual sovereignty doctrine** a person can be prosecuted in both federal and state courts for the same offense or in multiple state courts for the same offense. Double jeopardy does not apply in these situations because a different sovereign, or jurisdiction, is prosecuting the person. However, a person may not be tried for the same crime in both a municipal court and a state court, as these two courts derive their authority from the same source—the state constitution.

The Fifth Amendment also protects individuals from being forced to incriminate themselves. The privilege against self-incrimination, so familiar to those who have watched television shows and seen police officers read Miranda warnings to suspects, is a right we often take for granted today but that did not exist at early common law. The privilege allows a defendant to refuse to speak to police about the crime charged and to refuse to testify at trial. Furthermore, the prosecution is barred from commenting on a defendant's refusal to testify, as the Supreme Court has determined that doing so would limit the privilege against self-incrimination by suggesting that asserting a constitutional right was somehow evidence of something to hide (*Griffin v. California*, 1965).

The privilege is not total, however. The Supreme Court has held that the privilege protects a person from compelled testimonial communications—meaning spoken admissions (*Malloy v. Hogan*, 1964). The privilege does not apply to obtaining evidence from a suspect by other means, such as from blood samples, from fingerprints, or in a lineup.

Finally, the Fifth Amendment also provides for due process of law. Exactly what constitutes due process is highly debated. Essentially, **due process** means the state must follow certain procedures, designed to protect individual rights, before they deprive an individual of their liberty or property.

Sixth Amendment. The Sixth Amendment, like the Fifth, contains a laundry list of rights. These rights are also associated with the criminal trial and include the right to a speedy trial, the right to a public trial, the right to a trial by an impartial jury, the right to notice of the charges against oneself, the right to representation by counsel, and the right to confront the witnesses against oneself.

The right to a speedy trial means the defendant must be brought to trial without "unnecessary delay" (*Barker v. Wingo*, 1972). The right to a public trial means the defendant has a right to have the public attend the trial if they so wish. The right to notice of the charges against the defendant simply means the prosecution must inform the defendant prior to trial what he or she is accused of, so a defense may be prepared. This notification can occur through the filing of an information or the handing down of an indictment by the grand jury.

The right to a trial by an impartial jury means the right to a jury, selected from the community where the crime occurred, that is not predisposed to believe the defendant is guilty. In other words, the members of the jury need not be unaware of the events that led to the trial, but they must not have formed an opinion as to the guilt (or innocence) of the accused—this right is the presumption of innocence. Trial by jury is an ancient right, mentioned in the Assize of Clarendon (1166) and affirmed in the Magna Carta (1215).

The Sixth Amendment also provides for the assistance of counsel. The Supreme Court has interpreted this provision to include the right to assistance of counsel not only at trial but at any proceeding deemed a "critical stage" (*Kirby v. Illinois*, 1972) in the proceedings. Precisely what constitutes a critical stage is subject to some dispute but includes the preliminary hearing, the arraignment, the trial itself, and the appeal of right.

The Supreme Court has also determined that the right to counsel means indigent persons who cannot afford to hire a lawyer must be provided one at the state's expense, as long as the defendant faces the possibility of incarceration for six months or more. Additionally, the Supreme Court has held that the right to counsel includes the right to effective assistance of counsel (*Strickland v. Washington*, 1984).

Seventh Amendment. The Seventh Amendment provides for the right to a trial by jury in federal civil trials. This amendment applies only to federal trials; it has not been incorporated into the Fourteenth Amendment by the Supreme Court.

Eighth Amendment. The Eighth Amendment prohibits several things, including excessive bail, and cruel and unusual punishment. Both of these prohibitions are written broadly, and the courts have struggled with interpreting them.

Regarding the prohibition on excessive bail, this provision does not expressly state that bail must be set in all cases—it just says bail cannot be excessive. While the Eighth Amendment does not clearly provide for a right to bail, such a right existed as common law and has been codified in state statutes. What constitutes excessive bail, according to the Supreme Court, is bail set at a figure higher than necessary to ensure the presence of the defendant at trial (*Stack v. Boyle*, 1951).

The prohibition on cruel and unusual punishment limits the type and form of punishment imposed by a state after conviction of a crime. It prohibits torture, as well as punishment that is disproportionate to the offense. The cruel and unusual punishment clause does not prohibit the death penalty it is deemed to be in accord with contemporary standards of decency, and the death penalty existed at the time of the passage of the Eighth Amendment.

Ninth Amendment. The Ninth Amendment simply states that the listing of some rights in the Constitution should not be construed as a listing of *all* the rights retained by individual citizens. In other words, the rights provided in the Bill of Rights should not be taken as the only rights that citizens have—these are merely some of the rights retained by the people.

The obvious question, then, is if the Bill of Rights is not all-inclusive, what exactly are the other rights retained by the people? The Supreme Court has struggled to provide a framework for delineating these rights, as the discussion on incorporation (later in this chapter) indicates. In at least one case, the Supreme Court expressly mentioned the Ninth Amendment as providing a basis for giving individual citizens other unenumerated rights, such as a right to privacy (*Griswold v. Connecticut*, 1965). Generally, however, the Court has ignored the Ninth Amendment.

Tenth Amendment. The Tenth Amendment, like the Ninth, has been largely ignored by the Supreme Court. It simply states that the rights not delegated to the federal government by the Constitution are reserved for the states or individual citizens. This codifies the principle of *federalism* and *constitutionalism*—the federal government is a government of enumerated powers. That is, it has no authority unless so granted by the Constitution. And where the federal government has no authority, the states and individual citizens retain the authority.

Other amendments. In addition to the individual rights enumerated in the Bill of Rights, several other later-enacted constitutional amendments directly implicate individual rights. These include the

Reconstruction Amendments, passed shortly after the Civil War and intended to protect the recently freed slaves from abuse at the hands of state governments.

Thirteenth Amendment. The Thirteenth Amendment prohibits slavery in the United States. Since its passage it has been used to uphold civil rights legislation passed by Congress to prevent racial discrimination by private citizens. Where other amendments prohibit discrimination by state governments, no such limiting language appears in the Thirteenth Amendment. Courts have thus interpreted it as not merely outlawing slavery but forbidding so-called badges of slavery, or practices intended to keep blacks at lower social and economic levels than whites.

Fourteenth Amendment. The Fourteenth Amendment is very important. It is the first amendment that specifically forbids states from mistreating their citizens. The Bill of Rights was intended to apply only to actions of the federal government. After the Civil War, congressional leaders realized that individual states were just as capable of oppressing individual citizens as the federal government was. They responded by enacting the Fourteenth Amendment, which forbids states from denying citizens *due process* of law or *equal protection* of the laws. These two clauses have dramatically altered the way states deal with citizens.

The due process clause is identical to the clause in the Fifth Amendment. It has been interpreted to incorporate the various provisions of the Bill of Rights, making them applicable to the states.

The **equal protection** clause has been interpreted to preclude states from making unequal, arbitrary distinctions between people. It does not ban reasonable classifications, but it does prohibit classifications that are either without reason or based on race or gender. These are sometimes referred to as **suspect classifications.**

Not all classifications are a violation of equal protection. States may treat people differently if they have a legitimate reason to do so. Thus, states may refuse to issue a drivers' license to a minor or may limit the age at which a person can lawfully consume alcoholic beverages. Classifications based on age are not suspect (meaning likely illegal), because (1) the state can demonstrate an interest in the health and safety of minors who are a peculiarly vulnerable segment of society, and (2) there is no history of "invidious" discrimination of minors, as there is for minorities and women. Furthermore, juveniles are seen as possessing fewer rights, or lesser rights, than adults. Thus a juvenile curfew might be upheld whereas a general curfew including adults would be struck down.

Standard of Review

Often in constitutional law, the outcome of a case is determined as much by the standard of review the court uses as by the facts of the case. Not all of the individual protections set forth in the Bill of Rights are accorded the same respect—rather, there is a hierarchy of rights. The court uses either *strict scrutiny* or *rational basis* review, depending on whether a fundamental right is implicated or a suspect classification is involved.

Fundamental rights are those freedoms essential to the concept of ordered liberty—rights without which neither liberty nor justice would exist (*Palko v. Connecticut,* 1937). Examples include virtually all of the various provisions of the Bill of Rights, as well as the Fourteenth Amendment guarantees of due process and equal protection. To date, the Supreme Court has held that only race and religion are suspect classifications in all circumstances, although gender, illegitimacy, and poverty have occasionally been treated as suspect classifications.

Under strict scrutiny review, the state may not enact legislation that abridges a fundamental right unless (1) it has a compelling interest that justifies restricting a fundamental right, and (2) the legislation is "narrowly tailored" so that the fundamental right is not abridged any more than absolutely necessary to effectuate the state's compelling interest. An example of a compelling interest is the state's interest in the health and safety of its citizens. Additionally, the Supreme Court requires that for legislation to be narrowly tailored, a sufficient nexus must exist between the legislative body's stated interest and either the classification drawn or the means chosen to advance the state's compelling interest.

This standard of review is referred to as the **strict scrutiny test** because the court looks closely at the purpose and effect of the legislation rather than merely accept the claims of the legislature that the legislation is needed or accept the legislation as presumptively valid. The reason for using a higher standard of review when legislation affects a fundamental right or suspect classification is that closer analysis is required when individual liberties are threatened.

If neither a fundamental right nor a suspect classification is implicated, a state may enact legislation abridging that right or affecting that class as long as there is a rational basis for the legislation. This standard of review is generally referred to as the **rational basis test** because the court will not strike down legislation that appears to have some rational basis. The court does not look closely at the effects of the legislation, unlike with the strict scrutiny test. Under this standard of review, state actions are presumptively valid. This standard of review is obviously a much easier one to pass. The legislature need not choose the best possible means; it must merely appear that it has chosen means that are not wholly unrelated to achievement of the legislative purpose.

Incorporation of the Bill of Rights

Originally the Bill of Rights applied only to the federal government, and state and local governments were not bound by its various provisions. This distinction arose out of a fear of a strong centralized government. State governments were viewed much more favorably, and many state constitutions contained protections of individual rights similar to those in the Bill of Rights. In 1833 the Supreme Court, in *Barron v. Baltimore,* expressly held that the Bill of Rights applied only to the federal government.

After the Civil War and the failed attempt by the Southern states to secede from the Union, federal legislators felt it was necessary to amend the Constitution to provide greater protections for individuals from the actions of state governments. In particular, there was a fear that the Southern states would attempt to limit the ability of the recently freed slaves to become equal citizens. The result was the 1868 passage of the Fourteenth Amendment.

The Fourteenth Amendment, as discussed above, contains three clauses: the privileges and immunities clause, the due process clause, and the equal protection clause. The essence of each of these clauses is that they bar states, not the federal government, from infringing on individual rights. The amendment was expressly intended to control state action, but it was unclear exactly how far the amendment went. The original spur for it was a desire to protect the rights of the freed slaves, but the language of the amendment was broad and not specifically limited to state actions infringing on the rights of blacks.

An early attempt to apply the language of the privileges and immunities clause to other persons failed in the *Slaughterhouse cases* (1873). During the later part of the eighteenth century, however, the Supreme Court began to use the due process clause of the Fourteenth Amendment to strike down state action involving economic regulation. Under a theory known as *substantive due process* the Court repeatedly held that states could not impose regulations such as minimum wage laws and child labor laws on private businesses because doing so violated due process. The violation of due process consisted of the regulatory taking of a right, such as the right to work, or to enter into a contract.

During the 1930s, the use of the due process clause to protect economic interest fell into disfavor, in part because the Supreme Court used it to strike down much of President Roosevelt's New Deal legislation, which was intended to ease the burden of the Great Depression. At the same time, however, the Supreme Court began to use the due process clause of the Fourteenth Amendment to protect individual rights from state action. Beginning in the late 1930s, the Supreme

Court incorporated most of the provisions of the Bill of Rights into the Fourteenth Amendment's due process clause and applied them to the states. Many of the criminal law provisions were applied to the states during the 1960s by the Supreme Court under the leadership of Chief Justice Earl Warren.

The term **incorporation** refers to the justices interpreting the due process clause of the Fourteenth Amendment, which says that no state shall deprive a person of life, liberty, or property without "due process of law," as prohibiting states from abridging certain individual rights. Many of these rights are included in the Bill of Rights (which originally applied only to the federal government), hence these rights were included (or incorporated) in the definition of "due process." Several approaches to incorporation have been advocated by various Supreme Court justices during the twentieth century. These are each discussed below.

Total incorporation. Under the **total incorporation** approach, the due process clause of the Fourteenth Amendment made the entire Bill of Rights applicable to the states. In essence, the phrase "due process of law" was interpreted to mean "all of the provisions of the Bill of Rights." This approach has never commanded a majority of justices on the Court. Prominent supporters of this approach include Justice Hugo Black.

Total incorporation plus. As the name implies, the **total incorporation plus** approach goes a step further than the total incorporation approach. Under total incorporation plus, the due process clause of the Fourteenth Amendment includes all of the Bill of Rights and, in addition, includes other, unspecified rights. A principal advocate of this approach was Justice William Douglas, who argued that the provisions of the Bill of Rights created the penumbras of privacy emanating from the First, Third, Fourth, and Fifth Amendments allowing one to interpret the Ninth Amendment to include the right to privacy (*Griswold v. Connecticut*, 1965) meaning the whole was greater than the sum of the parts—that the individual rights contained in the Bill of Rights, when examined together, created other rights. Thus, he argued that the various provisions limiting the ability of the government to intrude into a person's private life (such as the Fourth Amendment prohibition on unreasonable searches and the Third Amendment prohibition on quartering troops in private residences) created a general right to privacy.

Fundamental rights. In *Twining v. New Jersey* (1908) the Supreme Court suggested that some of the individual rights in the Bill of Rights might also be protected from state action, not because the Bill of Rights applied to the states but because these rights "are of such a nature that they are included in the conception of due process of law." This became known as the "fundamental rights" or "ordered liberty" approach.

Under this approach, there is no necessary relationship between the due process clause of the Fourteenth Amendment and the Bill of Rights. The due process clause has an independent meaning, which prohibits state action that violates rights "implicit in the concept of ordered liberty" or those rights that are "fundamental" (*Palko v. Connecticut,* 1937). Exactly what constitutes a fundamental right is left to the justices considering the history and tradition of the law. Additionally, justices consider the "totality of the circumstances" (*Illinois v. Gates,* 1983), of each case in determining whether a right is fundamental. This approach provides justices with greater discretion, and they may interpret it either narrowly or broadly. This approach enjoyed strong support on the Court until the late 1960s. A principal advocate of this approach was Justice Felix Frankfurter.

Selective incorporation. The **selective incorporation** approach combines elements of the fundamental rights and total incorporation approaches, in modified form. Selective incorporation rejects the notion that all of the rights in the Bill of Rights are automatically incorporated in the due process clause of the Fourteenth Amendment but does look to the Bill of Rights as a guide for which rights are incorporated. Selective incorporation rejects the "totality of the circumstances" component of the fundamental rights approach and instead incorporates rights deemed fundamental to the same extent and in the same manner as applied to the federal government.

As an example, under the total incorporation approach, the Fourth Amendment prohibition on unreasonable searches and the exclusionary rule, which states that evidence seized in violation of the Fourth Amendment cannot be used at trial, apply to both the federal government and the states. Under the fundamental rights approach, the Fourth Amendment was deemed fundamental and applied to the states, but the exclusionary rule was deemed nonfundamental and not applied to the states. Consequently, state law enforcement was told by the Court to obey the Fourth Amendment, but failure to do so would not result in the exclusion of the evidence sought to be obtained through a violation of the Fourth Amendment. Under selective incorporation, the Court holds both the right (freedom from unreasonable searches) and the means of enforcing the right (the exclusionary rule) to be part of the due process clause of the Fourteenth Amendment.

Selective incorporation became popular in the 1960s with the Warren Court. A principal advocate was Justice William Brennan. While selective incorporation accepts the idea that the due process clause protects only "fundamental rights" and that not every right in the Bill of Rights is necessarily fundamental, over time it has led to the incorporation of virtually everything in the Bill of Rights. The criminal protections not yet included are the right to an indictment by a grand jury and the prohibition on excessive bail.

Judicial Review

Given the varied sources of law, and the ambiguous language of many statutes and constitutional provisions, it is inevitable that laws will come into conflict or that interpretations of statutes will differ. When this happens, who decides which law is paramount? In the United States, the answer to that question is the courts, through the power of judicial review.

Judicial review simply means the power of the court, specifically judges, to examine a law and determine whether it is constitutional. If a judge determines the law to be constitutional, he or she upholds the law. If the judge determines the law to not be constitutional, he or she declares it unconstitutional and therefore void. To make this determination, judges must examine the law and compare it with the Constitution. This process requires them to interpret the language of both the statute and the constitution.

For example, the Fourth Amendment prohibits "unreasonable" searches. Suppose a state legislature passes a law allowing police officers to search anyone they encounter on a public street. Is this law constitutional? Or does it violate the prohibition on unreasonable searches? To answer this question, judges must examine the history and meaning of "unreasonable" as contained in the Fourth Amendment. They do so by examining precedent.

Judicial review is not specifically provided for in the Constitution. Rather, judicial review is judge-made law. *Marbury v. Madison* (1803) established the authority of the United States Supreme Court to engage in judicial review of the acts of the other branches of government. The Supreme Court stated in *Marbury* that it is the duty of the judiciary to interpret the Constitution and to apply it to particular fact situations. The Court also said that it is the job of the courts to decide when other laws (acts of Congress or state laws) are in violation of the Constitution and to declare these laws null and void. This is the doctrine of judicial review.

Marbury v. Madison. *Marbury v. Madison* is perhaps most important case ever decided by the Supreme Court, because it established the authority of the high court. Article III of the Constitution created the Supreme Court but did not discuss whether the Supreme Court could review legislation or interpret the Constitution.

At the time of the adoption of the Constitution, there was heated debate concerning which branch of government had the authority to declare an act void. There were three suggestions on how to handle such a situation: (1) Each branch within its sphere of authorized power has the final say, (2) the Supreme Court has the final say, but only as to the parties in cases before the court, and (3) the Supreme Court has the final say. This controversy was finally resolved by the opinion in *Marbury*. An examination of the case provides insight into this controversy and how the Supreme Court handled the situation.

The Facts of *Marbury v. Madison:*

1. President John Adams, a Federalist, appointed 42 of his fellow Federalists as justices of the peace for the District of Columbia just days before turning over the office to incoming President Thomas Jefferson, a Democrat. Adams' secretary of state, John Marshall, delivered most of the commissions to the newly appointed justices of the peace but failed to deliver Marbury's.

2. The newly elected president's secretary of state, James Madison, refused to deliver Marbury's commission, so Marbury applied directly to the Supreme Court for a writ of mandamus (a writ compelling a public official to perform his duty). The Supreme Court was granted original jurisdiction in such matters by the Judiciary Act of 1789. The Supreme Court agreed to hear the case but was unable to for 14 months because Congress passed a law that stopped the Supreme Court from meeting.

3. In 1803 the Supreme Court reconvened, heard the case, and decided that Marbury was entitled to his commission but that the Supreme Court could not issue a writ of mandamus. Chief Justice John Marshall (formerly Adams' secretary of state!) wrote the opinion of the court.

Marshall said that: (1) Marbury was entitled to his commission, as he had a legal right that was not extinguished by the change in office of president, (2) a writ of mandamus was proper legal remedy for enforcing Marbury's right, but (3) the Supreme Court lacked the constitutional authority to issue such a writ. The Judiciary Act of 1789 gave the Supreme Court original jurisdiction in such cases, but this grant of authority was unconstitutional because Article III of the Constitution defined Supreme Court jurisdiction. The Judiciary Act of 1789 had the effect of changing (by enlarging) the jurisdiction of the Supreme Court, and Congress cannot pass a statute that changes the Constitution. The only way to change the Constitution is through a constitutional amendment. As stated by Chief Justice Marshall, "An act of the legislature, repugnant to the Constitution, is void." In other words, the Constitution is superior to Congressional legislation.

Prior to the decision in *Marbury,* Democrats argued the Supreme Court lacked the authority to declare acts of other branches of the federal government unconstitutional, while Federalists supported judicial review. If the Supreme Court had issued a writ of mandamus, it could not have forced Madison to honor it. The Supreme Court was thus faced with a serious challenge to its authority. Marshall's opinion saved the court's prestige while allowing the Democrats to claim a political victory (not having to appoint any more Federalists as justices of the peace). More important, the decision established as law that the Supreme Court has the authority to review the constitutionality of congressional activity (and presidential acts)—this is judicial review.

This was obviously a major victory for the Supreme Court, and was not unopposed at the time, but it was accepted at least in part because the result in the case was satisfactory to opponents of a strong Supreme Court. The Supreme Court did not use power of judicial review to invalidate congressional legislation again until 1857, so Congress had little reason to complain. However, the Supreme Court did use judicial review to invalidate state legislation as violative of the Constitution.

How do the rules of evidence promote a fair trial?

Rules of Evidence

As noted at the beginning of this chapter, evidence law is the set of rules that govern what the jury can hear (and see) during a trial. These rules place limits on the type of testimony that may be presented as well as the forms of physical evidence that may be admitted. Evidence law may be confusing to a person who does not understand the rationale for a particular evidentiary rule. Evidence law has a long history, built in large part on past experience.

Generally speaking, *evidence* is the information presented to the jury during a trial that allows the jury to render a verdict. Jurors are not supposed to consider any information they obtain outside the courtroom, such as news reports or gossip from friends. Rather, jurors are supposed to base their verdict solely on what they learn in the courtroom, during the course of the trial.

The Purpose of Evidence Law

Persons not familiar with evidence law are often shocked to discover that information that appears relevant may not be admitted at trial. The variety of objections to the types and forms of evidence is at first glance bewildering. Evidence law has developed over a long period of time. It is created by judges as well as through the passage of statutes. Why a particular evidence rule exists today is not always

Table 1-2	Categories Included in the Federal Rules of Evidence (FRE)

Article I. General Provisions
Article II. Judicial Notice
Article III. Presumptions In Civil Actions and Proceedings
Article IV. Relevancy and Its Limits
Article V. Privileges
Article VI. Witnesses
Article VII. Opinions and Expert Testimony
Article VIII. Hearsay
Article IX. Authentication and Identification
Article X. Contents of Writings, Recordings, and Photographs
Article XI. Miscellaneous Rules

For more information go online: *http://www.law.cornell.edu/rules/fre/overview.html.*

clear; in some instances it is because the rule has an ancient origin and purpose that may not apply to the world of today.

Evidence law is intended to ensure the jurors hear or see only the information that is both relevant and competent. **Relevant evidence** is evidence that pertains to the matter at hand, that has some bearing on the trial. For example, evidence about a defendant's feelings about the murder victim might be useful in explaining why the defendant killed (or did not kill) the victim. **Competent evidence** is evidence that is in a form the jury is permitted to hear or see. For example, hearsay evidence is sometimes deemed incompetent because it lacks reliability. Evidence must be both relevant and competent for it to be deemed admissible at trial. It is evidence law that helps the court sort out what evidence the jury will be allowed to see and hear.

The Development of Evidence Law

Evidence law developed over a long period of time. In medieval times, trials as we now understand them did not exist. Different societies used a variety of methods for determining the "truth." For instance, in eleventh-century England, guilt was often determined through *trial by battle,* in which an accused would fight his accuser; if the accused won, he was determined to be innocent. Other societies appealed to God to reveal guilt or innocence. A person might be tied to a heavy stone and placed in a lake. If the person did not drown, it was seen as evidence that the person was corrupted by the devil. If the person did drown, it was assumed that he or she was innocent. Obviously this determination was of little use to the drowned person, at least in this life.

A movement toward trial by jury began in the thirteenth century in England. A person accused of crime gathered people who would swear to his innocence. These persons were known as oath helpers. Over time, oath helpers began to not only swear not just to the innocence of the accused but also provide facts relevant to his guilt or innocence. This was the beginning of the use of witnesses at trial. In 1215 the Magna Carta was adopted, which provided for criminal jury trials.

Several different legal systems are in existence today. The United States follows the common law system brought over to the colonies from England. During the common law period, evidence rules developed sporadically, on a case-by-case basis. Today, evidence law in virtually every state is governed by statute, or code. The *evidence code* is a compilation of the common law evidence rules, written down (or codified) by the legislature. The best-known example is the Federal Rules of Evidence, or FRE, which apply in all federal courts; more than 40 states have also adopted the FRE in whole or part.

The FRE were enacted by Congress in 1975. While the rules have been in existence for less than 30 years, they are the product of many years of discussion, research, and deliberation by lawyers, judges, scholars, and legislators. Additionally, there were earlier attempts at evidence codes, such as the Model Code of Evidence, created by the American Law Institute (ALI) in 1942 (the same body that developed the Model Penal Code, which is still in use today).

While many states have adopted the FRE others have not. It is crucial the student know whether his or her state follows the FRE, or has its own evidence law. The rules of evidence may vary widely among the states.

Summary

This chapter introduced some important developments and issues in the law, both in general and with respect to evidence law. It discussed the history and development of the law, in early times, during the common law period, and in the modern era.

The chapter also reviewed the sources of law and the sources of individual law. Particular attention was paid to the Bill of Rights and the incorporation of the Bill of Rights into the Fourteenth Amendment. This incorporation of the individual rights contained in the Bill of Rights is vitally important, for without it many individual rights would not be protected from infringement by state agencies. In criminal justice, this applies to the actions of the police, courts, and corrections.

The chapter also discussed the concepts of judicial review, precedent, and *stare decisis*. These concepts play an important role in the development of the law. Additionally, it discussed the development of evidence law and the Federal Rules of Evidence. While each state writes its own evidence code, the FRE have had a profound influence on evidence law.

Discussion Questions

1. Explain *Marbury v. Madison* (1803) and the impact the case had on the judicial system.

2. Explain the concepts of precedent and *stare decisis.*

3. Give a detailed description of the Fourth Amendment and explain why it is particularly important in evidence law.

4. Why is the Fourteenth Amendment one of the most important to the rights of citizens? What are the three clauses, and why are they so important?

5. Explain the two standards of review mentioned in the text.

6. What is a fundamental right? Give some examples.

7. Explain relevant evidence and give two examples.

8. Explain competent evidence and give two examples.

9. In thirteenth-century England there were people known as "oath takers." What was their function, and what did their function evolve into?

10. What is meant by FRE?

11. Does your state follow the FRE? Cite references supporting your answer.

12. Give arguments for and against using the FRE.

13. What is a bill of attainder and why was it prohibited by the Constitution?

14. Explain the importance of *stare decisis.*

15. Explain the difference between strict scrutiny and rational basis of review.

16. Explain the total incorporation approach. What does the total incorporation plus approach add to total incorporation?

17. How does the selective incorporation approach differ from total incorporation?

18. Explain the importance of rules of evidence. Give examples.

19. Explain the importance of common law to our system of law today.

20. Give an example of a situation that might convince a court to overturn a previous case.

Further Reading

Amar, Akhil Reed. (1998). *The Bill of Rights*. New Haven, CT: Yale University Press.

Anastaplo, George. (1989). *The Constitution of 1787: A Commentary*. Baltimore, MD: The Johns Hopkins University Press.

Anastaplo, George. (1995). *The Amendments to the Constitution: A Commentary*. Baltimore, MD: The Johns Hopkins University Press.

del Carmen, Rolando V. (1998). *Criminal Procedure*. Belmont, CA: Wadsworth.

Domino, John C. (1994). *Civil Rights and Liberties*. New York: HarperCollins.

Kelly, Alfred H., Winfred A. Harbison, and Herman Belz. (1983). *The American Constitution: Its Origins and Development* (6th edition). New York: W. W. Norton.

Massey, Calvin R. (1995). *Silent Rights: The Ninth Amendment and the Constitution's Unenumerated Rights*. Philadelphia: Temple University Press.

Peltason, J. W. (1991). *Understanding the Constitution*. New York: Harcourt Brace.

Tribe, L. H. (1988). *American Constitutional Law*. Mineola, NY: Foundation Press.

Cases Cited

Barker v. Wingo, 407 U.S. 514 (1972)

Barron v. Baltimore, 32 U.S. (7 Pet.) 243 (1833)

Chaplinsky v. New Hampshire, 315 U.S. 568 (1942)

Everson v. Board of Education, 330 U.S. 1 (1947)

Griffin v. California, 380 U.S. 6091 (965)

Griswold v. Connecticut, 381 U.S. 489 (1965)

Hurtado v. California, 110 U.S. 516 (1884)

Illinois v. Gates, 462 U.S. 213 (1983)

Kirby v. Illinois, 406 U.S. 682 (1972)

Lemon v. Kurtzman, 1,403 U.S. 602 (971)

Malloy v. Hogan, 378 U.S. 1 (1964)

Marbury v. Madison, 5 U.S. (1 Cranch) 137 (1803)

Miller v. California, 413 U.S. 15 (1973)

Palko v. Connecticut, 302 U.S. 319 (1937)

Slaughter-House Cases, 83 U.S. (16 Wall.) 36 (1873)

Stack v. Boyle, 342 U.S. 1 (1951)

Strickland v. Washington, 466 U.S. 668 (1984)

Texas v. Johnson, 491 U.S. 397 (1989)

Twining v. New Jersey 211 U.S. 78 (1908)

Virginia State Board of Pharmacy v. Virginia Citizens Consumers Council, Inc., 425 U.S. 748 (1976) ✦

Chapter Two

The American Criminal Court System

Key Terms

- Appellate jurisdiction
- Appointed counsel
- Appointment
- Article Three Courts
- Attorney general
- Change of venue
- Defense attorneys
- Diversity of citizenship
- Election
- En banc
- Federal court of appeals (circuit courts)
- General jurisdiction
- Geographic jurisdiction
- Hierarchical jurisdiction
- Judge

- Judiciary Act of 1789
- Jurisdiction
- Limited jurisdiction
- Magistrates
- Merit system or Missouri plan
- Original jurisdiction
- Personal jurisdiction
- Prosecutors
- Public defenders
- Retained counsel
- Rule of four
- Subject matter jurisdiction
- Supreme Court
- Trial de novo
- United States district courts
- Venue
- Writ of certiorari

Courts perform several functions. First, courts settle disputes by providing a forum for obtaining justice and resolving disputes through the application of legal rules and principles. It is in court that injured parties may be heard and that the state may seek to punish wrongdoers. Private parties may seek redress in civil court, while the state may seek to punish violators of the criminal law in criminal court. Although

29

the courtroom is obviously not the only place that people may go to settle disputes, Americans traditionally have turned to the courts for redress. Other countries, such as Japan, use the courts much less frequently.

Second, courts make public policy decisions. Policy making involves the allocation of limited resources (such as money, property, and rights) to competing interests. America has a long tradition of settling difficult policy questions in the courtroom rather than the legislature. This is because politicians often avoid settling complex or difficult problems. Additionally, the rights of minorities are often unprotected by the legislature, so courts are forced to step into the breach. Finally, litigation is accepted as a tool for social change.

Third, courts serve to clarify the law through interpretation of statutes and the application of general principles to specific fact patterns. Courts are different from the other branches of government in many ways, but perhaps the most significant difference is that courts are reactive: Courts do not initiate cases but rather serve to settle controversies brought to them by others—plaintiffs and defendants, in legal parlance. This function frequently involves the interpretation of statutes written by the legislature.

In this chapter, we examine the structure of the American court system. It is a bit misleading to think of America as having just one court system—actually there are fifty state court systems and the federal court system. The court systems of the various states and the federal system share a number of characteristics but also can be quite different. First, we review some key concepts that all of the court systems share. Next, we examine the federal and state court systems. After our discussion of court structure, we discuss the trial process, focusing on the criminal trial and the appeals process.

Jurisdiction

In order to appreciate how and why court systems are set up the way they are, it is important to understand the concept of jurisdiction. **Jurisdiction** involves the legal authority of a court to hear a case. Jurisdiction is conferred by statutory or constitutional law. There are four primary types of jurisdiction: personal, subject matter, geographic, and hierarchical.

Personal jurisdiction involves the authority of the court over the person. A court may acquire personal jurisdiction over a person if that person comes in contact with the court, either by being a citizen of the state or by committing an act (criminal or non-criminal) or series of acts within the state.

Subject matter jurisdiction involves the authority conferred on a court to hear a particular type of case. Some courts may hear only a specified type of case, such as a juvenile court or probate court. Other courts are given broad subject matter jurisdiction and may hear both civil and criminal proceedings of all kinds.

Geographic jurisdiction refers to the authority of courts to hear cases that arise within specified boundaries, such as a city, county, state, or country. Geographic jurisdiction is also sometimes referred to as **venue.** For a court to have jurisdiction over an event, that event must have taken place, in whole or part, within the geographic jurisdiction of the court. Thus, a person who kills someone in Idaho could not be prosecuted in North Carolina for that killing. The proper forum would be in Idaho. Furthermore, the proper court within Idaho would be that for the county in which the killing occurred.

Precisely where a crime occurs is not always clear-cut. For instance, a person may be kidnapped in California and taken to Texas. In this case, the kidnapping is a continuing offense—that is, each state into which the victim is taken could charge the kidnapper with a crime. Furthermore, both California and Texas may prosecute without violating the prohibition on double jeopardy, as they are each separate sovereign governments. This means each state derives its authority from a different source—its own state constitution. While two states can prosecute a person for the same offense, a state and a county in that state cannot do so because the county derives its jurisdiction from the same source as the state (that state's constitution).

Within each state there are jurisdictions, usually defined by county boundaries. A state crime must be tried both within the proper state and the proper district within the state. Occasionally a defendant in a criminal case may request a **change of venue.** Such a request must be based on evidence that it is impossible for the defendant to get a fair trial in the original court, perhaps because of substantial adverse publicity.

Hierarchical jurisdiction involves the division of responsibilities and functions among the various courts. Jurisdiction can be general or limited, original or appellate.

General jurisdiction means a court has the authority to hear a variety of cases, that it is not limited to hearing only a particular type of case. An example is the state trial court, which often has the authority to hear all manner of civil and criminal cases. Civil cases involve a dispute between two private parties, such as in contract or property law. Criminal law involves a prosecution of an individual by the state for violating state criminal law.

Limited jurisdiction means that a court is limited to hearing only a particular class of cases. Examples include traffic court, juvenile court, and probate court. Thus, a juvenile court would hear only matter involving juveniles. Smaller jurisdictions often do not have such courts, instead they combine all the specialized courts in one court because of limited resources.

Original jurisdiction means the power of the court to hear the case initially. For example, in federal court, all felony-level cases begin in the district court, while a suit between two states would start at the Supreme Court level. The court of original jurisdiction is where the trial takes place.

Appellate jurisdiction means the power of the court to review a decision of a lower court. Appeals courts may affirm or reverse lower court judgments and either enter a new judgment or send the case back down to the lower court for reconsideration in light of its decision. Appellate courts do not conduct a retrial; rather, they are generally limited to a review of the trial record to determine if there were any major legal errors. The court hears oral arguments by the attorneys for each side, reads legal briefs filed with the court, and bases its decision on these materials rather than new evidence.

Table 2-1 The Three Tiers of the Federal Court System and Their Purposes	
Court	**Purpose**
District courts	Trial court, court of original jurisdiction
Courts of appeals (circuit courts)	Federal circuit: Appeals from several administrative agencies, patent claims, and decisions of the Claims Court and the Court of International Trade District of Columbia and the 50 states: Appeals from lower courts
Supreme Court	Original jurisdiction: suits between states, suits between the United States and a state, and suits between a state and a foreign citizen Appellate: almost entirely discretionary, based on the rule of four.

The Federal Courts

There are essentially two court systems in the United States: the court systems of the fifty states, and the federal court system. The jurisdictions of the federal and state courts frequently overlap when a crime in a state may also be punishable under federal law.

The Constitution drawn up at the Constitutional Convention in 1787 created a federal government with three branches: the legislative, executive, and judicial. The duties of each branch were set forth in separate articles of the Constitution. The duties of the judicial branch were listed in Article Three. This article established the Supreme Court and authorized "such inferior courts as Congress" chose to create. Neither the number of members of the Supreme Court nor the form of any potential "inferior" (meaning lower) courts were described.

At first, the idea of creating inferior federal courts met with much resistance from supporters of states rights, who were afraid federal courts would infringe on the jurisdiction and authority of state courts. Several contributors to the Federalist Papers argued for a strong federal court system, as a bulwark against the actions of a democratically elected legislature. Additionally, these writers saw the Constitution as fundamental, paramount law and believed the job of the courts to be interpreting it and preventing the legislature from passing laws that took away fundamental rights.

One of the first acts of the newly elected Congress was to pass the **Judiciary Act of 1789.** This act established Supreme Court membership at six justices and created three federal circuit courts and 13 district courts, one in each state. From this act an entire federal system has grown, today encompassing some 13 federal circuit courts and 94 district courts. The first set of intermediate-level appellate courts with purely appellate jurisdiction was established over a hundred years later, in 1891. Courts created under the authority of Article Three of the Constitution are sometimes referred to as **Article Three Courts.**

The federal court system today consists of three primary tiers: district courts, intermediate appellate courts, and the Supreme Court. Each of these courts has different functions.

District Courts

The district court is the trial court, or court of original jurisdiction, for the federal court system. There are currently over 100 federal judicial districts. Each state has at least one district court; some, such as California and Texas, have as many as four. With minor exceptions, no judicial district crosses state lines.

In each district there is a **United States District Court.** The number of judges in each district ranges from 2 to 32, depending on the population of the individual district. While each district has more than one judge, only one judge presides over a particular trial. There are approximately 650 federal district judges.

Within each district court there are subordinate judicial officers, referred to as **magistrates.** These judicial officers conduct preliminary proceedings in cases before the district court and issue warrants. Judgments entered by magistrates are considered judgments of the district court. Federal magistrate courts are similar to courts of limited jurisdiction in state courts.

Federal district courts have original jurisdiction over both civil matters and criminal cases involving federal statutes. Their jurisdiction is defined by both the Constitution and federal statute. District courts conduct trials for all federal criminal offenses and have jurisdiction to hear civil cases in which there is diversity of citizenship between the parties. **Diversity of citizenship** refers to situations in which the opposing parties are from different states. Until recently, much of the federal court docket was made up of civil cases, but this balance has begun to shift as Congress has greatly increased the number of federal crimes. Although the number of civil cases filed in federal district court still far outnumbers criminal cases, criminal trials take up a significant potion of the district court's time. Some jurisdictions have been forced to postpone all civil proceedings in order to deal with the backlog of criminal cases. Because the Constitution requires a "speedy trial," criminal cases take precedence, and civil cases are often delayed.

Federal district courts are not courts of general jurisdiction. Rather, they have jurisdiction to hear only those types of cases specified by acts of Congress, and Congress may authorize district courts to hear only those cases and controversies specified in Article Three. The majority of cases in federal court deal with claims arising out of federal law, either civil or criminal. These may be based on federal statutes or the Constitution. The other major category of cases heard in federal courts are civil cases arising out of the court's diversity jurisdiction. District courts are authorized to hear any civil matter, even if it involves state law, if the amount in question exceeds $50,000 and the parties are citizens of different states. Federal courts were originally given diversity jurisdiction because the founding fathers feared state courts would be biased in favor of their residents when presented with a suit between a resident and a non-resident. Allowing the non-resident to shift the case to federal court was seen as a means of ensuring a fair trial.

Federal judges are appointed for life. Furthermore, their salary cannot be reduced during their term of office. This policy protects the independence of the federal judiciary and sets it apart from state court judges, most of whom are appointed or elected to a defined term of years.

Courts of Appeals

The next level in the federal system is the **federal court of appeals,** also referred to as *circuit courts.* There are today thirteen courts of appeals: eleven for the fifty states, one for the District of Columbia and one for the federal circuit.

The jurisdiction of the Court of Appeals for the Federal Circuit is defined by stat-

Why are appeals permitted in criminal cases?

ute to include appeals from several federal administrative agencies, patent claims, and decisions of the Claims Court and the Court of International Trade, two specialized federal trial courts. The District of Columbia has its own appeals court in part because of the large volume of cases filed in the District of Columbia. Federal judges are appointed to their positions for life.

The 11 remaining courts of appeals are organized on a territorial basis, with each covering several states. For instance, the Eleventh Circuit encompasses the states of Florida, Georgia, and Alabama, while the Ninth Circuit, the largest of the courts of appeals, includes the states of Alaska, Hawaii, California, Nevada, Arizona, Idaho, Oregon, Washington, and Montana, as well as Guam, and the Northern Marianas Islands.

The number of judges on each of the courts of appeals varies from 6 in the First Circuit to 32 in the Ninth Circuit. Appeals are heard by three-judge panels. The makeup of these panels is constantly changing, so that Judge A does not repeatedly sit with Judge B. If conflicting decisions involve the same legal issue between two panels, the entire circuit may sit **en banc** ("as a group") and rehear the case. Doing so can obviously be a bit unwieldy in those circuits that have a large number of judges; consequently, federal law permits courts of appeals with more than 15 active judges to sit *en banc* with less than all of its members. The Ninth Circuit may hold en banc hearings with as few as 11 of its 32 judges. As with district court judges, courts of appeals judges are appointed for life.

The Supreme Court

The final tier in the federal court system is the **Supreme Court.** This is the "court of last resort" for all cases arising in the federal system as well as for all cases in state courts that involve a federal constitutional issue. The Supreme Court has original jurisdiction over a very small number of situations, including suits between states, suits between the United States and a state, and suits between a state and a foreign citizen. These cases rarely occur. The bulk of the Court's docket consists of cases taken on appeal from either the federal courts of appeal or state supreme courts.

The Supreme Court's appellate docket is almost entirely discretionary—that is, the Court may chose which cases it takes and which it refuses to hear. When a party asks the Court to accept a case, it submits a petition for a **writ of certiorari.** A writ of certiorari is an order issued by the Supreme Court to the lower court to send the record of the case up to the Supreme Court. The justices vote on whether to accept a case. If four or more justices vote to accept a case, it is placed on the Court's docket. This is known as the **rule of four.** If four votes are not obtained, the petition for a writ of certiorari is denied, and the decision of the lower court is left undisturbed. Refusal to accept an appeal is not considered a decision on the merits and has no binding precedential value. It simply means the Court has chosen not to hear the case, for whatever reason.

The Supreme Court has three main purposes: (1) to resolve disputes between states, (2) to resolve conflicting opinions of lower federal and state courts, and (3) to resolve constitutional questions. The Court uses its discretionary docket to take only those cases that fit into these categories. Thus, the Court may refuse to grant certiorari in a case because there is no difference of opinion on the issue among the circuit courts or because no federal constitutional issue is raised.

The Court is currently composed of nine justices, one of whom is designated the chief justice. Congress has the authority to either enlarge or reduce the number of justices on the Supreme Court and has at times done so. Congress has not changed the number of justices in over 100 years, however, so it seems unlikely Congress would try to do so now, in the face of a longstanding tradition of having nine justices on the Court.

Although it was created as a third branch of the federal government, the Supreme Court did not immediately establish a significant presence in the affairs of the country. In fact, there was so little for the Court to do that the first chief justice, John Jay, resigned to take a position as an ambassador. It was not until the term of John Marshall that the Supreme Court was able to establish its role in the government. Today, the Supreme Court plays a significant role in public affairs, through its exercise of the power of judicial review (discussed in Chapter 1).

Table 2-2 State Courts and Their Purposes	
Court	**Purpose**
Courts of limited jurisdiction	Less serious offenses and civil cases
Courts of general jurisdiction or court of original jurisdiction	Trial courts for civil and criminal matters; generally authorized to hear any matters not exclusively designated for the court of limited jurisdiction. Trial de novo

The State Courts

Although the federal courts, particularly the Supreme Court, capture much of the attention of the media and the general public, the reality is that state courts are the workhorses of the American judicial system. State courts process in excess of 100 million cases a year. These cases range from the most serious of criminal cases to complex civil litigation to routine divorces and traffic violations.

The structure of state courts is much more varied than the structure of the federal court system. The 50 states have created a multiplicity of court structures. Some court systems are unified and clearly organized, while others are a jumble of overlapping jurisdiction and confusion. In this section we present a "typical" state court system, but your state court structure may differ.

The most common state court system consists of four levels, or tiers: courts of limited jurisdiction, courts of general jurisdiction, intermediate appellate courts, and a final appellate court, or court of last resort.

Courts of limited jurisdiction are those courts that deal with the less serious offenses and civil cases. These courts are referred to by a variety of names, including justice of the peace court, magistrate's court, municipal court, and county court. These lower courts handle a wide variety of matters, including minor criminal cases, traffic offenses, violations of municipal ordinances, and civil disputes under a certain amount. On the criminal side, these courts may also be responsible for issuing search and arrest warrants and conducting the preliminary stages of felony cases, such as the preliminary hearing and arraignment. On the civil side, these courts may handle a variety of matters, including juvenile delinquency, family law, and probate.

Proceedings in lower courts are often more informal than those in appellate or trial courts. There is generally no right to trial provided in these courts; a losing party who wishes to appeal an adverse decision must do so through a trial de novo in the court of original jurisdiction. A **trial de novo** is not like a standard appeal in which the higher court concerns itself only with a review of the trial record and consideration of any possible legal errors. Instead, a trial de novo is an entirely new trial.

While courts of limited jurisdiction receive little attention, they are important for several reasons. First, they are the only experience that most citizens will have with the court system. Second, these courts process a tremendous number of cases, and there are a lot of these courts. The National Center for State Courts reports that there are almost 14,000 lower courts, and these courts process some 71 million cases each year. Third, these courts are often involved in the crucial early stages of criminal cases, in the issuance of warrants and the determination whether to set bail and to hold the suspect over for trial.

The next level in a typical state court system are the *courts of general jurisdiction*. These are the trial courts for civil and criminal matters. They are also *courts of original jurisdiction*, and it is here that trials for felonies are held. They are generally authorized to hear any matters not exclusively designated for courts of limited jurisdiction; in some states they may even have concurrent jurisdiction with lower courts on some matters, such as misdemeanors. They may also hear appeals, in the form of a trial de novo, from lower courts.

Trial courts are usually referred to as the district court, circuit court, or superior court, although at least one state, New York, refers to its trial court as the supreme court and its court of last resort as the court of appeals. While there is no hard evidence that New York did this with the express purpose of confusing students, the authors do have their suspicions.

The precise workload of the trial courts varies by jurisdiction. In less populous areas, the trial court may hear all manner of cases, including civil and criminal. In other more populated areas, there may be a greater specialization with one court handling only felony trials and another handling only civil matters.

Currently, at least 38 states have two levels of appellate courts consisting of an intermediate appellate court and a court of last resort. Intermediate appellate courts are largely a creation of the twentieth century. As jurisdictions became more crowded and court dockets increased, officials saw a need to relieve the state supreme court of the burden of hearing all appeals of right. The states that have not created an intermediate court tend to be either small or not densely populated.

The intermediate appellate courts are referred to by a variety of names, but by far the most common is court of appeals. The primary purpose of the intermediate court of appeals is to hear felony appeals of right. The number of judges on the intermediate appellate court varies. Additionally, many states have more than one intermediate appellate court.

The court of last resort is in most states called the state supreme court. Forty-eight states have one court of last resort; two states (Oklahoma and Texas) have two (Meador 1991). These states have a court of last resort for all civil cases and a court of last resort for all criminal cases. The number of judges on the court of last resort varies by state from three to nine.

The court of last resort usually hears the majority of appeals on a discretionary basis, similar to the United States Supreme Court. This allows them to control their docket and focus on cases involving significant legal issues. The exceptions are those states that do not have an intermediate appellate court and, in other states, death penalty cases. In states without an intermediate appellate court (usually the smaller and less populous states), the state supreme court is the only appellate court and thus is mandated by law to hear all appeals. Most states also require their supreme court hear all appeals in cases involving the death penalty. This requirement is provided as an extra safeguard because the punishment in these cases is obviously the most severe possible, and the states wish to be absolutely sure the defendant has received a fair trial.

For most cases, the state supreme court is the end of the line, the final arbiter of the dispute. The only option for a losing party in the state supreme court is to appeal directly to the United States Supreme

Court, and to do so the party must be able to identify a legal issue that involves the Constitution or a federal law. Defendants who lose in state courts also have the option of filing a writ of habeas corpus in federal district court.

Court Actors

There are three key actors in court: judges, prosecutors, and defense attorneys. Each of these actors are attorneys trained in the law, but each performs different tasks.

Judges

The **judge** serves as a referee, responsible for enforcing court rules, instructing the jury on the law, and determining the law. Judges are expected to be completely impartial. Trial judges have tremendous power to control a case. As a whole, judges are not representative of American society. They are mostly white, male, and upper middle class; women and minorities are underrepresented. A number of commentators have argued that this underrepresentation results in bias, either intentional or unintentional. Others have suggested that even if bias does not in fact exist, there is a perception among many segments of the population that justice is not obtainable because minorities and women are underrepresented on the bench (Slotnick 1984).

Why are trial court judges given the authority to decide what evidence is admissible?

There are three common methods of selecting judges: appointment, election, and the merit system. Different jurisdictions use different methods of selecting judges. Some jurisdictions use more than one method, while others, such as the federal system, use only one method.

Appointment by the chief executive of the jurisdiction (the president of the United States or the governor of an individual state) is the oldest method of selecting judges. All thirteen of the original colonies used it, and it is used today in the federal system and about 20 states.

Election of judges became popular during the 1830s when Democrats under the leadership of Andrew Jackson gained control of Congress from the Federalists. Jackson and his supporters believed wholeheartedly in popular democracy and thought appointment of judges was undemocratic. Georgia (1824) was the first state to implement judicial elections. Currently, 29 states use popular elections to select judges.

These elections take one of two forms. Some states have partisan (meaning aligned with a particular party) elections, in which candidates for judicial office run in the party primary and their political affiliation is listed on ballot; 13 states use this method. In 16 other states, judges are selected in nonpartisan elections, in which no political affiliation is listed.

A third method of selecting judges is the **merit system.** This system is based on system originally developed by the American Judicature Society in 1909 and endorsed by the American Bar Association in 1937. It was first adopted by Missouri in 1940 and consequently is sometimes referred to as the *Missouri plan.*

The merit system has become popular only recently. In 1960 only four states used the system, but by 1998 about half the states were using it. The merit system has three parts. First, a nonpartisan nominating commission selects a list of potential candidates, based on the candidates' legal qualifications. Second, the governor makes a selection from this list. Finally, the person selected as a judge stands for election (this is referred to as *retention*) within a short time after he or she is selected, usually within one year.

Prosecutors

Under the early common law, there were no public **prosecutors.** Instead, private citizens were responsible for litigating their criminal cases. Private prosecution gave way to public prosecution as society came to view crime as an offense not just against the person, but against society as well. Today, private prosecution is no longer permitted in any state; in its place are prosecutor's offices. There are over 25,000 prosecutors today, although about half of them are part-time (primarily in small jurisdictions).

The 1789 Judiciary Act provided a United States attorney for each court district (appointed by the U.S. president.) In 1870 Congress authorized the creation of the Department of Justice, with an attorney general and assistants (Meador 1991). The **attorney general,** a political appointee, is an administrator who sets prosecution priorities for deputy attorney generals. *Deputy attorney generals* are appointed by the president and confirmed by the Senate and serve at the pleasure of the president. *Assistant United States attorneys* are not political appointments.

State prosecutors are called by various names, such as district attorney, solicitor, county attorney, state's attorney, and commonwealth attorney. State prosecutors are usually elected officials, with appointed assistants who do most of the trial work. Only four states (Alaska, Connecticut, Delaware, and New Jersey) do not have an elected district attorney. The district attorney's duty is to not only prosecute cases in the name of the people but also to do justice by pursuing only those who have in fact committed crimes. District attorneys have tremendous power to decide whether to prosecute, and this power is largely unreviewable.

Defense Attorneys

Defense attorneys are expected to represent their client as effectively as possible while acting within the rules of court. The right to counsel existed at common law and in state constitutions. The Sixth Amendment codified this right. The Supreme Court has interpreted the Sixth Amendment as requiring the right to counsel as applying at any "critical stage" of the prosecution, not just at trial. Thus, a defendant has been held to have the right to counsel at a lineup that takes place after indictment, at the preliminary hearing, and during pretrial discovery.

The role of defense counsel is primarily: (1) to ensure that the defendant's rights are not violated (intentionally or in error) by the police; (2) to make sure the defendant knows all his or her options before making a decision; (3) to provide the defendant with the best possible defense, without violating ethical and legal obligations; (4) to investigate and prepare the defense; and (5) to argue for lowest possible sentence or best possible plea bargain.

There are several types of defense counsel. These include private, retained counsel, public defenders, and appointed counsel. **Retained counsel** are attorneys selected and paid by the defendant. **Public defenders** are hired by the state but work for defendants who cannot afford to hire their own lawyer. **Appointed counsel** are private attorneys who are paid by the state on a case-by-case basis to represent indigent defendants.

While the Supreme Court has held that there is a right to counsel, the Court has not held that this means a right to the counsel of the defendant's choice in all cases. A person who can afford to hire a lawyer may do so; those who cannot afford a lawyer will be provided one but there are limits on when the appointment will occur, and the defendant has little or no say in who is selected to represent them.

Overview of the Criminal Process

This section provides a brief overview of the major stages in a typical criminal trial. The process begins with the arrest of a suspect and ends with the verdict at trial or, potentially, an appeal. Evidentiary issues may arise at any point during the proceeding, although the bulk of evidence law deals with the conduct of the trial.

Pretrial Proceedings

The criminal process begins either with the filing of a *complaint* or an *arrest*. A complaint may be filled out by a police officer, a prosecutor, or a private citizen. If an arrest is made first, a complaint will be sworn out afterward, usually by the arresting officer. The complaint serves as the charging document for the preliminary hearing.

Search and arrest warrants are obtained by police officers who first must fill out an *affidavit* stating the facts relied upon to create what is called probable cause. There must be probable cause to arrest or search. As noted in Chapter 1, *probable cause* is a legal concept referring to the amount of proof a police officer must have in order to search or arrest someone. This concept is discussed further in Chapter 6.

After someone is arrested, he or she is booked. *Booking* is an administrative procedure that involves entering of the suspect's name, arrest time, and offense charged, into the police blotter and taking fingerprints and photographs.

The first court appearance is referred to as the *initial appearance*. Once a person is arrested, he or she must be brought before a magistrate "without unnecessary delay." It is here that bail is set. The next stage in the proceedings is the *preliminary examination*, sometimes referred to as the *preliminary hearing*. Here the magistrate determines whether there is probable cause to believe that an offense was committed and that it was defendant who committed it. If probable cause is established, the defendant is "bound over" for trial. The preliminary examination is a formal adversarial proceeding conducted in open court. The Supreme Court has defined it as a "critical stage" of the prosecution, which means the defendant has a right to have a lawyer present.

There are two ways that charges may be filed against a defendant— either by an *information* filed by the prosecutor or by an *indictment* issued by a grand jury. An information is adequate if it informs the defendant of the facts and the elements of the offense charged. It is a more efficient way to proceed than a grand jury indictment because it eliminates the need to organize a grand jury and present evidence.

On the federal level, the Fifth Amendment requires the government to proceed via an indictment handed down by a grand jury. This clause of the Fifth Amendment is one of the few that has not been applied to the states however, so states may use an information instead. Fewer than half the states require an indictment; 12 states require indictment by a grand jury only for felonies, while 3 states require indictment by a grand jury only for capital offenses. Four states require indictment by a grand jury for all felonies and misdemeanors.

The typical *grand jury* is comprised of 23 people, and its proceedings are not open to the public. The only persons present aside from the members of the grand jury are the district attorney and any witnesses the prosecutor calls. The rationale behind requiring indictment by a grand jury is that this body can act as a check on an overzealous prosecutor, preventing him or her from prosecuting cases for which there is not sufficient evidence. In reality the grand jury today is unlikely to refuse to indict anyone. This fact does not necessarily mean that the jury is not achieving its purpose of preventing improper prosecutions because its very existence may prevent prosecutors from taking shaky cases to the grand jury. In this way, the grand jury does check the prosecutor's power. If the grand jury returns an indictment it is referred to as a *true bill*. If the grand jury refuses to indict the defendant, it is referred to as a *no bill*.

At the *arraignment* the defendant enters a *plea*. Possible pleas include guilty, not guilty, no contest, and standing mute. *Standing mute* means refusing to plead—in these instances the court enters a "not guilty" plea for the defendant, thus preserving the defendant's constitutional right to trial. A no contest plea, also referred to as *nolo contendre*, means the defendant accepts whatever punishment the court would impose on a guilty defendant but refuses to admit liability. This plea is frequently used by defendants who fear being exposed to civil liability for their criminal misdeeds.

Pretrial Motions

Prior to trial, both the prosecution and defense may file motions with the court. These motions may cover a variety of issues. Common *pretrial motions* in criminal cases include a *motion to compel discovery* and a *motion to suppress evidence*. These motions are usually made by the defense. The judge rules on these motions before the trial begins.

The period of time between arraignment and trial is often referred to as the *discovery period*, this is the time when both sides may seek to discover what evidence the other side has. This is typically done via a pretrial motion. The defendant has a constitutional right to any *exculpatory evidence* (evidence that tends to suggest the defendant is innocent) in the possession of the prosecution.

Jury Selection

The next step in the process is the trial itself. Once a trial date is set, jury selection begins. The *jury* is selected from the eligible members of the community who are selected at random, usually from voting records or automobile registration records. These records are used to obtain as complete a list as possible of all the residents of a community. Prospective jurors are examined by the judge or the attorneys to determine whether there is any bias, prejudice, or interest that would prevent the potential juror from being impartial. This process of questioning the jurors is referred to as the *voir dire*.

It should be noted that while the purpose of the voir dire is to obtain an unbiased jury, in reality each side seeks not only to excuse potential jurors who are biased against their side but also to keep on the jury those individuals who are biased toward their own side. Attorneys sometimes use the services of professional jury consultants to help them determine what type of person is more likely to favor the prosecution or defense.

Jurors may be *challenged for cause* or removed through the use of a peremptory challenge. A *peremptory challenge* is one for which no reason need be given. While challenges for cause are unlimited, peremptory challenges are usually limited to a certain number. The Supreme Court has held that peremptory challenges may not be used to exclude potential jurors on the basis of race (*Batson v. Kentucky*, 1986) or gender (*J. E. B. v. Alabama*, 1994).

The Supreme Court has also held that the jury need not be composed of the traditional 12 members. Juries as small as 6 have been approved for both civil and criminal trials (*Williams v. Florida*, 1970). Furthermore, there is no constitutional requirement that the jury verdict be unanimous, even in criminal cases. The Supreme Court has approved both 9–3 and 10–2 verdicts (*Johnson v. Louisiana*, 1972; *Apodaca v. Oregon*, 1972). However, a six-person jury must be unanimous. Finally, the requirement of a "jury of one's peers" has been interpreted simply to require that the jury be selected from the community in which the crime takes place. It does not mean the jury must share any other similarities with the defendant. To hold otherwise would be next to impossible. A perfect example is the O. J. Simpson case. If the jury should have been made up of people with similar attributes, how would we have defined them? As black men, rich people, ex-football players, or bad actors? Instead, jury members simply had to be Los Angeles county residents.

The Trial

Once the jury is selected and sworn in, the trial can begin. The first step is the making of *opening statements*—first by the prosecution and then by the defense. The defense may choose to reserve its opening statement until after the prosecution has presented its evidence. This is referred to as the prosecution's *case-in-chief*. During this phase, the prosecution must establish each element of crime charged beyond a reasonable doubt.

Once the prosecution has presented its evidence and called its witnesses, the defense has an opportunity to present its case-in-chief. The defense is not required to put on any case, but if defense chooses to, it may raise several types of defenses. These include either an alibi or an affirmative defense such as insanity or self-defense.

Witnesses may be called to testify by both the prosecution and the defense. The side that calls the witness to testify conducts what is called the *direct examination*. The other side conducts the *cross examination*. There are many limitations on what a witness may testify about, such as whether a witness can give an opinion or whether the witness may mention what someone told him or her. If an attorney believes a witness is asked an improper question, the attorney may make an *objection* (this process is discussed in Chapters 10 and 11).

Next are *closing arguments* in which each side has the opportunity to sum up its case. Here the prosecution gets to go last, since it has the burden of proof. There are some states, such as Florida, where the defense gets to argue first and last if no evidence is offered by the defense except the defendant's testimony. After closing arguments (or in some jurisdictions *before* them), the judge will give the *jury instructions* on the applicable law. These include instructions on the elements of the crime charged, the presumption of innocence, and the burden of proof—which in criminal trials is proof beyond a reasonable doubt.

Once the jury has received its instructions, it retires to the jury room to deliberate. It remains there until a *verdict* is reached. In most jurisdictions, criminal verdicts must be unanimous. Failure to achieve a unanimous jury means the case is declared a mistrial. If a mistrial occurs, the defendant may be retried without violating the prohibition against double jeopardy.

Sentencing

If a jury returns a verdict of "not guilty," the defendant is set free. The constitutional prohibition on double jeopardy prevents the state from prosecuting the defendant again for the same act. If the verdict is "guilty," then *sentence* must be imposed. In most instances the judge imposes the sentence. The exception is death penalty cases in which the jury traditionally imposes, or at the very least recommends, the sentence. The sentence is usually not handed down immediately after verdict. Instead the judge orders a presentence investigation and sentencing recommendation, written by officers in a probation department.

A number of sentences are possible, including probation, a suspended sentence, or a fine. Factors influencing sentence include the information contained in the *presentence report*, the attitude of defendant, and the defendant's prior criminal and personal history. In recent years, there has been a move to increase sentence length and require incarceration. The result has been a tremendous increase in the number of persons incarcerated.

Appeals

Once a person has been convicted and sentenced, there are two ways for a defendent to challenge the trial outcome: a *direct appeal* or an indirect appeal, also known as a *writ of habeas corpus*. Habeas corpus translates as "you have the body," and the writ requires the person to whom it is directed to either produce the person named in the writ or release that person from custody. There is no federal constitutional right to an appeal, but every state allows a direct appeal by either statute or state constitutional provision.

The writ of habeas corpus is considered an indirect appeal because it does not directly challenge the defendant's conviction but instead challenges the authority of the state to incarcerate the defendant. The state defense to a habeas writ is based on the conviction—that is the basis for the defendant's incarceration. Habeas corpus is an ancient legal remedy, dating back at least to the Magna Carta. It is often referred to as the "Great Writ."

There is no time limit for filing of habeas petitions unlike direct appeals, which in most jurisdictions must be filed within a set period, usually several months. However, Congress has recently restricted the use of habeas corpus by imposing time limits on federal habeas petitions if there is evidence of intentional delay by the defendant that does injury to the prosecution's case. Additionally, Congress and the Supreme Court have recently restricted habeas corpus by imposing limits on how such appeals are filed and pursued, such as requiring that inmates include all their appealable issues in one writ, rather than doing separate, consecutive writs for each issue.

Summary

While justice may be an elusive concept—one with different meanings for different people—in the United States it is clear that the court system is intended to provide a forum for doing justice. There are many different types of courts, but all share this common feature. Courts serve as a forum for settling disputes between private parties, as a means of prosecuting individuals who break the law, and as a place where public policy is sometimes made. The common refrains "I'll sue you" and "I'll take it all the way to the Supreme Court" are evidence that courts are a popular forum.

This chapter has examined the structure of the federal and state courts. Both the federal and state court systems typically have three levels—the trial court, an intermediate appellate court, and a supreme court. The United States Supreme Court is the court of last resort, the final arbiter of legal disputes.

The courtroom is populated with a number of actors, all of whom are crucial to its operation. For our purposes, the three most important courtroom actors are the judge, the prosecutor, and the defense attorney. These are the individuals who will organize the presentation of evidence and conduct the examination of witnesses. The jury hears the evidence and makes a determination of whether the defendant is guilty as charged.

There are a number of steps in the trial process, which begins with an arrest or the filing of a complaint and the issuance of an arrest warrant. Each of these stages requires different actions by the courtroom actors. Evidence law is most prominently displayed during trial, but evidentiary issues may also arise and be dealt with in pretrial proceedings.

Discussion Questions

1. Explain the concept of jurisdiction and give four examples of the different types of jurisdiction.

2. How does a case get to the Supreme Court? What is the basis for acceptance of an appeal?

3. What are the three main purposes of the Supreme Court?

4. Who are the three key actors in court? What are the duties of each?

5. What is the Missouri plan and how does it work?

6. When a trial begins, which side presents its case first and why?

7. What causes a mistrial? What happens after a mistrial is declared?

8. What information might be included in a pre-sentence investigation? What do you think is the purpose of the pre-sentence investigation?

9. Briefly explain the different types of appeals.

10. What is *voir dire*?

11. What are the three types of functions courts provide?

12. What is the Judiciary Act of 1789 and what did it do?

13. What is the function of the district courts?

14. What does the phrase "court of last resort" mean and which courts does it apply to?

15. Who is the current chief justice of the Supreme Court and how long has he or she been chief justice? Who are the other eight members of the Supreme Court?

16. What is the purpose of a jury consultant, and who would be the most likely to hire one? Give an example of a real-life case where a jury consultant was likely involved in the jury selection process.

17. What are the methods of selecting judges?

18. List the process involved in pretrial proceedings in the order that they occur after arrest.

19. What is the purpose of a grand jury?

20. What are the different challenges available during *voir dire*? Have any of them been abused in the past?

Further Reading

Abraham, Henry J. (1987). *The Judiciary: The Supreme Court in the Governmental Process* (7th edition). Boston: Allyn and Bacon.

Blumberg, L. (1967). "The Practice of Law as Confidence Game: Organizational Co-optation of a Profession." *Law and Society Review* 15(1): 18–21.

Brigham, John. (1987). *The Cult of the Court*. Philadelphia: Temple University Press.

Graham, Barbara L. (1990). "Judicial Recruitment and Racial Diversity on State Courts." *Judicature* 74(1): 28–34.

Harris, David A. (1992). "Justice Rationed in the Pursuit of Efficiency: De novo Trials in the Criminal Courts." *Connecticut Law Review* 24: 382–431.

Horwitz, Morton J. (1977). *The Transformation of American Law 1780–1860*. Cambridge, MA: Harvard University Press.

Kelly, Alfred H., Winfred A. Harbison, and Herman Belz. (1983). *The American Constitution: Its Origins and Development* (6th edition). New York: W. W. Norton.

Meador, Daniel J. (1991). *American Courts*. St. Paul, MN: West Group.

Shreve, Gene R., and Peter Raven-Hansen. (1994). *Understanding Civil Procedure* (2nd edition). New York: Matthew Bender.

Slotnick, Elliot E. (1984). "The Paths to the Federal Bench: Gender, Race, and Judicial Recruitment Variation." *Judicature* 67(8): 370–388.

Smith, Christopher E. (1992). "From U.S. Magistrates to U.S. Magistrate Judges: Developments Affecting the Federal District Courts' Lower Tier of Judicial Officers." *Judicature* 75(4): 210–215.

Uphoff, Rodney J. (1992). "The Criminal Defense Lawyer: Zealous Advocate, Double Agent, or Beleaguered Dealer?" *Criminal Law Bulletin* 28(5): 419–456.

Wasby, Stephen L. (1993). *The Supreme Court in the Federal Judicial System*. Chicago: Nelson-Hall.

Cases Cited

Apodaca v. Oregon, 406 U.S. 404 (1972)
Batson v. Kentucky, 476 U.S. 79 (1986)
Hurtado v. California, 110 U.S. 516 (1884)
J. E. B. v. Alabama ex rel T.B., 511 U.S. 127 (1994)
Johnson v. Louisiana, 406 U.S. 356 (1972)
Williams v. Florida, 399 U.S. 78 (1970) ✦

Chapter Three

Some Important Underlying Concepts

Key Terms

* Affirmative defense
* Burden of persuasion
* Burden of production
* Consent
* Directed verdict
* Duress
* Exclusionary rule
* Excuse defenses
* Execution of public duties
* Good faith exception
* Inevitable discovery exception
* Insanity
* Intoxication
* Justification defense
* Mistake of fact
* Mistake of law
* Prima facie
* Proof beyond a reasonable doubt
* Proof by a preponderance of the evidence
* Proof by clear and convincing evidence
* Reasonable doubt
* Self-defense
* Silver platter doctrine

This chapter examines some concepts that are crucial to understanding how a criminal trial is organized. These concepts include procedural matters, such as which side has the burden of proof and the burden of production. The chapter also examines the typical affirmative defenses that may be raised by the defense.

Burdens of Production and Proof

In the United States, the criminal courts use the adversary system to establish the guilt of a criminal defendant. Both the prosecution and the defense are expected to do everything they can to win the case while playing by the rules set forth by the court system. In theory, this adversary system is intended to ensure that all relevant evidence will be brought out and that each side will have an opportunity to fully and adequately present its case. The prosecution has both the burden of production and the burden of persuasion.

The Burden of Production

The **burden of production** refers to the obligation placed on one side in a trial to produce evidence—to make a prima facie showing on a particular issue. A *prima facie showing means having enough evidence to justify submission of the matter to the jury if unchallanged by the other side. It is also called burden of going forward.*

In a criminal case, the prosecution has the burden of production. Placing the burden of production on the prosecution means a criminal defendant cannot be found guilty unless the prosecution introduces evidence to show that the defendant committed the crime. The defendant is under no obligation to introduce evidence that he or she is innocent. A failure by the prosecution to introduce evidence of each element of the crime charged will result in a **directed verdict** for the defendant, without any requirement that the defense introduce evidence or call any witnesses.

The Burden of Proof

The **burden of persuasion** is the burden placed on the party to convince the jury with regard to a particular issue. It is more commonly referred to as the *burden of proof.* Whereas the burden of production merely requires the prosecution to provide some evidence, the burden of proof requires the prosecution to provide evidence sufficient to justify a conviction.

There are different levels of the burden of proof depending on the type of trial. In civil matters, the burden of proof is typically **proof by a preponderance of the evidence.** This means that the facts asserted are more probably true than false. This burden is a relatively easy one to meet. The burden of proof in a criminal trial is **proof beyond a reasonable doubt.** This means that the facts asserted are highly probable. This burden is a very difficult one to meet. Another burden used in some civil and criminal matters (such as civil commitment proceedings and deportation hearings) is **proof by clear and convincing evidence.** This means that the facts asserted are quite likely true. It lies somewhere between proof by a preponderance of the evidence and proof beyond a reasonable doubt.

Every state has a statutory provision, usually found in the penal code, requiring that no defendant shall be found guilty in a criminal case unless guilt is established "beyond a reasonable doubt." Determining that the prosecution has failed to meet its burden of proof is different from determining that the defendant is innocent. That is why the verdict delivered is "not guilty" rather than "innocent." "Not guilty" is a legal finding that the prosecution has failed to meet its burden of proof, not necessarily a factual description of reality.

The reasonable doubt standard. The requirement that the prosecution prove the guilt of the defendant "beyond a reasonable doubt" is derived from the common law, and the Supreme Court has held that it is required by the due process clause of the Constitution (*In re Winship*, 1970). Precisely what constitutes "reasonable doubt" is less clear. Many courts have attempted to define it for the jury with varying degrees of success.

Table 3-1   Reasonable Doubt Standard Cases
In re Winship, 397 U.S. 357 (1970) *Commonwealth v. Webster* 59 Mass. 295 (1850) *Leland v. Oregon* 343 U.S. 790 (1952) *Victor v. Nebraska* 511 U.S. 1 (1994)

The reasonable doubt standard traces its roots as far back as the twelfth century. The phrase "moral certainty" was equated with "reasonable doubt" at that time. Achieving "moral certainty" meant that a juror was virtually certain of the defendant's guilt. The standard of persuasion at this time was often referred to as the "satisfied conscience test," meaning that jurors were to convict only if in their conscience they were sure that the defendant was guilty. While the language is different, the "satisfied conscience" standard is similar to the concept of "reasonable doubt" in that jurors were instructed that a guilty verdict should be delivered only if the evidence supporting it was very strong.

By the early eighteenth century, American courts commonly required proof of guilt beyond a reasonable doubt in criminal trials. There were few attempts to define the term. The most famous attempt came in *Commonwealth v. Webster* (1850). Most current definitions of **reasonable doubt** are derived from Chief Justice Shaw's oft-cited opinion, which states:

> [W]hat is reasonable doubt? It is a term often used, probably pretty well understood, but not easily defined. It is not mere possible doubt; because everything relating to human affairs, and depending on moral evidence, is open to some possible or imaginary doubt. It is that state of the case, which, after the entire comparison and consideration of all the evidence, leaves the minds of ju-

rors in that condition that they cannot say they feel an abiding conviction, to a moral certainty, of the truth of the charge.

Most states today have case law that provides some definition of reasonable doubt. While some states adhere to only one definition, other states accept multiple definitions. There are a number of commonly used definitions of reasonable doubt. They include "a doubt that would cause one to hesitate to act" (used in some form in at least 20 states), "a doubt based on reason" (used in 17 states), and "an actual and substantial doubt" (used in 10 states). Other less popular definitions include "a doubt that can be articulated" and "moral certainty" (Hemmens, Scarborough, and del Carmen 1997).

The United States Supreme Court has upheld several definitions of reasonable doubt. In *Leland v. Oregon* (1952), the Court recommended that courts define reasonable doubt using the "hesitate to act" formulation. In 1970, the Court in *In re Winship* applied the reasonable doubt standard to juvenile adjudications, and stated that the reasonable doubt standard is a constitutionally required protection for a criminal defendant. Justice O'Connor acknowledged in a more recent case (*Victor v. Nebraska*, 1994) that while the requirement of proof beyond a reasonable doubt "is an ancient and honored aspect of our criminal justice system, it defies easy explication." She noted, however, in upholding the jury instruction used in this case, that the Constitution does not require that any particular definition of reasonable doubt be used.

The Supreme Court has reason for concern over the definition of reasonable doubt. Researchers have conducted a number of studies of the abilities of juries to understand jury instructions. These studies have found that juror misunderstanding is created by the instruction's terminology, phrasing, and manner of presentation and by the general unfamiliarity of the jurors with legal terminology (Kassin and Wrightsman 1979; Severance and Loftus 1982). A study of Florida jurors found that half of the jurors who were given an instruction on the burden of proof erroneously believed a defendant was required to prove his innocence (Strawn and Buchanan 1976).

Several studies have attempted to determine how jurors quantify "reasonable doubt." One early study found that jurors quantified it as 87 percent sure of guilt (Simon and Mahan 1971), while a later study found jurors quantified it as 86 percent sure of guilt (Kassin and Wrightsman 1979). Interestingly, this result compares with an estimate of 90 percent or more by judges (McCauliff 1982). While these findings suggest that jurors understand the phrase "reasonable doubt" to mean something close to absolute certainty, it is unclear how different definitions of reasonable doubt might affect the quantification of the concept.

Other standards for the burden of proof. While the general rule is that the state has the burden of production and the burden of proof in a criminal trial, there are exceptions to the rule. If a defendant wishes to raise an **affirmative defense,** such as alibi, self-defense, or insanity, he or she must introduce evidence to support that defense. Thus the burden of production may be switched to the defense.

In most states, the burden of proof is also switched to the defense when an affirmative defense is raised. However, the general rule is that the burden of proof is by "a preponderance of the evidence" rather than "beyond a reasonable doubt." Proof by a preponderance of the evidence is the burden of proof used in civil trials and is often quantified as 51 percent sure, or if the jury believes it is more likely than not. This is a relatively easy burden of persuasion to meet. A few states do not switch the burden of proof to the defense but instead still require the state to disprove the affirmative defense beyond a reasonable doubt.

What is the purpose of the exclusionary rule?

Recently, a few states and the federal courts have changed the burden of proof for the affirmative defense of insanity, requiring the defense to prove it by "clear and convincing evidence." This quantum of proof lies somewhere between "a preponderance of the evidence" and "proof beyond a reasonable doubt." This shift in the level of the burden of proof was in response to several "not guilty by reason of insanity" verdicts in high-profile cases, such as the trial of John Hinckley Jr. for the attempted assassination of President Ronald Reagan. There was a feeling that defendants in such cases were finding it too easy to escape criminal liability for their actions.

The Exclusionary Rule

The **exclusionary rule** is a judicially created remedy for violations of the Fourth Amendment. It provides that any evidence obtained by law enforcement officers in violation of the Fourth Amendment guarantee against unreasonable searches and seizures is not admissible in a criminal trial to prove guilt. The rule was applied by the United States Supreme Court to the states in 1961, in *Mapp v. Ohio*.

The primary purpose of the exclusionary rule is to deter police misconduct. While some proponents argue that the rule emanates from the Constitution, the Supreme Court has indicated that it is merely a judicially created remedy for violations of the Fourth Amendment. Without a means of enforcing the prohibition on unreasonable searches and seizures through deterrence of police misconduct, the Fourth Amendment is reduced to a "form of words" (*Mapp v. Ohio,*) as police have no incentive to act lawfully.

The exclusionary rule is perhaps the most controversial legal issue in criminal justice. Application of the rule may lead to the exclusion of important evidence and the acquittal of persons who are factually, if not legally, guilty. Consequently, the exclusionary rule has been the subject of intense debate. Proponents argue it is the only effective means of protecting individual rights from police misconduct, while critics decry the exclusion from trial of relevant evidence. Despite calls for its abolition and shifts in the composition of the Supreme Court, the exclusionary rule remains entrenched in American jurisprudence. But while the rule has survived, it has not gone unscathed. Supreme Court decisions over the years have limited the scope of the rule and have created several exceptions.

History of the Exclusionary Rule

In 1914 the Supreme Court held that evidence illegally obtained by federal law enforcement officers was not admissible in federal criminal prosecutions (*Weeks v. United States,* 1914). Because the *Weeks* decision applied only against the federal government (the Fourth Amendment had not yet been incorporated), state law enforcement officers were still free to seize evidence illegally without fear of exclusion in state criminal proceedings.

Additionally, evidence seized illegally by state police could be turned over to federal law enforcement officers for use in federal prosecutions because federal law enforcement officers were not directly involved in the illegal seizure. This was known as the **silver platter doctrine** because illegally seized evidence could be turned over to federal law enforcement officers "as if on a silver platter." In 1960, in *Elkins v. United States,* the Supreme Court put an end to this practice, prohibiting the introduction of illegally seized evidence in federal prosecutions regardless of whether the illegality was committed by state or federal agents.

In 1949, the Supreme Court applied the Fourth Amendment against the states, incorporating it into the due process clause of the Fourteenth Amendment. However, the Court refused to apply the remedy of the exclusionary rule to the states (*Wolf v. Colorado,* 1949). Just three years later the Court modified its position somewhat, holding in *Rochin v. California* that evidence seized in a manner that "shocked the conscience" must be excluded as violative of due process. Exactly what type of conduct shocked the conscience was left to be determined on a case-by-case basis. The exclusionary rule thus became applicable to state criminal proceedings, but its application was uneven.

Finally, in 1961, in *Mapp v. Ohio,* the Supreme Court took the step it failed to take in *Wolf* and explicitly applied the remedy of the exclusionary rule to the states. The Court did so because it acknowledged that the states had failed to provide an adequate alternative remedy for violations of the Fourth Amendment. While there was language in *Mapp* suggesting that the exclusionary rule originated from the Constitution and was not merely a judicially created remedy, subsequent decisions indicate that the Court views the rule not as part of the Constitution but rather as a means of enforcing the Fourth Amendment prohibition against unreasonable searches and seizures.

Exceptions to the Exclusionary Rule

Table 3-2	Exceptions to the Exclusionary Rule and the Cases They Have Affected	
Exception	**Cases**
Good Faith Exception	*Illinois v. Krull,* 480 U.S. 340 (1987) and *Arizona v. Evans,* 514 U.S. 1 (1995)
Inevitable Discovery Exception	Nix v. Williams, 467 U.S. 431 (1984); *Mapp v. Ohio,* 367 U.S. 643 (1961); and *Weeks v. United States,* 232 U.S. 383 (1914)

The Supreme Court in *Mapp* stated that the exclusionary rule serves at least two purposes: the deterrence of police misconduct and the protection of judicial integrity. In recent years, however, the Court has emphasized almost exclusively the deterrence of police misconduct, leading to the creation of several exceptions to the rule. Additionally, the Court has held that the exclusionary rule does not apply to a variety of proceedings other than the criminal trial.

In 1984, the Court held in *Massachusetts v. Sheppard* and *U.S. v. Leon* that evidence obtained by the police acting in good faith, reliance on a search warrant ultimately found to be invalid may nonetheless be admitted at trial. The Court stressed that the primary rationale for the exclusionary rule—deterrence of police misconduct—did not warrant exclusion of evidence obtained by police who act reasonably and in good faith reliance on the actions of a judge. By "good faith" the Court meant the police were unaware that the warrant is invalid.

The Court emphasized that the **good faith exception** did not apply to errors made by the police, even if the errors were entirely inadvertent. The exception applies only to situations in which the police relied on others who, it later turns out, made a mistake. Subsequent cases reiterated this point. In 1987, in *Illinois v. Krull,* the Court extended the good faith exception to instances where the police act in reliance on a statute that is later declared unconstitutional. In 1995, in *Arizona v. Evans*, the Court refused to apply the exclusionary rule to evidence seized by a police officer who acted in reliance on a computer entry made by a court clerk that was later found to be in error.

The rationale for the good faith exception is that excluding evidence obtained by police who have not knowingly violated the Fourth Amendment and who relied in good faith on other actors in the criminal justice system does not serve the purpose of deterring police misconduct, the primary goal of the exclusionary rule. To summarize, the good faith exception does not apply to errors made by the police even if the errors were entirely inadvertent. It applies only to situations where the police relied on others who, it later turns out, made a mistake.

The Court has also established the **inevitable discovery exception** to the exclusionary rule. This exception, developed in *Nix v. Williams* (1984) permits the use at trial of evidence illegally obtained by the police if they can demonstrate that they would have discovered the evidence anyway by legal means. The burden is on the police to prove they would in fact have discovered the evidence lawfully even if they had not acted illegally. Police have only infrequently been able to successfully establish this exception.

Both the *Weeks* and *Mapp* decisions involved criminal trials. The Supreme Court has been reluctant to extend the exclusionary rule to other proceedings even if there is a potential for loss of liberty. The Court has held that illegally seized evidence may be admitted in a criminal trial if the purpose for admitting the evidence is not to prove guilt. Thus, illegally obtained evidence may be used to impeach a defendant's testimony or to determine the appropriate sentence. The Court has consistently refused to apply the exclusionary rule to evidence seized by private parties if they are not acting in concert with, or at the behest of, the police. The rule does not apply to evidence presented to the grand jury. An unlawful search does not bar prosecution of the arrestee, as the exclusionary rule is an evidentiary rule rather than a rule of jurisdictional limitation. The rule is inapplicable in both civil tax assessment proceedings and civil deportation proceedings. The exclusionary rule does not apply to parole revocation hearings.

Affirmative Defenses

A defense is a response made by the defendant to a charge in a criminal trial. It is raised after the prosecution has established its case and permits the defendant to avoid liability even when the government has met its burden of proof on the elements of the offense. There are two general defenses of justification and excuse. Justification and excuse defenses are referred to as *affirmative defenses* because the defendant must raise them in order for the jury to consider them (this is an example of the burden of production).

Generally, the defendant must also meet the burden of persuasion on an affirmative defense by a "preponderance of the evidence," although some states impose a greater burden of persuasion on the defendant for certain defenses such as the insanity defense, while other states require the prosecution to disprove an affirmative defense beyond a reasonable doubt.

Justification Defenses

A **justification defense** is raised when the defendant admits he or she is responsible for the act but claims that under the circumstances the act was not criminal—that it was lawful. Justified behavior precludes punishment because the conduct lacks blameworthiness. Examples of common justification defenses include self-defense, defense of others or property, consent, and the execution of public duties.

Self-defense. **Self-defense** may be successfully claimed if the defendant can demonstrate that he or she used force to repel an imminent, unprovoked attack that would have caused him or her serious injury. In such a situation the defendant may use only as much force as he or she honestly and reasonably believes is necessary to repel the attack—the defendant cannot use excessive force. Additionally, force may only be used against unprovoked attacks. This means the defendant cannot provoke the attack, or if he or she did, he or she must have withdrawn completely from the fight before asserting a right to self-defense. Force may be used only when the victim honestly and reasonably believes he or she is about to be killed or seriously injured. Threats that cannot be taken seriously do not justify the use of force. Force may be used only when an attack is either in progress or "imminent"—meaning it will occur immediately. It cannot be used to prevent a future attack. One cannot claim self-defense against someone who is justified in using force. Self-defense may be asserted only against an aggressor using unlawful force. Self-defense applies to both deadly and nondeadly uses of force. One may use deadly force only if faced with it. Less-than-deadly attacks authorize less-than-deadly responses.

There are a number of limitations and exceptions to the general rules of self-defense. The *retreat doctrine* requires that a person must retreat rather than use deadly force if it is possible to do so without endangering the retreator. This doctrine places a premium on human life and discourages the use of deadly force unless absolutely necessary and is endorsed by the majority of states. The *true man doctrine,* conversely, states that the victim of an attack need not retreat and may use whatever force is necessary to repel an attack, even if a safe retreat was possible. It is based on the idea that the criminal law should not force a victim to take a cowardly/humiliating position. Few states follow this doctrine today. The *castle doctrine* states that a person attacked in the home does not have to retreat, even if retreat is possible. This exception to the retreat doctrine is based on the idea that one's home is one's castle and that one should never be forced by the criminal law to abandon it.

Self-defense may also apply to defense of others and, in some circumstances, to the defense of property. Historically, defense of others was allowed only for family members. Most states have expanded this restriction to include other special relationships, such as lovers and friends, while other states have abandoned the special relationship requirement altogether. The "other" must have the right to defend himself or herself for the defender to claim the defense. Thus if A provokes an attack by B, C could not use force against B and claim defense of A. Most states restrict the use of deadly force to defense of the person or the home and allow only nondeadly force for defense of property. Some states, such as Texas, go further in allowing deadly force to protect land or certain types of property, such as natural gas.

Consent. Consent is a defense to some crimes. Most jurisdictions provide that persons may consent to suffer what would otherwise be considered a legal harm. The acts a person can consent to suffer are quite limited, however, and it must be demonstrated that the consent was voluntary, knowing, and intelligent. There can be no duress, trickery, or incompetence involved in the obtaining of consent. Additionally, one cannot consent after the fact to injuries already received.

Most jurisdictions allow consent only for minor injuries or for activities that society widely recognizes have a high potential for injury. An example of consent is professional athletes who choose to engage in activity in which injury similar to an assault may occur, as in a boxer punching another boxer. One cannot consent to serious injury, as to do so is assumed irrational. Thus, one cannot claim consent as a defense in mercy killing/euthanasia cases.

Execution of public duties. The common law allowed public officials to use reasonable force in the **execution of public duties.** This defense recognizes the value society places on obeying the law, and in permitting those charged with official duties the necessary authority to carry out those duties. Today an agent of the state, such as a police officer or soldier, is permitted to use reasonable force in the lawful execution of his or her duties. This defense allows the use of deadly force under the proper circumstances and also allows police to engage in activities that would otherwise be criminal if they are doing so as part of their law enforcement efforts, such as posing as a drug dealer.

At common law, police could use deadly force to apprehend any fleeing felon. At this time, felonies were capital offenses, and it was particularly difficult to apprehend fleeing criminals. This was known as the *fleeing felon rule*. The United States Supreme Court, in *Tennessee v. Garner* (1985), held that police use of deadly force to apprehend flee-ing criminal suspects was limited by the Fourth Amendment, which requires that all seizures be conducted in a reasonable manner.

Excuse Defenses

The second type of affirmative defense is the **excuse defense.** With an excuse defense the defendant admits that what he or she did was wrong but argues that under the circumstances is not responsible for the improper conduct. Examples of excuse defenses include duress, intoxication, mistake, age, and insanity.

Duress. **Duress** may be raised as a defense in a limited number of situations. For example, suppose A is forced by B to rob a store, who holds a gun to A's head and threatens to kill A unless A does as instructed. In this instance, A commits a serious crime, the robbery, but does so only to avoid a more serious crime, being murdered by B. Duress is allowed as a defense under the rationale that those forced to commit a crime in such circumstances do not act voluntarily, and the criminal law, as a practical matter, cannot force people to act irratio-nally against their own self-interest.

At common law, the defense of duress was permitted only when the defendant was threatened with both imminent and serious harm and when the act committed under duress resulted in less harm than the threatened harm. Most states now allow the defense for all crimes except murder (which is never excused), while some still limit the defense to minor crimes. Some states allow the duress defense only under fear of "instant harm," but most still follow the common law "imminent harm" rule. Threats to harm a third person or property do not constitute duress.

Intoxication. There are two forms of intoxication, voluntary and involuntary. **Intoxication** here refers to the effects of either alcohol or drugs. The effect of intoxication on criminal liability differs according to whether it was voluntary or involuntary. *Voluntary intoxication* never provides a complete defense, but it may be used to mitigate the punishment. Involuntary intoxication may provide a defense if it can be shown that the actor was unaware that he was being drugged. In such cases, the actor is excused because he or she is not responsible for becoming intoxicated; consequently, it would be unfair to hold him or her liable for the resulting uncontrollable and unintended action. Interestingly, the Supreme Court has held that due process does not require that states allow the defense of intoxication (*Montana v. Egelhoff*, 1996). Obviously, intoxication is also never recognized as a defense in situations where intoxication is an element of the crime, such as drunk driving or public intoxication.

Mistake. There are two types of mistake defenses—mistake of law and mistake of fact. The cliché "ignorance of the law is no excuse" is actually a misstatement. **Mistake of law** has always excused some (but very little) criminal responsibility. Ignorance is an excuse if the defendant undertakes reasonable efforts to learn the law but is still unaware that he or she has violated some obscure, unusual law. The constitutional prohibition on vague laws means persons must be provided with reasonable notice of what constitutes criminal conduct before they are punished for such conduct.

Mistake of fact excuses criminal liability when it negates a material element of the crime. The mistake must be both reasonable and honest. An example would be if a student took another student's notebook in class by mistake, thinking it was his or hers. While he or she has taken the property of another, as in larceny, he or she lack the requisite intent to deprive another of his or her property.

Age. Historically, youth has been treated as a defense to criminal liability on the ground that persons below a certain age lack the requisite mental capability to form *mens rea,* or criminal intent. At common law there was an irrebuttable presumption that children under the age of 7 years were incompetent. Children between the ages of 7 and 14 were presumed incapable, but this presumption could be rebutted by the prosecution. Children over the age of 14 were presumed to have mental capacity to form *mens rea,* but the defense could rebut this presumption. Today the various jurisdictions define the age of majority at different ages, ranging from 16 to 21.

Those classified as juveniles are dealt with not in the criminal justice system but rather in the juvenile justice system. The juvenile court was established as an alternate, more forgiving, approach to juvenile offenders and was based on the *parens patriae doctrine,* which holds that the state should act in the best interests of a child. Today the *parens patriae doctrine* of the juvenile court is slowly giving way to an increased desire to treat juveniles similarly to adult offenders; hence a number of states have removed juvenile court jurisdiction for serious crimes or repeat offenders, or have lowered the age at which a juvenile can be transferred to adult criminal court (Fritsch and Hemmens 1996).

Insanity. **Insanity** is a legal term that describes mental illness. It is not a medical term. Insanity excuses criminal liability by impairing the *mens rea* of the defendant. If a defendant is determined insane, then he or she is not blameworthy or culpable. Several legal tests for insanity have been developed over time, usually in response to a particularly egregious crime. They focus on the reason and willpower of the defendant. These tests include the right-wrong test (also called the M'Naghten rule), the irresistible impulse test, the Durham test, and the substantial capacity test. Each of the tests of insanity is slightly different.

The *M'Naghten test* for insanity focuses on the defendant's intellectual capacity to know what he or she is doing and to distinguish right from wrong. It is a two prong test: (1) the defendant must suffer from a disease or defect of the mind; and (2) this disease must cause the defendant either to not know the nature and quality of the criminal act or to not know right from wrong. Questions about this definition include the following: (1) What constitutes a "disease of the mind"? Is it any mental problem, or just a severe psychosis? (2) What does "know" mean? Most courts have held that it means intellectual awareness, which nearly everyone has. Other courts say it means being able to grasp an act's true significance. (3) What is "wrong"? Does it refer to what is defined as wrong by the law, or rather to what is considered immoral?

The *irresistible impulse* test for insanity is used when a defendant is unable to control his or her conduct because he or she suffers from a mental disease. This test holds that the defendant is not responsible if a mental disease kept him or her from controlling his or her conduct, even if the person knows the conduct is wrong. This test is broader than the right-wrong test, but critics have argued that it ignores mental illnesses that involve reflection.

The *Durham test* for insanity states that the defendant is not criminally responsible if his act was "the product of mental disease or defect." This is also called the *product rule*. It is an attempt to go beyond the right-wrong test's emphasis on intellectual cognition and the irresistible impulse test's emphasis on volition. This test has been widely criticized as too imprecise and has fallen out of favor.

The *substantial capacity test* defines insanity as when the defendant lacks substantial capacity to either control his or her conduct or appreciate the wrongfulness of his or her conduct. This test was developed by the American Law Institute, which drafted the Model Penal Code, and it became the majority rule during the 1970s. It is a modified version of the right-wrong and irresistible impulse tests. This test states that a defendant is not responsible if he or she lacks "substantial capacity to appreciate criminality of act or to conform his conduct." It requires that the defendant lack *substantial*, rather than *total*, capacity. The right-wrong and irresistible impulse tests are ambiguous on this point. It also uses "appreciate" instead of "know." Thus a defendant who knows right from wrong but doesn't appreciate the difference may be excused—unlike with the M'Naghten rule.

All of these tests have been criticized as either too difficult or too easy for the defense to prove insanity. Several states and the federal courts have recently limited the use of the insanity defense or have altered the burden of proof in establishing the defense. This movement stems from a fear that insane defendants will not be adequately punished or will be released too soon. An example is the 1984 Comprehensive Crime Control Act, passed shortly after John Hinckley Jr. was found not guilty by reason of insanity for attempting to assassinate President Ronald Reagan. This legislation shifted the burden of proof from requiring the government having to prove sanity beyond a reasonable doubt to requiring the defense to prove insanity by clear and convincing evidence (a tougher standard than the preponderance of the evidence standard usually applied to affirmative defenses). The Model Penal Code rejects this approach and requires the state to prove sanity beyond a reasonable doubt. Some states allow a verdict of "guilty but mentally ill" but require the state to treat the defendant in a hospital instead of putting him or her in prison. Some states have abolished the insanity defense altogether.

Summary

This chapter examined the burdens of production and proof. These burdens determine which side must present evidence, as well as the amount, or quantum, of evidence that must be presented in order to convince the jury. The burden of production in a criminal trial typically rests on the prosecution. It may shift to the defense, however, if the defense wishes to raise an affirmative defense.

Discussion Questions

1. Explain the exclusionary rule. What is it, and why do we have it? What case was before the Supreme Court when the exclusionary rule was applied to the states?

2. What is the "silver platter" doctrine?

3. What is the burden of proof? Who generally has to meet this burden? What are the exceptions to this rule?

4. Explain the good faith exception.

5. What is a justification defense? Give three examples and explain them.

6. What is an excuse defense? Give five examples and explain.

7. What is an affirmative defense?

8. Explain the M'Naughten rule.

9. Although there is no clear definition of "reasonable doubt," we do have many different interpretations of meaning. Why is there concern over having a definition?

10. Explain the inevitable discovery exception.

11. Explain the reasonable doubt standard. What cases has the Supreme Court used to define this standard?

12. Name and explain the different standards for the burden of proof.

13. Name the various exceptions to the exclusionary rule and the cases that established them.

14. What are the various definitions that have been used for the term reasonable doubt?

15. Give examples of what you believe to be the difference between a preponderance of the evidence and proof beyond a reasonable doubt.

16. What is the purpose of an affirmative defense?

17. What is the purpose of a justification defense?

18. What is the Durham test for insanity? What is the argument against this test?

19. What is the substantial capacity test?

Further Reading

Amar, Akhil Reed. (1997). *The Constitution and Criminal Procedure.* New Haven, CT: Yale University Press.

Brown, Richard Maxwell. (1991). *No Duty to Retreat: Violence and Values in American History and Society.* New York: Oxford University Press.

Bugliosi, Vincent. (1981). "Not Guilty and Innocent: The Problem Children of Reasonable Doubt." *Court Review* 20: 16–25.

DeLoggio, Louis. (1986). "Beyond a Reasonable Doubt—A Historic Analysis." *New York State Bar Journal* 58(3): 19–25.

Dressler, Joshua. (1995). *Understanding Criminal Law.* New York: Matthew Bender.

Fletcher, George. (1978). *Rethinking Criminal Law.* Boston: Little Brown.

Fritsch, Eric, and Craig Hemmens. (1996). *Juvenile Waiver in the U.S. 1977–1993: A Juvenile and Family Court Journal* 46: 3.

Gardner, Martin R. (1993). "The Mens Rea Enigma: Observations on the Role of Motive in the Criminal Law Past and Present." *Utah Law Review* 1993: 635.

Hart, Henry M. (1958). "The Aims of the Criminal Law." *Law and Contemporary Problems* 23: 401.

Hemmens, Craig, and Daniel Levin. (2000). "Resistance Is Futile: The Right to Resist Unlawful Arrest in an Era of Aggressive Policing." *Crime and Delinquency* 46: 472.

Hemmens, Craig, Katherine Scarborough, and Rolando del Carmen. (1997). "Grave Doubts About Reasonable Doubt: Confusion in State and Federal Courts." *Journal of Criminal Justice* 25: 231–254.

Kadish, Sanford. (1987). "Excusing Crime." *California Law Review* 75: 257.

Kassin, Sam, and Laura Wrightsman. (1979). "On the Requirements of Proof: The Timing of Judicial Instruction and Mock Juror Verdicts." *Journal of Personality and Social Psychology* 37: 1877–1887.

Katz, Leo, Michael S. Moore, and Stephen J. Morse. (1999). *Foundations of Criminal Law.* New York: Foundation Press.

Kerr, N., R. Atkin, G. Stasser, D. Meek, R. Holt, and J. Davis. (1976). "Guilt Beyond a Reasonable Doubt: Effects of Concept Definition and Assigned Decision Rule on the Judgments of Mock Jurors." *Journal of Personality and Social Psychology* 34: 282–294.

McCauliff, Carl. (1982). "Burden of Proof: Degrees of Belief, Quanta of Evidence, or Constitutional Guarantees?" *Vanderbilt Law Review* 35: 1293–1335.

Morano, Anthony. (1975). "A Reexamination of the Development of the Reasonable Doubt Rule." *Boston University Law Review* 55: 507–528.

Morris, Norval. (1982). *Madness and the Criminal Law.* New York: Oxford University Press.

Morse, Stephen J. (1985). "Excusing the Crazy: The Insanity Defense Reconsidered." *Southern California Law Review* 58: 777.

Schulhofer, Stephen J. (1974). "Harm and Punishment: A Critique of Emphasis on the Results of Conduct in the Criminal Law." *University of Pennsylvania Law Review* 122: 1497.

Severance, Louis, and Eric Loftus. (1982). "Improving the Ability of Jurors to Comprehend and Apply Criminal Jury Instructions." *Law and Society Review* 17: 153–197.

Shapiro, Barbara. (1991). *Beyond Reasonable Doubt and Probable Cause: Historical Perspectives on the Anglo-American Law of Evidence.* Berkeley: University of California Press.

Simon, Rita, and Linda Mahan. (1971). "Quantifying Burdens of Proof: A View From the Bench, the Jury, and the Classroom." *Law and Society Review* 5: 319–330.

Strawn, D., and R. Buchanan. (1976). "Jury Confusion: A Threat to Justice." *Judicature* 59: 478–483.

Ward, Patricia. (1997). "Judicial Activism in the Law of Criminal Responsibility: Alcohol, Drugs and Criminal Responsibility." *Georgetown Law Journal* 63: 69.

Cases Cited

Arizona v. Evans, 514 U.S. 1 (1995)
Boyd v. United States, 116 U.S. 616 (1886)
Commonwealth v. Webster, 59 Mass. 295 (1850)
Elkins v. United States, 364 U.S. 206 (1960)
Illinois v. Krull, 480 U.S. 340 (1987)
In Re Winship, 397 U.S. 357 (1970)
Leland v. Oregon, 343 U.S. 790 (1952)
Mapp v. Ohio, 367 U.S. 643 (1961)
Massachusetts v. Sheppard, 468 U.S. 981 (1984)
Montana v. Egelhoff, (1996)
Nix v. Williams, 467 U.S. 431 (1984)
Pennsylvania Board of Probation and Parole v. Scott, 118 S. Ct. 2014 (1998)
Rochin v. California, 342 U.S. 165 (1952)

Tennessee v. Garner, (1985)
United States v. Leon, 468 U.S. 897 (1984)
United States v. Calandra, 414 U.S. 338 (1974)
Victor v. Nebraska, (1994)
Weeks v. United States, 232 U.S. 383 (1914)
Wolf v. Colorado, 338 U.S. 25 (1949) ✦

Chapter Four

Forms of Evidence

Key Terms

- Actus reus
- Ascertainable fact
- Blank pad rule
- Circumstantial evidence
- Common knowledge
- Conclusive presumption
- Demonstrative evidence
- Direct evidence
- Indisputable fact
- Inference
- Judicial notice
- Judicial notice of adjudicative facts
- Judicial Notice of Law
- Judicial Notice of Legislative Facts

- Mens rea
- Modus operandi
- Motive
- Presumption
- Presumption against suicide
- Presumptions of fact
- Presumption of innocence
- Presumption of law
- Presumption of sanity
- Real evidence
- Rebuttable presumption
- Stipulations
- Tacit judicial notice
- Testimonial evidence
- Uniform Judicial Notice of Foreign Law Act

Introduction

In this chapter we turn our attention to "forms" of evidence. We begin with types of evidence, notably real and testimonial evidence. Then we draw distinctions between direct and circumstantial evidence. The bulk of the chapter is devoted to judicial notice, presumptions and inferences, and stipulations. Each of these four can best be understood as "substitutes" for evidence.

The various topics covered throughout this chapter are not unrelated to one another. For example, real evidence can be direct and circumstantial. Jurors can draw inferences based on testimonial evidence. Judicial notice can be taken with reference to real evidence. In short, there is a great deal of overlap between the various evidentiary topics covered in the next few pages.

What are the different types of evidence?

Types of Evidence

Two types of evidence will be repeatedly referred to throughout this text. The first of these is *real evidence*. **Real evidence** refers broadly to any tangible item that can be perceived with the five senses. Real evidence can consist of physical items, such as articles of clothing, weapons, and drugs. It can also consist of documents, such as contracts, letters, newspaper articles, and so on. Photographs, videos, and the like are also considered real evidence.

One particularly important type of real evidence is known as *demonstrative evidence*. **Demonstrative evidence** is, as the term suggests, evidence intended to "demonstrate" a certain point. Examples of demonstrative evidence are drawings and diagrams, displays and demonstrations, computer simulations, and many others. Don't confuse demonstrative evidence with the various types of real evidence mentioned in the preceding paragraph. What sets demonstrative evidence apart from other forms of real evidence is its ability to help jurors sort through a complex matter. For example, a diagram may show how several pieces of real evidence are linked together.

The second type of evidence that we will consider in this book is testimonial. **Testimonial evidence** refers to what someone says. However, not just anything that is said can be considered testimonial evidence. Testimonial evidence is evidence given by a competent witness who is testifying in court and under oath. Other types of testimonial evidence include affidavits and depositions taken out of court. The key to testimonial evidence is that it be given under oath. If a statement is not made under oath, it may not be admissible as evidence. Certain exceptions to this rule exist. Some hearsay statements, for example, are admissible in court as evidence (see Chapter 12). Table 4-1 shows the relationships between the types of evidence covered in this book.

Table 4-1	Types of Evidence	
	Real Evidence	**Testimonial Evidence**
Definition	Tangible items	Things people say
Types	Demonstrations Physical evidence	In-court testimony Validly obtained confessions

Direct and Circumstantial Evidence

We have already seen that the two *types* of evidence are real and testimonial. Now it is time to distinguish between two varieties of real and testimonial evidence: direct and circumstantial. It is possible for real evidence to be either direct or circumstantial, and it is also possible for testimonial evidence to be either direct or circumstantial.

What is the difference between direct and circumstantial evidence? **Direct evidence** is evidence that proves a fact without the need for the juror to infer or presume anything from it. It is evidence that speaks for itself—that *directly* proves a certain fact. By contrast, **circumstantial evidence** is evidence that *indirectly* proves a fact. Circumstantial evidence requires jurors to draw their own conclusions concerning whether the evidence in question should be taken as proof of the defendant's guilt (or lack thereof). Circumstantial evidence does not speak directly to the defendant's involvement in a crime; it shows involvement in a roundabout way.

An example of direct evidence is testimony by a witness that the accused committed the crime. Assuming the witness can be believed, his or her statements in court do not require that jurors *infer* the defendant's guilt. More specifically, if a witness testifies that she saw the defendant shoot the victim, jurors need not make much of an intellectual leap between the witness's testimony and the defendant's guilt. Again, this assumes that the witness is to be believed.

Another example of direct evidence could be a convenience store videotape clearly showing the defendant robbing the teller. If the video is properly authenticated (see Chapter 13), the jurors will not have to infer the defendant's guilt. In other words, the video speaks for itself. Unfortunately, direct evidence is not very common. By far the most common type of evidence is circumstantial. Thus, we will devote attention here to examples of and rules surrounding the admissibility of circumstantial evidence.

We have already described circumstantial evidence as being "indirect" in nature. Return to our example of the witness who saw the accused shoot the victim. If, instead, the witness testified that she overheard—rather than observed—the accused and the victim fighting and, further, that she heard a gunshot, jurors could only *infer* that the victim was shot by the accused.

Importantly, circumstantial evidence does not require that an inference be drawn. That is, once circumstantial evidence is presented to the jury, it is up to individual jurors to decide on the merits of the evidence in question. Some circumstantial evidence is highly convincing and nearly direct. Other types require a substantial leap between the evidence and the conclusion. Given the many types of circumstantial evidence (some strong, others weak), we frequently say that jurors "may" infer the defendant's guilt.

The most common methods by which jurors can infer the guilt of a suspect include circumstantial evidence (1) of the accused's ability to commit the crime, (2) of intent or motive, (3) of consciousness of guilt, (4) involving the victim, or (5) involving the character of the suspect or victim. Let us now consider each type of circumstantial evidence in more detail.

Ability to Commit the Crime

Sometimes it is clear that the defendant possessed the ability to commit the crime. This information can assist jurors in concluding that the defendant is guilty. Assume that the defendant is on trial for bombing a government embassy. If the prosecution can show that the defendant had the technical knowledge to construct a bomb, the jury may able to infer his or her guilt. By contrast, if the defense can show that the accused *lacked* the technical knowledge to build the bomb, jurors may infer that he or she is not guilty.

Another method by which the accused could be shown to have the ability to commit the crime is if he or she has the *means* to offend. For example, if the prosecution shows that the defendant owns a gun that it is of the same type and caliber as that used in the killing of the victim, the jury may infer the defendant's guilt. Or, if a youth is arrested and found to have sparkplug porcelain (a burglary tool) in his possession, and this evidence is introduced at trial, the jury may be able to conclude that the youth is guilty of burglary.

A defendant's physical capacity can also be considered evidence of an ability to commit a crime. If the facts of the case show that only a person with a certain body makeup could commit the crime, jurors may infer guilt. More specifically, if a victim was killed by being crushed with a 500-pound barbell, then jurors may be able to infer the defendant's guilt if he is "big" enough to complete such a feat.

Finally, a defendant's mental capacity may be enough to constitute circumstantial evidence of guilt. If it can be shown that the defendant possessed the knowledge and intelligence to engage in a sophisticated insider trading scheme, the jury may infer the defendant's guilt. If, by contrast, a defendant of subnormal intelligence—with no understanding of the stock market—is put on trial for the same offense, it would be difficult for the jury to infer guilt. The defense would capitalize on this fact and strive to show that the defendant could not possibly have been involved in such a sophisticated crime.

Usually, the defendant's mental capacity is *not* treated as circumstantial evidence. Indeed, most of the time the defendant's mental status is irrelevant. This is because most crimes are not highly sophisticated and most are committed by people of "normal" intelligence. Mental capacity usually only "matters" when the defendant claims insanity, when perhaps a juvenile is involved, or when, as we have seen, the crime requires a level of sophisticated knowledge that the ordinary person probably does not possess.

Intent or Motive

Three types of circumstantial evidence are relied on in order to show intent or motive. The first is **modus operandi,** which literally means "the method of operation." The second is motive, and the third is threats. If it can be shown that one of these three is present, jurors may be able to infer guilt.

If the prosecutor points out that the defendant has committed past crimes that are similar to the present one, this is circumstantial evidence. For example, if a homicide defendant has been twice convicted of murdering his victims by decapitation, then jurors may be able to infer guilt if the same method was used in the homicide for which the defendant is currently being tried. It is not enough for the prosecution to show that the defendant was convicted of similar crimes in the past; rather, it must show that the *method of operation* was the same. Importantly, evidence of prior crimes is usually not admissible. Thus, the prosecutor will need to convince the judge before circumstantial evidence of modus operandi will be allowed.

Motive can also provide circumstantial evidence of guilt. Motive rarely needs to be proven by the prosecution, unless it is an element of the underlying offense, but it can still help convince jurors that the defendant is guilty. For example, if the prosecution shows that a husband took out a $1 million life insurance policy on his wife before her murder, then it may also seek to convince the jury that the defendant sought to profit from his wife's death. Motive can also come from a need for revenge or retaliation and it can come from hate and prejudice. Countless other forms of motive can be identified depending on the nature of the underlying offense.

Finally, if it is clear that a defendant has threatened the victim of a crime on several occasions, the jury may infer that he or she is guilty. For example, if in a trial for aggravated assault, the prosecution shows that the defendant repeatedly threatened to "beat up" the victim, jurors may be inclined to infer guilt from this pattern of activity. Again, the decision on whether to assign value to such evidence is the jury's. It could be that the defendant has a pattern of making empty threats and never carrying them through to fruition. If the defense shows that this is the case, the jurors would probably downplay this form of circumstantial evidence. The prosecution would then need to introduce other evidence and make a more convincing case that the defendant is guilty of aggravated assault.

Consciousness of Guilt

If the prosecution can show that the defendant is demonstrating the habits of a guilty person, jurors may be inclined to infer guilt from such evidence. Guilt can be demonstrated in several ways, including flight, concealing or destroying evidence, possession of the fruits of crime, sudden wealth, and threats against witnesses. Let us briefly elaborate on each.

First, if a person flees in an effort to avoid punishment, guilt can sometimes be inferred. Why else would someone who is about to tried for a crime flee? Flight from the police, after being released on bail, and at other stages of the criminal process can be used to infer guilt. For example, if a securities fraud defendant flees the country following his release on bail—and assuming he doesn't seek refuge in a nonextradition country— when he is brought back to the United States for trial, the prosecution will probably point out to the jury that the defendant fled and that he should be considered guilty of the crime for doing so.

Next, if the prosecution can show that the defendant took steps to conceal evidence, jurors may again be inclined to infer guilt. Also, if it can be shown that the defendant consciously destroyed evidence, guilt may be inferred. Even falsifying or tampering with evidence can provide circumstantial evidence of guilt. For example, if the police find a discarded pistol with the defendant's fingerprints on it, the jury may conclude that his decision to throw the gun away is evidence of some criminal act; why else would someone throw away a perfectly good gun? Likewise, if the prosecution shows that the defendant attempted to flush illegal narcotics down the toilet, the jury may conclude that he or she is guilty.

Clearly, if the defendant is caught with the fruits of a criminal act, it may be tempting to infer guilt. Say, for example, that a burglary defendant is caught with stolen stereo equipment. If the prosecution introduces evidence of this at trial, the jury may conclude that the defendant is guilty of the crime. What about someone who possesses the fruits of crime but honestly does not know that the material was illegally obtained? Rarely is ignorance a defense, and it is still a criminal act in most jurisdictions to be caught in possession of stolen property.

Either way, when a defendant possesses material that he or she did not legally acquire, juries can easily infer a certain measure of guilt.

Circumstantial evidence of guilt also exists when the defendant appears to amass sudden wealth. For example, if the defendant in a narcotics trial recently bought a $2 million mansion—and does not appear to be engaged in any legitimate business activities—the jury may conclude that such sudden wealth is indicative of guilt. Indeed, in many such situations the government will seek forfeiture use of the defendant's property either civilly or criminally. All states as well as the federal government have laws that provide for the forfeiture of property that is used to facilitate a crime or is derived from criminal activity. Forfeiture applies to many offenses other than narcotics violations.

Finally, let us consider a hypothetical trial of a mafia kingpin. If the prosecution can show that the defendant repeatedly threatened to kill witnesses who would testify against him (perhaps through their own testimony), jurors may conclude that the defendant is guilty. The very fact that he would not want witnesses to say anything at trial suggests that he has something incriminating to hide.

Evidence Involving the Victim

Most circumstantial evidence directly involves the defendant: something about the defendant, such as his or her habits, life changes, experiences, and so on, points to guilt. However, circumstantial evidence can also involve other parties to a criminal case. In particular, if something has happened to a victim, this can provide circumstantial evidence of the defendant's guilt. Let us consider some examples.

First, assume a defendant is on trial for rape. His defense attorney claims that the victim consented to intercourse. However, the prosecution introduces expert medical testimony to the effect that the injuries suffered by the victim were not indicative of a consensual sexual encounter. In this instance, the victim's injuries help provide circumstantial evidence of the defendant's involvement in the crime.

As another example, let us assume that a man is on trial for first degree murder. He is accused of forcing the victim to get on his knees and shooting the victim in the back of the head, execution style. Assume further that the defense argues that the victim's injuries were self-inflicted and that the defendant could not have been involved in the crime because he was at the movies with friends. However, the prosecution introduces expert testimony to the effect that the victim's injuries were not consistent with suicide. That is, the prosecution argues that the injuries suffered by the victim were a result of an intentional shooting. With this information, the jury may be inclined to conclude that the defendant is guilty. And with additional evidence by the prosecution, such as evidence pointing to a gap in the defendant's alibi, and perhaps gun shot residue on the defendant's hands, its case would be substantially more persuasive.

Evidence Involving the Character of the Suspect or Victim

In Chapter 9 we will discuss the important topics of witness competency, credibility, and impeachment. Of these topics, credibility is important to our current discussion. Credibility refers to whether a witness should be believed. Credibility is basically synonymous with character. If a person is of questionable character, he or she may not be credible. Evidence concerning a person's character is not direct evidence. Rather, it requires that an inference be drawn. In other words, character evidence is circumstantial evidence.

Issues of character can be brought into a criminal trial in one of two ways. First, the defendant's character may be questioned. However, before a defendant's character can be attacked by the prosecution, the defense must first present testimony to the effect that the defendant is of solid moral character. Only when the defendant plays the character card can the prosecution attack his or her character. Whether the defense or prosecution is more convincing does not matter here; either way, the jury will be forced to infer that the defendant is of good character or not.

The character of victims is also called into question from time to time. For example, if the defendant in a criminal trial argues that he killed the victim in self-defense, he or she may attempt to show that the victim lacked character and was, perhaps, prone to violent outbursts. The character of rape victims has also been questioned in some criminal trials, but rape shield laws curtail this practice to a certain extent. Regardless of how victim character is called into question, jurors again must weigh this form of circumstantial evidence and reach their own conclusions concerning the defendant's involvement in the criminal act at issue.

Practice Pointer 4-1

It is sometimes necessary to use circumstantial evidence to prove guilt, but direct evidence is always preferable. Direct evidence is preferable because it does not require any inferences on the part of jurors.

Judicial Notice

Judicial notice is a procedure that courts use to determine the truth or falsity of a matter *without* having to follow the normal rules of evidence. Another common definition of judicial notice is any use by a court of a fact that has not been proved by ordinary evidentiary means. The normal rules of evidence are the main topic of this book. We turn later to specific rules for determining what types of evidence are admissible and when. Judicial notice, by contrast, does not require attention to any of these guidelines.

Why judicial notice? Without it, courts would be bound to the **blank pad rule.** This rule provides that the court and jury in a criminal case know nothing about the dispute between the two parties involved. The only way that the court and the jury come to know about the dispute is through evidence properly introduced. However, if *every* shred of information relevant to the case had to be introduced in accordance with the formal rules of evidentiary procedure, trials would take years.

Another way to understand the need for judicial notice is to put yourself in the shoes of a person with absolutely no knowledge or awareness of anything, except the English language. Without judicial notice, judges and jurors would have to be educated on every minute detail relevant to the case, from proving the sun rises every day, to showing where Idaho is located, to showing that gravity causes objects to fall to the earth, and so on.

Judicial notice is therefore best understood as a method for saving time. In this vein, judicial notice is something of a substitute for evidence; it gives all parties involved in any case—jurors, judges, and the attorneys—a means of agreeing on a particular fact without undue delay and debate. Understood in yet another way, judicial notice is legalese for preexisting or common knowledge.

Who Is Responsible for Judicial Notice?

Judicial notice is always taken by the judge in a case. That is, the judge gives judicial notice of certain facts. The term *judicial notice* itself suggests that a judge gives notice of something. The "something" that notice refers to is, again, anything that is common knowledge and that does not need to be presented to the court in accordance with the formal rules of evidence.

Varieties of Judicial Notice

There are several varieties of judicial notice. One is **tacit judicial notice,** which occurs when the judge does not make any statements to the effect that judicial notice is being given with regard to a certain fact. It is unspoken judicial notice. An example of tacit judicial notice could occur when jurors hear from a witness to a vehicle accident that the victim died in the crash. The court will give tacit judicial notice by allowing the jurors to infer that the term "vehicle" refers to some sort of automobile with four or so wheels. In such an instance, the judge will not interrupt the witness and explain to the jury what a vehicle is; every potential juror already knows.

Tacit judicial notice probably accounts for almost all facts that the court takes notice of. Rarely is it actually the case that a judge will pause to give judicial notice to a certain fact. Common knowledge is what it is—knowledge that almost everyone has. There seems little need to stop or otherwise interrupt a trial to reinforce common knowledge. Thus, it is not totally inaccurate to state that judicial notice is an academic exercise. It is hardly ever explicitly mentioned outside the pages of textbooks such as this.

The second type of judicial notice is **judicial notice of law,** which occurs when courts accept what is written in statutes, constitutional provisions, and court cases. A court could be given judicial notice that the penal code contains two elements for the crime of second degree murder: (1) intentional (2) killing of another. It would be a significant distraction if the parties were required to stop and convince the court that the penal code is authentic as well as written and enacted by the legislature.

What about the laws and rules of other jurisdictions? Judicial notice of law must be taken in the area that law covers. The very purpose of the laws of a particular state, for example, is that they be used and enforced by the courts. Many states have also adopted the **Uniform Judicial Notice of Foreign Law Act,** which requires that every court in a specific state give notice of the common law or statutes of every other jurisdiction in the United States. Next, because federal law is—to quote Article VI of the U.S. Constitution—"the supreme law of the land," all federal and state courts must given judicial notice of its provisions. Judicial notice can also be taken of municipal ordinances and administrative regulations, but it is typically limited to the courts that enforce them. Finally, judicial notice of foreign laws is hardly ever taken.

Closely connected to judicial notice of law is **judicial notice of legislative facts.** Legislative facts are the facts that courts rely on when interpreting statutes, constitutional provisions, and the like. Think of legislative facts as those bits of information legislators assume to be true when passing laws. For example, federal guidelines requiring that firearm retailers be licensed implicitly assume that guns are dangerous and can kill people. Accordingly, a court may give judicial notice that firearms are inherently dangerous.

The next type of judicial notice is **judicial notice of adjudicative facts.** Adjudicative facts constitute a catchall category. They are matters of general knowledge not otherwise connected to statutes, constitutions, administrative rules, or other sources of law. Given that there are so many types of adjudicative facts, we will explain them in a separate subsection.

Judicial Notice of Adjudicative Facts

According to Rule 201 of the Federal Rules of Evidence, a court can only take judicial notice of an adjudicative fact if it is (1) indisputable, (2) common knowledge, and (3) an ascertainable fact. Let us consider each of these criteria in some detail.

The "indisputable" component. An **indisputable fact** is one that speaks for itself and requires virtually no interpretation or debate as to its truthfulness (FRE 201[b]). We have included the terms "reasonably" and "virtually" in this definition because there are certain facts that can be disputed, however far-fetched the argument. For example, most educated people know that the earth is round, but some people still believe it is flat. Likewise, some organized groups steadfastly believe that humans were put on earth by aliens, even though there is no publicly available evidence—other than blind faith—to support such an outlandish claim.

The common knowledge component. "Common knowledge" seems simple enough, but it can be fairly difficult to define with precision (see FRE 201[b]). A fact is considered **common knowledge** if it is (a) generally known (b) by informed individuals (c) within the jurisdiction of the trial court. These three elements are discussed in the next three paragraphs.

The notion of an "informed individual" is somewhat abstract. For example, informed individuals know that the Supreme Court is made up by nine justices, even though many Americans are ignorant of this fact. Likewise, it is well known that exceeding the posted speed limit in one's car by 30 miles an hour is risky, but it can be quite a feat to convince young drivers that this is true.

Next, the phrase "within the jurisdiction of the trial court" refers to the district, county, or state within which the court sits. This limitation on judicial notice is important because there are certain bits of common knowledge in one area but not another. For instance, it would be common knowledge to Seattle residents that the Redhook brewery originated in Ballard, Washington. Jurors in other cities or states may not know this.

What, then, are facts that are "generally known"? Perhaps some specific examples from actual court cases will prove illustrative. Courts have considered it general knowledge that pistols are deadly weapons (*State v. Taylor*, 1916) and that full-choke shotguns scatter more than open-bore shotguns (*Sanders v. Allen*, 1911). Courts have also taken notice that automobiles cause extensive injury and loss of life (*State v. Przybyl*, 1937).

Generally known facts can have a historical dimension as well. For example, that the stock market crash of 1929 actually occurred is considered generally known. In fact, almost any documented historical event with a date attached to it can be considered general knowledge, even though many jurors' understanding of history is sketchy. Similarly, geographical facts can be considered general knowledge. Courts take judicial notice of the location of prominent geographic features, the division of the country into states, the division of states into counties, distances between certain points, and the like. It would be a waste of the court's time for the parties to prove such matters.

Other types of generally known facts include facts relating to nature and science as well as facts connected to language, symbols, and abbreviations. Certain natural events and varieties of scientific knowledge—even if not known to the layperson—can be considered generally known. Examples of such knowledge can be found in the laws of physics. With regard to language and symbols, courts usually take judicial notice of words defined in the dictionary. It would be a distraction to say the least if the parties to a case had to debate the meaning of certain words. They also take notice of symbols such as road signs; a red octagon with the word STOP in the middle is "noticed" as a stop sign. Similarly, courts take judicial notice of certain abbreviations—provided they are generally known. An example is the abbreviation Ph.D. after someone's name. Most people know that Ph.D. is an advanced degree known as a doctorate of philosophy in some subject (such as criminal justice).

The ascertainable fact component. Finally, getting back to our definition of an adjudicative fact, an **ascertainable fact** is one that can be determined by looking it up in some source (such as a dictionary), the accuracy of which cannot be easily disputed (FRE 201[b]). An example of an ascertainable fact is the distance in miles between Seattle and Los Angeles. The mileage can easily be determined by consulting a popular road atlas.

A fact cannot be considered ascertainable if it is exceedingly difficult to locate a source to back it up. Some facts are ascertainable only by experts trained to identify the information in question. For example, the periodic table of elements is a source whose accuracy cannot be easily disputed, but most laypeople cannot understand most of what it contains.

Obviously, certain sources cannot be trusted. A source is considered accurate if its accuracy cannot reasonably be questioned. Thus, a claim that someone's destiny is based on the day's horoscope is not a fact that courts will take judicial notice of; the accuracy of astrology can easily be questioned. Finally, with regard to the nature of the source, courts generally prefer to consult written documents when taking judicial notice of certain facts that need to be "looked up." Sometimes, however, people can serve as the source for factual information, provided their knowledge cannot reasonably be disputed.

Procedure for Judicial Notice

As indicated already, judicial notice will sometimes go without mention. The court and the parties to the case will automatically assume, without reflection, that certain facts are true. However, when the court opts to take formal judicial notice of a certain fact, it is required to follow a certain procedure according to the Federal Rules of Evidence (notably Rules 201[c]–[f]).

First, a court may take judicial notice of a certain fact without anyone requesting that the court do so. That is, neither attorney in the case has asked the court to take notice of a fact. Rather, the judge informs the parties to the case that the court has noticed, or intends to notice, a certain fact. This allows both parties an opportunity to contest the court's decision to take notice of the fact.

Both parties to a case can also formally request that the court take judicial notice of some fact. There are two components to such a request. First, the party seeking judicial notice of some fact must formally request notice. Second, the party must also provide the source of the fact and prove that the source is accurate. This method of securing judicial notice is also open to contest. For example, one party may succeed in securing judicial notice but the other may disagree.

What if one of the parties disputes the court's decision to take judicial notice on some fact? Usually, both parties and the judge will confer on the matter—outside the hearing range of the jury—on the judge's decision. There are two methods of contesting judicial notice. First, one or more parties can challenge the "propriety" of taking notice by showing that the fact is not generally known. Alternatively, one or more parties can challenge the "tenor" of the fact noticed. "Tenor" refers not to whether the fact is generally known but rather to whether the fact, as the court has interpreted it, is wrong.

It is conceivable that, even with a persuasive argument to the contrary, a court could wrongfully take judicial notice of a certain fact. If this situation occurs, the issue can be resolved at the appellate level. That is, appellate courts can decide whether the lower court's decision to take judicial notice was valid. Appellate courts can also take judicial notice of facts themselves— say, in the event that the lower court failed to do so. Parties cannot, however, request judicial notice at the appellate level; it is entirely within the discretion of appellate courts to do so.

More Benefits of Judicial Notice

As we have seen, judicial notice is something of an efficiency mechanism; it speeds events up. How precisely does it do so? First, judicial notice bars contrary evidence. That is, it prohibits the opposing party (if one party contests notice) from introducing evidence to contradict the fact. Second, judicial notice makes jury members' duties easier.

The court instructs the jury that it is to assume that a fact is true, which avoids time-consuming deliberations on its truthfulness. (See Table 4-2.)

Criticisms of Judicial Notice

Although judicial notice has advantages, haste can make waste. In particular, some critics of judicial notice have argued that it violates the Constitution. The Sixth Amendment guarantees the right to a jury trial, but when courts take judicial notice of facts, they essentially circumvent this provision. Similarly, when a court takes notice of a certain fact, it threatens the right of confrontation. Defendants are given the constitutional right to confront witnesses against them, but judicial notice—even if both parties to a case agree on the court's decision—essentially bars argument to the contrary. Table 4-2 summarizes these criticisms.

Table 4-2 Arguments for and Against Judicial Notice	
For	**Against**
Speeds events up	May violate Sixth Amendment
Bars contrary evidence	May threaten confrontation
Makes jury members' job easier	

Despite criticisms, judicial notice is here to stay. Without it, court cases would drag on indefinitely. Judicial notice is actually much like plea bargaining in this way. Both save the court's time. If every criminal defendant asserted his or her right to trial, or if every fact were subject to dispute, the wheels of justice would grind to a screeching halt; little, if anything, would ever be accomplished in our nation's courts.

Practice Pointer 4-2
While judicial notice is not without criticism, it behooves the parties to a case to seek judicial notice, especially judicial notice for adjudicative facts. Judicial notice of adjudicative facts saves time.

Presumptions and Inferences

Jurors rarely have occasion to witness the acts that call them to service. For example, jurors who have to decide the fate of a murder defendant rarely—in fact, probably never—witness the murder firsthand. If an individual juror *did* witness the murder firsthand, he or she would probably be a witness rather than a juror in the case. What happens in the real world is that jurors are presented evidence by both par-

Why do courts utilize presumptions and inferences?

ties and must make their own decisions as to whether the defendant actually committed the crime. Two methods of doing this are presumptions and inferences.

Distinguishing Between Presumptions and Inferences

With a **presumption,** a person draws a conclusion from one or more facts presented during a case. Understood differently, a presumption is a legal practice whereby a court accepts the existence of one fact from the existence of another fact that has already been proven. A presumption can also be understood as a substitute for evidence; it is a logical decision based on human knowledge, a decision that connects two or more important facts together in some fashion. Presumptions are covered in rule 301 of the Federal Rules of Evidence.

Inferences are often confused with presumptions, but there is a subtle distinction between the two. Presumptions are typically mandatory, meaning that the jury is *required* to draw some conclusion. **Inferences,** by contrast, are not mandatory. It is up to each jury member to draw inferences. As one court has put the matter:

> [an] inference is merely a logical tool which permits the trier of fact to proceed from one fact to another, whereas a "presumption" is a procedural device which not only permits an inference of the "presumed" fact, but also shifts to the opposing party the burden of producing evidence to disprove the presumed fact. (*Commonwealth v. DiFrancesco,* 1974)

Another court has drawn a distinction between inferences and presumptions in this way:

> Presumptions are one thing; inferences another. Presumptions are assumptions of fact which the law requires to be made from another fact or group of facts; inferences are logical deductions or conclusions from an established fact. Presumptions deal with legal processes, whereas inferences deal with mental processes. (*State v. Jackson,* 1989)

Because it is up to each individual juror to draw inferences, the rules of evidence make it difficult to restrict them. Presumptions, by contrast, are subject to several important restrictions. We therefore devote more attention to presumptions in the following sections.

Conclusive Versus Rebuttable Presumptions

Two types of presumptions can be identified. The first is a "conclusive" presumption. **Conclusive presumptions** require that all parties in the case agree with the decision. Further, conclusive presumptions are presumptions that cannot be challenged by either the prosecution or the defense. Finally, conclusive presumptions are used where the law demands that the presumption be drawn. They are sometimes called irrebuttable presumptions.

The second type of presumption is a **rebuttable presumption,** in which the party against whom the presumption operates may introduce evidence to disprove the presumption. Let us consider an example. It is reasonable to conclude that a letter that was stamped, addressed, and mailed arrived at the addressee. This is a *rebuttable presumption* because one party could argue that the letter never arrived. Another example of a rubuttable presumption would be asking the jury to infer that a person's disappearance for five years means that the person is dead. The party who would be harmed by this presumption—say, a murder defendant—would vehemently attempt to rebut such a presumption because people can disappear for five years and not be dead.

Presumptions of Law Versus Presumptions of Fact

Presumptions can also be divided into presumptions of law and presumptions of fact. With a **presumption of law,** the law requires that an inference or deduction be drawn. An example of one such presumption is the **presumption of innocence**: Our criminal justice system requires that accused persons be presumed innocent until proven guilty.

Presumptions of law do not require that members of the jury draw some conclusion in all cases and at all times. Rather, juries must assume the presumption is factual until evidence is introduced to the contrary. Thus, when the prosecution introduces evidence suggesting that the defendant is guilty, the jury can change its mind and declare that the accused is guilty. Another way to understand presumptions of law is to think of them as applying at the *outset* of a criminal case.

Presumptions of fact are not required by law. Instead, they deal with facts, issues, and circumstances as they arise. Presumptions of fact cannot be made at the outset of a criminal case, like presumptions of law can. The need for presumptions of fact arises once both parties to a case begin to present evidence. The presumption that a stamped, addressed, and mailed letter reached its addressee is a presumption of fact and is not necessary until such evidence is brought to light at trial.

The Effect of Presumptions

The effect of presumptions varies depending on whether the case is civil or criminal. We focus here on the effect of presumptions in criminal cases because the rules of civil procedure would make the discussion unnecessarily complex. There are two important effects of presumptions in criminal cases: (1) the effect on the jury and (2) the effect on the burden of proof.

First, presumptions have the effect of causing the jury to draw some inference. Returning to our example of the mailed letter, if the opposing party does not claim that the letter was not received, then the judge will instruct the members of the jury to conclude that the letter reached its recipient. That is, the judge will instruct the jury that it *must* conclude that the letter arrived.

The second effect of presumptions is on the burden of proof (see Chapter 4). First, however, it is important to remember that the burden of proof in a criminal case almost always falls on the prosecution; it is proof beyond a reasonable doubt that the accused committed the crime (see *In re Winship,* 1970). This means that the state cannot put the burden of proof of any elements of the crime on the defense (see *Sandstrom v. Montana,* 1979). However, when a rebuttable presumption is offered by the prosecution, the burden of proof shifts to the defense. In such an instance the presumption effectively "disappears," and the jury will be instructed by the judge to decide whether the presumption is factual.

A Sixth Amendment violation occurs when a conclusive presumption is required by law. This issue arose in the case of *Leary v. United States* (1969). In that case, Timothy Leary was convicted of "possession of marijuana knowing it was imported into the United States." The statute under which he was convicted required the presumption that people who possess marijuana *know* it was imported illegally. The Supreme Court held that the statute was unconstitutional because it did not leave it up to the jury to decide whether knowledge of illegal importation existed.

The Need for Presumptions and Inferences

Presumptions, like judicial notice, serve important purposes. First, since presumptions—especially conclusive presumptions—are substitutes for evidence, they speed up proceedings. Without certain presumptions, juries would be required to weigh every shred of evidence introduced by either side in the case. This process would be time-consuming and distracting.

Second, presumptions can serve important purposes for public policy outside the courtroom. As an example, it is commonly assumed that a child born in wedlock by two parents who live together (and by parents who are capable of having children) is legitimate. To assume otherwise would open a Pandora's box requiring that every child's parents be identified by DNA analysis. As another example, it is presumed that all people in the United States know criminal law (*Bakody Homes v. City of Omaha*, 1994). To assume otherwise would mean that every criminal defendant could claim ignorance as a defense.

Finally, presumptions are necessary for the normal functioning of governments and public organizations. For example, it is necessary to presume that public organizations and governments keep adequate records. Without such a presumption, the accuracy of records at all levels of government and in all public organizations could easily be disputed, causing unnecessary delay in daily functioning. If, for instance, a student could claim that her grade point average is really a 4.0, and not the 2.8 listed in her transcript, because a new person is working in the records office, universities would be an awkward predicament (and everyone would graduate with highest honors).

What purpose is served by the presumption of innocence?

Types of Presumptions

Rebuttable presumptions are much more common than conclusive presumptions. Also, because conclusive presumptions are mandated by law, a complete review of such presumptions would require an extensive search of each state's statutes. We devote most of our attention in the rest of this chapter to rebuttable presumptions. Such presumptions pop up in courts throughout the country and do not require knowledge of each state's statutory provisions.

Examples of rebuttable presumptions include: (1) the presumption of innocence, (2) the presumption of sanity, (3) the presumption against suicide, (4) the presumption of a guilty mind following possession of fruits of the crime, (5) the presumption of the regularity of official acts, (6) the presumption that young children are not capable of committing crime, (7) the presumption that people intend the consequences of their voluntary actions, and (8) the presumption of death following a lengthy unexplained absence. An example of a conclusive presumption is the presumption of knowledge of the law.

The presumption of innocence. As indicated earlier, because the presumption of innocence can be refuted it is a type of rebuttable presumption. As we also indicated, the presumption of innocence is required by law and exists until evidence is offered (by the prosecution) to the contrary. The rebuttable presumption of innocence requires that the prosecution prove beyond a reasonable doubt that the accused is guilty. One court has pointed out that the presumption of innocence

> is not a mere belief at the beginning of the trial that the accused is probably innocent. It is not a will-o'-the-wisp, which appears and disappears as the trial progresses. It is a legal presumption which the jurors must consider along with the evidence and the inferences arising from the evidence, when they come finally to pass upon the case. In this sense, the presumption of innocence does accompany the accused through every stage of the trial. (*Dodson v. United States,* 1928)

The presumption of innocence is not one that jurors are expected to know coming into the trial. It is the judge's responsibility to instruct the jury members that the accused should be presumed innocent until it is proven otherwise. Here is an example of such instructions that were upheld by the U.S. Court of Appeals for the Fifth Circuit:

> I remind you that the indictment is merely the formal charge against the defendants; it is not evidence of guilt. Indeed, the defendants are presumed to be innocent. The law does not require a defendant to prove innocence or produce any evidence at all, and no inference whatever may be drawn from the election of a defendant not to testify . . . The government has the burden of proving a defendant's guilt beyond a reasonable doubt, and if it fails to do that, you must acquit the defendant.(*United States v. Castro,* 1989)

The presumption of sanity. Another common presumption is the **presumption of sanity,** which means that every person tried for a criminal offense is assumed to be of sound mind—absent evidence to the contrary. You may be asking, what about defendants who are clearly insane? Nothing prohibits defendants from raising defenses such as sanity, but the salient point is that, *going into the trial,* the defendant is presumed sane. Also, if the defense attorney cannot show that the defendant is insane, the jury must *continue to presume* that the defendant is sane. Remember that the prosecution does not need to show that the defendant is sane; only the burden of proving guilt falls on the prosecution.

The presumption of sanity can more easily be understood with reference to the Fifth Circuit's decision in *United States v. Lyons* (1983). In that case the defendant sought to show that he was not guilty by reason of insanity. Specifically, the defendant tried show that he was involuntarily addicted to drugs. With regard to the presumption of sanity, the court stated:

> It is equally well established that the defendant is presumed sane, and where no evidence to the contrary is presented, that presump-

tion is wholly sufficient to satisfy the required proof that the defendant is sane, and hence responsible for his actions . . . however, should the defendant produce even slight evidence tending to prove his insanity at the time of the alleged offense, the government has the burden of proving the defendant's sanity beyond a reasonable doubt. (*United States v. Lyons*, 1983)

What is necessary to overcome the presumption of sanity? The answer depends on the state. Several different tests are used, and you will need to consult a criminal law text for the answer. Also, some states require that once the defendant has presented evidence to overcome the presumption of sanity, the prosecution must then show that the defendant was sane at the time the alleged offense was committed. Again, the reader should familiarize himself or herself with each state's requirements as necessary.

The presumption against suicide. When a person dies, it is presumed that the person did not die by his or her hand. That is, it is assumed that all people have an inherent respect for their own lives (and themselves) and, as such, are unlikely to contribute directly to their own mortality. Clearly this assumption is wrong some of the time, but the **presumption against suicide**—like the presumption of sanity—operates in such a way that someone is presumed to die by causes other than suicide unless evidence is offered to the contrary.

The presumption against suicide rarely arises in criminal cases. The reason should be quite obvious: One who has committed suicide cannot be charged for engaging in that act (suicide is a criminal act in most states). Rather, the presumption against suicide often arises in cases where a person's death may result in a life insurance payment. Under normal circumstances, the deceased will be presumed to have died of natural causes. The burden will then fall on the insurance company to show otherwise. In other words, the insurance company will be required to show that the deceased killed himself or herself.

The presumption of a guilty mind following possession of the fruits of crime. If the accused is caught with stolen property or the fruits of the crime, it is often presumed that the jury can infer guilt. As one court explained,

> Possession of recently stolen property, if not satisfactorily explained, is ordinarily a circumstance from which you may reasonably draw the inference and find, in light of the surrounding circumstances shown by the evidence in the case, that the person in possession knew the property had been stolen. (*Barnes v. United States*, 1973)

Without this presumption it would be exceedingly difficult to convict criminal defendants in the absence of full confessions. Let us consider an example. If a person is caught driving a stolen automobile and is tried for grand theft auto, and assuming the presumption we are referring to did not exist, the suspect would probably be acquitted. The only way to secure a conviction—absent the presumption that he who possesses the fruits of the crime is guilty—would be for the police to obtain a confession.

This presumption operates in the same way the others we have already discussed do. In particular, if the defense introduces evidence to the contrary, the presumption can be overcome. This is the very essence of a rebuttable presumption; the defense can try, and succeed, to sway the jury in another direction. If in our example the defense attorney were able to show that the accused thought he was borrowing a friend's car, the presumption of his guilt would be overcome and the jury would find the defendant not guilty of grand theft auto.

Can you think of an instance where a presumption can be misused in court?

The presumption of knowledge of the law. It is commonly said throughout criminal law that ignorance is not a defense. This statement carries some weight with regard to evidentiary procedure as well. Specifically, it is presumed that all persons in the United States know the law. In reality, thorough knowledge of the law is beyond even the most erudite lawyer, but without this presumption, guilty criminals would simply appeal to their own stupidity and escape conviction. Of course, accused persons are not presumed to know the law of other states or of other countries. This type of presumption is not rebuttable.

The presumption of the regularity of official acts. This presumption refers to the official acts engaged in by public officials. It is presumed that public officials going about their official duties do, in good faith, what is required of them. An example is the chain of custody. It is presumed that police officers who seize evidence from crime scenes do so properly. It is further presumed that the evidence is properly logged and stored until which point it is needed in court. Of course, this presumption can be overcome by evidence of tampering supplied by the defense. Absent such evidence, however, the jury will be required to infer that the evidence was not tampered with or improperly handled in any way whatsoever.

The presumption that young children are not capable of committing crime. Some states make it a conclusive presumption that children under a certain age—say, seven—are not capable of committing crime. Obviously, some very young children commit serious crimes. As a result, some states have changed this presumption to a rebuttable one. That is, if the prosecution can show that the child knew that the act he or she committed was wrongful, the jury would decide that the child-defendant is guilty.

The presumption that people intend the consequences of their voluntary actions. It has often been presumed that a person intends the consequences of his or her voluntary actions. To use a specific example, this presumption assumes that a person who kills another intended to do so. In at least two important cases (*Sandstrom v. Montana*, 1979; *Francis v. Franklin*, 1986) the Supreme Court has considered the constitutionality of instructions to the jury that it is required to presume that persons intend what they voluntarily set out to do. In both cases, the Supreme Court held that this presumption violates the Fourteenth Amendment's due process clause.

In the former case, the Supreme Court concluded that the Fourteenth Amendment was violated with a jury instruction "that the law presumes that a person intends the ordinary consequences of his voluntary acts." In the latter case, the unconstitutional jury instructions were "the acts of a person of sound mind and discretion are presumed to be the product of the person's will, but the presumption may be rebutted." Thus, it is unconstitutional to require (or even allow) juries to presume that defendants intend the results of their voluntary actions.

Why is this presumption unconstitutional? Recall that the burden of proof in a criminal case falls on the prosecution; its responsibility is to prove beyond a reasonable doubt that the accused committed the crime. Going back to basic criminal law, this requires that the state prove both important elements of a criminal act: *actus reus* and *mens rea*. **Actus reus** refers to the criminal act itself; **mens rea** refers to intent. This means that the burden falls on the prosecution to prove that the defendant intended to commit the crime. It is a violation of due process to require the defense to show that the defendant *did not* intend to commit the crime for which he or she is charged.

The presumption of death following a lengthy unexplained absence. Many states have so-called "presumed decedents laws." These laws permit a presumption that someone is dead after he or she has been missing for several years. Where this presumption is recognized and used, it is usually rebuttable. That is, the party against whom the presumption operates can introduce evidence to the contrary—evidence that the person who has disappeared is still alive somewhere.

In general, this presumption does not apply to fugitives from justice. The reason is that fugitives from justice seek to hide from authorities for as long as possible. However, at least one court has held that a person who was a fugitive from justice could still be presumed dead for life insurance purposes (*Blodgett v. State Mutual Life Assurance Co.*, 1961). Of course, the presumption remains rebuttable.

A Quick Summary

The reader may be somewhat confused concerning the distinctions between rebuttable and conclusive presumption vis-à-vis presumptions of law and presumptions of fact. Table 4-3 attempts to sort out the distinctions using some of the discussed presumptions as examples. Note that we have not discussed the conclusive presumption of fact (that today's date is accurate) is not listed above. Even so, it is clear that today's date cannot reasonably be disputed by an opposing party.

Table 4-3	Distinguishing Between Types of Presumptions (with Examples)	
	Conclusive Presumptions	Rebuttable Presumptions
Presumption of law	Presumption of knowledge of the law	Presumption of innocence
Presumption of fact	Presumption that today's date is accurate	Presumption of death following extended absence

Constitutional Requirements for Presumptions

When legislatures mandate specific presumptions in criminal statutes, they are bound by constitutional restrictions. In particular, the due process clauses of the Fifth and Fourteenth Amendments limit legislatively mandated presumptions. Basically, for the presumption to be considered constitutional, a rational connection must exist between some fact and a presumption that follows from it. Let us consider an example.

In the famous case of *Tot v. United States* (1943), the Supreme Court had occasion to decide on the constitutionality of a statute providing that "the possession of a firearm or ammunition by any such person shall be presumptive evidence that such firearm or ammunition was shipped or transported or received, as the case may be, by such person in violation of this Act." The Court declared that this legislatively mandated presumption was unconstitutional:

> Under our decisions a statutory presumption cannot be sustained if there be no rational connection between the fact proved and the ultimate fact presumed, if the inference of the one from proof of the other is arbitrary because of lack of connection between the two in common experience. This is not to say that a valid presumption may not be created upon a view of relation broader than that a jury might take in a specific case. But where the inference is so strained as not to have a reasonable relation to the circumstances of life as we know them, it is not competent for the legislature to create it as a rule governing the procedure of courts. (pp. 467–8)

Two important summary propositions can be gleaned from this quote. First, the presumption needs to logically follow some specific fact. If it is a stretch for the jury to presume something, then the presumption will be unconstitutional. Second, legislatively mandated presumptions should not shift the burden of proof to the defense in any way whatsoever. That is, the defense should not be forced to *prove* the defendant's innocence. The only time the defense should be required to offer proof against some presumption is if that presumption is specifically rebuttable, not conclusive or legislatively mandated.

Stipulations

Stipulations are agreements between opposing attorneys about some important fact. Stipulations can also be viewed as "concessions" made by either side to a case. Stipulations are usually made with regard to facts that have little bearing on the outcome of the trial. An agreement is reached in the interest of expediency and efficiency; it would be too time-consuming to debate trivial facts.

Some stipulations are made over relatively serious facts. For example, both sides often stipulate in advance that the defendant has one or more prior convictions. The advantage of doing so is that it minimizes potential for prejudice against the defendant if the issue is raised at trial. There are, however, important restrictions on the prosecution bringing in evidence of other convictions (see Chapter 10).

There are limitations on stipulations. One is that the defense should not stipulate to the prosecution on all points. To do so would be to put on an inadequate defense. Second, if either side stipulates in error, the court is not bound to accept the stipulation. In this vein, the court is not required to accept a stipulation that would be damaging to the defendant's case (see, for example, *United States v. Grassi*, 1979). Finally, stipulations can be withdrawn if the need arises.

Practice Pointer 4-3

Do not confuse stipulations with judicial notice. Stipulations are agreements between the parties to a case—usually the defense and the prosecution. The *court* is responsible for giving judicial notice.

Summary

There are two general types of evidence, real and testimonial. Testimonial evidence refers to what people say under oath. Real evidence is any tangible item and can also consist of demonstrative evidence. The latter refers to the use of demonstrations to prove a point. A computer simulation is demonstrative evidence, as would be the use of a diagram to outline a suspect's presumed patterns of movement.

Real or testimonial evidence can be either direct or circumstantial. Direct evidence is evidence that proves a fact without the need for the juror to infer or presume anything from it. It is evidence that speaks for itself. A knife with the victim's blood on it is direct evidence. Circumstantial evidence requires an inference that a certain assertion is true. For instance, it would be reasonable to conclude that a defendant is guilty if he or she had the ability and opportunity to commit the crime, along with intent to do so, motive, and consciousness of guilt. Other types of circumstantial evidence exist.

Judicial notice is best understood as a substitute for evidence. When a court takes judicial notice of something, it is concluding that something is true and need not be debated by the opposing parties in open court. It is a procedure that courts use to determine the truth or falsity of a matter *without* having to follow the normal rules of evidence. Without judicial notice, judges and jurors would have to be educated on every minute detail relevant to every case.

A presumption occurs when a person draws a conclusion from one or more facts presented during a case. Inferences are often confused with presumptions, but there is a subtle distinction between the two. Presumptions are usually mandatory, which means that the jury is *required* to draw some conclusion. Inferences, by contrast, are not mandatory. It is up to each jury member to draw inferences. Presumptions and inferences are also understood as substitutes for evidence, much like judicial notice.

We referred primarily to presumptions throughout this chapter, largely because they can be controlled by the courts. Individual jurors' inferences are somewhat beyond the control of the court. That said, there are two types of presumptions, conclusive and rebuttable. Conclusive presumptions are required, which means the opposing party cannot argue against the presumption. Rebuttable presumptions can be challenged by the opposing party. Presumptions are essential to the smooth operation of criminal trials. As such, they come in several varieties.

Stipulations are agreements between opposing attorneys about some important fact. They can be understood as "concessions" made by either side to a case. Stipulations can also be understood as substitutes for evidence, much like judicial notice and presumptions and inferences. They expedite trials and spare jurors the headache of having to decide inconsequential facts.

Discussion Questions

1. What is the difference between real evidence and testimonial evidence?

2. What is the difference between direct and circumstantial evidence?

3. What are the three types of circumstantial evidence relied on in order to show intent or motive?

4. What are the two ways that issues regarding the character of the defendant or victim can be brought into trial?

5. Explain three types of judicial notice.

6. What are the criticisms of judicial notice? Do you agree or disagree? Why?

7. Explain the main differences between inferences and presumptions. What purpose is served by the use of presumptions or inferences?

8. What are the constitutional requirements for presumptions?

9. What are stipulations, and why are they used?

10. What are the three procedures that are used as substitutes for evidence in court?

Further Reading

Fishman, C. S. (1992). *Jones on Evidence, Civil and Criminal* (7th ed.). Eagan, MN: West Group.

Graham, M. H. (1992). *Federal Practice and Procedure: Evidence* (interim ed.). Eagan, MN: West Group.

Lilly, G. C. (1996). *An Introduction to the Law of Evidence* (3rd ed.). Eagan, MN: West Group.

Mueller, C. B., and L. C. Kirkpatrick. (1999). *Evidence* (2nd edition). Gaithersburg, MD: Aspen Publishers Inc.

Strong, J. W. (1992). *McCormick on Evidence* (4th ed.). Eagan, MN: West Group.

Weinstein, J. B., J. H. Mansfield, N. Abrams, and M. A Berger. (1997). *Evidence: Cases and Materials* (9th edition). Westbury, NY: Foundation Press.

Cases Cited

Bakody Homes v. City of Omaha, 516 N.W.2d 244 (1994)
Barnes v. United States, 412 U.S. 837 (1973)

Blodgett v. State Mutual Life Assurance Co., 32 Ill. App. 2d 155 (1961)
Commonwealth v. DiFrancesco, 329 A.2d 203 (1974)
Dodson v. United States, 23 F.2d 401 (1928)
Francis v. Franklin, 471 U.S. 307 (1986)
In re Winship, 397 U.S. 358 (1970)
Leary v. United States, 395 U.S. 6 (1969)
Sanders v. Allen, 65 U.S. 220 (1911)
Sandstrom v. Montana, 442 U.S. 510 (1979)
State v. Jackson, 112 Wash. 867 (1989)
State v. Przybyl, 6 N.E.2d 848 (1937)
State v. Taylor, 182 S.W. 159 (1916)
Tot v. United States, 319 U.S. 463 (1943)
United States v. Castro, 874 F.2d 230 (1989)
United States v. Grassi, 602 F.2d 1192 (1979)
United States v. Lyons, 704 F.2d 743 (1983) ✦

Section II

Arrest and Search Procedure

Chapter Five

An Introduction to the Fourth Amendment

Key Terms

- Administrative justification
- Actual possession
- Constructive possession
- Curtilage
- Effects
- Enhancement devices
- House
- Justification
- Nonsearch
- Open field
- Papers
- Person
- Probable cause
- Reasonable expectation of privacy
- Reasonable suspicion
- Reasonableness clause
- Search
- Seizure
- Standing

Introduction

The Fourth Amendment to the U.S. Constitution is an outgrowth of the early colonists' fear of the English Crown. Prior to our nation's independence, the British Parliament issued so-called *writs of assistance*, which permitted English authorities to conduct unlimited searches of colonists without any justification. After independence was declared, the framers of the Constitution placed significant restrictions on government searches by adopting the Fourth Amendment.

On its face, the Fourth Amendment does not seem difficult to understand. However, it is likely that no amendment to the Constitution has been interpreted as much as the Fourth Amendment. The

Fourth Amendment has been subjected to intense scrutiny and commentary in courts' opinions and legal treatises, and literally millions of pages of text have been devoted to its interpretation. Everything from the meaning of "probable cause" to the intentions of the framers with respect to the warrant requirement have been debated by a host of legal and social commentators.

It is nearly impossible to develop a complete understanding of the scope and reach of the Fourth Amendment for at least two reasons. First, our Constitution continues to evolve; second, the composition of our nation's courts continue to change over time.

We have all heard that the Constitution is a "living document." The amendments to the constitution are "living" in the same sense. That is, they continue to evolve and change as the courts are faced with unique and perplexing cases. The Supreme Court has interpreted the meaning of the Fourth Amendment in a host of cases, but by no means has it addressed every unique search or seizure situation. For example, the courts are just beginning to address the issue of searches and seizures in cyberspace.

The composition of the courts, especially the Supreme Court, also continues to change, making it more difficult still to develop a firm grasp of the framers' intentions in adopting the Fourth Amendment. It is common knowledge that the Supreme Court has adopted a more conservative stance in the past three decades than it did during the 1960s. As a result, the Court has frequently handed down decisions favorable to law enforcement. As the composition of the Court continues to change, the Fourth Amendment will continue to be interpreted in different ways than it has in the past.

Two Clauses

The Fourth Amendment contains two basic clauses, the "reasonableness clause" and the "warrant clause," which help simplify the complex body of Fourth Amendment jurisprudence. The **reasonableness clause** proscribes unreasonable searches and seizures. As a result, many cases (thousands perhaps) have focused on the meaning of "reasonableness." The **warrant clause** requires that no warrants be issued without probable cause, supported by oath or affirmation, and particularly describing the place to be searched and the persons or things to be seized. Another broad category of cases, then, has addressed the meaning of "probable cause" and the components of a valid search warrant.

Our approach to the Fourth Amendment will roughly be divided into these two categories. This chapter will give special attention to the reasonableness requirement of the Fourth Amendment. It will also focus on the circumstances in which the Fourth Amendment does and does not serve to restrict the activities of law enforcement officials.

Chapter 6 will discuss warrants, particularly the requirements of a valid warrant, the process for serving warrants, and when warrants are required. Chapter 7, which continues our Fourth Amendment analysis, considers a number of unique situations where police searches and seizures can occur without warrants.

A question frequently asked about the relationship of the Fourth Amendment's warrant clause to the reasonableness clause is if warrants should be required for a search to be considered reasonable. The two Fourth Amendment clauses are separated by the conjunction "and," which has led to a great deal of debate concerning the relationship of one to the other.

Some have argued that the warrant clause is designed to give meaning to the reasonableness requirement, such that any search that is not conducted with a warrant should automatically be considered unreasonable. This view was expressed by Justice Frankfurter in *United States v. Rabinowitz* (1950, p. 83), where he asked:

> What is the test of reason which makes a search reasonable? . . .
> There must be a warrant to permit search, barring only inherent
> limitations upon that requirement when there is a good excuse for
> not getting a search warrant. . . .

Known as the "warrant requirement" interpretation, this view is subscribed to by many critics of warrantless searches. Those subscribing to this interpretation believe that a neutral magistrate should always come between the authority conducting the search and the citizen who is subjected to the search.

Another view is that the two clauses should be read independently of each other. According to this view, the reasonableness of a search should not depend on whether a warrant was obtained *or* whether there was a good excuse for not obtaining a warrant. Instead, those who believe that both clauses should be read separately focus on the factual circumstances justifying the police conduct in question. In other words, they look to the specifics of the case, focusing on the manner in which the search was executed, not on whether a warrant was secured prior to the police action. According to this view, the reasonableness of a search should be judged *after the search,* not before it, as with the strict requirement that a warrant be required *a priori.* This view is somewhat controversial, because it suggests that courts should be reactive instead of preventive when it comes to evaluating police misconduct.

A third and final perspective on the relationship between the warrant clause and the reasonableness clause is known as the "warrant preference" interpretation. This interpretation has become the most popular in recent years. In fact, much of the confusion surrounding the relationship of both Fourth Amendment clauses has been cleared up because of the compromise the warrant preference interpretation achieves. According to the Supreme Court in *Mincey v. Arizona* (1978, p. 390): "The Fourth Amendment proscribes all unreasonable searches and seizures, and it is a cardinal principle that searches conducted outside the judicial process, without prior approval by judge or magistrate, are per se unreasonable under the Fourth Amendment, subject to a few specifically established and well delineated exceptions" (see also *Vale v. Louisiana* 1970, p. 34). In other words, warrants should always be secured whenever it is practical to do so. If, however, an emergency presents itself, those in support of the warrant preference perspective are inclined to give the police a certain amount of deference and freedom with respect to searches and seizures.

What is the primary purpose of the Fourth Amendment?

Four Important Issues in Fourth Amendment Jurisprudence

The Fourth Amendment places distinct limitations on police activity. However, not all police actions are bound by the Fourth Amendment. It is important, therefore, to make sure that any constitutional analysis of police conduct proceed appropriately. Generally, four separate issues are to be considered.

Pre-fourth amendment analysis. To the ordinary, untrained person, the Fourth Amendment may seem to apply in any situation where the police look for or seize evidence. Nothing could be further from the truth. With regard to searches, for example, the Fourth Amendment applies only when the conduct in question is governmental and violates a reasonable expectation of privacy. When analyzing the Fourth Amendment, then, it is important to take into account the fact that the Fourth Amendment is not blanket protection against any form of law enforcement activity.

Reasonableness. On its face, the Fourth Amendment proscribes searches and seizures that are unreasonable. Unfortunately, there is no specific definition of "reasonableness." This is because the term has undergone significant interpretation by the Supreme Court in recent decades. In some situations, the Court has done away with the reasonableness requirement altogether. For example, airport metal detector searches can be conducted without any basis for suspicion. In other situations, the courts permit the police to stop and question people suspected of involvement in crime without probable cause.

The definition of reasonableness is often expressed in terms of "justification." Courts will ask what level of justification is required for a search to be considered reasonable. Three broad standards of justification will be introduced toward the end of this chapter: probable cause, reasonable suspicion, and administrative justification. It is important, therefore, to be able to (1) distinguish among different levels of justification and (2) determine which level of justification is required for the police conduct in question.

Warrant requirement. There are a number of situations in which the police can search for evidence (or people) and make arrests *without* a warrant. In fact, the courts continue to create exceptions to the Fourth Amendment's warrant requirement. The third important theme in a Fourth Amendment analysis is to understand which forms of police activity require warrants and which do not. One needs to ask, when is a warrant required? The next question for a search is, did the conduct fall within one of the established exceptions to the Fourth Amendment's warrant requirement? Or, for an arrest, did the arrest occur in a home or a public place? The answers to these questions naturally help determine whether the police activity in question comports with Fourth Amendment requirements.

Despite the conflicting arguments concerning the Fourth Amendment's warrant requirement, there are a number of situations where warrants are always required, such as arrests in a home absent exigent circumstances. Also, a number of essential features of the warrant requirement are scarcely disputed: (1) warrants require oath or affirmation, (2) warrants require probable cause, and (3) warrants must particularly describe the place to search and the items to be seized. Each of these topics will be discussed in this and the next two chapters.

Scope of police action. The Fourth Amendment also places significant restrictions on what the police can do when they conduct searches and seizures. Searches, if conducted with a warrant, are limited in terms of time and space. Even searches and seizures that can legally take place without a warrant, such as following a "hot pursuit," are limited. That is, there is a fixed amount of time the police have to serve a warrant, and they cannot look anywhere they choose for the items of interest. As a general rule, a search or seizure, whether or not conducted with a warrant, should be as minimally intrusive as possible. Thus, the fourth and final theme in our Fourth Amendment analysis requires us to give special attention to the scope of the police action permitted.

Basic Terminology

The Fourth Amendment protects "persons, houses, papers, and effects" from unreasonable searches and seizures. Very few court cases have focused directly on the meaning of these terms, but they nevertheless deserve mention. The reason these terms are important is that if the police activity in question is not directed toward a person, house, paper, or effect, no Fourth Amendment protections exist.

The term **person** describes individual people, whether citizens or not. "Person" also refers to the individual as a whole, both internal and external. The definition of *person* has recently been extended to include oral communications. In the case of *Olmstead v. United States* (1928), the Supreme Court declared that oral communications fell outside the scope of the Fourth Amendment. Examples of oral communications include confessions and admissions. Nowadays, however, following the Supreme Court's decision in *Katz v. United States* (1967), certain oral communications *do* trigger Fourth Amendment protections. Thus, a person's physical being, as well as anything a person communicates, falls within the meaning of "person" as described in the Fourth Amendment.

Houses, another Fourth Amendment term, is broadly construed to include any structure a person can occupy on a temporary or long-term basis. A hotel room is considered a "house," for purposes of the Fourth Amendment, even though a hotel room is generally used on a temporary basis. In addition, garages and other structures not connected to a "house" can nevertheless be considered "houses" for Fourth Amendment purposes. Whether specific structures can actually be considered "houses" depends on the notion of curtilage, which is defined later in this chapter.

Finally, "papers and effects" include all conceivable personal items. Business records, diaries, memos, and similar documents are considered **papers.** While **effects,** include such personal items as containers, purses, luggage, briefcases, cars, clothing, weapons, and any other tangible piece of property that a person possesses.

Given these broad definitions of persons, houses, papers, and effects, it is difficult to point to an item that is none of these. More than likely, *any* item that can be thought of or imagined falls within the meaning of the Fourth Amendment. This does not mean, however, that the Fourth Amendment always applies. For example, if a person discards a murder weapon (which is an effect), and if the weapon is found in an open field, as opposed to inside the person's house, the Fourth Amendment would not apply.

A Framework for Analyzing the Fourth Amendment

It is tempting to dive headlong into the meaning of reasonableness, the warrant requirement, and related Fourth Amendment topics. However, it is important to first "step back" from the Fourth Amendment itself and focus on when it applies. Not all forms of police activity are bound by the Fourth Amendment. If the police activity in question does not amount to a search or a seizure, the protections granted by the Fourth Amendment do not apply. This is one of the first important inquiries in any analysis of the Fourth Amendment. The second inquiry focuses on the justification required for conducting a search or seizure.

To define when a **search** takes place, three important factors need to be considered: (1) whether the presumed search is a product of government action; (2) whether the intrusion violated society's "reasonable expectation of privacy"; and (3) whether it infringes on an individual's "legitimate expectation of privacy." By way of preview, if the activity in question is not a product of government action, does not violate society's reasonable expectation of privacy, and does not infringe on an individual's legitimate expectation of privacy, the Fourth Amendment does not apply. Alternatively, if the activity is governmental and an expectation of privacy is violated, a search is said to have occurred.

Seizure, on the other hand, has a dual meaning. First, the fruits of searches are "seized." For example, if a search warrant authorizes officers to look for stolen televisions at 123 Oak Street and, upon service of the warrant, officers find stolen televisions in that location, the TVs may be seized. Seizures are not always limited to tangible evidence, though. The second meaning of the term *seizure,* refers to seizures of persons. Arrests are the most common form of seizure, but other seizures of persons can take place as well. For example, investigative stops, while not considered arrests, still fall within the meaning of seizure. Accordingly, this chapter devotes special attention to the definition of seizure.

The next step in the Fourth Amendment analysis is to focus on whether the search (or seizure) in question is reasonable. In other words, once the protections of the Fourth Amendment are triggered, the next step is to focus on whether the police acted in line with Fourth Amendment requirements. As we indicated, when courts focus on the reasonableness of a search or seizure, they speak in terms of *justification.* The question usually asked is, were the police justified in their actions?

The only justification mentioned in the Fourth Amendment is probable cause. The uninitiated reader may be inclined to think that any search or seizure based on a lesser degree of certainty than probable cause would violate the Fourth Amendment. For a time, this was the case. In recent decades, however, the Supreme Court has carved out exceptions to the Fourth Amendment's probable cause requirement. Basically, the Court has ruled that there are certain situations in which the police can seize people or look for evidence with a lesser degree of certainty than probable cause.

The remainder of this chapter is broken into four sections. First, we define searches, drawing distinctions between searches and "nonsearches." Second, we define seizures. By far the most complex of both definitions is that of a search, so our section defining seizure is comparatively brief. Third, we will focus on the doctrine of justification, introducing three specific standards of justification recognized by the courts: probable cause, reasonable suspicion, and administrative justification. Finally, we conclude this chapter with an introduction to the doctrine of standing.

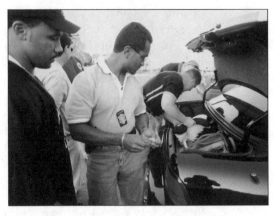

When may police officers search a suspect for contraband?

This chapter is intended to supply the foundation for further analysis of the Fourth Amendment. focusing (1) *when* the Fourth Amendment applies and (2) what justification is needed before looking toward the propriety of police action. In other words, this chapter focuses on what occurs *before* the police act. What the police do once the Fourth Amendment is applied and once justification is (or is not) in place is the focus of Chapters 6 and 7.

When a Search Occurs

A search can be defined, for our purposes, as the act of looking for evidence (e.g., police looking for narcotics during the service of a search warrant). However, not every act of looking for evidence can be considered a search *within the meaning of the Fourth Amendment.*

In drafting the Fourth Amendment, the framers sought to restrict police activity, but they did not express concern that everything the police (or government) do to look for evidence infringes on people's privacy. It is not the case, then, that the term *search* itself is difficult to define; it has a very simple definition. It is more difficult, rather, to define *when* a search occurs. Doing so involves drawing a distinction between searches and so-called nonsearches. A **nonsearch** occurs when the police look for evidence but their activity cannot be considered a search within the meaning of the Fourth Amendment.

To distinguish a search from a nonsearch, it is important to focus on (1) who is looking for evidence and (2) where they are looking for it. The "who" in this analysis requires that we distinguish between government actors and private parties. Basically, if a private party looks for evidence—even "searches" for it, it is not considered a search within the meaning of the Fourth Amendment, because the party looking for the evidence is not governmental. (Recall that the Bill of Rights is only binding on government actors, not private citizens.)

Second, *where* evidence is looked for has a direct bearing on whether the act of looking for evidence can be considered a search. The focus is on people's so-called reasonable expectation of privacy. To determine whether there is a reasonable expectation of privacy in a place to be searched, the courts almost always look to the place (house versus open field) in making their decision. The following subsections address the topics of (1) governmental versus private searches and (2) reasonable expectation of privacy.

Governmental Versus Private Action

The Fourth Amendment's protection against unreasonable searches and seizures has been limited by the courts to action that is governmental. When a private individual searches or seizes evidence, the person subjected to that activity is not protected by the Fourth Amendment. For example, assume that a man knows that his neighbor has a cache of illegal firearms in his garage. He could enter his neighbor's garage, seize the weapons, and turn them over to the police, and the neighbor would not be able to claim Fourth Amendment protection. This situation assumes the man acts independently of the police. Of course, the man could be prosecuted for trespassing, but the Fourth Amendment does not apply in such a situation. The evidence the man seizes could be used against his neighbor in a criminal trial and, unfortunately for the neighbor, there is *nothing* he can do that would lead to exclusion of the evidence.

The inapplicability of the Fourth Amendment to searches or seizures conducted by private individuals was first recognized by the Supreme Court in *Burdeau v. McDowell* (1921). In that case, some people illegally entered McDowell's business and seized a number of documents. The documents were then turned over to the attorney general of the United States, who planned to use the documents against McDowell at trial. McDowell sought return of the documents, and the district court granted his petition, but the Supreme Court ultimately declared that the Fourth Amendment's "origin and history clearly show that it was intended as a restraint upon the activities of sovereign authority, and was not intended to be a limitation upon other than governmental agencies" (*Burdeau v. McDowell*, p. 475).

Other Supreme Court cases have reaffirmed the *Burdeau* decision. For example, in *Coolidge v. New Hampshire* (1971, p. 487) the Court stated that if a private person "wholly on [his] own initiative" turns over evidence to the government "[t]here can be no doubt under existing law that the articles would later [be] admissible in evidence." And, in *Walter v. United States* (1980, p. 656), the Court declared that "a wrongful search and seizure conducted by a private party does not violate the Fourth Amendment and . . . does not deprive the government of the right to use evidence that it has acquired [from the third party] lawfully" (see also *State v. Oldaker,* 1983). A determinative factor is that the private party acts independently.

The issue of governmental versus private searches has been litigated extensively in the courts. Three broad categories of such cases can be identified. The first category of cases focuses on the characteristics of government actors. The second focuses on situations when private persons *not* acting wholly on their own initiative can be considered governmental actors for purposes of the Fourth Amendment. Finally, the third category of cases focuses on the types of actions authorized by private searches.

Government officials. Generally, it is not difficult to distinguish between a governmental actor and a private person. Most situations are fairly clear-cut. A uniformed police officer acting in his or her official capacity is clearly a governmental actor within the meaning of the Fourth Amendment. But what of other officials whose duties include law enforcement but who are not police officers? They too can be considered government actors. In the case of *Camara v. Municipal Court* (1967), for example, the Supreme Court declared that searches by regulatory officials conducting health and safety inspections can be considered governmental actions. This ruling has been expanded to include a number of other types of "government" workers, such as fire inspectors (*Michigan v. Tyler,* 1978), Occupational Health and Safety (OSHA) inspectors (*Marshall v. Barlow's Inc.,* 1978), federal mine inspectors (*Donovan v. Dewey* 1981), public school teachers (*New Jersey v. TLO,* 1985), and others.

The situation is not as clear for individuals who perform law enforcement functions but cannot be considered governmental officials. These types of individuals include store detectives (e.g., *Gillett v. State,* 1979), security guards (*Stanfield v. State,* 1983), and insurance inspectors (*Lester v. State,* 1978). The general rule is that when a private source is used *deliberately* in place of public law enforcement officials, Fourth Amendment protections are triggered.

When private individuals become government agents. A private person becomes a governmental actor when acting at the "behest" of the government. In *Coolidge v. New Hampshire* (1971, p. 487), the Supreme Court declared that "[t]he test . . . is whether [the private person] in light of all the circumstances of the case, must be regarded as having acted as an 'instrument' or agent of the state." In other words, when governmental actors join in on a private search or instruct the private party what to do during the course of the search, the private actor becomes a governmental actor for purposes of the Fourth Amendment.

A somewhat confusing situation is occurs when a governmental official does not actively participate in or order a private search but nevertheless provides information that leads to the private search or seizure. Consider the case of *People v. Boettner* (1974). In that case, a court upheld a search conducted by private university officials based on information supplied to them by the police, who, at the time, were proceeding with their own investigation of the incident. In another controversial case, *United States v. Lamar* (1977), the Fifth Circuit Court of Appeals declared that a search conducted by airline officials of an unclaimed bag was private, even though a police officer expressed interest in learning of the bag's contents. Both decisions seem to suggest that in certain circumstances it is appropriate for law enforcement officials to supply information leading to searches by private parties, provided they do not expressly order, request, or encourage the private search.

Practice Pointer 5-1

Police officers should be careful when relying on private parties to perform search functions when the police themselves cannot. Private parties can be government actors when they are used in place of the police, and any resulting search will be deemed unconstitutional if it is not supported by appropriate justification and/or a warrant.

What is authorized by a private search. A private search can evolve into a governmental search in certain situations. In *Walter v. United States* (1980), for example, sealed film canisters with suggestive labels were mistakenly sent to a company whose employees opened them but could not ascertain what was on the film. They turned the containers over to the FBI, which subsequently viewed the film and determined that it contained pornographic images. The Court ruled that because the FBI agents expanded on the private search by viewing the images on the film, the private search became governmental.

In another case, *United States v. Jacobsen* (1984), Federal Express employees opened a damaged package and found several packages containing white powder. They then closed the package and summoned federal agents, who reopened the package and conducted a field test on the powder. The Supreme Court upheld this action because the agents did not "significantly expand" on the private search. In the Court's words, "The agent's viewing of what a private party had freely made available for his inspection did not violate the Fourth Amendment" (p. 119). In addition, the field test of the substance (which turned out to be narcotics) had no more than a "*de minimus* [minimal] impact on any protected property interest."

The Supreme Court's opinion in *State v. Von Bulow* (1984, p. 1012) offers further clarification on the subject of private searches becoming governmental when government agents subject the fruits of private searches to additional scrutiny:

> No matter how egregious [the searchers'] actions may appear in a society whose fundamental values have historically included individual freedom and privacy, the exclusionary rule cannot be invoked by defendant to bar the introduction of evidence that was procured by [persons] while acting as private citizens. . . . Similar principles do not, however, govern our review of the evidence-gathering techniques employed by the state [the subsequent chemical testing of the fruits of the private search] . . . [W]hen the government *significantly expands a prior private search* . . . the independent governmental search is subject to the proscriptions of the Fourth Amendment [emphasis added].

Generally, a private party can turn evidence over to authorities without such action being considered a search. However, private parties become governmental when government actors encourage or order the private party to turn over evidence. Similarly, if a private party is deliberately used in place of a government actor, any evidence turned over by the private party will be considered the fruit of a governmental search. Finally, if the government "significantly expands" on a prior private search, the private search will be considered governmental. The situation is considerably less clear, however, when government actors supply information to a private party or know of or acquiesce to a private party's decision to search for evidence.

Reasonable Expectation of Privacy

Government action alone is not enough for the Fourth Amendment to be implicated. There are many things the police can do to look for evidence without such action being considered a search. Only when government action infringes on a **reasonable expectation of privacy** can a search be said to have occurred.

Prior to 1967, the definition of a search was closely tied to property interests. In particular, if the police were looking for evidence, their actions would not be considered a search unless they physically infringed on an individual's property. In essence, the police had to be trespassing in order for their actions to be considered a search. Conversely, any police activity that was not trespassory was not considered a search.

The property-based definition of a search became outdated in the landmark decision of *Katz v. United States* (1967). In that case, federal agents placed a listening device outside a phone booth in which Katz was having a conversation. When Katz made incriminating statements, the police sought to have them used against him at trial (on the grounds that the act of listening was not considered a search). The lower court declared that the police did not engage in a search because there was no actual entry into the phone booth. The Supreme Court reversed the lower court's decision, holding that the Fourth Amendment "protects people, not places" so its reach "cannot turn upon the presence or absence of a physical intrusion into any given enclosure" (p. 353). In the Court's words, "The Government's activities in electronically listening to and recording words violated the privacy upon which [Katz] justifiably relied while using the telephone booth and thus constituted a 'search and seizure' within the meaning of the Fourth Amendment" (p. 353).

An important feature of the *Katz* decision deserves mention. The Supreme Court stated that "[w]hat a person knowingly exposes to the public, even in his own home or office, is not subject to Fourth Amendment protection" (p. 351). Protection is only granted for "what he seeks to preserve as private" (p. 351). In a later decision the court stated, in a similar fashion, that what one voluntarily conveys to a third party (as in a conversation) does not enjoy an expectation of privacy, either (see *Hoffa v. United States*, 1966, and below). Still other decisions have suggested that there is an "assumption of risk" in certain activities, such as leaving one's garbage at the curb for pickup, (see *California v. Greenwood*, 1988).

Despite the significant change in the definition of search created in *Katz*, subsequent decisions have interpreted that decision rather narrowly. For example, in *California v. Greenwood* (1988), the Supreme Court ruled that a search or seizure occurs only where (1) a citizen has a manifested subjective expectation of privacy and (2) the expectation of privacy is one that society (through the eyes of the court) is prepared to accept as objectively reasonable. A *subjective* expectation is one in which an individual believes he or she enjoys privacy whereas, an *objective expectation* of privacy focuses on what a reasonable person (or in this case, society) would perceive as reasonable. Thus, according to *Greenwood*, it is not enough for a person to feel he or she should enjoy privacy in certain activity—the person's activity also needs to be one that society is prepared to construe as reasonable.

Today, courts rarely look at individuals' subjective expectation of privacy, opting instead to focus on a more general societal expectation of privacy. Therefore it is easy to determine how *Greenwood* narrowed the scope of *Katz*. *Katz* focused on privacy rather than property; *Greenwood* defined what is meant by privacy.

Despite the relatively narrow definition of a search offered in *Greenwood*, there remains no clear-cut definition of a search. Many important cases have focused on people's reasonable expectation of privacy with regard to certain forms of conduct. Four categories of such cases can be identified: (1) the "undercover agents" cases, (2) the "physical characteristics" cases, (3) the "open fields" and "curtilage" cases, and (4) the "enhancement devices" cases.

Undercover agents. When a person voluntarily conveys incriminating information during the course of a conversation, he or she cannot expect that the party to whom he or she is communicating will not go to the police with the information. What happens though when the third party is an undercover agent? In the case of *Hoffa v. United States* (1996), the Supreme Court took the opportunity to answer this question. In that case, the defendant, Hoffa, had a conversation with a union official who was in Hoffa's private suite by invitation. The union official turned out to be a government informant, and when he turned the information supplied by Hoffa over to the police, they sought to use it against Hoffa at trial. Hoffa sought to have the evidence excluded on the grounds that the government had engaged in an unlawful search. The Supreme Court disagreed, noting that the informant "was not a surreptitious eavesdropper" and "was in the suite by invitation and every conversation which he heard was either directed to him or knowingly carried on in his presence" (p. 302).

A somewhat more difficult question was posed in *On Lee v. United States* (1952). *On Lee* focused on the question of whether an informant could wear a recording device during a conversation with a suspected criminal. The majority ruled that such activity could not be considered a search, but only because the informant was invited into the area where the conversation took place. Justice Burton dissented, however, pointing out that the use of the recorder "amount[s] to [the agent] surreptitiously bringing [the police] with him" (p. 766). By contrast, the majority supported the use of the recording device on the grounds that it was designed solely to improve the accuracy of the evidence obtained by the informant. Other cases have yielded similar results (e.g., *United States v. White*, 1971; *Lopez v. United States*, 1963), but if the surveillance of the conversation is *not* consensual or is done in a surreptitious fashion, it will be considered a search (see *Katz*).

Similar questions have been raised with respect to so-called institutional agents. Institutional agents are people who work in some form of institution (such as a bank) and turn evidence over to authorities. They are not considered informants or undercover agents, just people who in the course of their work feel compelled to supply the police with incriminating evidence against certain individuals.For example, in *United States v. Miller* (1976), the Supreme Court ruled that a subpoena of records of financial information that was voluntarily surrendered to a bank could not be considered a search within the meaning of the Fourth Amendment. In other words, the Court argued that because the customer supplied the bank with financial information, he had no reasonable expectation of privacy that the bank would not turn the incriminating evidence over to authorities.

In *Smith v. Maryland* (1979), the Court declared that a person does not have a reasonable expectation of privacy regarding phone numbers he or she dials. In that case, authorities obtained a list of phone numbers the man called from the phone company. The Court stated that Smith should have known that a record of his phone calls would be maintained by the phone company. Finally, in *California v. Greenwood* (1988), the Court ruled:

> . . . garbage bags left on or at the side of a public street are readily accessible to animals, children, scavengers, snoops, and other members of the public. Moreover, respondents placed their refuse at the curb for the express purpose of conveying it to a third party, the trash collector, who might himself have sorted through respondents' trash or permitted others, such as the police, to do so. Accordingly, having deposited their garbage in an area particularly suited for public inspection and, in a manner of speaking, public consumption, for the express purpose of having strangers take it, respondents could have no reasonable expectation of privacy in the inculpatory items they discarded. (p. 40)

In sum, when people voluntarily convey or provide material to third parties (institutions or otherwise), they do not have a reasonable expectation of privacy. This is true even if the third party is a trusted friend who begins providing evidence for the state. Similarly, when people abandon their property (as in the *Greenwood* case), a Fourth Amendment search does not take place. In either situation, one cannot assume that the evidence will not be turned over to the authorities for further investigation.

Physical characteristics on public display. Another category of cases concerning reasonable expectation of privacy has focused on individuals' physical characteristics. In particular, the courts have held that a person's external physical characteristics are knowingly exposed to the public and thus not protected by the Fourth Amendment. For example, in *United States v. Dionisio* (1973), the Supreme Court opined that "No person can have a reasonable expectation that others will not know the sound of his voice, any more than he can reasonably expect that his face will be a mystery to the world" (p. 13). In *Dionisio*, the lower court required a handwriting sample from Dionisio. He objected on the grounds that requiring a handwriting sample is a search unsupported by probable cause. The Court disagreed. Subsequent cases have relied on the Supreme Court's ruling in *Dionisio* to justify the collection of additional forms of physical evidence, including locks of hair, voice exemplars, and fingerprints (e.g., *Davis v. Mississippi*, 1969).

Naturally, people possess physical characteristics that are not on public display. These usually fall within the protection of the Fourth Amendment. For example, in *Skinner v. Railway Labor Executives' Association* (1989, p. 616), the Supreme Court declared that blood, urine, and breath analysis all amounted to searches because "they intrude upon expectations of privacy as to medical information" (see also *Schmerber v. California*, 1966; *Winston v. Lee*, 1985; and *Cupp v. Murphy*, 1973).

Basically any part of a person's physical being that he or she displays to the public (even his or her voice) does not enjoy a reasonable expectation of privacy. A search does not occur, therefore, when a person is recognized by sight or other means of *external* physical identification.

Just because people's external physical characteristics are not protected by the Fourth Amendment does not mean that the Fourth Amendment fails to provide protection in other ways. Assume, for example, that the police wish to obtain fingerprints from a man who is suspected of homicide, but the man is home asleep in his home. The police cannot just waltz into the man's house without justification. Instead, they need a warrant in order to enter the man's house, arrest him, and take him to the station. In this example, the Fourth Amendment protects the man, but in a different way. In particular, the Fourth Amendment does not protect a person's external physical characteristics that are on display, so it is still essential to consider *where* the man is located. Because he is in his home—and because people always enjoy a reasonable expectation of privacy in their homes—the police need appropriate justification before entering. Referring back to the basic Fourth Amendment terminology introduced at the beginning of this chapter, the man's "person" may not be subject to Fourth Amendment constraints, but his "house" clearly is.

Open fields and curtilage. As we have indicated the physical setting in which police activity takes place is important when determining whether the Fourth Amendment applies. The inside of a person's home or residence is *always* protected by the Fourth Amendment, but what about the outside of the home? If the outside of the home falls within Fourth Amendment protection, how far beyond the home does the Fourth Amendment continue to remain in effect? When attempting to answer these questions, the Supreme Court has referred to the notions of "curtilage" and "open fields."

Curtilage has been defined by the Supreme Court as the "area to which extends the intimate activity associated with the sanctity of a man's home and the privacies of life" (*Oliver v. United States*, 1984, p. 225). This is in contrast to an **open field** which has been defined as any unoccupied or undeveloped real property outside the curtilage of a home (*Oliver v. United States*, 1984).

The term *open field* should not be taken literally. The property in question does not have to be "open" or a "field" to fall outside the scope of the Fourth Amendment. Instead, the property merely needs to fall beyond the curtilage of a home. For example, assume that a shed located 100 yards from a house is not used for "intimate activities." The shed can be considered an open field, even if it is on private property (see *United States v. Dunn*, 1987). The reason is that the shed does "not provide a setting for those intimate activities that the [Fourth] Amendment is intended to shelter from government interference or surveillance" (*Oliver v. United States*, 1984), the Supreme Court went on to point out:

> [T]here is no societal interest in protecting the privacy of those activities, such as the cultivation of crops, that occur in open fields. Moreover, as a practical matter, these lands usually are accessible to the public and the police in ways that a home, office, or commercial structure would not be. It is not generally true that fences or [No Trespassing] signs effectively bar the public from viewing open fields in rural areas. (p. 179)

It is troubling to some students of criminal procedure that private property can be considered an open field. Keep in mind that private property still enjoys a measure of protection. If a police officer or private citizen knowingly enters private property, the property owner may be able to pursue trespassing charges. In addition, in the case of a police officer illegally entering a person's property, the property owner may complain to the officer's supervisor or sue if circumstances permit.

To distinguish between open fields and curtilage, the courts often consider four separate factors: (1) the proximity of the area to the house, (2) whether the area is surrounded by a fence or other enclosure, (3) the nature of the use to which the land or property is being put, and (4) the steps taken by the property owner to protect the area from observation (*United States v. Dunn*, 1987). In *United States v. Dunn*, the police entered the defendant's property without a warrant, climbed over several fences, and then looked inside his barn. The Court ruled that this activity constituted a search within the meaning of the Fourth Amendment. See Table 5-1 for a summary of the discussion thus far.

Table 5-1 Question Asked When Distinguishing Between Open Fields and Curtilage
1. Is the area close to a house or a residence?
2. Is the area enclosed within a fence or similar enclosure?
3. To what use is the area being put?
4. What steps were taken to protect the area from observation?

An interesting subcategory of open fields/curtilage cases has arisen in recent years. It concerns occasions when the police perform fly-overs or aerial surveillance. For example, in *California v. Ciraolo* (1986), the Supreme Court ruled that naked-eye observation of a fenced-in backyard from a height of 1000 feet could not be considered a search. The Court argued that in "an age where private and commercial flight in the public airways is routine, it is unreasonable for respondent to expect that his marijuana plants were constitutionally protected" (p. 215). In essence, the Court suggested that fly-overs were analogous to "searches" of open fields. This is because airways are generally open to the public in much the same way unenclosed parcels of real property are accessible.

In another case, *Florida v. Riley* (1989), the Supreme Court ruled that the Fourth Amendment did not apply when the police flew a helicopter at an altitude of 400 feet over a person's partially covered greenhouse that was found to contain marijuana. According to the Court, "Riley no doubt intended and expected that his greenhouse would not be open to public inspection, and the precautions he took [including placing a wire fence around the greenhouse and a Do Not Enter sign] protected against ground-level observation" (p. 450), but he could not reasonably expect that any person would not position him or herself *over* the greenhouse in a helicopter. Had the police hovered over Riley's house at a lower altitude, their actions would have almost certainly been illegal. The Court noted that because the helicopter's altitude was within parameters established by the Federal Aviation Administration, the officers' actions were appropriate.

Another significant fly-over case was *Dow Chemical Co. v. United States* (1986). There, the Environmental Protection Agency (EPA) hired an aerial photographer to take pictures of the defendant's chemical plant. Even though the photographer was hired for the express purpose of observing the plant and did so with a camera instead of the naked eye, the Supreme Court ruled that a search did not occur (see also *Air Pollution Variance Bd. v. Western Alfalfa Corp.*, 1974).

Enhancement devices. It becomes considerably more difficult to decide if a search occurs when law enforcement officials rely on sensory **enhancement devices,** which include everything from flashlights and K-9s to satellite photography and thermal imagery. In determining whether the use of sensory enhancement devices constitutes a search, the courts usually focus on six separate factors: (1) the nature of the place surveilled, (2) the nature of the activity surveilled, (3) the care taken to ensure privacy, (4) the lawfulness of the vantage point, (5) the availability of sophisticated technology, and (6) the extent to which the technology enhances or replaces the natural senses.

With regard to the first consideration, the Supreme Court in *United States v. Knotts* (1983) decided on the constitutionality of federal agents' actions of placing a "beeper" (a tracking device) in a container and tracking that container to the defendant's cabin. Before entering the defendant's cabin, the police obtained a warrant. The question before the Supreme Court was, did the act of tracking the beeper on public roads constitute a search within the meaning of the Fourth Amendment? The Court answered "no," declaring that "[a] person traveling in an automobile on public thoroughfares has no reasonable expectation of privacy in his movements from one place to another" (p. 281). Important to this case was the fact that the "nonsearch" took place *outside* the defendant's residence. Had the police entered Knotts' residence without a warrant, the outcome almost certainly would have differed.

The lawfulness of the police vantage point is another determining factor with regard to sensory enhancement. In particular, if the police are not in a lawful vantage point (i.e., not authorized by law to be where they are), then a search occurs. Examples of lawful vantage points include sidewalks, streets, and, of course, public airways. As the Supreme Court declared in *United States v. Dunn* (1987), the police can take up position anywhere outside the curtilage of a home and be in a lawful vantage point. Therefore, if the police use a sensory enhancement device (such as binoculars) but are in a lawful vantage point, it is possible that the courts will not rule that a search occurs.

Interestingly, the Second Circuit decided otherwise in *United States v. Taborda* (1980). In that case, the police obtained lawful entry into the defendant's neighbor's house and peered into the defendant's house with a telescope. Drugs were spotted, but the court declared that the use of the telescope to view the interior of a person's home impairs a legitimate expectation of privacy.

Another factor in determining whether the use of sensory enhancement devices constitutes a search is the extent to which such devices are available to the general public. As discussed earlier in the *Dow Chemical* case, we saw that the use of camera equipment from publicly navigable airspace did not amount to a search because the "open fields" logic applied. Also, the Court suggested that the use of the camera equipment in *Dow Chemical* did not constitute a search because the camera equipment was available on the "open market." The Supreme Court did state, however, that "using highly sophisticated surveillance equipment *not* generally available to the public, such as satellite technology, might be constitutionally proscribed absent a warrant" (p. 238, emphasis added). Additionally, the use of "an electronic device to penetrate walls or windows so as to hear and record confidential discussion of chemical formulae or other trade secrets would raise very different and far more serious questions" (p. 238).

In a recent case, *Kyllo v. United States* (2001), the Supreme Court held that the Fourth Amendment is violated when "the Government uses a device [without a warrant] that is not in general use, to explore details of a private home that would previously have been unknowable without physical intrusion." In that case, the Court disallowed the warrantless use of a thermal imaging device to determine whether a home was radiating abnormal heat, because such a use is a search under the Fourth Amendment.

Courts will also give consideration to the extent to which enhancement devices "enhance" or "replace" the natural senses. Generally, the use of a device that enhances the senses, instead of replaces the senses, is not considered a search. Binoculars, for example, enhance the senses, which means that under certain circumstances, their use cannot be considered a search. Similarly, flashlights are devices that enhance the natural senses (by allowing people to see in the dark), and the courts have ruled that their use does not constitute a search (e.g., *Texas v. Brown,* 1983; *United States v. Dunn,* 1987). Devices such as satellites and thermal imagers are much more controversial, not only because they are not readily available to the general public but because they arguably replace the natural senses.

Another controversial sensory enhancement device is a "drug dog." Most courts have ruled that drug dog sniffs (such as in airports) do not violate the Fourth Amendment but their use is restricted if the police do not have justification *and* are on or close to private property (e.g., *United States v. Place,* 1983). For example, the Second Circuit ruled that the use of a drug dog adjacent to the defendant's apartment to determine the presence of narcotics *within* the apartment amounted to a search, thus triggering Fourth Amendment protections (*United States v. Thomas,* 1985). However, in *United States v. Colyer* (1989), the D.C. Circuit held that a dog sniff of a defendant's sleeper unit on a train did not trigger the Fourth Amendment because it was only inconsequently more intrusive than a luggage sniff in an airport.

The drug dog issue is not resolved, though, because one can argue that drug dogs are used to replace instead of enhance the natural senses. One court declared that the use of drug dogs is unconstitutional because "a free society will not remain free if police may use this, or any other crime detection device, at random and without reason" (*Commonwealth v. Johnston,* 1987, p. 465).

The final two issues courts consider when deciding whether the use of sensory enhancement devices constitutes a search are (1) the nature of the activity they are designed to uncover and (2) the care taken to ensure privacy. In general, if the activity in question takes place in a private home and significant steps are taken to ensure privacy (e.g., the curtains are drawn), the courts will be less inclined to give the police wide latitude in their use of sensory enhancement devices. However, if the activity takes place out in the open or does not enjoy a reasonable expectation of privacy, and if few if any steps are taken to ensure privacy, the use of sensory enhancement devices is more likely to be constitutional.

In closing, it needs to be underscored that throughout this section we have been dealing with the threshold question of whether the Fourth Amendment applies. In other words, was the activity governmental, and did it violate a reasonable expectation of privacy? If the answer to both parts of this question is no, the Fourth Amendment does not apply. If, however, the conduct in question *does* constitute a search, the Fourth Amendment does apply, and an additional question must be answered as to the type of justification required for the intrusion.

Table 5-2 summarizes the discussion in this section. It focuses specifically on where and when individuals enjoy an expectation of privacy. Remember, the "expectation of privacy" discussion pertains to only one element of a search; the other is government action.

Table 5-2 Where and When Does One Have a Reasonable Expectation of Privacy?	
Privacy Enjoyed	**Privacy Usually Not Enjoyed**
In one's residence In the curtilage of one's residence In cars and containers When one has the right to exclude others When one has continuing access In a private place of employment	In items/features knowingly exposed to the public In open fields In *abandoned* cars, containers, and other items When one is a temporary guest When one is "passing through" In most public places of employment

Practice Pointer 5-2
It is important for police officers to realize that the Supreme Court has, in recent years, taken significant steps to preserve personal privacy. The use of thermal imagers and other detection devices has been drastically curtailed. It is therefore advisable for police officers to obtain a warrant before using enhancement devices to detect evidence of criminal activity.

Next we briefly offer a definition of seizure. Just as a "nonsearch" fails to implicate the Fourth Amendment, so too does a "nonseizure" fail to grant constitutional protection.

Definition of Seizure

As far as the Fourth Amendment goes, seizure does not necessarily refer to the act of physically grasping something. Many things that law enforcement officials do fall short of actually touching a person but are still considered seizures. At the other extreme, the police can do many things to inconvenience people *without* triggering the Fourth Amendment. Two categories of seizures invariably arise: seizures of property and seizures of persons.

Seizures of Property

As the Supreme Court declared in *United States v. Jacobsen* (1984, p. 113), a seizure of tangible property occurs "when there is some meaningful interference with an individual's possessory interest in that property."

In determining whether a piece of property is seized, courts often refer to "actual" or "constructive" possession. A person has **actual possession** of a piece of property if he or she is physically holding or grasping the property. **Constructive possession,** by comparison, refers to possession of property without physical contact (e.g., a bag that is next to a person on the ground but not in his or her hands). A piece of property is seized within the meaning of the Fourth Amendment if the police remove it from a person's actual or constructive possession. An example would be the police taking a person's luggage at an airport and moving it into another room to be searched (see *United States v. Place,* 1983).

What is the difference between an arrest and a seizure?

We will encounter relatively few cases concerning seizures of property. Usually, property is seized *after* a search occurs. There are certain cases where seizures occur apart from a search. For example, in *Soldal v. Cook County* (1992), the Supreme Court had the opportunity to decide whether a landlord who removed a tenant's trailer from a trailer park (while the police looked on) "seized" the trailer. The Court ruled that a seizure did in fact take place.

Seizures of Persons

The seizure of a *person* occurs when a police officer, by means of physical force or show of authority, intentionally restrains an individual's liberty in such a manner that a reasonable person would believe that he or she is not free to leave (*Terry v. Ohio,* 1968; *United States v. Mendenhall,* 1980).

Seizure of a person can take place by a number of means. For example, a person is seized when he or she is arrested and taken to the police station for questioning (*Dunaway v. New York,* 1979). A person is also seized if he or she is physically restrained on the street in order to be frisked (e.g., *Terry v. Ohio,* 1968) or if he or she is pulled over by the police. The seizure of a person does not have to be "physical" for the Fourth Amendment to be implicated. For example, a seizure can occur when a police officer simply questions a person. The Supreme Court stated in *Terry v. Ohio*, that "[N]ot all personal intercourse between policemen and citizens involves 'seizures' of persons" (p. 20, n. 16), but a seizure *does* occur when the officer's conduct in conjunction with the questioning would convince a reasonable person that he or she is not free to leave.

Seizures of persons have also been considered in the context of foot pursuits. For example, in *California v. Hodari D.* (1991), the Supreme Court decided whether an officer who chased a suspect on foot had "seized" the suspect within the meaning of the Fourth Amendment. The officer did not have justification to stop or arrest the suspect but chased him anyway. The suspect discarded an item during the chase, which the officer stopped to pick up. The Supreme Court upheld the officer's action because the suspect was still in flight at the time the officer picked up the object.

As the Supreme Court noted in *California v. Hodari D.* (1991), when an officer chases a person but does not lay hands on the suspect, a seizure does not occur until which point the suspect submits to police authority. The Supreme Court also stated in *Hodari D.*, however, that a seizure *does* occur the instant a police officer lays hands on a suspect during a chase, even if the suspect is able to break away from the officer's grasp.

Important Clarification

Who decides when a search or seizure is "reasonable"?

The definitions of seizure offered in this section are general. We will discuss specific types of seizures in later chapters. While it is relatively easy to define when property has been seized, it is important to remember that there are different types of seizures of persons. An arrest is perhaps the most commonly understood form of seizure, but a seizure does not have to be an arrest. Accordingly, the following chapters will revisit seizures of persons, primarily in the sections on arrest (Chapter 6) and stop and frisk (Chapter 7).

When a Search Is Reasonable: The Doctrine of Justification

So far in this chapter we have focused on when the Fourth Amendment is implicated. We have done so by focusing on the definitions of search and seizure. Basically, the Fourth Amendment is implicated when a search or seizure occurs. But our Fourth Amendment analysis does not end there. The next step is to ascertain what the Fourth Amendment requires. As the Fourth Amendment states, people are protected from *unreasonable* searches and seizures. What, then, is unreasonable? To answer this question, the courts speak in terms of **justification.** Simply put, the police need to have justification, or cause, before a person (or property) is sought in an area that is protected by the Fourth Amendment.

Justification needs to be in place *before* the police act. In the case of a warrantless search, for example, the police need reason to believe that the item sought will be where they expect to find it *before* they start looking. Law enforcement officials cannot conduct searches without justification and then argue, after the fact, that they were justified in their actions. Thus, our discussion of justification is pre–Fourth Amendment in nature—it focuses on what needs to be in place before a search or seizure takes place.

The only standard of justification mentioned in the Fourth Amendment is probable cause. However, the Supreme Court has created a number of exceptions to the Fourth Amendment's probable cause requirements by focusing on the reasonableness clause. The Court has declared that there are certain situations in which searches or seizures can be considered reasonable even in the absence of probable cause. Generally, though, such searches or seizures are substantially less intrusive than those that must be premised on probable cause.

Justification can be understood in terms of gradations. The more intrusive the police action, the higher the level of justification required. Alternatively, the lower the level of intrusion, the lower the level of justification that is required. Three levels of justification can be identified: (1) probable cause, (2) reasonable suspicion, and (3) administrative justification. Probable cause is the most difficult of the three to establish, reasonable suspicion is the second most difficult, and administrative justification the third.

Probable Cause

Probable cause has the same meaning, regardless of the type of conduct the police engage in. It has been defined by the Supreme Court as more than bare suspicion. It exists when "the facts and circumstances within [the officers'] knowledge and of which they [have] reasonably trustworthy information [are] sufficient to warrant a prudent man in believing that the [suspect] had committed or was committing an offense" (*Beck v. Ohio*, 1964, p. 91). The Court later added that "the substance of all the definitions of probable cause is a reasonable ground for belief of guilt" (*Brinegar v. United States*, 1949, p. 175).

The Supreme Court has a tendency to be somewhat obtuse in its definitions of relatively simple concepts. Probable cause is no exception. Basically, probable cause exists when an officer has more than 50 percent certainty of guilt (for an arrest) or that the evidence will be found (for a search). Probable cause lies somewhere below absolute certainty and proof beyond a reasonable doubt and somewhere above a hunch or reasonable suspicion. It is about as certain as certain can get without the benefit of hindsight and a full-blown adversarial trial to determine guilt.

When the Supreme Court referred to the "prudent man" in *Beck v. Ohio,* it was basically speaking in terms of objective reasonableness. The Court was arguing that probable cause needs to be defined in terms of what the average "person on the street" would believe, not what a person who has received special training would believe. This is not to suggest that officers' training is irrelevant. Indeed, the Supreme Court has stated that "officers are entitled to draw reasonable inferences from these facts in light of their knowledge of the area and their prior experience . . ." (*United States v. Ortiz,* 1975, p. 897). Nevertheless, probable cause, if present, should be more or less apparent to the layperson and police officer alike.

Despite the uniform definition of probable cause set forth by the Supreme Court, the ingredients in the probable cause recipe differ depending on the type of conduct the police engage in. For example, when an arrest occurs, the police need probable cause that the person to be arrested has committed the offense. With regard to searches, though, the police need probable cause to believe the evidence sought will be found in the area to be searched.

It is critical to understand that probable cause can be required at different stages of the same encounter. Probable cause to search does not necessarily create probable cause to arrest. Alternatively, probable cause to arrest does not always lead to probable cause to search. If, for example, the police serve an arrest warrant at 123 Main Street and arrest the suspect, they are not automatically allowed to search the residence; they can only search the arrestee's grabbing area (see Chapters 6 and 7). The courts have placed significant restrictions on how searches and seizures are to be carried out. So probable cause to engage in one form of intrusion does not create probable cause to engage in another.

Probable cause is required in four separate situations: (1) arrests with warrants, (2) arrests without warrants, (3) searches and seizures of property with warrants, and (4) searches and seizures of property without warrants. When warrants are required, a judge decides whether probable cause exists by issuing the warrant. In situations where warrants are not required (or are impractical to obtain), the police officer on the scene makes the probable cause determination. In the latter case,

Probable cause can be obtained from police radio bulletins, tips from "good citizen" informers who have happened by chance to see criminal activity, reports from victims, anonymous tips, and tips from "habitual" informers who mingle with people in the underworld and who themselves may [even] be criminals. (Miles et al. 1988–89, p. 6:4)

The courts have devoted considerable effort to the definition of probable cause and to what types of information can satisfy the probable cause burden. The courts have had occasion to consider when the following sources of information give rise to probable cause: (1) informants, (2) third parties other than informants, (3) officers' firsthand knowledge, and (4) mistakes.

The role of informants in the probable cause determination. An informant is generally someone who calls the police or contacts them and supplies them with information about a crime. There are three varieties of such informants: (1) anonymous, (2) confidential, and (3) "known." Anonymous informants do not supply their name to the police. Confidential informants are known to the police, but the police do not supply such informants' names in warrant applications. "Known" informants' names are supplied in warrant applications. Naturally, courts are somewhat cautious about anonymous and confidential informants.

The courts have created tests to ensure that information supplied by informants is reliable and accurate. In *Aguilar v. Texas* (1964), the Supreme Court developed a two-prong test that required police officers who apply for warrants based on information supplied to show (1) information to demonstrate how the informant knows what he or she knows, and (2) information to establish the credibility and reliability of the informant. These criteria came to be known as the *Aguilar* test.

For both prongs of the *Aguilar* test to be satisfied, the Court required police officers to be specific. For example, a statement to the effect that "this informant has provided reliable information in the past" would not be enough. Instead, to demonstrate the credibility of an informant, the officer would need to point to specific information. The officer should instead state something to the effect that "this informant has supplied information in the past that led to the conviction of Jane Doe" (see *United States v. Freitas*, 1983).

In *Spinelli v. United States* (1969), the Supreme Court attempted to clarify the first prong of the *Aguilar* test, the so-called credibility prong. It declared that if an informant has insufficient knowledge about the details of the reported criminal activity, the deficiency can be overcome if "the tip describe[s] the accused's criminal activity in sufficient detail that the magistrate knows that he is relying on something more substantial than a casual rumor . . . or an accusation based merely on an individual's general reputation" (p. 416).

In *Draper v. United States* (1959), the Court declared that the credibility prong of *Aguilar* may also be satisfied when the informant implicates himself or herself in criminal activity, provided that such a statement is not in the informant's self-interest. If, for example, an informant implicates herself in an effort to curry favor with the prosecution or the police, she is not viewed as possessing the same credibility as a non-self-interested informant (see *United States v. Harris*, 1971; *United States v. Jackson*, 1987, p. 349).

The *Aguilar* test was heavily modified (and, according to some, abandoned) in the landmark case of *Illinois v. Gates* (1983). In that case, the Supreme Court abandoned the two-prong *Aguilar* test, substituting it with a "totality of circumstances" analysis. In the Court's words, if ". . . a particular informant is known for the unusual reliability of his predictions of certain types of criminal activities in a locality, his failure, in a particular case, to thoroughly set forth the basis of his knowledge surely should not serve as an absolute bar to a finding of probable cause based on his tip" (p. 233). Stated differently, a deficiency in one of the *Aguilar* prongs can be compensated for with a substantial showing of proof in the other prong.

The courts now give consideration to five separate factors when determining whether information supplied by informants constitutes probable cause (see *Draper v. United States*, 1959). These factors include: (1) the extent to which the informant describes how he or she came to learn of the criminal activity; (2) the extent to which the informant supplies detailed information about the criminal activity; (3) whether the informant is reliable, based on past information he or she supplied; (4) whether the informant predicts criminal activity that is corroborated by additional police work (information plus corroboration, as it is commonly described); and (5) whether the informant selflessly implicates himself or herself in criminal activity. Unlikely is the situation where one of these factors is enough to establish probable cause, but such a situation *is* possible.

Third parties other than informants. Naturally, information supplied by third parties other than informants can be used to establish probable cause. The two most common types of third parties are (1) victims and witnesses and (2) other police officers or government officials. More often than not, information supplied by victims, witnesses, and other police officers is not scrutinized to the extent that information supplied by informants is.

When a person has been a victim or has witnessed a crime, the courts generally relax the *Aguilar-Spinelli* tests discussed in the preceding section. For example, in *Jaben v. United States* (1965, p. 224), the Supreme Court held that "whereas some supporting information concerning the credibility of informants in narcotics cases or other common garden varieties of crime may be required, such information is not so necessary in the context of the case before us [where third parties provided information about the defendant's tax evasion case]." Because victims and witnesses are rarely self-interested, there is usually no incentive for questioning the truthfulness of their observations. Still, however, information supplied solely by witnesses or victims, provided that there is no evidence independent from either source, must still establish probable cause before the police can act.

The same rules apply to other police officers. In *United States v. Ventresca* (1965), the Supreme Court pointed out that "[o]bservations of fellow officers of the Government engaged in a common investigation are plainly a reliable basis for a warrant applied for by one of their number" (p. 111). Again the information supplied by other officers must establish probable cause before an arrest or search can take place. For example, a police officer cannot rely on a warrant that has been issued for a suspects' arrest if that warrant has been declared invalid because the warrant affidavit failed to establish probable cause (see *Whiteley v. Warden*, 1971).

The role of firsthand knowledge. A second source of information that the courts consider is police officers' firsthand knowledge. The courts are not usually as concerned with the accuracy or truthfulness of police officers' observations (when compared to that of informants), but they still give careful consideration to whether probable cause was in place prior to acting. A clear-cut case for probable cause being created by an officer's firsthand knowledge is when a person commits a crime in the officer's presence.

There have been a number of situations, however, in which the courts have had to decide whether probable cause to arrest or search can be based on an officer's firsthand knowledge about criminal activity but in which such activity does not necessarily take place in the officer's presence. With some exceptions, there are three categories of cases in which the courts have had to decide whether probable cause to arrest or search is created by firsthand knowledge. First, the courts have had to decide if postdetention information can be used to create probable cause. Second, courts have considered whether proximity to criminal conduct can create probable cause. Finally, courts have tried to decide whether criminal profiles can meet the probable cause burden.

With regard to the postdetention cases, courts have expressly stated that probable cause to arrest must be in place *before* the arrest takes place. Justification must be in place prior to police action, not afterward. Also, in *Sibron v. New York* (1968, p. 63), the Supreme Court stated, "It is axiomatic that an incident search may not precede an arrest and serve as part of its justification." Simply put, this means that the police cannot search people and seize evidence *before* probable cause is in place to arrest.

Of course, police activity that does not implicate the Fourth Amendment is exempt from these requirements. If a police officer stops a person on reasonable suspicion and frisks him because the officer fears for his or her safety, any evidence seized during the course of that frisk, such as a weapon, can be seized. Assuming a weapon is seized, the seizure can justify an arrest. Usually, however, arrests cannot be preceded by the type of search justified in the course of a stop and frisk.

In *United States v. Di. Re* (1948), the Supreme Court ruled that a suspect's proximity to criminal activity is not enough to create probable cause to arrest. In *Di. Re,* officers arrested a man on the grounds that there were two other men exchanging counterfeit ration coupons in close proximity to him. However, the Court pointed out that had the man even seen the illegal activity that "it would not follow that he knew they were ration coupons, and if he saw that they were ration coupons, it would not follow that he would know them to be counterfeit" (p. 593).

In another case, *Ybarra v. Illinois* (1979), the Supreme Court declared that just because the police had a warrant to search a bar, the warrant did not authorize them to search the bar patrons. Just because the patrons were in a location known for criminal activity, the police could not use such proximity to criminal conduct to justify a Fourth Amendment intrusion. According to the Supreme Court:

> [A] person's mere proximity to others independently suspected of criminal activity does not, without more, give rise to probable cause to search that person. Where the standard is probable cause, a search or *seizure of a person* must be supported by probable cause particularized with respect to that person. This requirement cannot be undercut or avoided by simply pointing to the fact that coincidentally there exists probable cause to search or seize another or to search the premises where the person may happen to be. (p. 91, emphasis added)

Another controversial form of firsthand knowledge concerns criminal profiles. In *United States v. Sokolow* (1989), the defendant was stopped, according to an airport agent, because his behavior displayed "all the classic aspects of a drug courier." As the Court remarked, the agent knew, among other things, that "(1) [the defendant] paid $2,100 for two airplane tickets from a roll of $20 bills; (2) he traveled under a name that did not match the name under which his telephone number was listed; (3) his original destination was Miami, a source city for illicit drugs; (4) he stayed in Miami for only 48 hours, even though a round-trip flight from Honolulu to Miami takes 20 hours; (5) he appeared nervous during his trip; and (6) he checked none of his luggage" (p. 3). Even so, the Court declared that the man's behavior did not justify arrest; however, it did justify an investigative stop (see below).

Mistakes in hindsight. There have been a number of cases in which information known to the police that helps establish probable cause turns out to be false. The courts have held, though, that as long as the officer *believes* the information to be true at the time of arrest, it is immaterial whether the information turns out to be mistaken in hindsight (see *Henry v. United States* 1959; *United States v. Garofalo,* 1974; *Franks v. Delaware,* 1978). However, if the officer's faith in untruthful information turns out to be *unreasonable,* probable cause may be found lacking.

In *Albright v. Oliver* (1994), the Supreme Court had the opportunity to decide whether a police officer's testimony against Albright violated the due process clause because the testimony was based on uncorroborated information from an informant who had proven to be unreliable on some 50 previous occasions. The Court pointed out that "[i]f Oliver gave misleading testimony at the preliminary hearing, that testimony served to maintain and reinforce the unlawful hauling of Albright into court, and so perpetuated the Fourth Amendment violation" (p. 279).

To summarize, probable cause is the justification required for arrests and searches with or without warrants. Probable cause can be established by various sources of information. It is most easily established when a crime is committed in a police officer's presence. However, since most crimes are *not* committed in the presence of the police, other sources of information are necessary. These sources include (1) anonymous informants, (2) confidential informants, (3) known informants, (4) victims and witnesses, (5) other police officers, and (6) firsthand knowledge. Information supplied by victims and witnesses as well as other police officers is generally regarded with a high level of credibility. On the other hand, the police need to be cautious when relying on information supplied by informants or firsthand knowledge that does not result from a crime being committed in the officer's presence. See Table 5-3 for a listing of "ingredients in the probable cause recipe."

Table 5-3 Some Ingredients In the Probable Cause Recipe
1. Prior record
2. Flight from the scene
3. Suspicious conduct
4. Admissions
5. Incriminating evidence
6. Unusual hour
7. Suspect resembles perpetrator
8. Evasive response to questions
9. Physical cues
10. Presence in high-crime area
11. Suspect's reputation of being involved in criminal activity

Reasonable Suspicion

When we discussed the definition of seizure earlier in this chapter, we emphasized that there are different types of seizures. Some fall short of arrest, or are not as intrusive as an arrest, and thus do not require probable cause. Lesser seizures require **reasonable suspicion.** For example, when a police officer pulls a motorist over for a traffic violation, probable cause is not required because such a stop is not considered an arrest or search. Similarly, if a police officer wishes to question a person on the street about suspected involvement in criminal activity, probable cause is not required, as long as the person is not arrested or searched. If probable cause were the standard of justification required for all contacts between the police and citizens, crime control would be seriously hampered.

Recognizing the importance of police-citizen contact for the purpose of investigating crime, the Supreme Court in *Terry v. Ohio* (1968) established the standard of justification commonly known as "reasonable suspicion." In *Terry,* an officer's attention was drawn to two men on a street corner who appeared to be "casing" a store for a robbery. The officer approached the men and asked them to identify themselves. He then patted the men down and found a gun on each man. The men were placed under arrest. They tried to have the guns suppressed when their case went to trial, but the Supreme Court ruled that the officer's actions were valid in the interest of "effective crime prevention and detection" (p. 22). Moreover, the court stated that a lesser standard of justification than probable cause is required in certain circumstances because "street encounters between citizens and police officers are incredibly rich in diversity" (p. 13).

There is no easy way to define reasonable suspicion. Instead, it is useful to think of where reasonable suspicion falls relative to other types of justification. In general, reasonable suspicion falls below probable cause but above a hunch. In *United States v. Cortez* (1981), the Supreme Court called attention to the difficulty of settling on a definition of reasonable suspicion and attempted to clarify some of the confusion courts had in defining the concept:

> Courts have used a variety of terms to capture the elusive concept of what cause is sufficient to authorize police to stop a person. Terms like "articulable suspicion" and "founded suspicion" are not self-defining; they fall short of providing clear guidance dispositive of the myriad factual situations that arise. But the essence of all that has been written is that the totality of circumstances—the whole picture—must be taken into account. Based upon that whole picture the detaining officers must have a particularized and objective basis for suspecting the particular person stopped of criminal activity. (p. 417)

Later, in *United States v. Sokolow* (1989, p. 7), the Supreme Court defined reasonable suspicion as "considerably less than proof of wrongdoing by a preponderance of evidence" but more than an unparticularized hunch.

Just as probable cause can be based on various sources of information, so too can reasonable suspicion. Naturally not as much information is required for reasonable suspicion, because it is a lesser standard of justification than probable cause. For example, in *Alabama v. White* (1990), the Court stated: "Reasonable suspicion is a less demanding standard than probable cause not only in the sense that reasonable suspicion can be established with information that is different but also in the sense that reasonable suspicion can arise from information that is less reliable than that required to show probable cause" (p. 330). Thus, many of the same sources of information that can help police officers show probable cause can help establish reasonable suspicion.

Several recent cases have focused on the types of conduct that give rise to reasonable suspicion to stop. For example, in *United States v. Brignoni-Ponce* (1975), the Supreme Court held that border patrol agents are prohibited from randomly stopping people while engaged in roving patrols on roads near the border. In that case, officers stopped a man because he appeared to be of Mexican descent, but the Court declared that "[t]he likelihood that any given person of Mexican ancestry is an alien is high enough to make appearance a relevant factor, but standing alone it does not justify stopping all Mexican-Americans to ask if they are aliens" (p. 887).

In another case, *Delaware v. Prouse* (1979), the Court ruled that marijuana seized while a police officer stopped a car to check the driver's license and registration was inadmissible in court. The officer's decision to stop the car was without justification. As a result, the Court declared that police officers may undertake license/registration checks only when there is an "articulable and reasonable suspicion that a motorist is unlicensed or that an automobile is not registered, or that either the vehicle or an occupant is otherwise subject to seizure for violation of the law" (p. 662).

In the same terms as *Prouse*, the Supreme Court decided *Brown v. Texas* (1979). In that case, officers stopped two men because, in their words, the situation "looked suspicious and we had never seen that subject in that area before." The Court ruled that reasonable suspicion did not exist on these facts:

> There is no indication in the record that it was unusual for people to be in the alley. The fact that the appellant was in a neighborhood frequented by drug users, standing alone, is not a basis for concluding that the appellant himself was engaged in criminal conduct. In short, the appellant's activity was no different from the activity of other pedestrians in that neighborhood. (p. 52)

The Supreme Court's recent decision in *Illinois v. Wardlow* (2000) provides further clarification as to the meaning of reasonable suspicion. In *Wardlow,* Chicago police officers were patrolling an area known for its narcotics traffic. When Wardlow spotted the officers, he ran in the opposite direction. He was chased by the officers, caught, and patted down. The officers found a pistol and arrested him. Wardlow appealed his conviction by arguing that the stop and frisk were illegal because the officers did not have reasonable suspicion to stop him. The Court disagreed with Wardlow's argument and held that "a location's characteristics are relevant in determining whether the circumstances are sufficiently suspicious to warrant further investigation." Moreover, "it was Wardlow's unprovoked flight that aroused the officers' suspicion, and headlong flight is the consummate act of evasion."According to the Court, the officers *did* have reasonable suspicion to chase Wardlow down.

Practice Pointer 5-3

There are innumerable methods of developing probable cause and reasonable suspicion. Police officers can often consult their department policy manuals and other state-specific peace officer publications for additional examples. For example, California's *Peace Officers Legal Sourcebook* lists dozens of sources of acceptable information for probable cause and reasonable suspicion.

Administrative Justification

Another standard of justification that courts have come to recognize is **administrative justification.** Actually, administrative justification is not justification at all. Instead of searches being based on probable cause or reasonable suspicion, under certain circumstances the courts permit select types of unjustified searches by weighing society's safety interests and individuals' interests in being free from unreasonable searches.

One of the first cases to recognize administrative justification was *Camara v. Municipal Court* (1967). *Camara* involved unjustified health code inspections of residential apartment units. The Supreme Court declared that such inspections did not need to be premised on reasonable suspicion or probable cause. In its opinion, the Court balanced the public interest in enforcing safety codes with the "relatively limited invasion of the urban citizen's privacy," given that "the inspections [were] neither personal in nature nor aimed at the discovery of evidence of crime" (p. 537).

The Court went on to note that such searches are permissible so long as "reasonable legislative or administrative standards for conducting an area inspection are satisfied with respect to a particular dwelling" (p. 538). Stated differently, administrative searches should be undertaken in a routine and predictable manner to avoid giving the appearance of arbitrariness or selective enforcement.

In a more recent case, *Colorado v. Bertine* (1987, p. 371), the Supreme Court stated that the:

> Standard of probable cause is peculiarly related to criminal inves-
> tigations, not routine, noncriminal procedures. . . . The probable
> cause approach is unhelpful when analysis centers upon the rea-
> sonableness of routine administrative caretaking functions, par-
> ticularly when no claim is made that the protective procedures are
> a subterfuge for criminal investigations.

A good example of weighing the balance between public safety and individual privacy is the case of *Veronia School District v. Acton* (1995). In that case, the Supreme Court decided on the constitutionality of a school policy that required athletes to submit to random urinalysis for drugs. The Court declared that such searches are constitutional, as long as they are not geared toward particular individuals. Also, the Court noted that student athletes enjoy a lesser expectation of privacy than ordinary citizens because they must participate in other examina-tions (e.g., health exams), dress together in the locker room, and par-ticipate in sports voluntarily. The public safety interest the court referred to in *Veronia School District* was "drug use by our nation's school children" (p. 2395).

Administrative justification has been applied in a variety of other situations as well. For example, in *New York v. Burger* (1987) the Supreme Court authorized a warrantless search of an automobile junkyard. In *Donovan v. Dewey* (1981), the Court upheld a warrantless inspection of a mine. And, in *United States v. Biswell* (1972), the Court upheld a warrantless search of a gun dealership. What these three cases have in common is that each involves a highly regulated form of business. Basically, the Supreme Court has stated that people who con-duct business in highly regulated environments do not enjoy the same expectation of privacy as ordinary citizens.

Still other administrative justification cases have involved arson investigations (*Michigan v. Clifford*, 1984), border checkpoints for the purpose of detecting illegal aliens (*United States v. Martinez-Fuerte*, 1976), searches of impounded vehicles (*Colorado v. Bertine*, 1987), other searches of personal items in need of inventorying (e.g., *Illinois v. Lafayette*, 1983), and mandatory drug testing of various public and pri-vate employees (e.g., *National Treasury Employees Union v. Von Raab*, 1989).

The Supreme Court offered further logic for administrative justifi-cation in the case of *Skinner v. Railway Labor Executives' Association* (1989):

In light of the limited discretion exercised by the railroad employers under the [drug testing] regulations, the surpassing safety interest served by toxicological tests in this context, and the diminished expectation of privacy that attaches to information pertaining to the fitness of covered employees, we believe it is reasonable to conduct such tests in the absence of a warrant or reasonable suspicion that any particular employee may be impaired. (p. 602)

Given the lack of suspicion with regard to administrative justification, the courts *have* placed significant restrictions on the scope of administrative searches. For example, in *Marshall v. Barlow's Inc.* (1978), the Court ruled that searches of businesses (by OSHA officials) that had not been highly regulated in the past were unconstitutional. At the other extreme, once an administrative search is authorized, if contraband or evidence of a crime is discovered during the course of the search, it can be seized. According to the Supreme Court, "The discovery of evidence of crimes in the course of an otherwise proper administrative inspection does not render that search illegal or the administrative scheme suspect" (*New York v. Burger*, 1987, p. 716).

However, in the recent case of *City of Indianapolis v. Edmond* (2000), the Supreme Court held that highway checkpoint programs with the primary purpose of detecting evidence of ordinary criminal wrongdoing violates the Fourth Amendment. Without some measure of individualized suspicion, only a limited line of exceptions exists to the Fourth Amendment's prohibition of suspicionless seizures, such as a sobriety checkpoint with the primary purpose of removing drunk drivers from the roadways (e.g., *Michigan Dept. of State Police v. Sitz*, 1990).

Another standard of justification similar to administrative justification has been applied to searches based on "special needs beyond the normal need for law enforcement" (*Skinner v. Railway Executives' Association*, 1989). In such situations, courts go a step beyond the balancing approach already discussed and focus on whether there are "reasonable grounds" for conducting such searches. For example, in *New Jersey v. TLO* (1985), the Supreme Court declared that a school principal's search of a student's purse was permissible in the absence of probable cause or reasonable suspicion when balancing "the schoolchild's legitimate expectation of privacy and the school's equally legitimate need to maintain an environment in which learning can take place" (p. 340).

Similarly, in *O'Connor v. Ortega* (1987), a case involving the warrantless search of a government employee's office, and *Griffin v. Wisconsin* (1987), a case in which a probation officer searched the home of a probationer, the Supreme Court invoked the "special needs beyond law enforcement" logic to abandon the warrant requirement. It did decide, however, that in these situations "reasonable grounds" for the search were required. In special needs searches, the courts also give special attention to the nature of the intrusion and the scope of the search. If the intrusion is significant and the scope of the search excessive, a warrant may be required.

In summary, most administrative searches are constitutional when the interest in public safety outweighs the individual's privacy interest. Searches that are based on "special needs beyond law enforcement," however, need to be based on "reasonable grounds." In either case, it is useful to think of both standards as falling below probable cause and reasonable suspicion. The logic for a lower standard of justification in the administrative and special needs contexts is that these types of searches are usually conducted by officials other than the police.

Administrative searches are restricted in three primary ways. First, they must conform to established procedures. Second, they cannot be geared toward the discovery of criminal evidence. Finally, they cannot be used as a pretext for a full-blown search. These restrictions do not apply to "special needs beyond law enforcement" searches. However, special needs searches are restricted in other ways. First, the courts will decide whether the search was justified at its inception, then they will decide whether the search as actually conducted was reasonably related to the circumstances that justified the search in the first place. Table 5-4 compares the levels of justification just discussed.

Table 5-4 Levels of Justification Compared	
Level of Justification	**Degree of Certainty**
Proof beyond a reasonable doubt	Approximately 99 percent
Probable cause/preponderance of evidence*	Above 50 percent
Reasonable suspicion	Below 50 percent and above 0 percent
Hunch	0 percent

*Probable cause is associated with criminal proceedings; preponderance of evidence is associated with civil proceedings.

Standing

Usually, standing is a topic covered near the end of an evidence or criminal procedure class. It makes more sense, though, to address standing before proceeding with a detailed Fourth Amendment analysis, because standing is a threshold issue. A defendant cannot successfully raise a Fourth Amendment objection until he or she can show standing to bring the issue to the court's attention. Stated differently, a person who does not have standing will not even be able to set foot inside the courtroom to object to the police conduct.

A person has **standing** if he or she is the "victim" of a Fourth Amendment violation. Basically, this means that A cannot complain about an infringement on B's rights. According to the Supreme Court in *Jones v. United States* (1960, p. 261), the "victim" of a Fourth Amendment violation should be distinguished from one "who claims prejudice only through the use of evidence gathered as a consequence of a search or seizure directed at someone else." Or, as stated in *Rakas v. Illinois* (1978, p. 134), "[a] person who is aggrieved by an illegal search and seizure only through the introduction of damaging evidence secured by a search of a third person's premises or property has not had any of his Fourth Amendment rights infringed."

Originally, standing was tied to property interests. Only if one had a *possessory interest* in the thing seized or the place to be searched was the person considered to have standing. However, in *Jones v. United States* (1960), the Supreme Court declared that "it is unnecessary and ill-advised to import into the law surrounding the constitutional right to be free from unreasonable searches and seizures subtle distinctions, developed and refined by the common law in evolving the body of private property law" (p. 266). The Court conferred standing, instead, on anyone "legitimately on the premises." Also, in *Jones* the Court declared that when defendants are charged with possessory offenses (e.g., possession of an illegal firearm), they automatically enjoy standing. The reason was that certain defendants, in order to establish standing, had to admit that the contraband was theirs and incriminate themselves.

The automatic standing doctrine was overturned in *United States v. Salvucci* (1980), and the "legitimately on the premises" standard has been replaced with a new standard based on a person's expectation of privacy (*Katz v. United States*, 1967). The courts now focus on the "totality of circumstances" to determine whether a person has a *reasonable expectation of privacy.*

The courts have referred to at least three specific situations in which a person can be said to have standing. First, if a person has the right to exclude others from the premises, that person has standing (e.g., *Rawlings v. Kentucky*, 1980). Second, if a person has continuing access plus possessory interest, he or she can be said to have standing. For example, in *United States v. Jeffers* (1951), the Court declared that a man who had a key to his aunt's apartment as well as possession of some items within the apartment had standing, even though he could not technically exclude others from the premises. Third, in *Minnesota v. Olson* (1990), the Supreme Court ruled that a person who is legitimately on the premises and has a possessory interest in the item seized can also have standing. An example of such a person is a woman who visits a friend in her friend's house. Although the guest cannot exclude anyone from the house and does not have continuing access, she can still have standing if an item in her possession is seized unlawfully.

In *Rakas v. Illinois* (1978), the Supreme Court recognized the similarity between the standing analysis and the definition of a search. Both focus on a person's reasonable expectation of privacy. In essence, the standing and search analyses collapses into one when there is a questionable search on the part of the police.

Why discuss standing separately from the definition of a search? There are three reasons. First, it is important to realize that while a search may occur, it is not always the case that the person targeted by that search has a reasonable expectation of privacy. In other words, a search may occur, but if evidence is not seized and used against that person at trial, the person cannot claim any Fourth Amendment protection. Second, there may be situations in which a search is legal but a seizure illegal, thus requiring that the search and seizure be analyzed separately. Finally, as Justice Blackmun observed in *Rawlings v. Kentucky* (1980, p. 112), it is possible for a defendant to demonstrate standing to challenge a search but fail to prove that the search was unlawful. Alternatively, a defendant may show that a Fourth Amendment violation took place but not have standing to contest it.

For all practical purposes, the standing analysis is subsumed into the Fourth Amendment search analysis and rarely requires discussion in and of itself. Rare are the situations in which standing and the Fourth Amendment will receive individual attention.

Summary

This chapter introduced the Fourth Amendment, beginning with definition of search and seizure. Searches occur when government actors infringe on a legitimate expectation of privacy while looking for evidence. Seizures of property occur when a meaningful possessory interest is interfered with. Seizures of persons occur when a reasonable person would believe he or she is not free to leave.

The chapter identified three standards of justification. Probable cause, which falls between 50 and 100 percent certainty, is required for arrests and searches with and without warrants. Reasonable suspicion, which falls below 50 percent certainty but above a hunch, is required for stops and investigative detentions that fall short of arrests. Finally, administrative justification is required in administrative and "special needs beyond law enforcement" searches. The constitutionality of searches based on administrative justification is determined by balancing the interests of society with the privacy interests of the individual.

The chapter ended with a brief discussion of standing. A person has standing when he or she has a reasonable expectation of privacy in the property seized or the place to be searched. Without standing, a person cannot contest a Fourth Amendment violation. The search and standing analysis frequently combine into one single analyses, which is why it is more important to give attention to the definition of a search.

Discussion Questions

1. Explain the "warrant clause" and the "reasonableness clause" of the Fourth Amendment.

2. Explain when a seizure has occurred.

3. What are the three standards of justification recognized by the courts? Give a brief explanation of each.

4. Explain the concept of "reasonable expectation of privacy."

5. The courts have established tests to ensure that information supplied by informants is reliable and accurate. Explain the *Aguilar* test.

6. Explain the concept of "totality of the circumstances."

7. In a number of cases, information known to the police that helped establish probable cause later turns out to be false. What has the Supreme Court said about this issue? What three cases does the book cite in support of your answer?

8. The Supreme Court made a very important ruling that established a new standard of justification in *Terry v. Ohio* (1968). Explain.

9. Give a brief description of *Veronia School District v. Acton* and what was decided by the Court in this case.

Further Reading

Dressler, T., and Thomas, G. C. III. (2001). *Criminal Procedure: Principles, Policies, and Perspectives.* Eagan, MN: West Group.

Katz, L. (1990). "In Search of a Fourth Amendment for the Twenty-First Century," *Indiana L. Rev.* 65:549.

Maclin, T. (1996). "Informants and the Fourth Amendment: A Reconsideration." *Wash. U. L.Q.* 74:573.

Miles, J. G. Jr., D. B. Richardson, and A. E. Scudellari. (1988–1989). *The Law Officer's Pocket Manual,* p. 6:4. Washington, DC: Bureau of National Affairs.

Slobogin, C. (1991). "The World Without a Fourth Amendment." *UCLA L. Rev.* 39:1.

Whitebread, C. H., and C. Slobogin. (2000). *Criminal Procedure: An Analysis of Cases and Concepts* (4th ed.). New York: Foundation Press.

Worrall, J. L. (2004). *Criminal Procedure: From First Contact to Appeal.* Boston, MA: Allyn and Bacon.

Cases Cited

Aguilar v. Texas, 378 U.S. 108 (1964)
Air Pollution Variance Bd. v. Western Alfalfa Corp., 416 U.S. 861 (1974)
Alabama v. White, 496 U.S. 325 (1990)
Albright v. Oliver, 510 U.S. 266 (1994)
Beck v. Ohio, 379 U.S. 89 (1964)
Brinegar v. United States, 338 U.S. 160 (1949)
Brown v. Texas, 443 U.S. 47 (1979)
Burdeau v. McDowell, 256 U.S. 465 (1921)
California v. Ciraolo, 476 U.S. 207 (1986)
California v. Greenwood, 486 U.S. 35 (1988)
California v. Hodari D., 499 U.S. 621 (1991)
Camara v. Municipal Court, 387 U.S. 523 (1967)
City of Indianapolis v. Edmond, 99-1030 (2000)
Colorado v. Bertine, 479 U.S. 367 (1987)
Commonwealth v. Johnston, 515 Pa. 454 (1987)
Coolidge v. New Hampshire, 403 U.S. 443 (1971)
Cupp v. Murphy, 412 U.S. 291 (1973)
Davis v. Mississippi, 394 U.S. 721 (1969)
Delaware v. Prouse, 440 U.S. 648 (1979)
Donovan v. Dewey, 452 U.S. 594 (1981)
Dow Chemical Co. v. United States, 476 U.S. 227 (1986)
Draper v. United States, 358 U.S. 307 (1959)
Dunaway v. New York, 442 U.S. 200 (1979)
Florida v. Riley, 488 U.S. 445 (1989)
Franks v. Delaware, 438 U.S. 154 (1978)
Gillett v. State, 588 Tex. Crim. App. S.W.2d 361 (1979)
Griffin v. Wisconsin, 483 U.S. 868 (1987)
Henry v. United States, 361 U.S. 98 (1959
Hoffa v. United States, 385 U.S. 293 (1996)
Illinois v. Gates, 462 U.S. 213 (1983)
Illinois v. Lafayette, 462 U.S. 640 (1983)
Illinois v. Wardlow, No. 98-1036 (2000)
Jaben v. United States, 381 U.S. 214 (1965)
Jones v. United States, 362 U.S. 257 (1960)
Katz v. United States, 389 U.S. 347 (1967)
Kyllo v. United States, 99-8508 (2001)
Lester v. State, 145 Ga. App. 847 (1978)
Lopez v. United States, 373 U.S. 427 (1963)
Marshall v. Barlow's Inc., 436 U.S. 307 (1978)
Michigan v. Clifford, 464 U.S. 286 (1984)
Michigan v. Tyler, 436 U.S. 499 (1978)
Michigan Dept. of State Police v. Sitz, 496 U.S. 444 (1990)

Mincey v. Arizona, 437 U.S. 385 (1978)
Minnesota v. Olson, 495 U.S. 91 (1990)
National Treasury Employees Union v. Von Raah, 489 U.S. 656 (1989)
New Jersey v. T.L.O., 469 U.S. 325 (1985)
New York v. Burger, 482 U.S. 691 (1987)
O'Connor v. Ortega, 480 U.S. 709 (1987)
Oliver v. United States, 466 U.S. 170 (1984)
Olmstead v. United States, 277 U.S. 438 (1928)
On Lee v. United States, 343 U.S. 747 (1952)
People v. Boettner, 80 Misc.2d 3 (1974)
Rakas v. Illinois, 439 U.S. 128 (1978)
Rawlings v. Kentucky, 448 U.S. 98 (1980)
Schmerber v. California, 384 U.S. 757 (1966)
Sibron v. New York, 392 U.S. 40 (1968)
Skinner v. Railway Labor Executives' Association, 489 U.S. 602 (1989)
Smith v. Maryland, 442 U.S. 735 (1979)
Soldal v. Cook County, 506 U.S. 56 (1992)
Spinelli v. United States, 393 U.S. 410 (1969)
Stanfield v. State, 666 P.2d 1294 (Okla. Crim. 1983)
State v. Oldaker, 172 W.Va. 258 (1983)
State v. Von Bulow, 475 A.2d 995, 1012 (1984)
Terry v. Ohio, 392 U.S. 1 (1968)
Texas v. Brown, 460 U.S. 730 (1983)
United States v. Biswell, 406 U.S. 311 (1972)
United States v. Brignoni-Ponce, 422 U.S. 873 (1975)
United States v. Colyer, 878 F.2d 469 (D.C. Cir. 1989)
United States v. Cortez, 449 U.S. 411 (1981)
United States v. Di. Re, 332 U.S. 581 (1948)
United States v. Dionisio, 410 U.S. 1 (1973)
United States v. Dunn, 480 U.S. 294 (1987)
United States v. Freitas, 716 F.2d 1216 (9th Cir. 1983)
United States v. Garofalo, 496 F.2d 510 (8th Cir. 1974)
United States v. Harris, 403 U.S. 573 (1971)
United States v. Jackson, 818 F.2d 345 (5th Cir. 1987)
United States v. Jacobsen, 466 U.S. 109 (1984)
United States v. Jeffers, 342 U.S. 48 (1951)
United States v. Knotts, 460 U.S. 276 (1983)
United States v. Lamar, 545 F.2d 488 (5th Cir. 1977)
United States v. Martinez-Fuerte, 428 U.S. 543 (1976)
United States v. Mendenhall, 446 U.S. 544 (1980)
United States v. Miller, 425 U.S. 435 (1976)
United States v. Ortiz, 422 U.S. 891 (1975)
United States v. Place, 462 U.S. 696 (1983)
United States v. Rabinowitz, 339 U.S. 56 (1950)
United States v. Salvucci, 448 U.S. 83 (1980)
United States v. Sokolow, 490 U.S. 1 (1989)
United States v. Taborda, 635 F.2d 131 (2d Cir. 1980)
United States v. Thomas, 757 F.2d 1359 (2d. Cir. 1985)

United States v. Ventresca, 380 U.S. 102 (1965)
United States v. White, 401 U.S. 745 (1971)
Vale v. Louisiana, 399 U.S. 30 (1970)
Veronia School District v. Acton, 115 S. Ct. 2386 (1995)
Walter v. United States, 447 U.S. 649 (1980)
Whiteley v. Warden, 401 U.S. 560 (1971)
Winston v. Lee, 470 U.S. 753 (1985)
Ybarra v. Illinois, 444 U.S. 85 (1979) ✦

Arrests and Searches With Warrants

Key Terms

- Administrative search warrants
- Deadly force
- Exigent circumstances
- Frisk

- Knock and announce
- Nonstop
- Particularity requirement
- Qualified immunity

Introduction

The Fourth Amendment places restrictions on six types of government action: (1) arrests with warrants, (2) arrests without warrants, (3) searches with warrants, (4) searches without warrants, (5) seizures of evidence without warrants, and (6) seizures of evidence with warrants. As you will recall from the previous chapter, evidence is seized when there is a meaningful interference with someone's possessory interest in a piece of property. Indeed, it is possible for a seizure to take place without a prior search (e.g., *Soldal v. Cook County,* 1992), but such seizures are relatively rare. More commonly, a seizure is preceded by a search. Thus, we limit our focus in this chapter to arrests and searches, particularly arrests and searches *with* warrants. Chapter 7 covers warrant*less* actions governed by the Fourth Amendment.

On its face, the Fourth Amendment is fairly clear about the search and arrest warrant requirement: "and no warrants shall issue, but upon probable cause, supported by Oath or affirmation, and particularly describing the place to be searched, and the persons or things to be seized." Like the Fourth Amendment's reasonableness clause though, the warrant clause has been the subject of intense scrutiny in the courts over the years. Many decisions have focused on the meaning of probable cause in the warrant context, the nature of an oath or affirmation, when warrants are required, how they are to be served, and what the framers intended in terms of particularity.

As a general rule, a warrant is preferred whenever it is practical to obtain one. The next chapter discusses warrantless searches and seizures, including some situations in which a warrantless search can occur even if there is plenty of time to obtain a warrant (such as automobile searches), but the courts still prefer warrants under *most* circumstances.

Search and Arrest Warrant Components

There are three requirements for a search or arrest warrant to be valid. First, it must be issued by a neutral and detached magistrate. Second, probable cause must be set forth in the warrant. Third, the warrant must conform to the Fourth Amendment's particularity requirement. The neutral and detached magistrate requirement is the same whether the warrant is for an arrest or a search. The probable cause and particularity requirements, however, differ depending on whether the warrant is issued for a search or an arrest. Each of these three requirements is considered in the subsections that follow.

Neutral and Detached Magistrate

The Supreme Court described the rationale for the "neutral and detached magistrate" requirement some 50 years ago:

> The point of the Fourth Amendment . . . is not that it denies law enforcement the support of the usual inferences reasonable men draw from evidence. Its protection consists in requiring that those inferences be drawn by a neutral and detached magistrate instead of being judged by the officer engaged in the often competitive enterprise of ferreting out crime. (*Johnson v. United States*, 1948, pp. 13–14)

Police officers, according to the Court, cannot be considered neutral and detached. The same applies to any other official charged with executing the law (such as prosecutors). For example, in *Coolidge v. New Hampshire* (1971), the Supreme Court ruled that state attorneys general cannot issue warrants. Because the attorney general of any given state is the chief law enforcement officer, the Court concluded (rightly) that such officials may be inclined to side with the police officer. Similarly, in *United States v. United States District Court* (1972), the Court concluded that the president, acting through the Attorney General of the United States, cannot authorize electronic surveillance without judicial approval. According to Justice Powell:

> The Fourth Amendment does not contemplate the executive officers of Government as neutral and detached magistrates. Their duty and responsibility is to enforce the laws, to investigate and to prosecute. . . . [T]hose charged with this investigative and prosecutorial duty should not be the sole judges of when to utilize constitutionally sensitive means in pursuing their tasks. The historical judgment, which the Fourth Amendment accepts, is that unreviewed executive discretion may yield too readily to pressures to obtain incriminating evidence and overlook potential invasions of privacy and protected speech. (p. 317)

In other words, *no* executive officials can issue warrants.

Who then can be considered neutral and detached? Most judges and some judicial officers are considered neutral and detached. This is not to say that all judges and similarly situated officials can be considered neutral and detached. For example, in *Lo-Ji Sales, Inc. v. New York* (1979), a magistrate issued a warrant for police officers to search for "obscene items." He also authorized the police to seize any other items that he might find obscene while he *accompanied* the officers during the service of the warrant. The judge pointed out items that he believed to be obscene, the officers seized them, and the evidence was admitted into trial against the defendants. The Supreme Court held that the magistrate was not acting in a neutral and detached capacity, but "as an adjunct law enforcement officer" (p. 327).

What is the definition of probable cause?

A magistrate or judge can also be considered other than neutral and detached if he or she has a financial interest in the issuance of warrants. This issue arose in the case of *Connally v. Georgia* (1977), in which the Supreme Court held that a Georgia statute providing for unsalaried magistrates to receive $5 for each warrant issued (but no money if the warrant was not issued) was unconstitutional. The Court decided unanimously that "judicial action by an officer of a court who has 'a direct, personal, substantial, pecuniary interest' in his conclusion to issue or to deny [a] warrant" (p. 250) cannot be considered neutral and detached within the meaning of the Fourth Amendment.

Probable Cause Showing

A definition of probable cause was offered in the previous chapter. It is worth pointing out here, however, that probable cause is the second important component of a valid search or arrest warrant. In other words, the law enforcement officer applying for a warrant must demonstrate that probable cause exists to search or arrest. The probable cause showing differs depending on whether the warrant is for an arrest or for a search.

Probable cause in an arrest warrant. The probable cause showing in an arrest warrant is straightforward. As the Court noted in *Beck v. Ohio* (1964), probable cause to arrest exists when "the facts and circumstances within [the police's] knowledge and of which they [have] reasonably trustworthy information [are] sufficient to warrant a prudent man in believing that the [suspect has] committed or was committing an offense" (p. 91). Specifically, the officer applying for the warrant must show probable cause that the person to be arrested committed the offense in question.

Probable cause in a search warrant. In the case of a search warrant, there are two elements to the probable cause showing. First, the officer applying for the warrant must show probable cause (sworn to by oath or affirmation) that the items to be seized are connected with criminal activity. Items connected with criminal activity are anything that could be used against a person in a criminal trial. Second, the officer must show probable cause that the items to be seized are in the location to be searched. This second requirement differs noticeably from an arrest warrant, from which the officer does not necessarily need to show *where* the arrestee will be found.

Particularity

The Fourth Amendment provides that warrants must "particularly describ[e] the place to be searched, and the persons or things to be seized." The purpose of this provision, known as the **particularity requirement,** is to prohibit "general warrants," such as those issued in England and the American colonies. Just as the probable cause showing differs between arrest and search warrants, particularity is defined differently depending on the police conduct in question.

Particularity in an arrest warrant. The particularity requirement in an arrest warrant depends on whether the police actually know the suspect's name. If they do, the suspect's name is sufficient to meet the Fourth Amendment's particularity requirement. If officials do not know the suspect's name, more detail is necessary. If a sufficiently detailed description of the suspect can be offered, then a "John Doe" arrest warrant may be issued.

For example, if police have in their possession a video from a bank security camera that was recently robbed and the video shows that the suspect is a white male, 6 feet tall, with a mustache, a bald head, a scar on his left cheek, and a tattoo of a skull and crossbones on his neck, a John Doe arrest warrant will almost certainly be issued and upheld if the man described is actually caught and arrested. The logic for John Doe warrants is quite clear; if police officers were required to know the name of every suspect prior to arrest, then their ability to enforce the law would be seriously compromised.

Particularity in a search warrant. The particularity requirement for a search warrant is far more complex than that for an arrest warrant. First, the warrant must clearly describe the place to be searched. Second, the warrant must set forth with sufficient detail the items to be seized during the search.

With regard to the place to be searched, it is not absolutely essential that exacting detail be provided. As the Court noted in *Steele v. United States* (1925), it "is enough of the description is such that the officer with a search warrant can, with reasonable effort, ascertain and identify the place intended" (p. 503). Thus, a warrant to search "150 Oak Street" is sufficiently precise if a single residence exists at that address. It will fail the particularity requirement, however, if a multi-unit complex, such as an apartment building, exists at 150 Oak Street. This is especially the case if the warrant does not offer additional detail as to which unit will be subjected to the search.

If a search warrant insufficiently describes the place to be searched, the warrant will not automatically be declared invalid. Instead, the courts will focus on the reasonableness of the officers' mistake. For example, in *Maryland v. Garrison* (1987), officers secured a warrant to search the person of Lawrence McWebb and "the premises known as 2036 Park Avenue third floor apartment." Unknown to the police officers, there were actually two apartment units on the third floor, one of which belonged to Garrison, the defendant. Garrison's unit was mistakenly searched, but the Court held that the warrant was sufficiently "particular" because (1) a "reliable" informant had provided information leading to the warrant, and (2) the police officers who inquired with the local utility company about the location were led to believe that there was only one apartment unit on the third floor.

The second particularity requirement for a search warrant concerns the items to be seized. Specifically, articles to be seized pursuant to a warrant should be described with sufficient detail that the officer or officers executing it can determine which objects are to be seized. Consider once again the case of *Lo-Ji Sales, Inc. v. New York* (1979), where the magistrate accompanied police officers while they served a search warrant. Recall that the magistrate authorized the police officers in that case to seize anything the magistrate thought to be "obscene." The Court unanimously held that the warrant in *Lo-Ji Sales* failed to "particularly describe . . . the things to be seized" (p. 319).

In stark contrast to *Lo-Ji Sales,* is the case of *Andreson v. Maryland* (1976). In that case, the Supreme Court upheld a warrant that authorized the seizure of several items "together with other fruits, instrumentalities and evidence of crime. . . ." (p. 479). The reason for this "sidestep" around that particularity requirement, according to the Court, was that the crime in question was complex and was one that "could be proved only by piecing together many bits of evidence" (p. 482). Thus, it would appear under certain circumstances that the Fourth Amendment's particularity requirement can be interpreted loosely, especially when it comes to the items named in the search warrant (see also *United States v. DeLuna,* 1985; *United States v. Alexander,* 1985).

Another means by which the particularity requirement can be avoided is by way of the plain view doctrine. *Plain view* is discussed in the next chapter, but for now suffice it to say that if the police have probable cause that an item is evidence of criminal activity—even if it is not named in the warrant, and even if it is not discovered inadvertently—it can be seized if it is in plain view. There are additional restrictions on the plain view doctrine (such as lawful access), which are discussed in more detail in Chapter 7.

The Court has also acknowledged something of a "good faith" exception to the requirement that a search warrant particularly describe the evidence to be seized. In *Massachusetts v. Sheppard* (1984), for example, the Court upheld a warrant that authorized a search for "controlled substances." The reason for the Court's decision was that the officer described the items to be seized with sufficient detail, but the judge neglected to fill out the appropriate form. Justice Stevens pointed out that the judge who issued the warrant, the police officers who executed it, and the reviewing courts were all able to determine the scope of the authorization provided by the court.

Practice Pointer 6-1

Police officers should take careful steps to detail their probable cause showing when applying for warrants. This is especially true if the probable cause showing relies on information supplied by informants. Likewise, officers should ensure that the Fourth Amendment's particularity requirement it satisfied, as doing so minimizes potential challenges to the warrant.

Figure 6-1   Arrest Warrant

Bail set at $_____ by Judge

WARRANT FOR ARREST

STATE OF MISSOURI   )
County of Cole   ) ss.

IN THE CIRCUIT COURT, DIVISION III WITHIN AND FOR SAID COUNTY

THE STATE OF MISSOURI TO ANY PEACE OFFICER IN THE STATE OF MISSOURI:

Upon consideration of the facts presented, the Court finds that sufficient facts have been stated therein to show probable cause that a crime has been committed and that the accused has committed it. You are therefore commanded to arrest

(DEFENDANT)
(ADDRESS)
(SSN/DOB)

who is charged with

(CHARGE)
(DATE/PLACE)

The statement has been alleged in a warrant request/complaint made under oath from which this Court finds probable cause to issue this warrant believing the alleged crime to have been committed within the jurisdiction of this court and in violation of the laws of the State of Missouri, and to bring him forthwith before this court to be here dealt with in accordance with law; and you, this officer serving this warrant, shall forthwith make return hereof to this court.

WITNESS THE HONORABLE _____ , Judge of the said court and the seal thereof, issued in the county and state aforesaid on this _____ day of_____, 1998.

_____
JUDGE

RETURN:
Served the within warrant in my County of _____, and in the State of Missouri on this _____ day of _____, 1998, by arresting the within named _____, and producing him before the said court on the _____ day of _____, 1998.

_____

Source: Courtesy of the Missouri Bar. Available at www.mobar.org/handbook/warrant.htm

Arrest Warrants

As Justice Powell noted in *United States v. Watson* (1976), "a search may cause only an annoyance and temporary inconvenience to the law-abiding citizen, assuming more serious dimensions only when it turns up evidence of criminality [but an] arrest . . . is a serious personal intrusion regardless of whether the person seized is guilty or innocent" (p. 428). By itself, however, an arrest has little significance in criminal procedure, because the result of an unlawful arrest—taken by itself—is a release from custody (and possibly civil recourse). The reason we focus on arrests is that the constitutionality of an arrest can determine whether evidence obtained during a subsequent search is admissible at trial.

Ultimately, it is unconstitutionally obtained evidence that cannot be admissible in a criminal trial. An unconstitutional arrest has no ramifications in court, apart from the possible exclusion of evidence thereby obtained. This is so because of the *fruit of the poisonous tree doctrine.* This doctrine provides that the exclusionary rule applies not only to evidence obtained as a direct result of a constitutional rights violation, but also to evidence indirectly derived from the constitutional rights violation.

Arrest Defined

It is important to remember that seizures, stops, and arrests are not the same. Stops—as in *Terry* stops—and arrests are different types of seizures. Furthermore, think of arrests and seizures as lying at opposite ends of a scale of intrusiveness; arrests are the most intrusive form of seizure, while stops are the least intrusive form. Consensual encounters, by contrast, are not considered seizures at all and are therefore exempt from Fourth Amendment requirements. The reason it is important to distinguish between stops and arrests is that a stop can evolve into a *de facto* arrest if it becomes too intrusive.

If the Supreme Court recognized a uniform definition of the term seizure, the definition of arrest would be the same as that for a seizure. Unfortunately, the Court has not been very clear on what constitutes an arrest versus a mere investigative stop. As noted in *Terry v. Ohio* (1968), the seizure of a person occurs when a police officer, by means of physical force or show of authority, intentionally restrains an individual's liberty in such a manner that a reasonable person would believe that he or she is not free to leave. Given this definition, the only way to distinguish between a stop and an arrest is to focus on the particulars of each case.

Why bother distinguishing between stops and arrests? Because arrests require probable cause, whereas stops only require reasonable suspicion. If the circumstances are such that a stop evolves into an arrest but the officer does not have probable cause to make the arrest (only reasonable suspicion to stop and frisk), any evidence obtained from such an illegal seizure will not be admissible in court.

At one point the Supreme Court intimated that *anything* the police did to restrain an individual's liberty would be considered an arrest. In *Henry v. United States* (1959), for example, the Court held that an arrest took place when a police officer stopped a car whose occupants were suspected of transporting illegal alcohol: "When the officer interrupted the two men and restricted their liberty of movement, the arrest, for purposes of this case, was complete" (p. 103). Because the police in that case did not have probable cause to stop the men, the "arrest" was considered unconstitutional.

More recently, the Supreme Court has held that the police must do much more than merely restrict a person's movement for such action to be considered an arrest. In *Terry v. Ohio* (1968), the court distinguished between arrests that "eventuate in a trip to the station house and prosecution for crime" and lesser intrusions that routinely occur "whenever a police officer accosts an individual and restrains his freedom to walk away" (p. 16). *Terry* ushered in an era of constitutionally permissible "stop and frisks," seizures that are bound by the Fourth Amendment but that do not require probable cause.

In some situations it is simple to distinguish between an arrest and a so-called *Terry* stop. If a suspect is handcuffed, led away to a patrol car, and driven to the stationhouse for booking, such activity is positively an arrest. At the other extreme, if a person is confronted on the street by a police officer who asks general questions, an arrest has *not* occurred. Unfortunately, there are untold numbers of police-citizen encounters that fall between both of these extremes. If a stop goes "too far," it will be considered an arrest, which requires probable cause.

Distinguishing between stops and arrests. The courts will weigh two important factors in determining when a stop evolves into an arrest: (1) the duration of the stop, and (2) the degree of intrusion. In addition to these two factors, the courts will sometimes focus on the officers' intentions as well as the "manner" in which the stop takes place (e.g., in public versus in a private place out of public view). Consider what the Supreme Court stated in the case of *Florida v. Royer* (1983):

> The predicate permitting seizures on suspicion short of probable cause is that law enforcement interests warrant a limited intrusion on the personal security of the suspect. The scope of the intrusion permitted will vary to some extent with the particular facts and circumstances of each case. *This much, however, is clear: an investigative detention must be temporary and last no longer than is necessary to effectuate the purpose of the stop. Similarly, the investigative methods employed should be the least intrusive means reasonably available to verify or dispel the officer's suspicion in a short period of time.* (p. 500, emphasis added)

The Supreme Court has had several opportunities to draw distinctions between stops and arrests. Four categories of cases can be identified (1) stationhouse detentions, (2) public encounters, (3) border detentions, and (4) detentions in the home. We briefly consider cases in each category to help the reader understand the differences between stops and arrests. Again, and perhaps unfortunately, we cannot (nor can the Court) offer a clear-cut definition of arrest, because of how varied police-citizen encounters tend to be.

In *Davis v. Mississippi* (1969), a stationhouse detention case, several youth were taken into custody on suspicion of being involved in a rape. The men were all fingerprinted. The officers did not have probable cause to detain the men. Davis, one of the suspects, was held for two days. Then, on the basis of the fingerprints and a confession, Davis was charged with rape, was convicted, and was sentenced to death. The Supreme Court reversed Davis' conviction because his detention was too long and was not supported by probable cause. In essence, the Court decided that an arrest took place and that the police did not act within Fourth Amendment guidelines. The Court did note, however, that "because of the unique nature of the fingerprinting process, [detentions for the purpose of obtaining fingerprints] might, under narrowly defined circumstances, be found to comply with the Fourth Amendment even though there is no probable cause in the traditional sense" (p. 727; see also *Hayes v. Florida*, 1985).

In another stationhouse detention case, *Dunaway v. New York* (1979), police officers without probable cause took a man into custody during the course of a robbery/murder investigation. They read the man his Miranda rights and then questioned him. Dunaway was convicted, but the Supreme Court reversed his conviction, not on the basis of an unlawful arrest this time, but on the grounds that custodial interrogations similar to that involving Dunaway must be supported by probable cause. The Court also observed that *Terry* was inapplicable in this case because *Terry* permits only a "limited violation of individual privacy" while ensuring "interests in both crime prevention and detection and in the police officer's safety" (p. 209).

In another case, *Florida v. Royer* (1983), the Court again ruled that certain types of detentions must be supported by probable cause, not reasonable suspicion. In *Royer*, police officers in an airport asked a man to accompany them into a room because he fit a drug courier profile. Royer was detained for only 15 minutes, but the Court ruled that this action constituted an arrest, requiring probable cause. According to Justice White, "What had begun as a consensual inquiry in a public place had escalated into an investigatory procedure in a police interrogation room, where the police, unsatisfied with previous explanations, sought to confirm their suspicions" (p. 503).

Not surprisingly, encounters on the street can also evolve into full-blown arrests. In *Terry*, the Court emphasized the stops must be brief, but it neglected to offer a definition of "brief." An excerpt from one important decision offers some clarification:

> While it is clear that "the brevity of the invasion of the individual's Fourth Amendment interests is an important factor in determining whether the seizure is so minimally intrusive as to be justifi-

able on reasonable suspicion," we have emphasized the need to consider the law enforcement purposes to be served by the stop as well as the time reasonably needed to effectuate these purposes. . . . Much as a bright line rule would be desirable in evaluating whether an investigative detention is unreasonable, common sense and ordinary human experience must govern over rigid criteria. (*United States v. Sharpe*, 1985, p. 685)

In one particularly interesting case, *United States v. Montoya de Hernandez* (1985), the Supreme Court upheld a 16-hour detention of a woman who was suspected of smuggling drugs in her alimentary canal. Officials detained Montoya de Hernandez in an airport after her arrival from Colombia because she fit a drug courier profile and was believed to be a "balloon swallower." Eventually nature took its course and she passed a large number of balloons filled with narcotics. The Court approved the actions of law enforcement officials in this case because the defendant's detention "resulted solely from the method by which she chose to smuggle illicit drugs into the country" (p. 559). The decision was not a unanimous one, however. As Justices Brennan and Marshall argued in their dissent, "indefinite confinement in a squalid back room cut off from the outside world, the absence of basic amenities that would have been provided to even the vilest of hardened criminals, [and] repeated strip searches" (p. 556)—all of which occurred in their view—should be considered an arrest that needs to be supported by probable cause.

It is also possible for a person detained in his or her house to be considered "arrested." It is not the case that *all* nonconsensual detentions in the home amount to an arrest, though. For example, in *Beckwith v. United States* (1976), the Supreme Court ruled that questioning by IRS agents of a man in his living room was not considered an arrest, or even a custodial detention. Compare this decision to the Court's decision in *Rawlings v. Kentucky* (1980), where it was decided that an in-home detention did amount to an arrest. In that case, officers detained several individuals at a house where they had served an arrest warrant. The officers did not find the man named in the warrant. The Court declared that the officers did not have probable cause to detain the other people who were not named in the warrant. In other words, their detention amounted to an arrest. Part of the reason for the Court's decision was that the detention lasted some 45 minutes.

The *Rawlings* decision was dealt a blow in *Michigan v. Summers* (1981), a case decided one year later. In that case, the Supreme Court held that an individual can be detained (involuntarily) in his or her home during a search of the house, even in the absence of probable cause. What is required, however, is a warrant to search the premises. In support of its decision, the Court pointed to two issues. First, it noted that in-home detentions are not as embarrassing as public detentions and should not need to be supported by the same level of justification as a lengthy public detention would. Second, when there is probable cause to search for evidence connected with criminal activity (manifested in the form a search warrant), it is reasonable to conclude that the person who owns or rents the residence is involved in criminal activity, so a detention is not unreasonable, even if unsupported by probable cause.

What is to be learned from these cases? That there are no "easy answers" as to when a stop evolves into a full-blown arrest. All that can be said is this: If the detention is excessively lengthy, considerably intrusive, and conducted in a manner where the intent is essentially to arrest, an arrest takes place. Each element by itself is not enough, usually, for a stop to become an arrest. In *Montoya de Hernandez,* a 16-hour detention was not considered an arrest. In *Summers* the detention took place in a person's home—an area that enjoys the most Fourth Amendment protection of any place—but the Court said that in-home detentions should not always be considered arrests. It is critical, therefore, to look at the facts and circumstances surrounding each individual case to determine when a stop evolves into an arrest; there are no clear rules. See Table 6-1 for a list of factors used to distinguish between a stop and an arrest.

Table 6-1	Factors Used to Distinguish Between a Stop and An Arrest*

1. Duration
   a. Short duration = seizure
   b. Long duration = arrest
2. Degree of intrusion
   a. Minimal intrusion (such as pat down) = frisk
   b. Significant intrusion (such as full body search) = arrest
3. Manner/location
   a. In public = more likely a frisk, although not necessarily a frisk
   b. In private (such as in the stationhouse) = more likely an arrest

*One factor may not be enough by itself for a stop to be considered an arrest. However, if a detention is lengthy, intrusive, and conducted out of public view, it will almost certainly be considered an arrest.

Stops versus nonstops. There are differences between stops and "nonstops" as well. A **nonstop** occurs when a person confronted by the police is still free to leave. A nonstop requires no justification at all, because it is not considered a seizure within the meaning of the Fourth Amendment. A stop occurs when a person confronted by the police is not allowed to leave. Only certain forms of police conduct can be considered an arrest. Consensual encounters that amount to "nonstops" as well as investigative detentions, by themselves, are not considered arrests.

When Arrest Warrants Are Required

At common law, if a police officer had probable cause that (1) a person was committing or had committed a felony or (2) a person was committing certain misdemeanors in the officer's presence, an arrest could be made without a warrant. This rule held true regardless of *where* the arrest was made, even if it was in a private place. The only situation where arrest warrants were truly required was when misdemeanors were committed out of a police officer's presence. In *Carroll v. United States* (1925), the Supreme Court set forth the reasoning for this almost unbridled arrest authority:

> The reason for arrest for misdemeanors without warrant at common law was to promptly suppress breaches of the peace . . . while the reason for arrest without a warrant on a reliable report of a felony was because the public safety and the due apprehension of criminals charged with heinous offenses required that such arrests should be made at once without a warrant. (p. 157)

Since the *Carroll* decision, the Supreme Court has deviated only slightly from the rule that warrantless arrests can be made for almost all offenses. In particular, it has placed three restrictions on the rule. First, arrests in people's private residences cannot be made without a warrant unless exigent circumstances exist (e.g., hot pursuit). Second, arrests in the homes of third parties are impermissible without a search warrant *and* an arrest warrant, again providing that no exigent circumstances exist. A third, less explicit, restriction, recognized in the case of *Gerstein v. Pugh* (1975), is that a judicial determination of probable cause must be made following arrests without warrants. This determination is usually accomplished in a postarrest "probable cause hearing."

Arrests in the home. In *Payton v. New York* (1980), the Court held that the Fourth Amendment prohibits warrantless, nonconsensual entries into private homes for the purpose of making an arrest. In that case, police officers had probable cause to believe that Payton had murdered the manager of a gas station. The officers went to Payton's apartment to arrest him. When no one answered the door, the officers pried open the door with a crowbar and entered the apartment, but they did not find Payton. They did, however, find—in plain view—a .30-caliber shell casing laying on the floor of the apartment. It was seized and entered into evidence against Payton at trial. Payton ultimately surrendered to the police and was indicted for murder. The Supreme Court observed

> In terms that apply equally to seizures of property and to seizures
> of persons, the Fourth Amendment has drawn a firm line at the en-
> trance to the house. Absent exigent circumstances, that threshold
> may not reasonably be crossed without a warrant. (p. 590)

Justice Stevens stated furthermore (citing *United States v. United States
District Court*, 1972, p. 313), that "physical entry of the home is the
chief evil against which the wording of the Fourth Amendment is directed" (p. 585). A bright-line rule was therefore set in place: Arrests in
the home must be accompanied by warrant if no exigent circumstances exist.

   Arrests in third-party homes. Shortly after *Payton*, the Supreme
Court decided the landmark case of *Steagald v. United States* (1981). In
that case Justice Marshall expressed some concern that while an arrest
warrant may protect a person "from an unreasonable seizure, it [does]
absolutely nothing to protect [a third party's] privacy interest in being
free from an unreasonable invasion and search of his home" (p. 213).
As such, the Court decided that when an arrest is to be made in a third-
party home, the police must obtain a separate search warrant (in addition to the arrest warrant) to search the premises of the third party for
purposes of locating the arrestee. In the Court's words:

> Two distinct interests were implicated by the search in this case—
> Ricky Lyons' interest in being free from unreasonable seizure and
> petitioner's [Steagald's] interest in being free from an unreason-
> able search of his home. Because the arrest warrant for Lyons ad-
> dressed only the former interest, the search of petitioner's home
> was no more reasonable from petitioner's perspective that it would
> have been if conducted in the absence of any warrant. (p. 216)

   The decision in *Steagald* was by no means unanimous. Justices
Rehnquist and White dissented, arguing that the police and judges
"will, in their various capacities, have to weigh the time during which a
suspect for whom there is an outstanding arrest warrant has been in
the building, whether the dwelling is the suspect's home, how long he
has lived there, whether he is likely to leave immediately, and a number
of related and equally imponderable questions" (p. 231). The majority
then countered by pointing out that if the police did not need separate
search warrants to enter third-party residences, then "[a]rmed solely
with an arrest warrant for a single person, [the police] . . . could search
all the homes of that individual's friends and acquaintances" (p. 215).

When Arrest Warrants Are Not Required

   By far the most common type of arrest is one made without a warrant. Therefore, we shall briefly consider situations where arrest warrants are not required. Two types of arrests do not require warrants: (1)

arrests in public and (2) arrests in the presence of exigent circumstances.

Arrests in public. Warrants are not required for public arrests. This was made clear by the Supreme Court's decision in *United States v. Watson* (1976). There, the Court upheld the common law rule that arrests made in public do not require warrants. In its opinion, the Court expressed confidence in the ability of police officers to make probable cause determinations in such situations: "We decline to transform [a] judicial preference [for arrest warrants] into a constitutional rule when the judgment of the Nation and Congress has for so long been to authorize warrantless public arrests on probable cause" (p. 423).

The Court has since extended this ruling to even include the curtilage of a person's home. That is, in certain situations an arrest warrant is not required for an arrest in the curtilage of a home. For example in *United States v. Santana* (1976), the police, with probable cause to arrest Santana, arrived at her house to find her standing in the opening of the front door of her house. She turned and entered the house, and the officers followed her into the house and made the arrest. The Court declared that the officers' conduct did not violate the Fourth Amendment because, when Santana was standing in the doorway "[s]he was not in an area where she had any expectation of privacy" (p. 42). Incidentally, the entry into Santana's house was supported by hot pursuit (see next section as well as next chapter).

Arrests in the presence of exigent circumstances. Warrants are not required to make arrests in the presence of **exigent** (i.e., emergency) **circumstances.** Five common types of exigencies justify warrantless arrest: (1) hot pursuit, (2) danger to officers, (3) danger to third parties, (4) possible escape, and (5) possible destruction of evidence. Any one of these exigencies, either in isolation or in conjunction with others, justifies warrantless arrest, assuming probable cause is in place to begin with.

In *Warden v. Hayden* (1967), the Supreme Court ruled that if police have probable cause to believe a suspect who is being pursued has fled into a private residence, the officers can follow that suspect into the residence (or other private structure). In that case, police officers followed a robbery suspect into his home and effected an arrest. The Court upheld this action, noting that the "Fourth Amendment does not require police officers to delay in the course of an investigation if to do so would gravely endanger their lives or the lives of others" (p. 299). The *Hayden* decision thereby ushered in the "hot pursuit" doctrine.

As we saw in the previous section, the Court's decision in *United States v. Santana* (1976) also clarified the role of exigencies with regard to arrest. The Court noted that in addition to potential danger to police officers and others, flight on the part of a suspect should permit warrantless arrest because of the potential for escape. Had the police been required to obtain a warrant in that case, it is likely that Santana would not have been found upon their return.

The potential for destruction of evidence is another exigency that justifies warrantless arrest. In *Minnesota v. Olson* (1990), the Supreme Court pointed out that "a warrantless intrusion may be justified by hot pursuit of a fleeing felon, or *imminent destruction of evidence*, . . . or the need to prevent a suspect's escape, or the risk of danger to the police or to other persons inside or outside the dwelling" (p. 100, emphasis added).

Interestingly, the Court has also pointed out that the seriousness of the offense in question can factor into the decision of whether a warrant should be obtained in order to make an arrest. In *Welsh v. Wisconsin* (1984), a witness observed Welsh's car being driven erratically. The car eventually swerved off the road and stopped in a field. Welsh, the driver, left the scene before the police could arrive. When the police arrived they checked Welsh's car registration in order to ascertain where he lived. They then went to Welsh's house, gained entry, and arrested him without a warrant. The Court held that such warrantless entry for the purpose of a making an arrest is in violation of the Fourth Amendment because the offense in question was *nonjailable:*

> Before government agents may invade the sanctity of the home, it must demonstrate exigent circumstances that overcome the presumption of unreasonableness that attaches to all warrantless home entries. An important factor to be considered when determining whether any exigency exists is the gravity of the underlying offense for which the arrest is being made . . . [A]pplication of the exigent circumstances exception in the context of home entry should rarely be sanctioned when there is probable cause that only a minor offense has been committed. (*Welsh v. Wisconsin*, 1984, p. 750)

The majority in *Welsh* cited another case, *McDonald v. United States* (1948), in support of its decision: "When an officer undertakes to act as his own magistrate, he ought to be in a position to justify it by pointing to some real immediate and serious consequences if he postponed action to get a warrant" (p. 460).

The *Welsh* decision has met with considerable criticism. In particular, it is not always clear what constitutes a "minor" offense. Drunk driving is obviously considered a serious offense by every state, but the Court intimated that such a crime is "minor" in the context of the Fourth Amendment's warrant requirement. *Welsh* is also controversial because, even though the Court did not state it directly, it *implied* that warrants are not required for warrantless arrests in homes for serious offenses.

Some confusion exists in the lower courts as to what constitutes an acceptable warrantless entry for the purpose of making an arrest. For example, in *Dorman v. United States* (1970) the D.C. Circuit decided that the following criteria may permit warrantless entry: (1) the offense is serious; (2) the suspect is believed to be armed; (3) the police have a high degree of probable cause for arrest; (4) there is an especially strong reason to believe the suspect is on the premises; (5) escape is likely; (6) the entry can be made peaceably; and (7) the entry is during the day. Other lower courts have applied these same criteria in their decisions (e.g., *United States v. Reed*, 1978; *State v. Gregory*, 1983), being illustrative of the confusion surrounding the issue of warrantless arrests in private locations. See Table 6-2 for a summary of the arrest warrant requirement.

Table 6-2   Arrest Warrant Requirement Summarized
When arrest warrants are required: 1. In homes/residences absent exigent circumstances 2. In third-party homes, but separate search warrant also required **When arrest warrants are not required:** 1. In public regardless of whether offense committed in the officer's presence 2. If one or more of the following exigencies is in place: 　(a) hot pursuit 　(b) danger to officers 　(c) danger to third parties 　(d) possible escape, and/or 　(e) possible destruction of evidence

Arrests for Offenses Committed Out of an Officer's Presence

It is a generally accepted rule that a police officer can, without a warrant, arrest any person for any offense as long as the arrest is made in a public place (or in the presence of exigent circumstances). However, it is often informative to distinguish between offenses committed in an officer's presence and offenses *not* committed in an officer's presence. The reason is that it is more controversial to make a warrantless arrest for a minor offense committed out of a police officer's presence than it is to arrest a person for a serious offense committed *in* an officer's presence. The courts tend to view the former activity with a measure of skepticism and caution.

As we saw in *Welsh*, the Court frowned on the warrantless arrest of a suspect in his home for drunk driving, an offense the Court deemed not particularly serious. Though it was not the focus of the Court's opinion in that case, it is important to note that the arrest in *Welsh* was based on a crime that was committed out of view of the police officer. The Supreme Court has not directly confronted the issue of warrantless arrests for misdemeanors committed out of a police officer's presence. At common law, however, the police could not make an arrest for a misdemeanor that was simply reported to them by a third party. In states that observe this rule, it is usually required that officers obtain warrants in such situations. There are exceptions, though, some of which include (1) if the misdemeanant will flee, (2) if evidence will be destroyed, or (3) if others will be harmed.

On the Seriousness of the Offense

Rarely will police officers arrest for certain minor offenses, especially traffic violations. However, this practice does not mean an arrest cannot be made. In the recent case of *Atwater v. Lago Vista* (2001) the Supreme Court held that a warrantless arrest for a misdemeanor is not a violation of the Fourth Amendment. Atwater, the petitioner, failing to secure her children and herself with a safety belt in violation of Texas law, was arrested without a warrant by an officer who witnessed the violation. The warrantless arrest for such a violation is expressly authorized by Texas statute. The Court upheld the arrest, even though the officer could have fined the woman instead.

Executing Arrest Warrants

Once a warrant is procured (if required), the police are required to follow strict procedures when serving it. For example, the use of deadly force is severely restricted. Also, the police cannot engage in excessive property damage while serving a warrant (e.g., they cannot break every window out of a house in which a warrant is to be served). The most significant restrictions concerning the service of warrants relate to (1) the knock and announce requirement, (2) deadly force, and (3) property damage during the service of search or arrest warrants.

The announcement requirement. At common law, the police were entitled to break into a house to make an arrest after announcing (1) their presence and (2) their reason for being there. Today, the common law requirement stands; subject to limited exceptions, the police officers are still required to announce their presence and state their authority (e.g., "Police officers, search warrant!"). The reasons for this so-called announcement requirement are threefold, according to the courts: (1) It helps in the prevention of needless property damage; (2) it helps prevent violence resulting from surprise entries; and (3) it helps preserve people's dignity and privacy. An announcement is not *always* required, however. Let us turn briefly to a few court cases setting forth "exceptions" to the **knock and announce requirement.**

Consider the case of *Wilson v. Arkansas* (1995). Wilson engaged in several narcotics transactions with a police informant over a period of several months. Based on the transactions, police officers obtained an arrest warrant for Wilson as well as a search warrant for her home.

When the officers arrived at Wilson's home, they identified themselves and stated that they had a warrant *as they entered the home through an unlocked door.* They did not wait until someone answered the door; instead, they entered as they were announcing their presence. The officers found evidence as well as Wilson in the bathroom flushing marijuana down the toilet. At trial, Wilson moved to suppress the evidence on the ground that the search was invalid because the officers did not follow the common law knock and announce requirement before entering her home. The Supreme Court agreed with Wilson and held that the officers *were* required to follow the knock and announce requirement:"An examination of the common law of search and seizure . . . leaves no doubt that the reasonableness of a search of a dwelling may depend in part on whether law enforcement officers announce their presence and authority prior to entering" (*Wilson v. Arkansas* 1995, p. 931).

The Court then refined its decision in the case of *Richards v. Wisconsin* (1997). In that case, the Court held that the police can abandon the knock and announce requirement if they have *reasonable suspicion* that such a requirement "would be dangerous or futile, or that it would inhibit the effective investigation of the crime by, for example, allowing the destruction of evidence" (p. 394). Simply put, if exigent circumstances exist, the knock and announce requirement is not necessary. Had the Court decided in this way in *Wilson,* the officers probably could have apprehended Wilson before she began to flush marijuana down the toilet.

In another case, *Ker v. California* (1963), the Court discussed the relation of exigencies to the common law knock and announce requirement:

> [T]he Fourth Amendment is violated by an unannounced police intrusion into a private home, with or without an arrest warrant, except (1) where the persons within already know of the officers' authority and purpose; or (2) where the officers are justified in the belief that persons within are in imminent peril of bodily harm, or (3) where those within, made aware of the presence of someone outside (because, for example, there has been a knock at the door), are then engaged in activity which justifies the officers in the belief that an escape or the destruction of evidence is being attempted. (p. 47)

Property damage during the service of warrants. In *Sabbath v. United States* (1968), the Supreme Court turned attention to the issue of property damage during the service of search and arrest warrants. Specifically, the Court focused on part of 18 U.S.C.A., Section 3109, which authorized law enforcement officials to "break and enter" for the purpose of serving a warrant. In that case, police officers entered a man's apartment, unannounced, through an unlocked door and arrested him. The Supreme Court held that "[a]n unannounced intrusion into a dwelling—what Section 3109 basically proscribes—is no less an unannounced intrusion whether officers break down a door, force open a chain lock on a partially open door, open a locked door by use of a passkey, or, as here, open a closed but unlocked door" (p. 590). Thus, mere entry without an announcement (absent exigent circumstances) constitutes "breaking and entering" in the eyes of the Supreme Court.

There are, of course, cases where police officers have forcibly entered for the purpose of serving warrants. What degree of physical force is acceptable? There is no clear answer to this question, except to say that when the damage becomes excessive, the Fourteenth Amendment's due process clause kicks in. If the police conduct in question shocks the conscience, their actions will be declared unconstitutional. This standard sets the bar for "excessive" property damage quite high, but there is at least some protection from serious damage.

The Supreme Court reaffirmed the "shocks the conscience" standard in *County of Sacramento v. Lewis* (1998), a case in which a police officer ran over a motorcycle passenger while in pursuit of the motorcycle. The woman was killed, and her surviving family members sued under 42 U.S.C. Section 1983, alleging, among other things, that the woman's Fourteenth Amendment rights were violated. The Court held that "[w]hile prudence would have repressed the [officer's] reaction, the officer's instinct was to do his job as a law enforcement officer, not to induce [the driver of the motorcycle's] lawlessness, or to terrorize, cause harm, or kill" (p. 855).

On the use of force. Almost every state has a law or regulation concerning police use of force. The American Law Institute's use-of-force policy, which resembles those of many states, holds that a police officer "may use such force as is reasonably necessary to effect the arrest, to enter premises to effect the arrest, or to prevent the escape from custody of an arrested person." **Deadly force,** by contrast, is only authorized when the crime in question is a felony and when such force "creates no substantial risk to innocent persons" and the officer "reasonably believes" that there is a "substantial risk" that the fleeing felon will inflict harm on other people or police officers.

In *Tennessee v. Garner* (1985), the Supreme Court adopted a rule similar to the American Law Institute's use-of-force rule. *Garner* involved the shooting death of a young, unarmed felon who was fleeing the scene of a suspected burglary. The result was the leading Supreme Court precedent concerning the use of deadly force to apprehend fleeing felons. In *Garner,* the Court declared that a Tennessee statute that authorized police officers who give notice of the intent to arrest to "use all the necessary means to effect the arrest" was unconstitutional.

The Court further held that deadly force may be used only when (1) it is necessary to prevent the suspect's escape and (2) the officer has probable cause to believe the suspect poses a serious threat of death or serious physical injury to other people or police officers.

One would think that the Supreme Court would be unanimous in a decision such as this, but three justices dissented, noting that the statute struck down by the majority "assist[s] the police in apprehending suspected perpetrators of serious crimes and provide[s] notice that a lawful police order to stop and submit to arrest may not be ignored with impunity" (p. 28).

Four years after *Garner*, the Supreme Court decided the landmark case of *Graham v. Connor* (1989). This case set the standard for the use of *nondeadly* force. The Court declared that all claims against police officers involving allegations of excessive force must be analyzed under the Fourth Amendment's reasonableness requirement. Further, the Court adopted an "objective reasonableness" test to decide when excessive force is used. This test requires focusing on what a *reasonable* police officer would do "without regard to [the officer's] underlying intent or motivation."

In helping to decide what a reasonable police officer would do, the Court looked to three factors: (1) the severity of the crime, (2) whether the suspect poses a threat, and (3) whether the suspect is resisting and/or attempting to flee the scene. Courts must, in focusing on these three factors, allow "for the fact that police officers are often forced to make split-second judgments—about the amount of force that is necessary in a particular situation." Therefore, if the crime in question is a serious one, or the suspect is dangerous and resists arrest, the suspect will have difficulty succeeding with an excessive force claim.

Wrongful arrests. Sometimes the police have a warrant to arrest someone but mistakenly arrest the wrong person. The most obvious consequence of arresting the wrong person is that the person is set free (and the officers are sued). However, because some "wrongful" arrests result in the arrest of people who themselves are acting criminally, a few decisions have focused on the admissibility of evidence resulting from wrongful arrest. To what extent would such evidence be admissible? It depends on the reasonableness of the police action.

For example, in *Hill v. California* (1971), the Supreme Court focused on an arrest of the wrong person. In that case, the police arrived at Hill's apartment to arrest him, but Miller answered the door. Miller fit Hill's description, so the police arrested Miller. Miller even provided identification to prove that he was not Hill, but the Court stated that "aliases and false identifications are not uncommon" (p. 803). While in the apartment, police officers spotted a pistol and ammunition clip in plain view. These items were seized and later admitted into evidence. The Supreme Court ruled that the police could have reasonably believed that Miller was Hill. Furthermore, the Court pointed out that "sufficient probability, not certainty, is the touchstone of reasonableness under the Fourth Amendment, and on the record before us the officers' mistake was understandable and the arrest a reasonable response to the situation facing them at the time" (p. 803).

Media Presence During the Execution of Arrest Warrants

People possess a reasonable expectation of privacy in their homes. As such, constitutional protections apply. Allowing members of the media to accompany police during the service of search warrants violates people's reasonable expectation of privacy, at least according to a recent Supreme Court decision.

The Supreme Court's decision in *Wilson v. Layne* (1999) serves as the foundation of this section. The facts in *Wilson* were as follows: Dominic Wilson was identified as a dangerous fugitive because he had apparently violated his probation on three previous occasions. The Circuit Court for Montgomery County, Maryland, issued three arrest warrants, one for each of his violations. The warrants were addressed to "any duly authorized peace officer." The warrants made no mention of media presence during the arrest. Early in the morning on April 16, 1992, Deputy U.S. Marshals and Montgomery County Police officers, who were joined by a *Washington Post* reporter and a photographer (as part of a Marshal's Service ride-along policy), entered the suspected home of Dominic Wilson.

Dominic's parents were asleep in bed when the officers arrived. They heard the officers enter the home and ran into the living room to investigate the disturbance. A verbal altercation ensued, and both the Wilsons were subdued. Dominic Wilson was never found. Throughout the ordeal, the reporter observed and the photographer took pictures of what occurred. The pictures were never published and a story was never printed. Nevertheless, Charles and Geraldine Wilson brought a Bivens lawsuit (a lawsuit against *federal* officials) against the Marshals, alleging the officers violated their Fourth Amendment rights by bringing the media into their home.

The case worked its way up through the lower courts, during which time the issue of qualified immunity (whether the officers could be immune from liability because of their "mistake") was hotly disputed. Then, on November 9, 1998, the Supreme Court granted the Wilsons writ of certiorari limited to the issues of (1) whether *law enforcement officers* violate the Fourth Amendment by allowing members of the media to accompany them on the service of warrants and (2) whether, if such activity violates the Fourth Amendment, the officers were nonetheless entitled to qualified immunity.

Clearly, the police were authorized to enter the Wilsons' home. However, it does not necessarily follow that they were entitled to bring the reporters into the residence. In *Horton v. California* (1990, p.140), for example, the Court held that "if the scope of the search exceeds that permitted by the terms of a validly issued warrant or the character of the relevant exception from the warrant requirement, the subsequent seizure is unconstitutional without more." This ruling does not mean that every police action during the service of the warrant should be explicitly set forth in the warrant (e.g., *Michigan v. Summers*, 1981, p.705), but it does mean that the police actions in the execution of the warrant should be related to the objectives of the intrusion (*Arizona v. Hicks*, 1987, p. 325).

Chief Justice Rehnquist, writing for the majority in *Wilson*, began by stating that the Fourth Amendment embodies the "centuries-old principle of respect for the privacy of the home" (p. 5). The court went on to state that although the law enforcement officers were authorized to enter the Wilsons' home, "it does not necessarily follow that they were entitled to bring a newspaper reporter and photographer with them" (p. 5). The Court then considered whether the actions of the reporters were related to the objectives of the intrusion into the Wilsons' home. It ruled that they were not. Because the reporters were in the Wilsons' residence for their own purposes, "they were not present for any reason related to the justification for police entry into the home" (p. 6).

The government offered arguments against this finding. First, it argued that the reporters *were* present to aid legitimate law enforcement purposes. The Supreme Court disagreed with this argument, claiming that Fourth Amendment protections would be "significantly watered down" (p. 6) if a media presence was to be seen as assisting in law enforcement objectives.

The government's second argument was that a media presence informs the public of law enforcement efforts to combat illegal activity. Previous Court decisions seemed to support this position. For example, in *Cox Broadcasting Corp. v. Cohn* (1975, pp. 491–492) the Court stated that "in a society in which each individual has but limited time and resources with which to observe at first hand the operations of his government, he relies necessarily upon the press to bring him in convenient form the facts of those operations" (see also *Richmond Newspapers, Inc. v. Virginia*, 1980). Despite past decisions that seemed to support the government's position on this point, the Court disagreed with this First Amendment argument, holding that "the Fourth Amendment also protects a very important right, and in the present case it is in terms of that right that media ride-alongs must be judged" (p. 6).

Finally, the government argued that media's presence aids in the reduction of police abuses, but the Court concluded that the reporters in *Wilson* were acting with their own interests in mind. "They were not there for the purpose of protecting the officers, much less the Wilsons . . . evidenced in part by the fact that the newspaper and not the police retained the photographs" (p. 7). The Court ruled that "it is a violation of the Fourth Amendment for police to bring members of the media or other third parties into a home during the execution of a warrant when the presence of the third parties in the home was not in aid of the execution of the warrant" (p. 7).

The second issue in *Wilson* concerned the concept of qualified immunity. Neither the language nor the legislative history of Section 1983 makes any mention of immunity from liability. However, courts now recognize a qualified immunity defense for conduct that, while unconstitutional, prevents the police from being held liable. Police officers charged with violating a plaintiff's constitutional rights may be entitled to **qualified immunity** if their conduct did not "violate clearly established statutory or constitutional rights of which a reasonable person would have known" (*Harlow v. Fitzgerald*, 1982, p. 818).

At one point, qualified immunity was determined by inquiring into whether the officer acted in good faith (*Wood v. Strickland* 1975); recently, however, the courts have substituted the subjective, good-faith test with a test of objective legal reasonableness (*Harlow v. Fitzgerald* 1982). The test for qualified immunity was set forth by the Court in *Anderson v. Creighton* (1987):

> Whether an official protected by qualified immunity may be held personally liable for an allegedly unlawful action generally turns on the "objective legal reasonableness" of the action, assessed in light of the legal rules that were "clearly established" at the time it was taken. (p. 639)

Qualified immunity can be extended to state law enforcement as well as federal law enforcement officials, as in *Wilson* (*Butz v. Economou*, 1978; *Malley v. Briggs*, 1986), and it owes its existence to the argument that the need for effective law enforcement outweighs the risk of police error (*Scheuer v. Rhodes*, 1974).

The issue in *Wilson*, according to the Supreme Court, was "whether a reasonable officer could have believed bringing members of the media into a home during the execution of an arrest warrant was lawful, in light of clearly established law and the information the officers possessed" (*Wilson v. Layne*, 1999, p. 8). The Court then set out to determine whether the right allegedly violated was defined at the "appropriate level of specificity" (*Anderson v. Creighton*, 1987:123). The Court concluded that it had not, and held that "it was not unreasonable for a police officer to have believed that bringing the media observers along during the execution of an arrest warrant (even in a home) was lawful" (p. 8).

In support of its position, the Court noted that there were no published federal opinions holding that media presence during the service of warrants was illegal, despite the fact that ride-alongs had become quite popular (*Florida Publishing Co. v. Fletcher*, 1976). The Court based its decision on case law published at the time of the entry into the Wilsons' residence, not in 1999, when the final decision was rendered.

One published state intermediate court decision supported the Court's position (*Prahl v. Brosamle*, 1980), and two unpublished District Court decisions seemed to also support the Court's position (*Moncrief v. Hanton*, 1984; *Higbee v. Times-Advocate*, 1980), but it still concluded that these cases cannot "clearly establish" that media entry into private homes violates the Fourth Amendment.

As part of their argument, the Wilsons cited a decision in *Bills v. Aseltine* (1992), in which the Sixth Circuit Court of Appeals denied summary judgment to law enforcement officers after they were sued for exceeding the scope of their warrant by bringing a private security officer along with them to identify stolen property. *Bills* was decided five weeks prior to the entry into the Wilsons' home; however, the Court stated that it "cannot say, even in light of *Bills*, [that] the law on third-party entry into homes was clearly established in April 1992" (*Wilson v. Layne*, 1999, p. 9).

The Court also argued that the Marshals acted legally by relying on a policy that permitted media ride-alongs, again because the law in this area was not entirely clear. On the issue of qualified immunity the Court thus ruled, quoting *Procunier v. Navarette* (1978), that "the officers in this case cannot have been 'expected to predict the future course of constitutional law'" and noted that "If judges . . . disagree on the constitutional question, it is unfair to subject police to money damages for picking the losing side of the controversy" (p. 9; see also *Pierson v. Ray*, 1967, p.557).

The Court's decision in *Wilson* seems to suggest that police officers have nothing to worry about when it comes to allowing the media to accompany them on the service of warrants, as they will be granted qualified immunity. The issue is hardly settled, however. Others, including the dissenters in *Wilson*, have argued that the law in the area of third-party ride-alongs is abundantly clear: It is unconstitutional invasion of privacy, a violation of the Fourth Amendment. For example, Justice Stevens, in his dissent from the majority's decision in *Wilson*, argued that the Court ruled mistakenly on the issue of qualified immunity. He stated that "the clarity of the constitutional rule, a federal statute (18 U.S.C. 3105), common-law decisions, and the testimony of the senior law enforcement officer" all support the claim that the officers violated the Wilsons' Fourth Amendment rights.

Other problems are evident with the Supreme Court's decision in *Wilson*. Arguably, the Court was mistaken in holding that it was *not* unreasonable for a police officer in April 1992 to believe that media accompaniment into a private residence was not constitutional. This is because the law in the area of media ride-alongs is limited; few published decisions have been reached on this issue. Nevertheless, generations of Fourth Amendment jurisprudence clearly determine that the right to privacy is of paramount importance. The Court could have easily turned to Fourth Amendment precedent in reaching their decision on qualified immunity, but it did not. Instead, the majority grasped at straws in citing three media-related cases decided prior to the invasion of the Wilsons' home.

According to the Court in *Ayeni v. Mottola* (1994), "the objectives of the Fourth Amendment are to preserve the right of privacy to the maximum extent consistent with reasonable exercise of law enforcement duties and that, in the normal situations where warrants are required, law enforcement officers' invasion of the privacy of a home must be grounded on either the express terms of a warrant or the implied authority to take reasonable law enforcement actions related to the execution of the warrant" (p. 686). The warrant in the Wilsons' case authorized "any duly authorized peace officer" to serve the warrant, not any third parties. And even though the Court could not defer to the decision in *Ayeni* (because the entry into the Wilsons' home occurred well before *Ayeni* was decided), the Court could have clearly adopted similar reasoning in its decision. Instead, the Court elected to undermine the protections provided by generations of Fourth Amendment jurisprudence.

Numerous court decisions attest that third parties cannot be present during the execution of a warrant, especially if their presence has little to do with the warrant (e.g., *United States v. Wright*, 1982; *United States v. Clouston*, 1980; *United States v. Gervato*, 1973). More specifically, several decisions attest that those not authorized by the warrant may not be present during its execution (*United States v. Gambino*, 1990; *In re Southeastern Equipment Co. Search Warrant*, 1990; *United States v. Schwimmer*, 1988). It is perplexing, therefore, that the officers in *Wilson* were immune from suit. Even so, it is a clear violation of the Fourth Amendment for police officers to allow members of the media to accompany them when they serve arrest warrants. *Wilson* did not address the issue of *search* warrants, but the same decision would almost certainly apply in such a situation.

Search Warrants

In many ways, the law governing search warrants is the same as that for arrest warrants. However, because the purpose of search warrants is to seize property, as opposed to persons, there are additional restrictions that we need to consider. For example, even though a search warrant may authorize a law enforcement officer to look for contraband in a particular location, he or she cannot necessarily look *anywhere* in that location for the evidence. Similarly, the courts have placed time restrictions on search warrants; usually, the police cannot take an unlimited amount of time to complete a search.

Figure 6-1 Sample Search Warrant

SUPERIOR COURT OF CALIFORNIA
County of _____

SEARCH WARRANT

THE PEOPLE OF THE STATE OF CALIFORNIA to: Warrant No. _____
Any peace officer in _____ **County**

The affidavit below, sworn to and subscribed before me, has established probable cause for this search warrant which you are ordered to execute as follows:

   Place(s) to be searched: Described in Exhibit 1A, *attached* hereto and incorporated by reference.
   Property to be seized: Described in Exhibit 1B, *attached* hereto and incorporated by reference.
   Night service: [If initialed by judge] For good cause, night service is authorized: _____
   Disposition of property: All property seized pursuant to this search warrant shall be retained in the affiant's custody pending further court order pursuant to Penal Code §§ 1528(a), 1536.

_____   _____
Date and time warrant issued   Judge of the Superior Court

✦ AFFIDAVIT ✦

Affiant's name and agency:
_____.

Incorporation: The facts in support of this warrant are contained in the Statement of Probable Cause which is incorporated by reference. Incorporated by reference and *attached* hereto are Exhibit 1A, describing the place(s) to be searched; and Exhibit 1B, describing the evidence to be seized.

Evidence type: (Penal Code § 1524)
   ☐ Stolen or embezzled property.
   ☐ Property or things used as a means of committing a felony.
   ☐ Property or things in the possession of any person with the intent to use it as a means of committing a public offense, or in the possession of another to whom he or she may have delivered it for the purpose of concealing it or preventing its being discovered.
   ☐ Property or things that are evidence that tends to show a felony has been committed, or tends to show that a particular person has committed a felony.
   ☐ Property or things consisting of evidence that tends to show that sexual exploitation of a child, in violation of Penal Code § 311.3, or possession of matter depicting sexual conduct of a person under the age of 18 years, in violation of Penal Code § 311.11 has occurred or is occurring.

   ☐ **Night Service:** [If checked] Authorization for night service is requested based on information contained in the Statement of Probable Cause, filed herewith.

Declaration: I declare under penalty of perjury that the information within my personal knowledge contained in this affidavit, including all incorporated documents, is true.

_____   _____
Date   Affiant

Source: www.co.alameda.ca.us/da/sw_affi.pdf

Executing Search Warrants

When police officers execute search warrants, they are required to abide by some of the procedures for arrest warrants already discussed. The "knock and announce" requirement applies to search warrants, provided no exigencies exist. Similarly, force can be used if a person "gets in the way," but force is not as much of an issue with regard to search warrants because it is property that is sought in such warrants. Finally, if the police mistakenly search the wrong residence, there can be consequences. If the mistake is truly a reasonable one, then the fruits of the (technically unconstitutional) search will be admissible as evidence under what amounts to a good faith exception to the Fourth Amendment's warrant requirement.

Without dwelling on these three issues any further (they were discussed at some length in the previous section), we now turn to additional restrictions governing the service of search warrants. Three important issues will be discussed: (1) time constraints, (2) the scope and manner of the search, and (3) the procedure after service of the search warrant.

Time constraints. There are three ways in which search warrants are restricted in terms of time. First, the service of a search warrant should take place promptly after its issuance. The reason for this first time constraint, according to the courts, is that probable cause could dissipate if too much time elapses between the time the warrant is issued and the time it is served. To avoid this potential problem, search warrants will sometimes specify that the search be conducted within a certain period of time.

Another time constraint that some courts have imposed concerns the time of day. Oftentimes judges will restrict the service of search warrants to daytime hours (e.g., *Gooding v. United States*, 1974). Even the Federal Rules of Criminal Procedure restrict the service of warrants to daytime hours, unless the issuing judge specifically authorizes service of the warrant at another time. "Daytime hours," according to the Federal Rules of Criminal Procedure, fall between 6:00 a.m. and 10:00 p.m.

The final time restriction placed on the service of search warrants addresses the amount of time the police can take to actually find the property named in the warrant. There are no clear indications of what constitutes a search that is "too lengthy," but the search cannot last indefinitely. Once the item or items named in the warrant are found, the search must be terminated. However, if authorities have difficulty finding the item named in the warrant, they can take as long as is necessary to find it. This includes looking *anywhere* that the item can reasonably be expected to be found. If the item cannot be found and the police decide to "come back later," they are usually required to obtain *another* search warrant that authorizes an entirely separate search.

The scope and manner of the search. In addition to imposing time constraints, the courts have also restricted the service of search warrants in their scope and manner. Scope refers to *where* the police can look for evidence. *Manner* refers to the actual physical actions the police can take find the item(s) named in the warrant.

As a general rule, the scope of a search must be reasonable based on the object of a search. In other words, the police can look for evidence only in places where such evidence could reasonably be found. To use an extreme (and obviously outlandish) example, the police could not look for a stolen circus elephant in a desk drawer. Alternatively, if the search warrant authorizes the police to search for stolen diamonds, the permissible scope of the search will be almost limitless. In the words of the Supreme Court, "[T]he same meticulous investigation which would be appropriate in a search for two small canceled checks could not be considered reasonable where agents are seeking a stolen automobile or an illegal still" (*Harris v. United States*, 1947, p. 152).

Even though a search warrant naming a small item authorizes the police to search almost anywhere within the premises specified in the warrant, this does not mean that the search can proceed without regard to a person's personal property. Usually, if property is damaged during the service of a search or arrest warrant (such as door kicked in, window broken), the police will not be held liable; however, the Supreme Court has stated that "[e]xcessive or unnecessary destruction of property in the course of a search may violate the Fourth Amendment, even though the entry itself is lawful and the fruits of the search not subject to suppression" (*United States v. Ramirez*, 1998, p. 71).

There are no clear decisions as to what constitutes appropriate conduct during a search—that is, how the manner of the search bears on the constitutionality of the police action. At least one case, however, suggests that the police can detain people during the service of a search warrant. This action is at least partially related to the manner in which a search can take place. Even though search warrants authorize the police to look for evidence, the manner by which they undertake such activity can include detaining people at the scene. This was the decision reached in the case of *Michigan v. Summers* (1981). According to the Court, "a warrant to search for contraband founded on probable cause implicitly carries with it the limited authority to detain occupants of the premises while a proper search is conducted" (p. 692). This ruling does not mean, however, that the people who are detained during the service of a search warrant can necessarily be searched (*Ybarra v. Illinois*, 1979). A **frisk** is permissible but can occur only if there is a reasonable fear for officer safety. And, of course, a frisk can give rise to search if, for example, a gun is found on a suspect during the course of a pat-down frisk. The point is that the police must guard against acting in too intrusive a fashion during the service of search warrants; they need to act, for lack of a better term, in a "reasonable" fashion. See Table 6-3 for a summary of this discussion.

Procedure after service of a search warrant. After a search is completed, the police are required to inventory the items seized during the search. Doing so helps protect against police theft and helps assure the person whose premises were searched that his or her property is accounted for (of course, this needn't apply in the case of property to which no one can claim legal ownership, such as contraband). A copy of the inventory will then be given to the person whose premises were searched. If no one was present during the search, a copy of the inventory must be left in a conspicuous place.

Table 6-3   Search Warrant Restrictions

1. Time constraints
   a. Search must be executed promptly after issuance.
   b. Search must be conducted during daylight hours if possible.
   c. Search must not last indefinitely.

2. Scope and manner
   a. Search must be based on object sought (cannot look for elephant in a desk drawer).
   b. Excessive and unnecessary property damage should be avoided.
   c. Guests/third parties cannot be searched if probable cause to do so is lacking.

Practice Pointer 6-2

In all cases, police officers should ensure that search warrants are executed in a reasonable manner. Specifically, they should minimize destruction to property and otherwise treat suspects "as though the news cameras are rolling." The Constitution does not become irrelevant once a warrant is secured.

Interestingly, the police are not required to notify people whose premises are searched of the procedures for getting their property back (e.g., *City of West Covina v. Perkins,* 1999). Also, the Supreme Court has stated that failure to provide a list of items seized does not invalidate the search under all circumstances. In particular, the Court has stated that failure to provide an inventory list is a matter of state law, not a constitutional concern (*Cady v. Dombrowski,* 1973).

Special Circumstances

There are some "special circumstances" where the blanket rules we have just discussed do not necessarily apply. We briefly consider three of these circumstances here: searches involving bodily intrusions, administrative searches, and anticipatory search warrants. The same rules we have discussed throughout this chapter apply in the circumstances that follow, but the courts have either added additional restrictions or "redefined" the requirements depending on the intrusiveness of the search/seizure in question.

Search Warrants and Bodily Intrusions

Certain searches involving intrusions into the human body cannot be conducted simply because the police have a warrant. The most well-known case that serves as an example is *Rochin v. California* (1952). In that case, the police had information that Rochin was selling narcotics. They entered Rochin's home and forced their way into his bedroom. The police then asked Rochin about two capsules that were lying beside his bed. At that point, Rochin put the capsules in his mouth. The officers unsuccessfully tried to remove the drugs from Rochin's mouth, so they took him to the hospital where his stomach was pumped. Drugs were found and Rochin was convicted in California state court for possession of morphine. *Rochin* was decided in 1952, prior to when the exclusionary rule was applied to the states. As a result, the Court ruled that the way the police handled Rochin "shocked the conscience," thereby violating his Fourteenth Amendment right to due process.

In another case, *Winston v. Lee* (1985), the Supreme Court decided whether the government could require a bullet to be surgically removed from a suspected robber. The Court required a warrant before such an intrusion but noted that the suspect's safety interests and privacy interests should be weighed against society's interest in capturing law breakers. The Court noted

> A compelled surgical intrusion into an individual's body for evidence . . . implicates expectations of privacy and security of such magnitude that the intrusion may be "unreasonable" even if likely to produce evidence of a crime. . . .The unreasonableness of surgical intrusions beneath the skin depends on a case-by-case approach, in which the individual's interests in privacy and security are weighed against society's interests in conducting the procedure. In a given case, the question whether the community's need for evidence outweighs the substantial privacy interest at stake is a delicate one admitting of few categorical answers. (p. 754)

The Court did not expressly decide the appropriate procedure before surgery is permitted, but it did cite a lower court decision (*United States v. Crowder*, 1977), in which the D.C. Circuit Court of Appeals decided that, before surgery is permissible (even if a warrant is obtained), an adversarial hearing with appellate review must occur. Thus, under certain circumstances, it would appear that with regard to certain types of bodily intrusions, warrants are not enough.

The Warrant Requirement for Administrative Searches

Warrants are required for administrative searches. **Administrative search warrants** are not issued on particularized probable cause (e.g., on probable cause that evidence will be found in a particular location).

Instead, they are issued once it is shown that the location to be inspected is chosen according to a prescribed plan, relying on neutral criteria (such as the date of the last search). This requirement is designed to overcome the appearance of bias or bad faith.

Anticipatory Search Warrants

Another special situation concerns anticipatory search warrants. In some situations, warrants will be issued based on *the expectation* that evidence will be present or arrive at a particular location. Assume, for example, that the police believe a freighter arriving from Colombia has drugs aboard but that they do not want to wait until the drugs arrive to obtain a warrant, for fear that the drugs will "disappear." In such a circumstance, a judge can issue a search warrant based on the expectation that the drugs will arrive, as long as the police have probable cause. According to a recent article in the *FBI Law Enforcement Bulletin:*

> Where officers have probable cause to believe that evidence or contraband will arrive at a certain location within a reasonable period of time, they need not wait until delivery before requesting a warrant. Instead, officers may present this probable cause to a magistrate before the arrival of that evidence, and the magistrate can issue an anticipatory search warrant based on probable cause that the evidence will be found at the location to be searched at the time the warrant is executed. (Dipietro 1990, p. 27)

A circuit court judge explained the reasons for the issuance of anticipatory search warrants:

> Courts—though not yet the Supreme Court, to be sure—have upheld the anticipatory warrant, in large part, because they see it as desirable, whenever possible, for police to obtain judicial approval before searching private premises. Indeed, the Fourth Amendment mandates that, with few exceptions, a warrant be obtained before any search of a dwelling occurs. Yet one of the major practical difficulties that confronts law enforcement officials is the time required to obtain a warrant. In many instances, the speed with which government agents are required to act, especially when dealing with the furtive and transitory activities of persons who traffic in narcotics, demands that they proceed without a warrant or risk losing both criminal and contraband. . . . [T]he purposes of the Fourth Amendment are best served by permitting government agents to obtain warrants in advance if they can show probable cause to believe that the contraband will be located on the premises at the time that search takes place. (*United States v. Garcia*, 1989)

Administrative search warrants are somewhat controversial because, when issued, they authorize the police to search for something on the belief that it will arrive, not on the belief that it is already in the place to be searched. This is somewhat akin to the problem of "pretext," where search warrants may be issued following a showing of probable cause that evidence will be found in a particular location but are then used as a "pretext" to look for other evidence not named in the warrant (such as that for which the police have less than probable cause to believe it will be found in the place to be searched).

Summary

This chapter introduced the essential components of any search or arrest warrant: (1) a neutral and detached magistrate, (2) a probable cause showing, and (3) particularity. A prosecutor or law enforcement official cannot be considered neutral and detached. Similarly, a judge who is paid for issuing warrants is not neutral and detached.

The chapter, stressed that the probable cause showing differs depending on the type of warrant. An arrest warrant requires probable cause that the person to be arrested committed the crime. A search warrant requires probable cause that the evidence to be seized was connected with a crime *and* that it will be found in the place to be searched.

Particularity in an arrest warrant requires only that a name or a detailed description of the suspect be provided. In contrast, particularity in a search warrant means (1) that the place to be searched be described and (2) that the item(s) to be seized are described in detail.

Arrest warrants are required in two situations: (1) arrests in the home and (2) arrests in third-party homes. Arrests in public do not require warrants. Similarly, arrests in the presence of exigent circumstances do not require warrants, regardless of location. The police are required to announce their presence during the execution of search warrants unless exigent circumstances are present.

The police will not be liable for property damage during the service of warrants unless the property damage is significant and unjustified; however, due process can be violated if the property damage is too excessive. Deadly force can be used to effect arrests, but only when the suspect seeks to escape and poses a significant threat to other officers or citizens. Finally, the courts will admit evidence resulting from a wrongful arrest as long as the mistake was a reasonable one.

Searches with warrants are subject to many of the same restrictions as arrests with warrants. However, search warrants are also constrained in terms of time insofar as the police cannot wait too long to serve the warrant or take too long to look for evidence. Also, the courts frequently require that search warrants be served during daylight hours. The *scope* of the search must be limited to the object of the search, the seized evidence must be inventoried and a list given to the homeowner, and the police cannot bring members of the media along when serving search warrants if the media presence serves no legitimate law enforcement objectives.

The Fourth Amendment's warrant requirement may not suffice in the case of bodily intrusions. Similarly, civil asset forfeiture is governed by restrictions beyond the Fourth Amendment's warrant requirement. This chapter concluded with a discussion of administrative search warrants and anticipatory search warrants.

Discussion Questions

1. Explain the differences among seizures, stops, and arrests. Why do we distinguish between stops and arrests?

2. When are arrest warrants required? When are they not needed?

3. Explain the three most significant restrictions concerning the service of arrest warrants.

4. Explain the precedent the Supreme Court set in the case of *Tennessee v. Garner* (1985).

5. What was the issue decided by the Supreme Court in *Wilson v. Layne* (1999). Provide a detailed explanation.

6. Explain the concept of "qualified immunity."

7. Explain the three most significant restrictions concerning the service of search warrants.

8. Give examples of the types of places police could search for stolen diamonds. For stolen welfare checks, for long rifles, for stereo equipment, for car parts, for automobiles.

9. Why is it a requirement that police must inventory seized items after a search? What types of items may be excluded from inventory?

10. What did the Supreme Court decide in *Winston v. Lee* (1985)? What was the issue and the outcome?

Further Reading

Amar, A. R. (1994). "Fourth Amendment First Principles." *Harv. L. Rev.* 107:757.

Dipietro, A. L. (1990). "Anticipatory Search Warrants." *FBI Law Enforcement Bulletin* 59:7, pp.27–32.

Dressler, T., and G. C. Thomas III. (2001). *Criminal Procedure: Principles, Policies, and Perspectives.* Eagan, MN: West Group.

Goldstein, A. (1987). "The Search Warrant, the Magistrate, and Judicial Review." *N.Y.U.L. Rev.* 62:1173.

Kamisar, Y. (1984). "Probable Cause, Good Faith, and Beyond." *Iowa L. Rev.* 69:551.

Stuntz, W. J. (1991). "Warrants and Fourth Amendment Remedies." *Va. L. Rev.* 77:881.

Whitebread, C. H., and Slobogin, C. (2000). *Criminal Procedure:An Analysis of Cases and Concepts* (4th ed.). New York: Foundation Press.

Williamson, R. A. (1982). "The Dimensions of Seizure: The Concepts of 'Stop' and 'Arrest.'" *Ohio St. L. J.* 43:771.

Worrall, J. L. (2004). *Criminal Procedure:From First Contact to Appeal.* Boston, MA: Allyn and Bacon.

Cases Cited

Anderson v. Creighton, 483 U.S. 635 (1987)

Andreson v. Maryland, 427 U.S. 463 (1976)

Arizona v. Hicks, 480 U.S. 321 (1987)

Atwater v. Lago Vista, 99-1408 (2001)

Ayeni v. Mottola, 35 F.3d 680 (2nd Cir. 1994)

Beck v. Ohio, 379 U.S. 89 (1964)

Beckwith v. United States, 425 U.S. 341 (1976)

Bills v. Aseltine, 958 F.2d 697 (6th Cir. 1992)

Butz v. Economou, 438 U.S. 478 (1978)

Cady v. Dombrowski, 413 U.S. 433 (1973)

Carroll v. United States, 267 U.S. 132 (1925)

City of West Covina v. Perkins, 525 U.S. 234 (1999)

Connally v. Georgia, 429 U.S. 245 (1977)

Coolidge v. New Hampshire, 403 U.S. 443 (1971)

County of Sacramento v. Lewis, 523 U.S. 833 (1998)

Cox Broadcasting Corp. v. Cohn, 420 U.S. 469 (1975)

Davis v. Mississippi, 394 U.S. 721 (1969)

Dorman v. United States, 435 F.2d 385 (D.C. Cir. 1970)

Dunaway v. New York, 442 U.S. 200 (1979)

Florida Publishing Co. v. Fletcher, 340 So.2d 914 (1976)

Florida v. Royer, 460 U.S. 491 (1983)

Gerstein v. Pugh, 420 U.S. 103 (1975)

Gooding v. United States, 416 U.S. 430 (1974)

Graham v. Connor, 490 U.S. 386 (1989)

Harlow v. Fitzgerald, 457 U.S. 800 (1982)

Harris v. United States, 331 U.S. 145 (1947)

Hayes v. Florida, 470 U.S. 811 (1985)

Henry v. United States, 361 U.S. 98 (1959)

Higbee v. Times-Advocate, 5 Media L. Rep. 2372 (SD Cal. 1980)

Hill v. California, 401 U.S. 797 (1971)

Horton v. California, 496 U.S. 128 (1990)

In re Southeastern Equipment Co. Search Warrant, 746 F. Supp. 1563 (S.D. Ga. 1990)

Johnson v. United States, 333 U.S. 10 (1948)

Ker v. California, 374 U.S. 23 (1963)

Lo-Ji Sales, Inc. v. New York, 442 U.S. 319 (1979)

Malley v. Briggs, 475 U.S. 335 (1986)

Maryland v. Garrison, 480 U.S. 79 (1987)

Massachusetts v. Sheppard, 468 U.S. 981 (1984)

McDonald v. United States, 335 U.S. 451 (1948)

Michigan v. Summers, 452 U.S. 692 (1981)

Minnesota v. Olson, 495 U.S. 91 (1990)

Moncrief v. Hanton, 10 Media L. Rep. 1620 (ND Ohio1984)

Payton v. New York, 445 U.S. 573 (1980)

Pierson v. Ray, 386 U.S. 547 (1967)

Prahl v. Brosamle, 98 Wis. 2d 130 (App. 1980)

Procunier v. Navarette, 434 U.S. 555 (1978)

Rawlings v. Kentucky, 448 U.S. 98 (1980)

Richards v. Wisconsin, 520 U.S. 385 (1997)

Richmond Newspapers, Inc. v. Virginia, 448 U.S 555 (1980)

Rochin v. California, 342 U.S. 165 (1952)

Sabbath v. United States, 391 U.S. 585 (1968)

Scheuer v. Rhodes, 416 U.S. 232 (1974)

Soldal v. Cook County, 506 U.S. 56 (1992)

State v. Gregory, 331 Iowa N.W.2d 140 (1983)

Steagald v. United States, 451 U.S. 204 (1981)

Steele v. United States, 267 U.S. 498 (1925)

Tennessee v. Garner, 471 U.S. 1 (1985)

Terry v. Ohio, 392 U.S. 1 (1968)

United States v. Alexander, 761 F.2d 1294 (9th Cir. 1985)

United States v. Clouston, 623 F.2d 485 (6th Cir. 1980)

United States v. Crowder, 543 F.2d 312 (1977)

United States v. DeLuna, 763 F.2d 897 (8th Cir. 1985)

United States v. Gambino, 734 F. Supp. 1084 (S.D.N.Y. 1990)

United States v. Garcia, 882 F.2d 699, 703 (2nd Cir. 1989)

United States v. Gervato, 474 F.2d 40 (3rd Cir. 1973)

United States v. Montoya de Hernandez, 473 U.S. 531 (1985)

United States v. Ramirez, 523 U.S. 65 (1998)

United States v. Reed, 572 F.2d 412 (2nd Cir. 1978)

United States v. Santana, 427 U.S. 38 (1976)

United States v. Schwimmer, 692 F. Supp. 119 (E.D.N.Y. 1988)

United States v. Sharpe, 470 U.S. 675 (1985)

United States v. United States District Court, 407 U.S. 297 (1972)

United States v. Watson, 423 U.S. 411 (1976)

United States v. Wright, 667 F.2d 793 (9th Cir. 1982)

Warden v. Hayden, 387 U.S. 294 (1967)

Welsh v. Wisconsin, 466 U.S. 740 (1984)

Wilson v. Arkansas, 514 U.S. 927 (1995)

Wilson v. Layne, 1999 U.S. LEXIS 3633 (1999)
Winston v. Lee, 470 U.S. 753 (1985)
Wood v. Strickland, 420 U.S. 308 (1975)
Ybarra v. Illinois, 44 U.S. 85 (1979) ✦

Chapter Seven

Arrests and Searches Without Warrants

Key Terms

- Arm span rule
- Common authority
- Evanescent evidence
- Exigencies
- Frisk
- Inventory
- Plain view
- Search incident to arrest
- Stationhouse detentions
- Terry stops

Introduction

In this chapter we turn our attention to arrests and searches *without warrants.* The actions discussed in this chapter are sometimes referred to as "exceptions" to the Fourth Amendment's warrant requirement. This means that they are actions the police can engage in that do not need to be supported by a search or arrest warrant. Interestingly, more warrantless actions have been upheld by the Supreme Court over the years than actions with warrants. Most criminal procedure books, for example, spend several chapters on exceptions to the warrant requirement. But our focus is primarily on the rules of evidence, so we will condense the discussion into a single chapter.

Given the complexity of case law concerning exceptions to the Fourth Amendment's warrant requirement, we approach the exceptions in an orderly progression. Recall from Chapter 5 that there are three standards of justification used to support a number of law enforcement tactics. Probable cause, the first one, is *always* required for searches and seizures, regardless of whether a warrant is required (D'Angelo 1998).

The second standard, reasonable suspicion, is required when the police engage in investigative stops, detentions, and "pat downs." Finally, several types of actions that may look like searches and seizures in the traditional sense, but are really not, have been upheld by the courts over the years. These actions are based on administrative justification. Administrative justification is not really justification at all; rather, it justifies certain police actions when the interest in public safety outweighs an individual's privacy concerns.

The warrantless actions discussed in this chapter that require probable cause include the following: (1) searches incident to arrests, (2) searches and arrests based on exigent circumstances, including hot pursuit, and (3) seizure of evidence based on plain view. The reasonable suspicion-based actions we discuss are stops and frisks. The administrative justification actions we discuss include (1) inventories, (2) inspections, (3) checkpoints, (4) school disciplinary searches, (5) searches of government employee offices, (6) drug and alcohol testing, and (7) probation supervision searches. Finally, we consider consent searches, which require no justification at all.

We frequently use the term "search" when discussing administrative justification. However, we use it simply to refer to the act of looking for something. The only searches within the meaning of the Fourth Amendment are those that require probable cause. The point is that it is important to not view administrative justification-based actions as searches in the traditional sense. Instead, they are special exceptions to the Fourth Amendment's warrant requirement that have been carved out over the years by the U.S. Supreme Court.

Warrantless Actions Based on Probable Cause

Searches Incident to Arrest

Imagine a situation in which a police officer lawfully (with probable cause) arrests a suspect, but the suspect reaches in his pocket. Imagine further what would be going through the police officer's mind as he or she observes this behavior. Such is the reasoning behind the **search incident to arrest** exception to the Fourth Amendment's warrant requirement. The logic for permitting police officers to engage in a search of a suspect incident to (i.e., following) arrest is that it would be impractical—even dangerous—to wait for a warrant.

The leading case in the area of incident searches is *Chimel v. California* (1969). As the Supreme Court stated, a search incident to arrest is permitted "to remove any weapons that the [arrestee] might seek to use in order to resist arrest or effect his escape" and to "seize any evidence on the arrestee's person in order to prevent its concealment or destruction" (p. 763).

The most basic requirement concerning searches incident to arrest—one that often goes overlooked—is that the arrest must be lawful. When the arrest itself is not lawful—that is, when it is not based on probable cause—any search that follows is unlawful (see *Draper v. United States,* 1959). Another basic requirement of the search incident to arrest exception is that the arrest *must* result in a person being taken into custody. This was the Supreme Court's decision in *Knowles v. Iowa* (1998).

Timing of the search. A key restriction pertaining to searches incident to arrest has to do with the timing of the search. In particular, *probable cause to arrest must precede the warrantless search* (*Sibron v. New York,* 1968). The reason for this requirement is to restrict officers from engaging in "fishing expeditions," searches based on less than probable cause that would presumably result in probable cause to make an arrest. Note, however, that if probable cause to arrest is in place, the officer is not required to formally arrest the suspect before engaging in the search (see *Rawlings v. Kentucky,* 1980).

Also, it is required that the warrantless search take place *soon* after probable cause to arrest. In legal parlance, the search must be *contemporaneous* to the arrest. In *Preston v. United States* (1964), the case establishing this rule, Justice Black observed that the "justifications [for the search incident to arrest] are absent where a search is remote in time or place from the arrest" (p. 367). In *Preston* police officers arrested the occupants of a car and took them to jail. After this, the officers searched the car, which had been towed to an impound lot. The Supreme Court noted that the possibilities of destruction of evidence or danger to the officers were no longer in place, as the suspects were no longer present to pose a threat (see also *Chambers v. Maroney,* 1970).

Scope of the search. The case of *United States v. Rabinowitz* (1950) was the first to set limits on the scope of a search incident to arrest. In that case, officers armed with a valid arrest warrant arrested Rabinowitz and then conducted a warrantless search of his one-room business, including the desk, safe, and file cabinets. The Supreme Court upheld the search because the room "was small and under the immediate and complete control of the respondent" (p. 64).

Nearly 20 years after *Rabinowitz,* however, the Supreme Court voted to overturn its earlier decision. In the case of *Chimel v. California* (1969), the Court argued that the *Rabinowitz* decision had been construed to mean that "a warrantless search 'incident to a lawful arrest' may generally extend to the area that is considered to be in the 'possession' or under the 'control' of the person arrested" (p. 759). Further, the Court noted that the *Rabinowitz* standard gave police "the opportunity to engage in searches not justified by probable cause, [but] by the simple expedient of arranging to arrest suspects at home rather than else-where" (p. 767). To get around this problem, Justice Stewart argued in favor of a new **armspan rule.** In the Court's words, a search incident to arrest is limited to the area "within [the] immediate control" of the person arrested—that is, "the area from within which he might have obtained either a weapon or something that could have been used as evidence against him" (p. 768). Table 7-1 summarizes the search incident to arrest exception to the Fourth Amendment's warrant requirement.

Table 7-1 Permissible Scope of Search Incident to Arrest*	
Level of Intrusion	**Justification Required**
Search of arrestee	None
Search of arrestee's grabbing area	None
Protective Sweep	Reasonable suspicion that confederates are present
Secure residence	Reasonable suspicion to fear destruction of evidence

*Assumes valid arrest.

Exigent Circumstances Searches (and Arrests)

The exceptions to the Fourth Amendment's search warrant requirement are premised on the impracticality of obtaining a warrant. Perhaps no other exception better illustrates this than exigent circumstances. Simply put, when the **exigencies** or emergencies of the situation require the police to act immediately at the risk of danger to themselves, danger to others, the destruction of evidence, or escape of the suspect, it would be unreasonable to require the police to take time to obtain a warrant. Generally, there are three types of exigencies recognized by the courts that authorize the police to act without a warrant: (1) hot pursuit, (2) likelihood of escape or danger to others, and (3) "evanescent" evidence. Despite the fact that these exceptions are such that the police can act without a warrant, the exceptions still require that probable cause be in place.

Hot pursuit. The Supreme Court first recognized the hot pursuit exception in the case of *Warden v. Hayden* (1967). In that case, the police were called by taxi cab drivers who reported that their taxi company had been robbed. The police then followed the suspect to a house. The police were granted entry to the house by the suspect's wife. The suspect was upstairs in the house, pretending to be asleep. While searching the house for the suspect, the police found and seized clothing, a shotgun, and a pistol that were used against the suspect at trial. The Court found the warrantless entry "reasonable" because the "exigencies of the situation made that course imperative" (p. 298). Several reasons were offered for the decision. First, Justice Brennan stated "[t]he Fourth Amendment does not require police officers to delay in the course of an investigation if to do so would gravely danger their lives or the lives of others" (pp. 298–299). Also, "[s]peed . . . was essential, and only a thorough search of the house for persons and weapons could have insured that Hayden was the only man present and that the police had control of all weapons which could be used against them or to effect an escape." (p. 299).

Warrantless action based on a hot pursuit exigency is only constitutional if the police have probable cause to believe (1) that the person they are pursuing has committed a serious offense; (2) that the person will be found on the premises the police seek to enter; (3) that the suspect will escape or harm someone, or evidence will be lost or destroyed; (4) the pursuit originates from a lawful vantage point; and (5) the scope and timing of the search are reasonable.

Practice Pointer 7-1

The most important component of a valid hot pursuit search/ arrest is that it originate from a lawful vantage point. This means that police officers cannot claim a hot pursuit exigency if they are on private property without proper justification.

Other exigencies. Hot pursuit is justified when, among other things, the suspect may escape or inflict harm on police officers or others. There are situations, however, in which a suspect can potentially escape or inflict harm *absent* hot pursuit. In *Minnesota v. Olson* (1990), for example, the prosecution sought to justify a warrantless entry and arrest of the suspect in a duplex that the police had surrounded. There was probable cause to believe that Olson had been the driver of a getaway car involved in a robbery-murder the day before. The Supreme Court ruled that the officers acted unconstitutionally under the circumstances because Olson was only the driver, not the murder suspect, and the weapon had been recovered, which diminished the urgency of the situation. In addition, it was unlikely that Olson would escape, because the building was surrounded. On its face, this case does not help us, however, the Court seemed to suggest that had Olson *not* been the driver (i.e., the murderer), had the weapon not been recovered, and had the building *not* been fully surrounded, the warrantless action would have been lawful.

In situations where the search incident to arrest or hot pursuit exceptions do not apply, the Supreme Court has also created an additional exception to the warrant requirement, one that permits warrantless searches for **evanescent** (i.e., disappearing) **evidence.** This can include evidence "inside" a person.

The best example of vanishing or disappearing evidence "inside" a person is alcohol in the blood. In *Breithaupt v. Abram* (1957), the Court upheld the warrantless intrusion (via a needle) into a man's body for the purpose of drawing blood to determine whether he had been drinking. The key in this case, however, was that medical personnel conducted a *routine* blood test. The majority noted that "the indiscriminate taking of blood under different conditions or by those not competent to do so" (p. 438) would not be allowed. (Indeed, this is why *Breithaupt v. Abram* is an isolated case; police officers rarely, if ever, draw blood from suspects. Breathalyzers usually provide sufficient evidence of intoxication anyway.)

The *Breithaupt* decision also established that warrantless searches for evanescent evidence are permissible only when (1) there is not time to obtain a warrant; (2) there is a "clear indication" that the search will result in obtaining the evidence sought; and (3) the search is conducted in a "reasonable manner."

Automobile Searches

In the landmark case of *Carroll v. United States* (1925), the Supreme Court carved out an "automobile exception" to the Fourth Amendment's warrant requirement. The Court declared that the warrantless search of an automobile is permissible when (1) there is probable cause to believe the vehicle contains evidence of a crime and (2) securing a warrant is impractical. *Carroll*, which was decided in 1925, resulted from the vehicle stop of a suspect who was known to have previously engaged in the sale of bootleg whiskey (during Prohibition). A warrantless search of the car revealed 68 bottles of illegal liquor. The Supreme Court upheld the warrantless search on the grounds that the evidence would be "lost" if they had been required to take the time to secure a warrant.

Requirements. Three general requirements must be met for a valid warrantless vehicle search: (1) the exception only applies to automobiles; (2) with one exception, such searches must be premised on probable cause; and (3) it must be impractical to obtain a warrant (i.e., the vehicle stop must be such that it is impractical, burdensome, or risky to take time to obtain a warrant). The third requirement is unresolved; courts have relied on lesser expectation of privacy analysis rather than an exigency argument to support warrantless searches of automobiles.

So far, we have been tossing the term *automobile* around with wild abandon. However, *automobile* has a very specific meaning. In other words, there are precise types of automobiles covered by the automobile exception. Cars, boats (e.g., *United States v. Lee*, 1927), and planes are all considered automobiles. However, what about the hybrid situation involving a vehicle serving the dual purpose of transportation and residence, such as a motor home or a tractor trailer with a sleeper cab? The Court was confronted with this question in the case of *California v. Carney* (1985). Unfortunately, the Court adopted another objective reasonableness standard and refused to explicitly define the types of automobiles covered by the automobile exception. The Court held that the test of whether a vehicle serves a transportation or residence function requires looking at the *setting* where the vehicle is located. If the setting "objectively indicates that the vehicle is being used for transportation," the automobile exception applies.

Factors used in determining whether a vehicle serves a transportation function are (1) whether it is mobile or stationary, (2) whether it is licensed, (3) whether it is connected to utilities, and (4) whether it has convenient access to the road. If, for example, a trailer is on blocks, unlicensed, connected to utilities, and in a trailer park, it will almost certainly be treated in the same way as a residence for purposes of the Fourth Amendment. Table 7-2 summarizes the automobile exception to the Fourth Amendment's warrant requirement.

Table 7-2 Automobile Searches	
Level of Intrusion	**Justification Required**
Search of entire car including containers	Probable cause to search
Search of passenger compartment and containers	Probable cause to arrest occupant
Weapons search of passenger compartment	Reasonable suspicion/fear for safety
Order occupants out of car	Reasonable suspicion to stop
Inventory search	Administrative

Scope. A number of court decisions have focused on the scope of the search authorized under the automobile exception. Most of the decisions have focused on whether containers in automobiles can also be searched if probable cause to search the vehicle exists. In *Arkansas v. Sanders* (1979), the Court ruled that the warrantless search of a suitcase was not permissible when the police waited for the suitcase to be placed in the vehicle. Similarly, in *Robbins v. California* (1981), the Court held that containers discovered during warrantless vehicle searches can be seized but not searched until a warrant can be obtained.

One year after *Robbins*, the Court handed down its decision in *United States v. Ross* (1982). That decision overturned *Robbins*. The Court declared that as long as the police have justification to conduct a warrantless vehicle search, they may conduct a search "that is as thorough as a magistrate could authorize in a warrant" (p. 800). The only limitation is "defined by the object of the search and the places in which there is probable cause to believe that it may be found" (p. 824). Accordingly, if the contraband sought is small (e.g., a syringe), the scope of the vehicle search exception is almost limitless.

Fewer cases have focused on precisely how far the police can go during vehicle searches in terms of inflicting damage to the vehicle. On the one hand, based on a reading of the previous chapter, a due process violation may occur if the damage inflicted is excessive. On the other hand, it would appear that a certain degree of physical damage to an automobile is permissible. The *Carroll* decision, for example, was based on a warrantless search in which the police sliced open the vehicle's upholstery to look for contraband.

Plain View

Untrained observers frequently suggest that "plain view" applies in situations where evidence can be seen without having to "search" for it. While this may be a *literal* interpretation of what it means for something to be in plain view, it is not the interpretation the courts use. Plain view has a very specific meaning in criminal procedure, and the doctrine applies only in certain situations.

Practice Pointer 7-2

Plain view does not mean the same thing in criminal procedure that it does in everyday use. For police officers to conduct a valid plain view search, they must (1) have lawful access to the object, and (2) the object must be immediately apparent as contraband.

The **plain view** doctrine first emerged in the Supreme Court's decision in *Coolidge v. New Hampshire* (1971). The issue in *Coolidge* was whether evidence seized during a search of cars belonging to Coolidge was admissible. The police had a warrant to search the cars, but it was later deemed invalid, so the state argued that the evidence should still be admissible because the cars were in "plain view" from a public street and from the house in which Coolidge was arrested. The Court did not buy this argument, pointing out that just because the police could *see* the cars from where they were was not enough to permit seizure of the evidence in question. However, the Court did point out that had the police been *in* an area such as a car or house, evidence that was "immediately apparent as such" and discovered "inadvertently" would be admissible. In other words, part of the reason the evidence was not admissible in Coolidge was that the police officers were not lawfully "in" the cars when the evidence was seized.

The lawful access requirement. For the plain view doctrine to apply, the police must have *lawful access* to the object to be seized. Consider what the Supreme Court had to say in *Coolidge:*

> [P]lain view *alone* is never enough to justify the warrantless seizure of evidence. This is simply a corollary of the familiar principle . . . that no amount of probable cause can justify a warrantless search or seizure absent "exigent circumstances." Incontrovertible testimony of the senses that an incriminating object is on premises belonging to a criminal suspect may establish the fullest possible measure of probable cause. But even where the object is contraband, this Court has repeatedly stated and enforced the basic rule that the police may not enter and make a warrantless seizure. (p. 468)

This excerpt from the Court's opinion in *Coolidge* reinforces the requirement that just because the police may *see* contraband does not necessarily mean they can seize it. If, for example, evidence is seen laying in a vacant lot or other public place, it may be seized. In such a situation, a search has not occurred. However, evidence that may be viewed from a public place but is in fact on private property cannot be seized unless a warrant is obtained or exigent circumstances are present. If a police officer on foot patrol observes a marijuana plant in the window of a private residence, he or she may not enter the premises and seize the plant, even though such observation establishes "the fullest possible measure of probable cause."

What is meant by *lawful vantage point?* There are four specific situations in which police officers can be found in a lawful vantage point for purposes of the plain view doctrine. The first is during a warranted search. For example, if an officer comes upon an article during the execution of a valid search warrant, the plain view doctrine may apply (subject to further restrictions described below). Second, officers are in a lawful vantage point during a valid arrest. Such situations include warrantless arrests in public, warrantless arrests based on exigent circumstances, and arrests with warrants. Third, when a warrantless search is conducted, the police officer is in a lawful vantage point, assuming of course that the warrantless search is based on probable cause. Finally, as illustrated in the previous paragraph, officers are always in a lawful vantage point during "nonsearches."

The "immediately apparent" requirement. In addition to the requirement that the police have lawful access to an object for the plain view doctrine to apply, it must also be immediately apparent that the object is subject to seizure. *Immediately apparent* means that the officer has probable cause to seize the object. This was the decision reached in *Arizona v. Hicks* (1987). In that case, the police entered the defendant's apartment without a warrant because a bullet had been fired through his floor into an apartment below, injuring a person. The warrantless entry was based on the exigency of looking for the shooter, for other potential victims, and for the weapon used in the incident. Once inside the apartment, the officer observed new stereo equipment that seemed out of place given the surroundings. The officer suspected the stereo equipment was stolen but did not have probable cause to believe as such, so he picked up a turntable to obtain its serial number. He then called in the information and confirmed that it was stolen. The Court held that this warrantless action did not satisfy the plain view doctrine. It was not immediately apparent to the officer that the stereo equipment was stolen.

Warrantless Actions Based on Reasonable Suspicion

Reasonable suspicion that criminal activity is afoot gives police officers the authority to stop and frisk people. These investigative encounters, also known as **Terry stops,** which can be traced to the Supreme Court's decision in *Terry v. Ohio,* (1968) do not require probable cause. Reasonable suspicion also gives police the authority to conduct so-called stationhouse detentions from time to time. Each of these two important police-citizen encounters are discussed in the following subsections.

Stop and Frisk

Stops are separate from frisks. A stop always precedes a frisk, but a stop *does not* give a police officer permission to conduct a frisk. Rather, the officer must have justification for each act. Reasonable suspicion is required to stop a person. Reasonable suspicion is also required in order to frisk a person.

The stop. In *Terry v. Ohio* (1968, n. 16), the Supreme Court stated that "obviously not all personal intercourse between policemen and citizens involves seizures of persons." Instead, the Fourth Amendment applies only "when the officer, by means of physical force or show of authority, has in some way restrained the liberty of [a] citizen" (p.20, n 16). Thus, there is an important distinction to be drawn between (1) a forcible seizure or a stop and (2) a less intrusive type of confrontation where, for example, the officer merely questions a person who is free to ignore the officer and leave. The seizure or stop requires reasonable suspicion (provided it is considered a *Terry* stop and not an arrest), but the simple questioning requires no justification.

There is no easy way to distinguish a stop from a "nonstop," but the Supreme Court has attempted to clarify the differences with an objective test. In *United States v. Mendenhall* (1980, p. 554), a case decided several years after *Terry*, the Court observed:

> [A] person has been "seized" within the meaning of the Fourth Amendment only if, in view of all the circumstances surrounding the incident, a *reasonable person would have believed that he was not free to leave.* Examples of circumstances that might indicate a seizure, even where the person did not actually attempt to leave, would be the threatening presence of several officers, the display of a weapon by an officer, some physical touching of the person of the citizen, or the use of language or tone of voice indicating that compliance with the officer's request might be compelled.(emphasis added)

The Court's decision in *Mendenhall* stemmed from a confrontation between plainclothes DEA agents and a 22-year-old black woman in the Detroit airport. They had asked the woman for her ticket and identification. The name on the ticket did not match her name, so the agents asked the woman to accompany them into a nearby private room. The Court did not actually decide whether Mendenhall had been "stopped," but it did create the objective test described in the foregoing quote.

Florida v. Royer (1983) was then the first case to apply the test set forth in *Mendenhall* to determine the conditions under which a seizure or stop takes place. The facts in *Royer* were virtually identical to the facts in *Mendenhall*, except that the officers did not return Royer's plane ticket or drivers' license. The Supreme Court held in a 5–4 decision that, given the circumstances, when the officers did not indicate that Royer was free to leave, a seizure had taken place. The Court wrote

> The predicate permitting seizures on suspicion short of probable cause is that law enforcement interests warrant a limited intrusion on the personal security of the suspect. The scope of the intrusion permitted will vary to some extent with the particular facts and circumstances of each case. This much, however, is clear: *an investigative detention must be temporary and last no longer than is necessary to effectuate the purpose of the stop. Similarly, the investigative methods employed should be the least intrusive means reasonably available to verify or dispel the officer's suspicion in a short period of time.* (p. 500, emphasis added).

Royer was subjected to the functional equivalent of an arrest and, as a result, the agents needed probable cause to detain him for as long as they did (which, incidentally, was only about 15 minutes). Moving the subject from a public location to a private location was one of the key factors that helped turn the encounter from a stop to an arrest.

Contrast *Royer* with the Supreme Court's decision in *Florida v. Rodriguez* (1984). In that case the Court ruled that a seizure had *not* taken place when a plainclothes officer approached a man in an airport, displayed his badge, asked permission to talk with the man, and requested that he move approximately 15 feet to where the man's companions were standing with other police officers. The Court described this type of confrontation as "clearly the sort of consensual encounter that implicates no Fourth Amendment interest" (p. 5). It seems, therefore, at least in the airport context, that certain confrontations that take place in common areas do not amount to stops within the meaning of the Fourth Amendment. See Table 7-3 for a summary of the discussion thus far.

Table 7-3 Factors Used to Distinguish a Stop as Opposed to a Consensual Encounter
1. Threatening behavior on the part of officers 2. Presence of several officers 3. Display of a weapon by an officer 4. Physical touching of the person by the officer 5. Orders as opposed to requests 6. Intimidating language or tone of voice 7. Lengthy time period 8. Intrusive actions (such as a full body search) 9. Use of lights or siren 10. Officer(s) blocks person's path 11. Coercive police behavior 12. Takes place out of public view

At the other extreme, a stop can evolve into a more serious intrusion, such as an arrest, if too much time elapses. For example, *Florida v. Royer* (1983) suggests that a 15-minute detention cannot fall within the meaning of a *Terry* stop. However, in certain exceptional circumstances, courts have permitted detentions lasting as long as 16 hours. For example, in *United States v. Sharpe* (1985) officers followed two vehicles suspected of involvement in drug trafficking. One vehicle was stopped and the driver was detained for 40 minutes while the officers sought out and stopped the second car and its driver. The Court did not establish a bright-line rule for what time period is considered permissible, but it did state that "in evaluating whether an investigative detention is unreasonable, common sense and ordinary human experience must govern over rigid criteria" (p. 685). Thus, the 40-minute detention of Sharpe was permissible.

In another case, *United States v. Montoya De Hernandez* (1985), a woman who was traveling from Colombia was detained for 16 hours in an airport because she was suspected of being a "balloon swallower," a person who hides narcotics in the alimentary canal. This case was a controversial one. Montoya De Hernandez was given two options: (1)

return on the next available flight to Colombia or (2) remain in detention until she was able to produce a monitored bowel movement. She chose the first option, but officials were unable to place her on the next flight, and she refused to use toilet facilities. Officials then obtained a court order to conduct a pregnancy test, an x-ray exam, and a rectal exam (she had claimed to be pregnant). The exam revealed 88 cocaine-filled balloons that had been smuggled in her alimentary canal. She was convicted of numerous federal drug offenses, but the Court of Appeals reversed, holding that her detention violated the Fourth Amendment. The Supreme Court, in turn, reversed the Court of Appeals decision and ruled that the 16-hour detention was permissible. According to the Court, "The detention of a traveler at the border, beyond the scope of a routine customs search and inspection, is justified at its inception if customs agents, considering all the facts surrounding the traveler and her trip, reasonably suspect that the traveler is smuggling contraband in her alimentary canal . . ." (p. 541).

The frisk. As indicated, the additional step of frisking a suspect is a Fourth Amendment intrusion that requires justification apart from that required to stop the person. Specifically, in order to conduct a **frisk,** the officer needs reasonable suspicion that the suspect is armed and dangerous. This requirement is in addition to the reasonable suspicion required to stop the person for questioning.

While *Terry* held that a frisk is permissible only when an officer reasonably fears for his or her safety, there is still considerable dispute over the situations in which a frisk is appropriate. What does it mean, in other words, to fear for one's safety? A number of court decisions have wrestled with this question.

For example, in *Pennsylvania v. Mimms* (1977), police officers observed Mimms driving a vehicle with expired plates. The officers stopped Mimms' vehicle in order to issue him a traffic summons. When the officers asked Mimms to step out of the car, the officers observed a large bulge in the pocket of Mimms' jacket. Fearing that the bulge might be a weapon, one of the officer frisked Mimms. It turned out that the bulge was a .38-caliber revolver. Mimms claimed at his trial that the gun was seized illegally, but the Supreme Court upheld the frisk. Even though a bulge in one's pocket is not necessarily indicative of a weapon, the Court granted some latitude to law enforcement personnel.

The Supreme Court in *Terry* described a frisk as "a carefully limited search of the outer clothing . . . in an attempt to discover weapons which might be used to assault him" (p. 30). In *Sibron v. New York* (1968), the Court offered additional clarification by declaring that the act of reaching into a suspect's pockets is impermissible when the officer makes "no attempt at an initial limited exploration for arms" (p. 65). Generally, a frisk is little more than an open-handed pat-down of outer clothing. Only if the officer feels something that resembles a weapon can he or she then reach into the suspect's pocket (or other area used to conceal it) to determine what the item is. And, as the Supreme Court observed in *United States v. Richardson* (1991), "When actions by the police exceed the bounds permitted by reasonable suspicion, the seizure becomes an arrest and must be supported by probable cause" (p. 856).

Next, the Supreme Court in *Ybarra v. Illinois* (1977) emphasized that frisks must be directed at discovering weapons, not criminal evidence. In *Ybarra,* one of the police officers had removed what he described as a "cigarette pack with objects in it" from *Ybarra.* The Court basically decided that the officer's actions were too intrusive; the package could not have been considered a threat to the safety of the officers conducting the search. Significantly, the Court declared the seizure illegal not because the officer was not looking for weapons but because the officer did not have reasonable suspicion to frisk every patron in the bar. Nevertheless, a frisk should not be used as a "fishing expedition" to see whether some kind of usable evidence can be found on the person.

Investigative Detentions

The Supreme Court has held that certain stationhouse detentions are justifiable on less than probable cause. **Stationhouse detentions** are detentions less intrusive than arrest but more intrusive than a *Terry* stop. They are used in many locations for the purpose of obtaining fingerprints or photographs, ordering lineups, administering polygraph examinations, or securing other types of evidence.

In *Davis v. Mississippi* (1969), the Court excluded fingerprint evidence obtained from 25 rape suspects, but it did note that detention for fingerprinting could have been permissible if "narrowly circumscribed procedures" were in place. In other words, the Court suggested that there had to be some objective basis for detaining a person, a clear investigation underway, and a court order stating that adequate evidence exists to justify the detention. In another case, *Hayes v. Florida* (1985), the Court stated

> Our view continues to be that the line crossed when the police, without probable cause or a warrant, forcibly remove a person from his home or other place in which he is entitled to be and transport him to the police station, where he is detained, although briefly, for investigative purposes. We adhere to the view that such seizures, at least where not under judicial supervision, are sufficiently like arrests to invoke the traditional rule that arrests may constitutionally be made only on probable cause. (p. 816)

The key in *Hayes,* however, is that the detention was not consensual. In cases where consent is obtained, probable cause is not necessary. In short, stationhouse detentions for the purpose of fingerprinting (the Supreme Court has not addressed stationhouse detentions not involving fingerprinting) are permissible when (1) there is reasonable suspicion to believe the suspect has committed a crime; (2) there is a reasonable belief that the fingerprints will inculpate or exculpate the suspect; and (3) the procedure is carried out promptly.

Warrantless Actions Based on Administrative Justification

Administrative searches, or those based on administrative justification, are those whose primary purpose is noncriminal. Because such "searches" intrude on people's privacy and can lead to the discovery of evidence, the Fourth Amendment is implicated. However, instead of focusing on probable cause or reasonable suspicion, the courts use a balancing test. This test involves weighing citizens' privacy interests against the interest in ensuring public safety. When the latter outweighs the former, administrative searches are allowed, subject to certain limitations (e.g., department policy).

This section briefly introduces several types of searches that the courts have authorized based on administrative justification. They are (1) inventories, (2) inspections, (3) checkpoints, (4) school disciplinary searches, (5) searches of government employee offices, (6) drug and alcohol testing, and (7) probation supervision searches.

Inventories

Like seizures based on plain view, inventory searches can be viewed as another fallback measure. Inventories can be of vehicles or of a person's personal items. Usually, a search occurs under the automobile exception (in the case of an automobile) or a search incident to arrest (when a person is involved), and an **inventory** is taken after the fact for the purpose of developing a record of what items are now in custody. Both types of inventory searches are fallbacks in the sense that they often occur *after* an earlier search.

What is the difference between an inventory and an automobile search?

Vehicle inventories. Vehicle inventories occur under a number of situations, usually after a car has been impounded for traffic or parking violations. In *South Dakota v. Opperman* (1976), the Supreme Court held that warrantless inventories are permissible on administrative/regulatory grounds; however, they must be (1) following a *lawful* impoundment; (2) of a routine nature, following standard operating procedures; and (3) not a "pretext concealing an investigatory police motive." Thus, even though inventory searches can be perceived as a fallback measure that permits a search when probable cause is lacking, inventory searches cannot be used in lieu of a "regular" search requiring probable cause.

Why did the Court opt for another standard besides probable cause for inventory searches, despite the fact that they are still searches in the conventional sense of the term? The Court noted that the probable cause requirement of the Fourth Amendment is "unhelpful" in the context of administrative care-taking functions (such as inventory searches) because probable cause is a concept linked to criminal investigations. Probable cause is irrelevant in such a context, "particularly when no claim is made that the protective procedures are a subterfuge for criminal investigations" (p. 371).

The Court offered three reasons in support of vehicle inventories. First, such searches protect the owner's property while it is in police custody. Second, inventory searches protect the police against claims of lost or stolen property. Finally, inventory searches protect the police and public from dangerous items (such as weapons) that might be concealed in a car.

Note that the inventory search exception includes containers discovered during the search. That is, the police may search *any* container discovered during the course of a vehicle inventory search, but searches of containers should be mandated by departmental procedures governing inventory searches. This was the decision reached in *Colorado v. Bertine* (1987). That decision also helped the police insofar as the Court refused to alter the vehicle inventory search exception to the Fourth Amendment when secure impound facilities are accessible. As the Court stated

> the security of the storage facility does not completely eliminate the need for inventorying; the police may still wish to protect themselves of the owners of the lot against false claims of theft or dangerous instrumentalities. (p. 373)

In *Bertine* the Court also rejected an argument that car owners should be able to make their own arrangements if their vehicles are impounded (have it towed by a private company, have a friend drive it home, and so on). The Court stated that "[t]he reasonableness of any particular governmental activity does not necessarily or invariably turn on the existence of alternative 'less intrusive' means" (p. 374).

By reading *Opperman* and *Bertine*, one would be led to believe that inventory searches are relatively standard and are intended mainly to take note of the car's contents. However, in *Michigan v. Thomas* (1982) the Supreme Court concluded that the police could go even further. In that case, officers found a loaded .38 revolver in one of the impounded vehicle's air vents. The Court upheld the officer's actions because marijuana had been found in the vehicle shortly before the gun was.

In conclusion, two important issues with regard to vehicle inventory searches must be understood. First, if during the course of a valid inventory search, the police discover evidence that gives rise to probable cause to search, a more extensive search is permissible. However, according to *Carroll v. United States* (1925), discussed above, one of the requirements for such action to be constitutional is the impracticality of securing a warrant.

Second, despite the Supreme Court's apparent willingness to give police wide latitude with vehicle inventory searches, what makes them constitutional is clear guidelines as to how the search should be conducted. In other words, the Court has authorized inventory searches without probable cause or a warrant only if, in addition to the other requirements discussed above, the search is conducted in accordance with clear departmental policies and procedures. Requiring the police to follow appropriate policies minimizes discretion and the concern that inventory searches may be used for criminal investigation purposes.

Person inventories. The inventory search exception to the Fourth Amendment's warrant requirement applies in the case of person inventories as well. Such searches are often called "arrest inventories." The general rule is that the police may search an arrestee and his/her personal items, including containers found in his or her possession, as part of a routine inventory incident to the booking and jailing procedure. Neither a search warrant nor probable cause is required (*Illinois v. Lafayette*, 1983). According to the Court

> Consistent with the Fourth Amendment, it is reasonable for police to search the personal effects of a person under lawful arrest as part of the routine administrative procedure at a police station incident to booking and jailing the suspect. The justification for such searches does not rest on probable cause, and hence the absence of a warrant is immaterial to the reasonableness of the search. Here, every consideration of orderly police administration—protection of a suspect's property, deterrence of false claims of theft against the police, security, and identification of the suspect—benefiting both the police and the public points toward the appropriateness of the examination of respondent's shoulder bag. (pp. 643–8)

Realize, however, that inventory searches of persons must follow a lawful arrest, so the probable cause-to-search requirement is essentially satisfied at the arrest stage.

The Supreme Court's decision in *Opperman,* discussed in the vehicle inventory search section, has essentially been extended to person inventories. That is, as part of inventorying a person's possessions pursuant to a valid arrest, the police may search containers. The Court felt that it would be unduly burdensome on the police to require them to distinguish between which containers may or may not contain evidence of criminal activity.

Inspections

A variety of "inspections" are permissible without a warrant or probable cause. For all practical purposes they are searches, but the courts have continually stressed that the justification for such "searches" is the invasion-versus-need balancing act; the benefits of some inspections outweigh the costs of inconveniencing certain segments of the population. Most of these exceptions to the warrant requirement are based on the Court's decision in *Camara v. Municipal Court* (1967), where it was concluded that "there can be no ready test for determining reasonableness other than by balancing the need to search against the invasion which the search entails" (pp. 536–537).

Home and business inspections. Two types of home inspections have been authorized by the Court. The first concerns health and safety inspections of residential buildings, such as public housing units. In *Frank v. Maryland* (1959), for example, the Court upheld the constitutionality of a statute designed to punish property holders for failing to cooperate with warrantless health and safety inspections. The Court noted that such inspections "touch at most upon the periphery of the important interests safeguarded by the Fourteenth Amendment's protection against official intrusion" (p. 367). In 1967, however, the Court overruled the *Frank* decision.

In *Camara v. Municipal Court* (1967), the Court noted that nonconsensual administrative searches of private residences amount to a significant intrusion upon the interests protected by the Fourth Amendment. Nowadays, then, warrants are required for authorities to engage in home inspections. However, the meaning of "probable cause" in such warrants differs from that discussed earlier. The Court has stated that if an area "as a whole" needs inspection, based on factors such as the time, age, and condition of the building, the probable cause requirement will be satisfied. The key is that probable cause in the inspection context is not "individualized" as in the typical warrant. That is to say, inspections of this sort are geared toward buildings, not persons.

A second type of home inspection is a welfare inspection. In *Wyman v. James* (1971), the Supreme Court upheld the constitutionality of a statute that allowed welfare caseworkers to make warrantless visits to the homes of welfare recipients. The reason for such inspections is to ensure that welfare recipients are conforming with applicable guidelines and rules. The Court declared that welfare inspections are not searches within the meaning of the Fourth Amendment, which means they can be conducted without a warrant *or* probable cause. Of course, such inspections should be based on neutral criteria and should not mask an intention to look for evidence of criminal activity.

More case law exists in the arena of business inspections. *See v. Seattle* (1967), which was a companion case to *Camara*, was one of the first to focus on the constitutionality of business inspections. *See* involved a citywide inspection of businesses for fire code violations. The Court noted that "[t]he businessman, like the occupant of a residence, has a constitutional right to go about his business free from unreasonable official entries upon his private commercial property" (p. 543) and, therefore, warrants are required to engage in business inspections.

However, soon after *See*, the Court created what came to be known as a "closely regulated business" exception to the warrant requirement set forth in *Camara* and *See*. Specifically, in *Colonnade Catering Corp. v. United States* (1970), the Court upheld a statute criminalizing refusal to allow warrantless entries of liquor stores by government inspectors.

Similarly, in *United States v. Biswell* (1972) the Court upheld the warrantless inspection of a firearms dealership. In *Biswell*, the Court observed that "When a dealer chooses to engage in this pervasively regulated business and to accept a federal license, he does so with the knowledge that his business records, firearms and ammunition will be subject to effective inspection" (p. 311). A key restriction on this ruling, however, is that authorities cannot use "unauthorized force" for the purpose of gaining entrance.

In a later case, *Donovan v. Dewey* (1981), the Court modified the "closely regulated business" exception. The Court decided that it is not enough that an industry be "pervasively regulated" for the business inspection exception to apply. Three additional criteria must be met: (1) the government must have a "substantial" interest in the activity at stake; (2) warrantless searches must be necessary to the effective enforcement of the law; and (3) the inspection protocol must provide "a constitutionally adequate substitute for a warrant."

The Court clarified the *Dewey* criteria in *New York v. Burger* (1987). In that case, the Court upheld the warrantless inspection of a vehicle junkyard for the purpose of identifying "vehicle dismantlers." Justice Blackman noted that Dewey's first criterion was satisfied because vehicle theft was a serious problem in New York. The second criterion was satisfied because "surprise" inspections were necessary if stolen vehicles and parts were to be identified, and the third criterion—adequate substitute—was satisfied because junkyard operators were notified that inspections would be unannounced and conducted during normal business hours.

Other inspections. In *Michigan v. Tyler* (1978), the Supreme Court authorized warrantless inspections of burned buildings and residences (i.e., fire inspections) immediately after the fire is put out. The key is that the search be contemporaneous, not several days or weeks after the fire. The justification offered by the Court was that it is necessary to determine the cause of a fire as soon as possible after it is extinguished. The court felt that a warrant in such an instance would be unduly burdensome.

In a related case, *Michigan v. Clifford* (1984), the Court decided on the constitutionality of a warrantless arson-related search that was conducted five hours after the fire was extinguished. The search began as an inspection, but when evidence of arson was turned up, a more extensive search was conducted. The Court required a warrant because the officials engaging in the search admitted it was part of a criminal investigation.

Interestingly, in *Clifford* the Court stated that "the home owner is entitled to reasonable advance notice that officers are going to enter his premises for the purposes of ascertaining the cause of the fire" (p. 303), which suggests that notice but not a warrant is required for the typical fire inspection. More extensive "searches," however, still require warrants supported by probable cause.

The Supreme Court has also permitted government officials to open incoming international mail. For example, in *United States v. Ramsey* (1977) customs agents opened mail that was coming into the United States from Thailand, a known source of drugs. Further, the agents felt that the envelope in question was heavier than usual. Considering these factors, the Supreme Court upheld the warrantless search:

> The border-search exception is grounded in the recognized right of the sovereign to control, subject to substantive limitations imposed by the Constitution, who and what may enter the country. It is clear that there is nothing in the rationale behind the border-search exception which suggests that the mode of entry will be critical. It was conceded at oral argument that customs officials could search, without probable cause and without a warrant, envelopes carried by an entering traveler, whether in his luggage or on his person. . . . Surely no different constitutional standard should apply simply because the envelopes were mailed, not carried. The critical fact is that the envelopes cross the border and enter this country, not that they are brought in by one mode of transportation rather than another. It is their entry into this country from without it that makes a resulting search "reasonable." (p. 620)

Checkpoints

Several types of checkpoints are constitutionally permissible without a warrant. Checkpoints are a means of investigating a large number of people and should be distinguished from inspections. Whereas inspections target a particular home or business, checkpoints have an element of randomness. Either everyone is stopped or every *n*th person (such as, every other or every 10th person) is stopped. Checkpoints are similar to investigations insofar as their purpose is not criminal in the sense that a typical search is. And, to the extent that some checkpoints border on looking for evidence of crime (e.g., illegal immigrants), they are often justified because they are not based on individualized suspicion.

Border and illegal immigrant checkpoints. In *Carroll v. United States* (1925), the Supreme Court stated that brief border detentions are constitutionally permissible. Further, it is in the interest of "national self protection" to permit government officials to require "one entering the country to identify himself as entitled to come in, and his belongings as effects which may be lawfully brought in" (p. 154).

More recently, the Court has reaffirmed the need for warrantless border inspections: "Routine searches of the persons and effects of entrants [at the border] are not subject to any requirement of reasonable suspicion, probable cause, or a warrant . . . one's expectation of privacy [is] less at the border" (*United States v. Montoya De Hernandez,* 1985).

Border checkpoints have also been upheld on the nation's waterways (*United States v. Villamonte-Marquez* (1983), at highway checkpoints well inside the international borders (*Almeida-Sanchez v. United States,* 1973), and at international airports (*Illinois v. Andreas,* 1983).

Next, in *United States v. Martinez-Fuerte* (1976), the Court upheld the Immigration and Naturalization Service (INS) decision to establish roadblocks near the Mexican border designed to discover illegal aliens. The Court offered a number of reasons for its decision. First, "The degree of intrusion upon privacy that may be occasioned by a search of a house hardly can be compared with the minor interference with privacy resulting from the mere stop for questioning as to residence" (p. 565). Second, motorists could avoid the checkpoint if they so desired. Third, the Court noted that the traffic flow near the border was heavy, so individualized suspicion was not possible. Fourth, the location of the roadblock was not decided by the officers in the field "but by officials responsible for making overall decisions." Finally, a requirement that such stops be based on probable cause "would largely eliminate any deterrent to the conduct of well-disguised smuggling operations, even though smugglers are known to use these highways regularly" (p. 557).

Drunk driving checkpoints. In *Michigan Dept. of State Police v. Sitz* (1990), the Court upheld warrantless, suspicionless checkpoints designed to detect evidence of drunk driving. In that case, police checkpoints were set up at which all drivers were stopped and briefly (approximately 25 seconds) observed for signs of intoxication. If such signs were found, the driver would be detained for sobriety testing and, if the indication was that the driver was intoxicated, an arrest would be made. The Court weighed the magnitude of the governmental interest in eradicating the drunk driving problem against the slight intrusion to motorists stopped briefly at such checkpoints. Key to the constitutionality of Michigan's checkpoint were two additional factors: (1) evenhandedness was ensured because the locations of the checkpoints were chosen pursuant to written guidelines, and every driver was stopped; and (2) the officers themselves were not given discretion to decide whom to stop. Significantly, the checkpoint was deemed constitutional even though motorists were *not* notified of the upcoming checkpoint *or* given an opportunity to turn around and go the other way.

Other types of checkpoints. In *Delaware v. Prouse* (1979), the Supreme Court held that law enforcement officials cannot randomly stop drivers for the purpose of checking their drivers' licenses. The Court did note, however, that "this holding does not preclude the State of Delaware or other States from developing methods for spot checks that involve less intrusion or that do not involve the unconstrained exercise of discretion" (p. 663). In particular, "Questioning of all oncoming traffic at roadblock-type stops is one possible alternative" (p. 663). If officers stopped every 5th, 10th, or 20th vehicle, this action would probably conform to the Court's requirement that roadblocks and checkpoints restrict individual officers' discretion to the fullest extent possible.

Other types of checkpoints have come to the Supreme Court's attention. In *United States v. Villamonte-Marquez* (1983), for example, the Court distinguished stops of boats from stops of vehicles on land. In that case, customs officers stopped and boarded a person's boat to inspect documents in accordance with 19 U.S.C.A. Section 1581(a), which permits officers to board any vessel at any time without justification to examine the vessel's manifest or other documents. While on board the defendant's boat, one of the customs officers smelled what he thought was marijuana. Looking through an open hatch, the officer spotted bales that turned out to contain marijuana. The Court noted that fixed "checkpoints" are not possible given the expansiveness of open water, so it relied on different reasoning. The Court noted that boardings such as that in *Villamonte-Marquez* are essential to ensure enforcement of the law in waters ". . . where the need to deter or apprehend drug smugglers is great. . . ." (p. 593). A key restriction the Court *did* impose, however, was that such detentions be (1) brief and (2) limited to the inspection of documents. The reason the seizure of the marijuana was upheld in *Villamonte-Marquez* was that the contraband was in plain view.

Airport checkpoints are also authorized. There is no need for probable cause or reasonable suspicion in such situations. According to the Ninth Circuit, "The need to prevent airline hijacking is unquestionably grave and urgent. . . . A pre-boarding screening of all passengers and carry-on articles sufficient in scope to detect the presence of weapons or explosives is reasonably necessary to meet the need" (*United States v. Davis*, 1973). Another court reached a similar conclusion (*United States v. Lopez* (1971).

Note that airport screenings are now conducted by public as opposed to private actors. Prior to the 2001 destruction of the World Trade Center by Al Qaida terrorists, airport searches were conducted by private security companies. Now, they are conducted by Transportation Safety Administration (TSA) officials, who are employed by the federal government. This change is of no consequence to the constitutionality of airport screenings, however, even though such searches are sometimes more intrusive than those prior to the attacks (e.g., "shoe searches" and searches at the boarding gate in addition to the main security checkpoint).

The administrative search rationale is *not* acceptable, by comparison, to detect evidence of criminal activity. This was the decision reached in the recent Supreme Court case, *City of Indianapolis v. Edmond* (2000). There the Court decided whether a city's suspicionless checkpoints for detecting illegal drugs were constitutional. Here is how the Supreme Court described the checkpoints:

> The city of Indianapolis operated a checkpoint program under which the police, acting without individualized suspicion, stopped a predetermined number of vehicles at roadblocks in various locations on city roads for the primary purpose of the discovery and interdiction of illegal narcotics. Under the program, at least one officer would (1) approach each vehicle, (2) advise the driver that he or she was being stopped briefly at a drug checkpoint, (3) ask the driver to produce a driver's license and the vehicle's registration, (4) look for signs of impairment, and (5) conduct an open-view examination of the vehicle from the outside. In addition, a narcotics-detection dog would walk around the outside of each stopped vehicle. (p. 32)

The Court held that stops such as those conducted during Indianapolis' checkpoint operations require individualized suspicion. In addition, "because the checkpoint program's primary purpose [was] indistinguishable from the general interest in crime control" (p. 44), it was deemed violative of the Fourth Amendment.

School Disciplinary Searches

Public school administrators and teachers may search students without a warrant if they possess reasonable suspicion that the search will yield evidence that the student has violated the law or is violating the law or rules of the school. However, such school disciplinary searches must not be "excessively intrusive in light of the age and sex of the students and the nature of the infraction" (p. 381). This was the decision reached in *New Jersey v. T.L.O.* (1985). In *T.L.O.*, a high school student was caught smoking in a school bathroom (in violation of school policy) and was sent to the vice principal, who proceeded to search the student's purse for cigarettes. During the search, the vice principal found evidence implicating the student in the sale of marijuana. The Supreme Court held that the evidence was admissible because the administrator had sufficient justification to search the purse for evidence concerning the school's antismoking policy.

In support of its decision in *T.L.O.*, the Court noted that a warrant requirement "would unduly interfere with the maintenance of the swift and informal disciplinary procedures needed in the schools . . . [and] . . . the substantial need of teachers and administrators for freedom to maintain order in the schools" (p. 376). The majority further stated that the reasonableness test for school disciplinary searches involves a twofold inquiry: "First, one must consider 'whether the . . . action was justified at its inception; second, one must determine whether the search as actually conducted' was reasonably related in scope to the circumstances which justified the interference in the first place."

Note that *T.L.O.* concerns students in grades K-12. A different story emerges when moving to public and private universities. The courts have generally held that the Fourth Amendment is applicable at the university level. That is, for university personnel to conduct searches of students' dorm rooms, lockers, and so on, some level of justification is required.

Searches of Government Employee Offices

In a case similar to *T.L.O.*, although not involving a public school student, the Supreme Court held that neither a warrant nor probable cause was needed to search a government employee's office, but the search must be "a noninvestigatory work-related intrusion or an investigatory search for evidence of suspected work-related employee misfeasance" (*O'Connor v. Ortega*, 1987). Justice O'Connor summarized the Court's reasoning:

> [T]he delay in correcting the employee misconduct caused by the need for probable cause rather than reasonable suspicion will be translated into tangible and often irreparable damage to the agency's work, and ultimately to the public interest. (p. 724)

It is important to note, however, that the Court was limiting its decision strictly to work-related matters: "We do not address the appropriate standard when an employee is being investigated for criminal misconduct or breaches of other nonwork-related statutory or regulatory standards" (p. 729). The Court further noted in *Ortega* that the appropriate standard with which to judge such searches is "reasonableness":

> We hold, therefore, that public employer intrusions on the constitutionally protected privacy interests of government employees for noninvestigatory, work-related purposes, as well as for investigations of work-related misconduct, should be judged by the standard of reasonableness under all the circumstances. Under this reasonableness standard, both the inception and the scope of the intrusion must be reasonable. (pp. 725–726)

At the risk of muddying the waters, it should be pointed out that "reasonableness" in the context of public school student and government employee searches is not the same as "reasonable suspicion." The latter refers to a certain level of suspicion, while the former focuses on the procedural aspects of the search (e.g., did authorities go "too far" in conducting the search). The distinction between reasonableness and reasonable suspicion is a subtle but important one, hence the reason for discussing disciplinary and work-related searches in the section on administrative justification. The searches in this section are based not on suspicion but on administrative need.

Perhaps more important, none of the foregoing applies to individuals employed in *private* companies. The reason should be fairly clear: Private employees work for private employers, which are not bound by the strictures of the Fourth Amendment. Stated simply, private employers can search private employees' lockers, desks, and the like without infringing on any constitutional rights.

Drug and Alcohol Testing

The Supreme Court has, especially recently, decided on the constitutionality of drug and alcohol testing programs. Three types of cases can be discerned: (1) employee testing; (2) hospital patient testing; and (3) school student testing.

First, The Supreme Court has permitted warrantless, suspicionless drug and alcohol testing of employees. In *Skinner v. Railway Labor Executives' Association* (1989) and *National Treasury Employees Union v. Von Raab* (1989), the Court upheld the constitutionality of certain regulations that permit drug and alcohol testing. The Court cited two reasons for its decision. The first was deterrence: without suspicionless drug testing, there would be no deterrent to employees to stay off of drugs. The second reason was that drug testing promotes businesses' interest in obtaining accurate information about accidents and who is responsible. In *Skinner,* Justice Stevens made this observation:

> Most people—and I would think most railroad employees as well—do not go to work with the expectation that they may be involved in a major accident, particularly one causing such catastrophic results as loss of life or the release of hazardous material requiring an evacuation. Moreover, even if they are conscious of the possibilities that such an accident might be a contributing factor, if the risk of serious personal injury does not deter their use of these substances, it seems highly unlikely that the additional threat of loss of employment would have any effect on their behavior. (p. 634)

Two interesting limitations should be noted about both these cases. The first is that the Court did not decide whether warrantless, suspicionless drug testing could be used for law enforcement purposes. Rather, such testing was held to be constitutional for regulatory reasons. Second, both cases focused on federal regulations (Federal Railroad Administration guidelines in *Skinner;* U.S. Customs Service policy in *National Treasury Employees Union*). Left open was the question of private business policy. Nevertheless, the courts have since upheld drug and alcohol testing of teachers, police officers, and several other types of government employees.

This line of cases would seem to suggest that employee drug testing is gaining full steam across the country. While it is certainly true that more employees are subject to drug testing now than in the past, the Supreme Court has clearly stated that certain drug testing policies are unconstitutional. For example, in *Chandler v. Miller* (1997), the Court struck down a Georgia statute that required every person seeking nomination or election to undergo a test for illegal drugs.

Second, in a recent case, *Ferguson v. Charleston* (2001), the Supreme Court addressed the constitutionality of drug testing of hospital patients. In the fall of 1988, staff at the Charleston, South Carolina public hospital became concerned over the apparent increase in the use of cocaine by patients who received prenatal treatment. Staff at the hospital approached the city and agreed to cooperate in prosecuting pregnant mothers who tested positive for drugs. A task force was set up, consisting of hospital personnel, police, and other local officials. The task force formulated a policy for conducting the tests, preserving the evidence, and using it to prosecute those who tested positive. Ferguson and several other women tested positive for cocaine. The question before the Supreme Court was, if the Fourth Amendment was violated when hospital personnel, working with the police, tested pregnant mothers for drug use without their consent? Not surprisingly, the Court answered yes.

Finally, the Supreme Court has recently extended drug testing decisions to include public school students. Specifically, in *Vernonia School District 47J v. Acton* (1995), the Court upheld a random drug testing program for school athletes. The program had been instituted because the district had been experiencing significant student drug use. Under the program, all students who wished to play sports were required to be tested at the beginning of the season and then to be retested randomly later in the season. The Court noted that athletes enjoy a lesser expectation of privacy given the semi-public nature of locker rooms where the testing took place. Also, athletes are often subject to other intrusions, including physical exams, so drug testing involved "negligible" privacy intrusions according to the Court.

Even more recently, the Supreme Court affirmed *Vernonia School District with Board of Education v. Earls* (2002), a case that dealt with another student drug testing policy. The Student Activities Drug Testing Policy implemented by the Board of Education of Independent School District No. 92 of Pottawatomie County required students who participate in extracurricular activities to submit to random suspicionless drug tests. Urine tests were intended to detect the use of illegal drugs. Together with their parents, two students, Lindsay Earls and Daniel James, brought a Section 1983 lawsuit against the School District, alleging that the drug testing policy violated the Fourth Amendment as incorporated to the states through the due process clause of the Fourteenth Amendment. The District Court found in favor of the school district, but the Tenth Circuit reversed, holding that the policy violated the Fourth Amendment. It concluded that random, suspicionless drug tests would only be permissible if there were some identifiable drug abuse problem. However, the Supreme Court held that random, suspicionless drug testing of students who participate in extracurricular activities "is a reasonable means of furthering the School District's important interest in preventing and deterring drug use among its schoolchildren and does not violate the Fourth Amendment."

Probation Supervision Searches

People on probation enjoy a lesser expectation of privacy than the typical citizen. In *Griffin v. Wisconsin* (1987), the Court held that a state law or agency rule permitting probation officers to search probationers' homes without a warrant and based on reasonable suspicion is not unconstitutional. The majority (of only five justices) concluded that probation supervision "is a 'special need' of the State permitting a degree of impingement upon privacy that would not be constitutional if applied to the public at large" (p. 875). The same almost certainly applies to parolees, but the Supreme Court has not addressed this issue.

The Court has also ruled that evidence seized by parole officers during an illegal search and seizure need not be excluded at a parole revocation hearing (see *Pennsylvania Board of Probation and Parole v. Scott,* 1998). This latter decision can be interpreted to mean that the exclusionary rule does not apply in parole revocation hearings. A warrant requirement, the Court noted, "would both hinder the function of state parole systems and alter the traditionally flexible, administrative nature of parole revocation proceedings" (p. 364).

Recently, in *United States v. Knights* (2001), the Supreme Court held that warrantless searches of probationers are permissible not only for probation-related purposes (such as to ensure that probation conditions are being conformed with) but also for investigative purposes. In that case, a probationer was suspected of vandalizing utility company facilities. A police detective searched the probationer's residence and found incriminating evidence. The Supreme Court held that "[t]he warrantless search of Knights, supported by reasonable suspicion and authorized by a probation condition, satisfied the Fourth Amendment."

Warrantless Actions Based on Consent

Technically, most of the "administrative" exceptions to the warrant require no justification. Rather, the courts focus on public safety versus individual privacy. That said, there is one clear-cut situation in which absolutely no justification or "balancing act" is required in order to decide on the constitutionality of a search. This situation is consent. When a person consents to a search, no justification is required. This is known as a *consent search.*

What are the requirements for a valid consent search?

Cases involving consensual searches can be placed into three categories. Consensual searches must be *voluntary,* so several cases have focused on the meaning of this term. Other cases have defined the *scope* of consent searches, and still others have focused on exactly whether third-party individuals can give consent in order to subject another person's private effects to a search.

The Voluntariness Requirement

The general rule is that validly obtained consent justifies a warrantless search with or without probable cause. However, for consent to be valid, it must be voluntary. If consent is the result of duress or coercion, express or implied, it is not voluntary (*Schneckloth v. Bustamonte*, 1973). When does duress or coercion take place? There is no clear answer to this question. Instead, the Supreme Court has opted for a "totality of circumstances" test.

Consent to search may be valid even if the consenting party is unaware of the fact that he or she can refuse consent (*Schneckloth v. Bustamonte*, 1973). As the Court stated in *Ohio v. Robinette* (1996), "just as it 'would be thoroughly impractical to impose on the normal consent search the detailed requirements of an effective warning,' so too would it be unrealistic to require police officers to always inform detainees that they are free to go before a consent to search may be deemed involuntary" (39–40). Nevertheless, the issue of one's aware-ness of the right to refuse consent is still factored into the totality of cir-cumstances of analysis (e.g., *United States v. Mendenhall*, 1980), although ignorance of the right to refuse is not enough in and of itself enough to render consent involuntary.

To err on the side of constitutionality, many police departments have suspects complete consent to search forms. An example of one such form is reprinted in Figure 7-1.

Scope of Consent Searches

The scope of a consent search is limited to the terms of the consent. In other words, the person giving consent "calls the shots." This was the decision reached in the case of *Florida v. Jimeno* (1991). For exam-ple, if a person says "you may look around," that does not necessarily mean the police can look *anywhere* for evidence of criminal activity.

Another issue concerning the scope of a consent search is whether consent can be withdrawn once given. In *State v. Brochu* (1967), the Maine Supreme Court held that a defendant's consent to search his house for evidence of his wife's murder did not extend to another search carried out the day after he was arrested as a suspect. Thus, although the man did not expressly request that the search terminate, the Maine court still decided that consent had been terminated. The Supreme Court has not decided whether consent can be withdrawn, however.

Third-Party Consent

A handful of Supreme Court cases have focused on whether third parties can give consent to have another person's property searched (such as a landlord consenting to have a tenant's apartment searched, parents consenting to have their child's room searched, and so on). As far as the immediate family is concerned, the general rule is that wives and husbands can give consent to have their partner's property

Figure 7-1 Example of a Consent to Search Form

FBISD Police Consent to Search form

STATE OF TEXAS
COUNTY OF FORT BEND

CONSENT TO SEARCH

I, _____, having been informed of my constitutional right not to have a search made of my person and property, hereinafter described, without a search warrant and my right to refuse consent to search, do hereby authorize:

_____ and _____ , law enforcement officers of the _____ (FORT BEND I.S.D. POLICE DEPARTMENT), or any agent acting on their behalf, including but not limited to officers with said agency, to conduct a complete search of the following described person and property, to wit:

_____

_____

_____

_____

_____

These officers are authorized by me to take from myself and my property and premises any items, papers, materials, or other property which they may desire, upon giving a receipt for the same.

This written consent to search is signed by me knowingly, intelligently and voluntarily and without any threats or promises of any kind.

DATED _____,20__ , TIME:_____

(DECLARANT)_____

WITNESSES

_____

_____

Source: www.fortbendisdpolice.com

searched and parents can give consent to have their children's property searched, but children cannot give consent to have their parent's property searched. The reason children cannot give consent is that they are considered "incompetent" to give voluntary consent because of their age.

More confusing is the situation of consent from a roommate, former girlfriend, friend, or extended family member. Two important Supreme Court cases are relevant here. First, third-party consent can be given if (1) the third party individual possesses "common authority" over the area to be searched and (2) the nonconsenting party (e.g., the roommate) is not present (*United States v. Matlock*, 1974). According to the Court, **common authority** rests on "mutual use of the property by persons generally having joint access or control for most purposes" (p. 172, n. 7). Thus, a third party could give consent to have a shared bathroom searched but not to have her roommate's bedroom searched. What happens, however, if the nonconsenting party is present and affirmatively objects to the search? The courts are divided on this issue.

There are some cut-and-dry situations in which two people possess common authority over a particular area, but what happens when it is not clear to officers at the scene whether common authority exists? In response to this question, the Supreme Court has held that warrantless entry of private premises by police officers is valid if based on the "apparent authority" doctrine. In other words, a warrantless entry of a residence is valid if it is based on the consent of a person who the police reasonably believe has authority to grant consent, even if their beliefs are erroneous (*Illinois v. Rodriguez,* 1990). The test for reasonableness in this situation, according to the Court, is: "[W]ould the facts available to the officer at the moment [of the entry] . . . warrant a man of reasonable caution in the belief that the consenting party had authority over the premises?" (p. 179) *Rodriguez* involved consent given by a former girlfriend who possessed apparent authority to grant consent because she still had a key to her ex-boyfriend's apartment.

Other cases have focused on whether other third-party individuals can give consent. Most cannot. For example, landlords cannot give consent to search property rented to another person (*Stoner v. California,* 1964), a lessor cannot give consent to search the premises of another lessor (*United States v. Impink,* 1985), hotel clerks cannot give consent to search guests' rooms (*Stoner v. California,* 1964), and college officials cannot give consent to search students' dormitories (*Piazzola v. Watkins,* 1971). Note, however, that consent given by the driver of a vehicle to search any part of the vehicle is valid, even if the driver is not the owner of the vehicle (*United States v. Morales,* 1988).

Summary

As this chapter indicates, the situations in which law enforcement officials *can* engage in searches or seizures without warrants nearly outnumber the situations in which they *cannot* search or seize without a warrant. The Supreme Court has carved out several exceptions to the Fourth Amendment's warrant requirement. While these exceptions vary considerably in their focus, they have in common the fact that the Court has decided that it is not always practical to obtain a warrant.

Practice Pointer 7-3

The consent search doctrine should not be abused. Where possible, it is advisable for police officers to secure written consent. Doing so protects them from possible claims that consent was not voluntary.

Searches incident to arrest are constitutionally permissible, but the arrest must be based on probable cause. Also, the arrest must result in someone being taken into custody. Next, the search must follow the arrest closely in time. Finally, the search incident to arrest is limited to (1) the person arrested and any containers discovered from that search and (2) the arrestee's immediate grabbing area or arm span. Prior to an arrest, the police *may* engage in a protective sweep of the premises if they have a reasonable belief that evidence may be destroyed by someone sympathetic to the arrestee. Police may also engage in a protective sweep following arrest; justification is required for such a postarrest sweep. Finally, the Supreme Court appears to agree that the premises can be searched for evidence that is likely to be destroyed, with probable cause not being required.

Hot pursuit, threats to persons, and threats to evidence are exigent circumstances that permit dispensing with the Fourth Amendment's warrant requirement. Warrantless searches and arrests based on hot pursuit are constitutional only if the police have probable cause to believe (1) that the person they are pursuing has committed a serious offense; (2) that the person will be found on the premises the police seek to enter; (3) that the suspect will escape or harm someone or evidence will be lost or destroyed; (4) that the pursuit originates from a lawful vantage point; and (5) that the scope and timing of the search are reasonable.

When hot pursuit does not apply, a warrantless search for evanescent evidence is permissible when (1) there is probable cause to believe that evidence will be destroyed, lost, or devalued; (2) the procedures employed are reasonable; and (3) the exigency was not police-created. Finally, if neither hot pursuit nor the potential for damage or destruction to evidence exists, a warrantless search is permissible if the police have probable cause to believe a person on the premises is in imminent danger of death or serious bodily harm.

Warrantless automobile searches are constitutionally permissible because (1) automobiles are mobile, making it difficult to obtain a warrant; (2) people enjoy a lesser expectation of privacy when in their cars; and (3) automobiles are subject to a host of government regulations. Even so, for an automobile search to be constitutional, it must be (1) directed at a vehicle ready to serve a transportation function; (2) premised on probable cause to believe the vehicle contains evidence of a crime; and (3) completed without unnecessary delay.

Items in plain view can be seized if the police have lawful access to the items and if it is immediately apparent that the items are contraband. The discovery of such items does not have to be inadvertent. The plain view doctrine has been extended to include plain smell and plain feel. The plain view doctrine should be viewed as something of a fallback measure. This is because the seizure of evidence can often be justified by other doctrines, such as hot pursuit, search incident to arrest, automobile searches, and so on.

The Fourth Amendment requires that probable cause be in place before a Fourth Amendment seizure can occur. However, the Supreme Court in *Terry* ruled that a person can be seized on less than probable cause to arrest. The second conclusion, focuses on when this can occur. Generally, a seizure based on less than probable cause (reasonable suspicion) can occur under three circumstances: (1) when the officer observes a person engaging in unusual activity and the officer can point to specific, articulable facts that contribute to reasonable suspicion that criminal activity is afoot; (2) when the officer receives information from an informant who is reliable; or (3) the officer receives a communication from another police department that the person to be stopped is suspected of involvement in criminal activity.

When reasonable suspicion is in place, in order for a police officer to make a stop the officer must make reasonable inquiries. These inquiries should be limited to testing the officer's suspicion. If the questioning becomes unreasonable, excessive, or too intrusive, probable cause may be required. Then, if the officer reasonably believes, during the course of questioning, that the person is armed and dangerous, he or she can frisk the person. Factors used in determining whether a frisk is reasonable include (1) whether the person has a reputation for dangerousness, (2) the type of criminal activity in which the person is presumably involved, (3) visual cues that suggest the presence of a weapon, and (4) suggestive or furtive gestures on the part of the suspect.

Frisks are limited. If one is authorized because the officer reasonably fears for his or her safety, the frisk is limited to a pat-down of the person's outer clothing. Recent decisions permit a limited search of the area immediately surrounding the person, such as in automobiles or in situations where several people may be found. Weaponlike objects can be removed during the course of the frisk, as can contraband, but both must be immediately apparent to the frisking officer. If a weapon or other item is not immediately apparent, the officer risks exceeding the limits of a frisk, especially if the officer feels, gropes, or otherwise manipulates the object in attempt to determine what it is. Such activity may arise to the level of a search, requiring probable cause.

Searches based on administrative justification and consent require neither reasonable suspicion nor probable cause. Administrative justification is not really "justification" at all. Instead, it is something of a euphemism. Searches based on administrative justification require that the government's interest in protecting public safety outweigh individual privacy interests. Consent searches need to be predicated on little more than validly given consent.

Table 7-4 summarizes our discussion, from this chapter as well as the previous two, concerning the Fourth Amendment.

Table 7-4   Guide to the Fourth Amendment

A. Does the Fourth Amendment apply? This is a four-part inquiry . . .
 1. Does the person have standing? If yes, then . . .
 2. Is the "evidence" in question a person, house, paper, or effect? If yes, then . . .
 3. Is the conduct governmental? If yes, then . . .
 4. Has a reasonable expectation of privacy been violated? If yes, then . . .
B. Was the conduct in question justified? Must match intrusion to correct level of justification . . .
 1. Identify the type of intrusion (search, stop, arrest, nonsearch, etc.).
 2. Identify level of justification required (probable cause, reasonable suspicion, administrative justification). If there is a mismatch, the conduct in question was *not* justified.
C. Was a warrant required? If yes, move to 1–3. If no, move to D.
 1. Was it issued by a neutral and detached magistrate? If yes, then . . .
 2. Was it supported by probable cause? If yes, then . . .
 3. Was the particularity requirement satisfied? If yes, then . . .
D. If a warrant was not required, were the prerequisites for a valid warrantless search or seizure complied with? The answer to this question requires revisiting the material set forth in this chapter.
E. "No" answers or inappropriate justification will result in exclusion of evidence.

Discussion Questions

1. Explain "exigent circumstances" and give examples.

2. Explain a "search incident to arrest." Be sure to address the timing and scope of the search.

3. What has the Supreme Court defined as "automobiles"? When can an automobile be searched without a warrant? What is the Court's opinion on hybrid vehicles, such as mobile homes or motor homes?

4. Give a detailed explanation of the plain view doctrine.

5. What is a *Terry* stop? What is the level of justification required?

6. Explain the difference between a "stop" and a "nonstop."

7. Explain in detail "third-party consent searches."

8. What level of justification is required for a consent search?

9. Briefly give the facts of the Supreme Court case *New Jersey v. T.L.O.* (1985) and explain the decision of the Court.

10. What has the Supreme Court decided regarding drunk driving checkpoints? Cite any relevant cases.

Further Reading

D'Angelo, C. (1998). "The Snoop Doggy Dogg Trial: A Look at How Computer Animation Will Impact Litigation in the Next Century." *U.S.F. L. Rev.* 32:561.

Donnino, W. C. and A. J Girese. (1980). "Exigent Circumstances for a Warrantless Home Arrest." *Albany L. Rev.* 45:90.

Dressler, T. and G. C. Thomas III. (2001). *Criminal Procedure: Principles, Policies, and Perspectives.* Eagan, MN: West Group.

Gardner, M. R. (1983). "Searches and Seizures of Automobiles and Their Contents: Fourth Amendment Considerations in a Post-*Ross* World." *Neb. L. Rev.* 62:1.

Poulin, A. B. (1997). "The Plain Feel Doctrine and the Evolution of the Fourth Amendment." *Vill. L. Rev.* 42:741.

Rigg, R. (1999). "The Objective Mind and Search Incident to Citation." *B.U. Pub. Int. L. J.* 8:281.

Saltzburg, S. (1998). "*Terry v. Ohio:* A Practically Perfect Doctrine." *St. John's L. Rev.* 72:911.

Whitebread, C. H. and C. Slobogin. (2000). *Criminal Procedure: An Analysis of Cases and Concepts* (4th ed.). New York: Foundation Press.

Worrall, J. L. (2004). *Criminal Procedure: From First Contact to Appeal.* Boston, MA: Allyn and Bacon.

Cases Cited

Almeida-Sanchez v. United States, 413 U.S. 266 (1973)

Arizona v. Hicks, 480 U.S. 321 (1987)

Arkansas v. Sanders, 442 U.S. 753 (1979)

Board of Education v. Earls, 536 U.S. 822 (2002)

Breithaupt v. Abram, 352 U.S. 432 (1957)

California v. Carney, 471 U.S. 386 (1985)

Camara v. Municipal Court, 387 U.S. 523 (1967)

Carroll v. United States, 267 U.S. 132 (1925)

Chambers v. Maroney, 399 U.S. 42 (1970)

Chandler v. Miller, 520 U.S. 305 (1997)

Chimel v. California, 395 U.S. 752 (1969)

City of Indianapolis v. Edmond, 531 U.S. 32 (2000)

Colonnade Catering Corp. v. United States, 397 U.S. 72 (1970)

Colorado v. Bertine, 479 U.S. 367 (1987)

Coolidge v. New Hampshire, 403 U.S. 443 (1971)

Davis v. Mississippi, 394 U.S. 721 (1969)

Delaware v. Prouse, 440 U.S. 648 (1979)

Donovan v. Dewey, 452 U.S. 494 (1981)

Draper v. United States, 358 U.S. 307 (1959)

Ferguson v. Charleston, 532 U.S. 67 (2001)

Florida v. Jimeno, 500 U.S. 248 (1991)

Florida v. Rodriguez, 469 U.S. 1 (1984)

Florida v. Royer, 460 U.S. 491 (1983)

Frank v. Maryland, 359 U.S. 360 (1959)

Griffin v. Wisconsin, 483 U.S. 868 (1987)

Hayes v. Florida, 470 U.S. 811 (1985)

Illinois v. Andreas, 463 U.S. 765 (1983)

Illinois v. Lafayette, 462 U.S. 640 (1983)

Illinois v. Rodriguez, 497 U.S. 177 (1990)

Knowles v. Iowa, 525 U.S. 113 (1998)

Michigan Dept. of State Police v. Sitz, 496 U.S. 444 (1990)

Michigan v. Clifford, 464 U.S. 287 (1984)

Michigan v. Thomas, 458 U.S 259 (1982)

Michigan v. Tyler, 436 U.S. 499 (1978)

Minnesota v. Olson, 495 U.S. 91 (1990)

National Treasury Employees Union v. Von Raab, 489 U.S. 656 (1989)

New Jersey v. T.L.O., 469 U.S. 325 (1985)

New York v. Burger, 482 U.S. 691 (1987)

O'Connor v. Ortega, 480 U.S. 709 (1987)

Ohio v. Robinette, 519 U.S. 33 (1996)

Pennsylvania Board of Probation and Parole v. Scott, 118 S.Ct. 2014 (1998)

Pennsylvania v. Mimms, 434 U.S. 106 (1977)

Piazzola v. Watkins, 442 F.2d 284 (5th Cir. 1971)

Preston v. United States, 376 U.S. 364 (1964)

Rawlings v. Kentucky, 448 U.S. 98 (1980)

Robbins v. California, 453 U.S. 420 (1981)

Schneckloth v. Bustamonte, 412 U.S. 218 (1973)

See v. Seattle, 387 U.S. 541 (1967)

Sibron v. New York, 392 U.S. 40 (1968)

Skinner v. Railway Labor Executives' Association, 489 U.S. 602 (1989)

South Dakota v. Opperman, 428 U.S. 364 (1976)

State v. Brochu, 237 A.2d 418 (Me. 1967)

Stoner v. California, 376 U.S. 483 (1964)

Terry v. Ohio, 392 U.S. 1, 20 (1968)

United States v. Biswell, 406 U.S. 311 (1972)

United States v. Davis, 482 F.2d 893 (9th Cir. 1973)

United States v. Impink, 728 F.2d 1228 (9th Cir. 1985)

United States v. Knights, 534 U.S. 112 (2001)

United States v. Lee, 274 U.S. 559 (1927)

United States v. Lopez, 328 F. Supp. 1077 (E.D.N.Y. 1971)

United States v. Martinez-Fuerte, 428 U.S. 543 (1976)

United States v. Matlock, 415 U.S. 164 (1974)
United States v. Mendenhall, 446 U.S. 544 (1980)
United States v. Montoya De Hernandez, 473 U.S. 531 (1985)
United States v. Morales, 861 F.2d 396 (3rd Cir. 1988)
United States v. Rabinowitz, 339 U.S. 56 (1950)
United States v. Ramsey, 431 U.S. 606 (1977)
United States v. Richardson, 949 F.2d 851 (6th Cir. 1991)
United States v. Ross, 456 U.S. 798 (1982)
United States v. Sharpe, 470 U.S. 675 (1985)
United States v. Skipwith, 482 F.2d 1272 (5th Cir. 1971)
United States v. Villamonte-Marquez, 462 U.S. 579 (1983)
Vernonia School District 47J v. Acton, 515 U.S. 646 (1995)
Warden v. Hayden, 387 U.S. 294 (1967)
Wyman v. James, 400 U.S. 309 (1971)
Ybarra v. Illinois, 444 U.S. 106 (1977) ✦

Chapter Eight

Self-Incrimination, Confessions, and Identification Procedures

Key Terms

- Custodial interrogation
- Custody
- Fair examination rule
- Immunity
- Lineups
- Miranda warnings

- Photographic arrays
- Self-incrimination clause
- Showup
- Transactional immunity
- Use and derivative use immunity

Introduction

In this chapter, we turn our attention to the law of confessions, self-incrimination, and identification. These often divergent topics can be tied together—at least in part—by the constitutional provisions that control them. For example, the Fifth Amendment's self-incrimination clause applies to both confessions and identification procedures. Also, the Fourteenth Amendment's due process clause affects what law enforcement officials can do as far as eliciting confessions and facilitating witness identification of criminals. The similarities end there, however.

We begin by focusing on the Fifth Amendment, then move into the law governing confessions. Finally, we consider eyewitness identification procedures, which include police lineups, showups, and photographic arrays.

The Fifth Amendment and Self-Incrimination

Although the Fifth Amendment protects against much more than self-incrimination, its protections are not particularly relevant in an evidence course. Thus, we focus squarely on the so-called **self incrimination clause,** which states in relevant part that no person "shall be compelled in any criminal case to be a witness against himself. . . ." This clause seems straightforward on its face but has actually been litigated extensively. The self-incrimination clause can be broken into four specific components. We focus here, following the text of the Fifth Amendment, on what it means to be (1) compelled, (2) in a criminal case, (3) to be a witness, (4) against oneself.

Compulsion

Former Chief Justice Burger once wrote that "absent some officially coerced self-accusation, the Fifth Amendment privilege is not violated by even the most damning admissions" (*United States v. Washington,* 1977, p. 187). What Justice Burger meant was that voluntary (noncompelled) admissions are not subject to Fifth Amendment protection. If a person fails to assert his or her Fifth Amendment protection against self-incrimination, and the waiver is "voluntary and intelligent," whatever that person says will be admissible (see *Garner v. United States,* 1976).

When, then, can a confession or admission be considered compelled? According to the Supreme Court, compulsion can occur in a number of formal as well as informal circumstances. As noted in the landmark case of *Miranda v. Arizona,* 1966, (discussed at length later in the chapter), if the Fifth Amendment applied only in formal settings (such as during trial), "all the careful safeguards erected around the giving of testimony, whether by an accused or a witness, would become empty formalities in a procedure where the most compelling possible evidence of guilt, a confession, would have already been obtained at the unsupervised pleasure of the police" (p. 466).

It is useful to distinguish between three types of situations in which compulsion can occur (1) during questioning, (2) in written documents, and (3) when threatened with noncriminal sanctions for failing to testify. We consider each of these situations in turn.

Compulsion during questioning. A person can be compelled to testify against himself or herself, in violation of the Fifth Amendment, in at least four questioning circumstances. One of these circumstances is **custodial interrogation.** For example, if a person is arrested and interrogated after asserting Fifth Amendment protection (and is not provided with counsel), the Fifth Amendment will be violated. This is the simple rule stemming from the *Miranda* decision. (Because *Miranda* is discussed later in this chapter, we will not dwell on compulsion during custodial interrogations at this point to avoid unnecessary redundancy.)

Aside from custodial interrogation, compulsion can take place during (1) trial, (2) questioning of grand jury witnesses, and (3) non-custodial questioning. First, in stark contrast to the *Miranda* decision, which requires officials to notify people of their right to counsel before custodial interrogation, the Supreme Court has held that trial witnesses are not entitled to notification of their "right to remain silent." Neither is assessment as to whether the person's testimony at trial is the product of a voluntary and intelligent waiver required. According to Justice Frankfurter in *United States v. Monia* (1943), "if [a witness] desires the protection of the [Fifth Amendment's privilege against self-incrimination], he must claim it or he will not be considered to have been 'compelled' within the meaning of the Amendment" (p. 427).

There is good reason that trial witnesses don't need to be advised of their privilege against self-incrimination. First, it is likely that testimony given at a (public) trial is less coercive than statements made out of view of the court. Second, because a trial witness is not the defendant, the process of questioning is less likely to be adversarial. Rather, the prosecution simply questions the witness.

Witnesses who testify before grand juries are likewise not required to be advised of their privilege against self-incrimination. This was the decision reached in the case of *United States v. Mandujano* (1976). There, the respondent was charged with perjury for making false statements while testifying before a grand jury. He moved to have his false statements suppressed in his criminal trial, but the Supreme Court held that the failure of the state to provide him with *Miranda*-like warnings did not violate the Fifth Amendment (see also *United States v. Wong*, 1977; *United States v. Washington*, 1977). The reasoning for this rule is simple: Since such testimony takes place before members of the public (the grand jury itself) and is usually monitored by the court, the potential for coercion is considerably less likely than that which is possible in a private setting.

Finally, noncustodial questioning of witnesses outside the courtroom creates the potential for coercion. However, the courts have held that out-of-court witnesses do not need to be advised of their privilege against self-incrimination. As Justice Scalia noted in *Brogan v. United States* (1998), it is "implausible" that people are not aware of their right to remain silent "in the modern age of frequently dramatized *Miranda* warnings" (p. 405).

We should point out, if it is not clear already, that the three situations just discussed concern *witnesses*, not defendants. The rules are considerably different with regard to criminal defendants. A defendant in a criminal trial cannot be compelled to testify under *any* circumstances. Defendants enjoy absolute Fifth Amendment protection from self-incrimination during criminal proceedings. However, once they "take the stand" they can be compelled to answer questions. Also, they can be held in contempt for failing to do so. Incidentally, the same rule applies to witnesses. The so-called **fair examination rule** ensures that witnesses at either a trial or a grand jury hearing can be compelled to answer questions once they waive their Fifth Amendment privilege and begin to testify (see, for example, *Brown v. United States*, 1958; *Rogers v. United States*, 1951).

Compulsion via written documents. Most states require citizens to fill out documents that can ultimately turn out to be incriminating. For example, information supplied in a tax return may serve as a basis for later criminal prosecution. A relevant case is *United States v. Sullivan* (1927). There the Supreme Court upheld a defendant's conviction for failing to file an income tax return. The defendant argued that the return would have been self-incriminating under the Fifth Amendment, but the Court disagreed. In the Court's words, "It would be an extreme if not an extravagant application of the Fifth Amendment to say that it authorized a man to refuse to state the amount of his income because it had been made in a crime" (pp. 263–264).

In a related case, *Garner v. United States* (1976), after being convicted for failure to adequately complete a tax form, the defendant argued that failure to submit a tax return would have led to criminal conviction but that returning an incomplete form would result in punishment under a federal statute that made it criminal to submit incomplete tax documents—a "Catch 22" in essence. The Court disagreed that the defendant's statements on his tax form were self-incriminating within the meaning of the Fifth Amendment. In defense of its decision, the Court observed that "a taxpayer, who can complete his return at leisure and with legal assistance, is even less subject to . . . psychological pressures . . . than a witness who has been called to testify in judicial proceedings" (p. 658). That is to say, one cannot succeed with an argument that questions on a tax form *compel* incriminating responses.

Both *Sullivan* and *Garner* dealt with questions on tax forms that were "innocent" (i.e., not prosecutorial in nature). There are certain situations in which a person can be compelled to supply incriminating information in a written document. This problem arose in the case of *Albertson v. Subversive Activities Control Board* (1965). At the heart of that case was a statute that required communists to register with the government. The petitioners argued that registration violated the Fifth Amendment's protection against self-incrimination because registering with the Communist party could result in criminal prosecution. The Supreme Court agreed with this reasoning and held that the petitioners are justified in their failure to register their membership in the Communist party:

> In *Sullivan* the questions in the income tax return were neutral on
> their face and directed at the public at large, but here they are di-

rected at a highly selective group inherently suspect of criminal activities. Petitioners' claims are not asserted in an essentially noncriminal and regulatory area of inquiry, but against an inquiry in an area permeated with criminal statutes, where response to any of the form's questions in context might involve the petitioners in the admission of a crucial element of a crime. (p. 79)

In another case, *Marchetti v. United States* (1968), the Court held that tax questions that applied only to gamblers violated the Fifth Amendment because they have the "direct and unmistakable consequence of incriminating" (p. 49) the people who are compelled to answer them (see also *Haynes v. United States*, 1968; *Grosso v. United States*, 1968).

A third type of written-document issue giving rise to self-incrimination questions concerns the so-called regulatory purpose doctrine. The leading case here is *Shapiro v. United States* (1948). The question before the Supreme Court in *Shapiro* was whether documents that a business owner was required to keep and provide to the government under the Emergency Price Control Act violate the Fifth Amendment's self-incrimination clause. The Court pointed out that:

(1) the purposes of the United States' inquiry must be essentially regulatory; (2), information is to be obtained by requiring the preservation of records of a kind which the regulated party has customarily kept; and (3), the records themselves must have assumed "public aspects" which render them at least analogous to public documents.

Interestingly, the Court upheld the business owner's conviction. However, in *California v. Byers* (1971), the Court modified its decision in *Shapiro*. It held that the required information must pose "substantial hazards of self-incrimination" (p. 427) before the Fifth Amendment will be violated. There, the defendant left the scene of an accident without reporting his name and was charged with, among other things, failure to stop and identify himself. He argued that had he stopped and identified himself, he would have supplied incriminating information in violation of the Fifth Amendment, but the Court held that such information did "not entail the kind of substantial risk of self-incrimination involved" (p. 431) in cases such as *Grosso* and *Haynes*. The Court noted furthermore that the state's vehicle code (which required Byers to stop and identify himself) was directed at the public at large rather than an inherently suspect group such as in *Albertson*.

In summary, then, compulsion can occur via written documents, but only in limited circumstances. In particular, if written documents require select groups to supply incriminating information, a Fifth Amendment violation will most likely occur. In most situations, however, the Fifth Amendment's self-incrimination clause is not violated by written documents. Compulsion via written documents is a relatively rare occurrence.

Threats of sanctions. What if a person is threatened with non-criminal sanctions for refusing to supply incriminating information? Just such a question arose in *Garrity v. New Jersey* (1967). In that case, police officers were summoned during an investigation of police corruption. They were told that they would be discharged if they failed to answer questions. The Supreme Court held that such compulsion violated the officers' rights, and it reversed the officers' convictions. Similarly, in *Lefkowitz v. Turley* (1973), the Court declared that a New York statute requiring public contractors to either waive immunity or suffer forfeiture of state contracts was unconstitutional.

In another interesting case (*South Dakota v. Neville*, 1983), the Supreme Court decided the constitutionality of a statute that required suspected drunken drivers to take a blood-alcohol test or risk revocation of their driver's license. The Court upheld admission of the defendant's refusal to take the test noting that "the state did not directly compel respondent to refuse the test, for it gave him the choice of submitting to the test or refusing" (p. 562). Furthermore, the Court noted that refusal to take a blood-alcohol test was admissible because the results of such tests are "nontestimonial."

Incrimination

What is an "incriminating" statement? The short answer is that any compelled statement might be used in a "criminal proceeding." The previous section considered several means by which the government can compel people to incriminate themselves. We now focus on the definition of "criminal proceeding." If a statement is compelled but is not used in a criminal proceeding, it cannot have been obtained in violation of the Fifth Amendment's self-incrimination clause.

As a general rule, any criminal defendant has the right to remain silent at grand jury as well as trial proceedings. In addition, however, such individuals can also refuse "to answer official questions put to him in any . . . proceeding, civil or criminal, formal or informal, where the answers might incriminate him in *future* criminal proceedings" (*Lefkowitz v. Turley*, 1973, p. 77). Thus, the definition of "criminal proceeding" is not limited to a criminal trial per se. However, just because an answer is compelled before a criminal proceeding does not mean it will be held in violation of the Fifth Amendment. For example, in *Estelle v. Smith* (1981), the Supreme Court held that the state may compel answers from a defendant during pretrial hearings to determine his or her competence to stand trial. Such questioning is not considered "criminal" for purposes of the Fifth Amendment.

The definition of "criminal proceeding." Determining whether a proceeding is criminal is not as easy as one might suspect. As such, the courts usually focus on the issue of "punitive" sanctions in determining whether the Fifth Amendment's self-incrimination clause applies. This way, there is no need to distinguish between civil and criminal proceedings. Both types of proceedings have the potential to hand down punitive sanctions (e.g., forfeiture of one's property or punitive damages in a liability lawsuit).

A civil proceeding can be considered "criminal" for self-incrimination purposes as evidenced in *In re Gault* (1967). In that case the Supreme Court had the opportunity to determine whether a state's "civil" designation of juvenile proceedings diminished the Fifth Amendment's applicability in such proceedings. The Court noted that "our Constitution guarantees that no person shall be 'compelled' to be a witness against himself when he is threatened with deprivation of his liberty" (p. 50). Because juveniles' liberty is often at stake in juvenile trials, even if they are designated "civil," the Fifth Amendment applies.

However, in *Minnesota v. Murphy* (1984), the Court noted that if questions asked of a probationer (person on probation) were relevant only to his or her probationary status and "posed no realistic threat of incrimination in a separate criminal proceeding" (p. 435, n. 7), the probationer cannot refuse to answer such questions.

There *are* types of proceedings in which a person's liberty can be deprived but where the Fifth Amendment does not apply. In one relevant case (*Allen v. Illinois*, 1986), the Supreme Court noted that the *Gault* decision's "deprivation of liberty" criterion was "plainly not good law" (p. 372). Instead, the Court focused on "the traditional aims of punishment—retribution or deterrence" (p. 370). Specifically, in *Allen* the Court determined the constitutionality of an Illinois statute that provided for the civil commitment of people deemed to be "sexually dangerous." The Court's decision was that civil confinement under the Illinois Sexually Dangerous Persons Act did *not* meet the traditional aims of punishment but was instead rehabilitative. Had the civil confinement imposed on the offenders included "a regimen which is essentially identical to that imposed upon felons with no need for psychiatric care, this might well be a different case" (p. 373).

Immunity. The government is permitted to compel answers from a criminal defendant, but only if (1) the nature of the information is irrelevant to any criminal matter; (2) a grant of **immunity** protecting the individual against the future use of any statements resulting from questioning is provided; or (3) some other guarantee that the information will not be used against the defendant is provided. Compelled testimony is admissible under these circumstances because it is considered nonincriminating. This section focuses on the second and third of these exceptions, known collectively as the *immunity exception* to the Fifth Amendment's protection against self-incrimination.

Stated simply, a person cannot claim the Fifth Amendment right to be free from compelled self-incrimination if the person's testimony is rendered "noncriminal" by a grant of immunity. This general rule arose out of the government's need to procure information from criminals about individuals considered more important. For example, the immunity exception allows the government to compel answers from low-level drug dealers in order to facilitate apprehension of a higher-level drug supplier.

Two types of immunity are recognized by the courts: use and derivative use immunity and transactional immunity. **Use and derivative use immunity** immunizes only answers to questions asked. **Transactional immunity** extends immunity to matters discussed far beyond the scope of the questions asked.

The 'Testimonial Evidence' Requirement

Still another restriction exists concerning the scope of the Fifth Amendment's protection against self-incrimination: the protection is limited to "testimonial evidence." So, not only must answers be compelled in a criminal proceeding, they must also give rise to "testimonial evidence." In other words, physical evidence is not protected by the Fifth Amendment. As Justice Holmes pointed out, "The prohibition of compelling a man in a criminal court to be witness against himself is a prohibition of the use of physical or moral compulsion to extort communications from him, not an exclusion of his body as evidence when it may be material" (*Holt v. United States,* 1910, pp. 252–253). More recently, in *Schmerber v. California* (1966), the Court held that "the privilege protects an accused only from being compelled to testify against himself, or otherwise provide the State with evidence of a testimonial or communicative nature" (p. 761).

As a general rule, the government can compel any criminal defendant to supply incriminating physical evidence without violating the Fifth Amendment. Indeed, the government can force the accused to wear a particular outfit (as in *Holt*), submit to the extraction of a blood sample (as in *Schmerber*), participate in a lineup (*United States v. Wade,* 1967), or produce a writing sample (*Gilbert v. California,* 1967; *United States v. Mara,* 1973) or voice exemplar (*United States v. Dionisio,* 1973). In addition, the Fifth Amendment "offers no protection against compulsion to submit to fingerprinting, photography, or measurements, . . . to appear in court, to stand, to assume a stance, to walk, or to make a particular gesture" (*United States v. Wade,* 1967, p. 223).

We should point out that *some* verbal responses to questions can be considered noncommunicative and thus exempt from the Fifth Amendment. For example, in *Pennsylvania v. Muniz* (1990) the Court held unanimously that the physical inability to articulate words in a clear manner was not testimonial evidence and could be used against the defendant. In that case, the state introduced the defendant's slurred responses to numerous routine booking questions in order to prove he was guilty of drunk driving.

The Meaning of 'Self' in Self-Incrimination

The fifth and last restriction on the Fifth Amendment's self-incrimination clause is that it is limited, not surprisingly, to the person making an incriminating statement. That is, the only person who can assert Fifth Amendment protection is the person being compelled to answer a question in an incriminating fashion. According to the Supreme Court, "The Constitution explicitly prohibits compelling an accused to bear witness 'against himself': it necessarily does not proscribe incriminating statements elicited from another. Compulsion upon the person asserting it is an important element of the privilege" (*Couch v. United States,* 1973, p. 328). Furthermore, the Court noted that "[w]e cannot cut the Fifth Amendment completely loose from the moorings of its language and make it serve as a general protector of privacy—a word not mentioned in its text and a concept directly addressed in the Fourth Amendment" (*Fisher v. United States,* 1976, p. 401). Thus, as in *Couch,* the Fifth Amendment did not protect a person whose accountant turned over documents that incriminated that person.

There are two exceptions to the rule that only the person being compelled can assert Fifth Amendment privilege. First, in *Couch* the Court pointed out that "situations may well arise where constructive possession is so clear or the relinquishment of possession is so temporary and insignificant as to leave the personal compulsions upon the accused substantially intact" (*Couch v. United States,* 1973, p. 341). The second exception concerns privileged communications. For example, when documents are transferred to an attorney for the purpose of obtaining legal advice, the attorney may assert Fifth Amendment protection in place of his or her client. This exception is not based on the Fifth Amendment, however. It lies in the attorney-client privilege discussed in Chapter 11.

Confessions

So far we have considered the general meaning of the Fifth Amendment's self-incrimination clause. We now consider precisely when it is implicated. That is, we focus in detail on the issue of compulsion. The question we will seek answers to is, When does compulsion occur for purposes of the Fifth Amendment?

Our analysis of the Fifth Amendment that follows pertains specifically to confessions and admissions. Realistically, a *confession* occurs when a person implicates himself or herself in criminal activity following police questioning or interrogation. An *admission,* by contrast, need not be preceded by police questioning; a person can simply admit to involvement in a crime without any police encouragement.

As indicated earlier, the Fifth Amendment's self-incrimination clause applies to a variety of forms of compulsion (such as written documents). We limit our focus now to confessions and admissions. This is not to suggest that incriminating verbal statements are more important than incriminating documents. Rather, we wish to emphasize that most of the law concerning confessions and admissions has arisen in the context of police interrogation. The courts have imposed a litany of restrictions on what law enforcement officials can do in order to elicit incriminating statements from suspected criminals.

The Various Approaches to Confession Law

Not only can confessions and admissions be protected by the Fifth Amendment, but they can also be protected by the Fourteenth Amendment's due process clause as well as the Sixth Amendment's right to counsel clause. Our focus here is on the Fifth Amendment, but for the sake of placing Fifth Amendment confession law into context, we will briefly consider the extent to which confessions are protected by other constitutional provisions. Indeed, the very fact that three constitutional amendments place restrictions on what the government can do in order to obtain confessions suggests that our country places a high value on people's rights to be free from certain forms of questioning.

The Due Process 'Voluntariness' Approach

One approach to confessions or admissions can be termed the due process voluntariness approach. In general, when a suspect makes an involuntary statement, his or her statement will not be admissible in a criminal trial (or as indicated earlier, in any other criminal proceeding) to prove guilt.

At one point, the Fifth and Sixth Amendments had not yet been applied to the states. An illustrative case is *Brown v. Mississippi* (1936), in which police officers resorted to whippings and other brutal methods to obtain confessions from three black defendants who were later convicted based on the confessions alone. The Supreme Court analyzed this case under the Fourteenth Amendment's due process clause and found the convictions invalid because the interrogation techniques were so offensive.

A confession is considered involuntary when, under the totality of circumstances that led to the confession, the defendant is deprived of his or her "power of resistance" (*Fikes v. Alabama*, 1957, p. 198). This answer, unfortunately, does not provide any uniform criteria for determining voluntariness. Instead, courts take a case-by-case approach to determine voluntariness. Usually, this requires focusing on two issues:

(1) the police conduct in questioning the suspect, and (2) the characteristics of the suspect.

It has been made patently clear that using physical brutality to coerce a confession violates the Fourteenth Amendment. As Justice Douglas stated in *Williams v. United States* (1951), confessions obtained by brutality and torture cannot be admissible under any concept of due process. In many other situations, however, the police conduct in question may not rise to the level of torture but could still be questionable. For example, in *Rogers v. Richmond* (1963), a man confessed after the police told him they were going to take his wife into custody. And in *Lynumm v. Illinois* (1963), a defendant confessed after being promised leniency. Both confessions were found to be coerced. This is not to suggest that deception on the part of the police necessarily gives rise to an involuntary confession—only that it is one of several considerations.

It is safe to conclude that psychological pressures, promises of leniency, and deception are rarely *by themselves* enough to render a statement involuntary, but two or more such acts (especially if coupled with physical force) will more than likely result in an involuntary confession (helpful cases in this regard include, but are not limited to, *Arizona v. Fulminante*, 1991; *Spano v. New York*, 1959; *Leyra v. Denno*, 1954; *Frazier v. Cupp*, 1969; *Fikes v. Alabama*, 1957; *Crooker v. California*, 1958; *Ashcraft v. Tennessee*, 1944; and *Chambers v. Florida*, 1940).

As far as characteristics of the accused are concerned, conditions such as disabilities and immaturity have resulted in excluded confessions. For example, in *Haley v. Ohio* (1948), the Supreme Court reversed a 15-year-old boy's confession. In the Court's words, "Mature men possibly might stand the ordeal from midnight to 5 a.m. but we cannot believe that a lad of tender years is a match for the police in such a contest" (pp. 599–600). In *Blackburn v. Alabama* (1960), the Court found that a confession by a man with a long history of mental problems could not have been considered voluntary. In some instances fatigue and pain (such as a result of an injury) can also render an accused's statement involuntary; however, such a result usually requires some questionable conduct on the part of the officials engaged in questioning the accused (see *Ashcraft v. Tennessee*, 1944; *Mincey v. Arizona*, 1978; and *Beecher v. Alabama*, 1972). See Table 8-1 for a summary of this discussion.

Table 8-1 Factors Considered in Determining Voluntariness	
Police Behavior	**Characteristics of the Suspect**
1. Psychological pressures by police	1. Disability
2. Promises of leniency	2. Immaturity
3. Deception	3. Intoxication
	4. Fatigue
	5. Pain

The Sixth Amendment Approach

The Sixth Amendment also places restrictions on what the police can do to extract confessions and admissions. In particular, the Supreme Court's decision in *Massiah v. United States* (1964) led to the rule that the Sixth Amendment's guarantee to counsel in all "criminal proceedings" is violated when the government "deliberately elicits" incriminating responses. Massiah, who was released on bail pending a trial for violations of federal narcotics laws, made an incriminating statement in the car of a friend who had allowed the government to install a radio designed to eavesdrop on the conversation. Justice Stewart, writing for the majority, argued that if the Sixth Amendment's right to counsel is "to have any efficacy it must apply to indirect and surreptitious interrogations as well as those conducted in the jailhouse" (p. 206). Furthermore, "Massiah was more seriously imposed upon . . . because he did not even know that he was under interrogation by a government agent" (p. 206).

A case closely related to *Massiah* (and decided shortly after) is *Escobedo v. Illinois* (1964). Escobedo was arrested for murder, questioned, and released. Ten days later, an accomplice implicated Escobedo, and he was rearrested. He requested to consult with his attorney, but that request was denied. Escobedo was convicted of murder, based partly on an incriminating statement he made while in police custody.

The Supreme Court reversed:

> We hold . . . that where, as here, the investigation is no longer a general inquiry into an unsolved crime but has begun to focus on a particular suspect, the suspect has been taken into police custody, the police carry out a process of interrogations that lends itself to eliciting incriminating statements, the suspect has requested and been denied an opportunity to consult with his lawyer, and the police have not effectively warned him of his absolute constitutional right to remain silent, the accused has been denied "the Assistance of Counsel" in violation of the Sixth Amendment . . . and that no statement elicited by the police during the interrogation may be used against him at a criminal trial. (pp. 490–491)

Unfortunately, *Escobedo* was cause for some confusion. In *Massiah* the Court held that the Sixth Amendment right to counsel applies once formal proceedings have begun (e.g., a preliminary hearing, trial, or anything in between). However, in *Escobedo* the Court seemed to broaden the scope of the Sixth Amendment by holding that it also applies once the accused becomes the focus on an investigation by the police. A question left unanswered was, When does a person become an accused? Fortunately, *Miranda*, the basis for the following sections, offered some answers.

The *Miranda* Approach

In a very important yet frequently overlooked case, *Malloy v. Hogan* (1964), the Supreme Court held that the Fifth Amendment applies to the states. The Court announced that "today the admissibility of a confession in a state criminal prosecution is tested by the same standard applied in federal prosecution since 1897" (p. 7). Not long after that decision, the Supreme Court essentially abandoned *Massiah*, *Escobedo*, and due process voluntariness, focusing instead on the Fifth Amendment. In *Miranda v. Arizona* (1966), the Court announced the following rule:

> [T]he prosecution may not use statements, whether exculpatory or inculpatory, stemming from *custodial interrogation* of the defendant unless it demonstrates the use of procedural safeguards effective to secure the privilege against self-incrimination. (p. 444; emphasis added)

This wording clearly established that the Fifth Amendment should serve as the basis for determining the constitutionality of confessions.

Understand that the Sixth and Fourteenth Amendments still apply in certain situations. For example, if the police conduct in question is not a custodial interrogation (as in *Miranda*) but formal charges have been filed, the Fifth Amendment will apply. Taken further, if custody and interrogation do not take place *and* formal charges are not filed, the due process voluntariness test can still kick in. In fact, think of the Fourteenth Amendment's due process clause in particular as being something of a fallback; if no other constitutional protections apply, the guarantee of due process almost always does.

We now turn to four issues surrounding *Miranda*. Because the Supreme Court limited its decision in *Miranda* to custodial interrogations, it is first important to understand the definitions of custody and interrogation. Next, we consider the substance and adequacy of the warnings. If they are not given "adequately," the police risk a confession being thrown out of court. Finally, like many rights, *Miranda* rights can be waived. That is, people can elect *not* to remain silent. We will consider what must be in place for a *Miranda* waiver to be considered valid in the eyes of the court.

Custody. Many people believe that *Miranda* rights apply whenever the police begin to question a person. This is not the case; if the person being questioned is not in **custody**, Miranda rights do not apply. Simple police questioning—even full-blown interrogation—is not enough to trigger the protections afforded by the Fifth Amendment. The person subjected to such questioning must be clearly in police custody.

What is custody? The Court announced that *Miranda* applies when "a person has been taken into custody or otherwise deprived of his freedom of action in any significant way" (p. 444). An arrest is a clear-cut case of police custody, but what about a lesser intrusion? Unfortunately, there is no easy answer to this question. Instead, courts focus on the circumstances surrounding each individual case. The Court has stated, however, that "the only relevant inquiry [in analyzing the custody issue] is how a reasonable man in the suspect's position would have understood his situation" (*Berkemer v. McCarty*, 1984, p. 442).

In the absence of a full-blown arrest, the courts have focused on four types of police-citizen encounters in determining whether custody exists for purposes of *Miranda*: (1) traffic and field stops, (2) questioning in the home, (3) questioning at the police station or equivalent facility, and (4) questioning for minor crimes. We briefly consider each of these encounters in the paragraphs that follow.

First, custody does not take place in the typical traffic stop. This was the decision reached in *Berkemer v. McCarty* (1984), in which a motorist was stopped for weaving in and out of traffic. After the driver admitted to drinking and smoking marijuana, the officer arrested him. The man argued that he should have been advised of his right to remain silent, but the Supreme Court disagreed, noting that vehicle stops are "presumptively temporary and brief" and sufficiently public to avoid the appearance of being coercive. "From all that appears in the stipulation of facts, a single police officer asked [the defendant] a modest number of questions and requested him to perform a simple balancing test at a location visible to passing motorists" (p. 442) and thus did not violate the Fifth Amendment.

The same applies to stops not involving vehicles. *Miranda* permits law enforcement officers to engage in "[g]eneral on-the-scene questioning as to facts surrounding a crime or other general questioning of citizens in the factfinding process . . . " (p. 477). With regard to *Terry* stops in particular, "[t]he comparatively nonthreatening character of [investigative] detentions explains the absence of any suggestion in our opinions that Terry stops are subject to the dictates of *Miranda*" (p. 440). However, if an investigative stop becomes more intrusive than a *Terry* stop (for example, by taking place over a long period of time or in a private setting), the Fifth Amendment's self-incrimination clause (made known to suspects through the *Miranda* rights) will almost certainly apply.

Next, it is possible for questioning in one's home to rise to the level of custody. In *Orozco v. Texas* (1969), the Supreme Court declared that custody existed when four police officers woke a man in his own house and began questioning him. However, in contrast to *Orozco* is *Beckwith v. United States* (1976), in which IRS agents interviewed a man in his home, an action that the Supreme Court declared noncustodial. The man argued that because he was the "focus" of a criminal investigation he should have been advised of his right to remain silent. However, Chief Justice Burger noted that "*Miranda* implicitly defined 'focus,' for its purposes, as 'questioning initiated by law enforcement officers *after* a person has been taken into custody or otherwise deprived of his freedom of action in any significant way" (p. 347).

Questioning at the police station or an equivalent facility can also rise to the level of custody. However, not all stationhouse questioning can be considered custodial. Consider what the Supreme Court said in *Oregon v. Mathiason* (1977), a case involving a man who agreed to meet officers at the police station for questioning. He admitted to involvement in a crime but later argued that his visit to the stationhouse was custodial because of its inherently coercive nature:

> Any interview of one suspected of a crime by a police officer will have coercive aspects to it, simply by virtue of the fact that the police officer is part of a law enforcement system which may ultimately cause the suspect to be charged with a crime. But police officers are not required to administer *Miranda* warnings to everyone whom they question. Nor is the requirement of warnings to be imposed simply because the questioning takes place in the stationhouse, or because the questioned person is one whom the police suspect. (p. 495)

In a later case, the Court offered some clarification concerning its decision in *Mathiason*. It pointed out that *Miranda* is not implicated "if the suspect is not placed under arrest, voluntarily comes to the police station, and is allowed to leave unhindered by the police after a brief interview" (*California v. Beheler*, 1983, p. 1121).

Interestingly, the *Beheler* decision seems to hold even if a person is pressured to come to the police station for questioning. For example, in *Minnesota v. Murphy* (1984), a probationer was ordered to meet with his probation officer for questioning. During the meeting, the probationer confessed to a rape and a murder. He argued that he should have been advised of his *Miranda* rights, but the Supreme Court disagreed, holding that Murphy's "freedom of movement [was] not restricted to the degree associated with formal arrest" (p. 430). Furthermore, while "[c]ustodial arrest is said to convey to the suspect a message that he has no choice but to submit to the officers' will and to confess . . . [i]t is unlikely that a probation interview, arranged by appointment at a mutually convenient time, would give rise to a similar impression" (p. 433). The Court stated

> Many of the psychological ploys discussed in *Miranda* capitalize on the suspect's unfamiliarity with the officers and the environment. Murphy's regular meetings with his probation officer should have served to familiarize him with her and her office and to insulate him from psychological intimidation that might overbear his desire to claim the privilege. Finally, the coercion inherent in custodial interrogation derives in large measure from an interrogator's insinuation that the interrogation will continue until a confession is obtained...Since Murphy was not physically re-

strained and could have left the office, any compulsion he might have felt from the possibility that terminating the meeting would have led to revocation of probation was not comparable to the pressure on a suspect who is painfully aware that he literally cannot escape a persistent custodial interrogator. (*Minnesota v. Murphy*, 1984, p. 433)

Fourth, the Supreme Court has had occasion to determine whether *Miranda* applies (specifically, whether people can be considered "in custody" for minor offenses). *Berkemer*, you will recall, was a case involving a traffic stop. The second issue before the Court in that case was whether an exception to *Miranda* should exist for relatively minor crimes such as misdemeanors. The Court declared that no distinction should be drawn between types of crimes as far as *Miranda* is concerned. Instead, the only relevant issue is whether a person is in custody (and, of course, interrogated). Even for misdemeanors, the incentive for police to try to induce the defendant to incriminate himself may be significant.

Before moving on we should stress that a key component of *Miranda* is that the questioning (and detention) be conducted by government actors. If the people engaged in questioning cannot be considered government actors, then Fifth Amendment protections do not apply. However, when a private individual conducts a custodial interrogation as an agent of the police (i.e., working for the police), *Miranda* applies (see, for example, *Wilson v. O'Leary*, 1990). See Table 8-2 for a list of factors used to distinguish between custodial and noncustodial situations.

Table 8-2 Distinguishing Between Custodial and Noncustodial Situations	
Custodial	**Noncustodial**
Arrest	Typical traffic stop
Excessively lengthy confrontation	General on-the-scene questioning
Not free to leave	Free to leave
Involuntary encounter	Voluntary encounter
Private place such as police station	Public place where movement not restricted

Interrogations. The second major component of *Miranda* is interrogation. Custody by itself is not enough to require that **Miranda warnings** be given. For a person to be afforded Fifth Amendment protection—and particularly to be advised of his or her right to remain silent—that person must be subjected to interrogation.

Miranda defined interrogation as "questioning initiated by law enforcement officers." Then, in *Rhode Island v. Innis* (1980), the Court noted that interrogation "must reflect a measure of compulsion above and beyond that inherent in custody itself" (p. 300). Thus, any questions that tend to incriminate—that is, those that are directed toward an individual about his or her suspected involvement in a crime—are considered interrogation.

Unfortunately, many "questions" are not always readily identifiable as such. In *Innis*, the Supreme Court noted that in addition to "express questioning," the "functional equivalent" of a question is also possible. The functional equivalent of a question includes "any words or actions on the part of the police (other than those normally attendant to arrest and custody) that the police should know are reasonably likely to elicit an incriminating response from the suspect" (p. 302, n. 8).

In *Innis*, while driving Innis to the police station after his arrest for armed robbery, police officers engaged in a conversation about the danger the missing robbery weapon posed to innocent individuals. Apparently in response to the conversation, Innis directed the officers to the location of the missing weapon. Interestingly, though, the Supreme Court held that the officers' conversation did not constitute interrogation: It was "nothing more than a dialogue between the two officers to which no response from the respondent was invited." The majority assumed implicitly that suspects will not respond to "indirect appeals to . . . humanitarian impulses" (p. 315), but Justice Stevens dissented and argued that such an assumption "is directly contrary to the teachings of police interrogation manuals, which recommend appealing to a suspect's sense of morality as a standard and often successful interrogation technique" (p. 315

Even though *Innis* did not ultimately involve the functional equivalent of a question, the Court essentially expanded the definition of questioning; a mere conversation between police officers designed to elicit an incriminating response—even if the conversation is not directed toward the suspect—can require *Miranda* warnings. Of course, the person must also be in custody for the *Miranda* warnings to apply. See Table 8-3 for a summary of how to distinguish between interrogation and general questioning.

Table 8-3	Distinguishing Between Interrogation and General Questioning
Interrogation	**General Questioning**
Guilt seeking-questions	Information gathering
Conversation intended to elicit a response	Conversation not intended to elicit response

Substance and adequacy of the warnings. Surprisingly, there is a long line of cases involving people who have sought to have their confessions excluded at trial because all or some of the *Miranda* warnings

---

Practice Pointer 8-1

The Supreme Court's *Miranda* decision does not require that rights be read unless custody and interrogation take place. To play it safe, however, police officers would be well advised to read suspects their *Miranda* rights immediately once they are taken into custody.

---

were not read adequately. For example, in *California v. Prysock* (1981), a juvenile was told, "You have the right to talk to a lawyer before you are questioned, have him present with you while you are being questioned, and all during the questioning" (p. 361). The defendant was then told that he had the right to a court-appointed lawyer but not that one would be provided for him if he was indigent. Prysock challenged his conviction, but the Court concluded that the warnings given him were sufficient and that "*Miranda* itself indicates that no talismanic incantation was required to satisfy its strictures" (p. 359).

In another interesting case, *Duckworth v. Eagan* (1989), the following warnings were given

> Before we ask you any questions, you must understand your rights. You have the right to remain silent. Anything you say can be used against you in court. You have the right to talk to a lawyer for advice before we ask you any questions, and to have him with you during questioning. You have this right to the advice and presence of a lawyer even if you cannot afford to hire one. We have no way of giving you a lawyer, but one will be appointed for you, if you wish, if and when you go to court. If you wish to answer questions now without a lawyer present, you have the right to stop answering questions at any time. You also have the right to stop answering at any time until you've talked to a lawyer. (p. 198)

Interestingly, even though the warnings in this version suggested that counsel would only be provided at court, the Supreme Court held, in a 5-4 decision, that these warnings "touched all the bases required by *Miranda*" (p. 203). Thus, simple departures from *Miranda*—as long as all the essential information is communicated—will not render confessions thereby obtained inadmissible in a criminal trial.

A second line of cases involving the substance and adequacy of the *Miranda* warnings concerns the role of additional unnecessary information. If more information besides the original *Miranda* warnings is provided to a suspect, will any subsequent confession be inadmissible? For example, must defendants be advised of the consequences of deciding to answer questions? *Colorado v. Spring* (1987) is a useful point of departure. There, the defendant was arrested and questioned on suspicion of transporting stolen firearms. He was also questioned about a homicide. Spring admitted that he had been given his *Miranda* warnings and that he understood them; however, he argued that the statements he made about the homicide were not admissible because he was not informed that he was going to be questioned about the homicide (because he was arrested on suspicion of transporting stolen firearms). Unfortunately for Spring, the majority held that "a suspect's awareness of all the possible subjects of questioning in advance of interrogation is not relevant to determining whether the suspect voluntarily, knowingly, and intelligently waived his Fifth Amendment privilege" (p. 577).

The public safety exception to Miranda. On some occasions custodial interrogation is permissible without *Miranda* warnings. Specifically, if public safety is in jeopardy, no warnings are required. This was the decision reached in *New York v. Quarles* (1984). There the Court held that the warnings need not be given if the suspect could have endangered public safety. The facts from *Quarles* are as follows: After receiving information that a man with a gun had just entered a supermarket, Officer Kraft, along with three other officers, entered the store. Kraft spotted the defendant, drew his gun, and ordered the man to stop and put his hands over his head. The officers found an empty shoulder holster on the man while they frisked him. They then asked the man where he had put the gun. He replied, "The gun is over there." Officer Kraft retrieved the revolver, then placed the man under arrest and read him his *Miranda* warnings. The trial court and the lower appellate courts excluded the gun on the grounds that it was obtained in violation of *Miranda* (because the man had not been advised of his right to remain silent at the time the gun was found). The Supreme Court disagreed. Justice Rehnquist wrote the majority opinion, arguing that rigid application of *Miranda* is not always warranted, particularly when public safety is a concern:

> [T]he need for answers to questions in a situation posing a threat to public safety outweighs the need for the prophylactic rule protecting the Fifth Amendment's privilege against self-incrimination. We decline to place officers such as Officer Kraft in the untenable position of having to consider, often in a matter of seconds, whether it best serves society for them to ask the necessary questions without the *Miranda* warnings and render whatever probative evidence they uncover inadmissible, or for them to give the warnings in order to preserve the admissibility of evidence they might uncover but possibly damage or destroy their ability to obtain that evidence and neutralize the volatile situation confronting them. (pp. 657–658)

The Court also made it clear that the appropriate test for determining whether a threat to public safety exists is an objective one—that is, one based on what a reasonable person in the same circumstances would believe. "Where spontaneity rather than adherence to a police manual is necessarily the order of the day, the application of the [public safety] exception . . . should not be made to depend on post hoc findings at a suppression hearing concerning the subjective motivation of the arresting officer" (p. 656). The majority in *Quarles* apparently believed that an objective threat to public safety existed. For officers to not know where the gun was located "obviously posed more than one danger to the public safety: an accomplice might make use of it [or] a customer or employee might later come upon it" (p. 657).

The *Quarles* decision is a controversial one. As Justice O'Connor noted in disagreement with the newly carved-out public safety exception to *Miranda* (though not with the majority's ultimate decision):

> *Miranda* has never been read to prohibit the police from asking questions to secure the public safety. Rather, the critical question *Miranda* addresses is who shall bear the cost of securing the public safety when such questions are asked and answered: the defendant or the state. *Miranda*, for better or worse, found the resolution of that question implicit in the prohibition against compulsory self-incrimination and placed the burden on the State. (p. 664)

Quarles, by contrast, appears to place the burden on the defendant. It does so, in O'Connor's view, not by ensuring that public safety is preserved but by creating a *Miranda* "loophole" that helps ensure that otherwise inadmissible evidence can be used against the defendant.

Waiver of Miranda. In *Miranda*, the Supreme Court stated that if a person talks after being read the warnings, "a heavy burden rests on the government to demonstrate that the defendant knowingly and intelligently waived his privilege against self-incrimination and his right to retained or appointed counsel" (p. 475). Furthermore, "a valid waiver will not be presumed simply from the silence of the accused after warnings are given or simply from the fact that a confession was in fact eventually obtained" (*Miranda v. Arizona*, 1966, p. 475). According to the Supreme Court,

> Whatever the testimony of the authorities as to waiver of rights by an accused, the fact of lengthy interrogation or incommunicado incarceration before a statement is made is strong evidence that the accused did not validly waive his rights. In these circumstances the fact that the individual eventually made a statement is consistent with the conclusion that the compelling influence of the interrogation finally forced him to do so. It is inconsistent with any notion of a voluntary relinquishment of the privilege. Moreover, any evidence that the accused was threatened, tricked, or cajoled into a waiver will, of course, show that the defendant did not voluntarily waive his privilege. (p. 476)

In recent years, the courts have interpreted this language loosely. That is, where *Miranda* declared that a waiver is to be viewed with considerable caution, later decisions have suggested that the burden of demonstrating a valid waiver is not difficult to meet. For example, in *Colorado v. Connelly* (1986), the Court held that the government need only show the validity of a waiver by a "preponderance of evidence." And in *Fare v. Michael C.* (1979) the Supreme Court held that the "totality of the circumstances approach is adequate to determine whether there has been a waiver" (p. 725). This latter test is not unlike the due process voluntariness test discussed earlier in this chapter.

Must the waiver be express? That is, must a person affirmatively state something to the effect that "I am willing to answer questions" for a waiver of *Miranda* to take place? The answer to this question is no. In the past, the Court preferred an express waiver. In *Miranda*, the Court noted that a valid waiver will not be presumed. Similarly, in *Westover v. United States*, (1966) (a case joined with *Miranda*) the Court stated that an "articulated waiver" is required before a confession will be considered admissible.

However, in *North Carolina v. Butler* (1979) the Court decided otherwise. According to Justice Stewart, "The question [of a waiver] is not one of form, but rather whether the defendant in fact knowingly and voluntarily waived his rights delineated in the *Miranda* case" (p. 373). Further, a "course of conduct indicating waiver" is sufficient for a valid waiver to take place. Based on this decision, the current rule is that the government show a valid waiver based on "the particular facts and circumstances surrounding [the] case, including the background, experience, and conduct of the accused" (pp. 374–375). In other words, courts now take a case-by-case approach in determining whether *Miranda* waivers are obtained legally.

As was made clear in *Butler*, a valid *Miranda* waiver requires a showing that the waiver was knowing and intelligent. What, then, is a knowing and intelligent waiver? There is no clear answer to this question, but the Court has noted that a full and complete understanding of the warnings is not necessary for a valid waiver to take place. This was the decision reached in *Connecticut v. Barrett* (1987). In that case, the defendant refused to give the police any written statements before he talked to an attorney. He did state, however, that he had no problem *talking* to the police. As it turned out, Barrett thought that only written statements could be used against him in court. The Court called his actions "illogical" but nonetheless held that his oral statements were admissible.

Another case focusing on the "knowing and intelligent" requirement was *Wyrick v. Fields* (1982). In that case, the defendant expressed some confusion about the duration of a *Miranda* waiver. He had agreed to take a polygraph examination without counsel present. After the polygraph examination, the defendant also answered questions from the examiner about his feelings about the examination, which led to him supplying incriminating information. When his statements were used against him, he argued that neither he nor his attorney believed that the polygraph procedure would also include postexamination questioning. However, the Supreme Court pointed out that "it would have been unreasonable for Fields and his attorney to assume that Fields would not be informed of the polygraph readings and asked to explain any unfavorable result" (p. 47). In addition, the Court concluded that "the questions put to Fields after the examination would not have caused him to forget the rights of which he had been advised and which he had understood moments before" (p. 49).

Two additional Supreme Court decisions focused on whether the police can use "trickery" to obtain a *Miranda* waiver or statement. In *Colorado v. Spring* (1987), the Court held that trickery *had not* taken place when the police failed to advise the defendant that he would be questioned about a different crime than the one for which he was arrested. The Court did point out, however, that "any evidence that the accused was . . . tricked . . . into a waiver will, of course, show that the defendant did not voluntarily waive his privilege" (p. 575).

In another interesting case, *Moran v. Burbine* (1986), the Supreme Court held that a confession was validly obtained, even though the police questioned the defendant after assuring his attorney that he would not be questioned until the following day. In a 6–3 decision, the Court held that this action did not result in a coerced confession. As Justice O'Connor noted, "the same defendant, armed with the same information and confronted with precisely the same police conduct, would have knowingly waived his *Miranda* rights had a lawyer not telephoned the police station to inquire about his status" (p. 422). In light of these two cases, it seems somewhat difficult to determine what constitutes trickery. A general rule is if officials lead a defendant to believe that he or she has no right to remain silent, trickery takes place; however, if the police merely lead a defendant to believe there is no point to remaining silent (as in *Butler, Barrett, Fields, Spring,* and *Burbine*), then subsequent incriminating statements will probably be viewed as knowing and intelligent.

It is worth mentioning before moving on that in addition to the requirement that it be "knowing and intelligent," a valid *Miranda* waiver must also be voluntary. The test for voluntariness is similar to the due process voluntariness test discussed earlier in this chapter. Threats, physical force, and the like can lead to involuntary confessions. However, in *Fare v. Michael C.* (1979), the Court held that the confession obtained from a 16-year-old was not involuntary. In a strongly worded dissent, Justice Powell argued that the juvenile in this case "was immature, emotional, and uneducated, and therefore was likely to be vulnerable to the skillful, two-on-one, repetitive style of interrogation to which he was subjected" (p. 733). A safe rule is that the police must engage in seriously questionable conduct for the voluntariness requirement of a *Miranda* waiver to be violated.

Questioning after assertion of one's right to remain silent. As a general rule, questioning must cease once an accused asserts his or her right to remain silent. According to the Supreme Court in *Miranda*:

> If the individual indicates in any manner, at any time prior to or during questioning, that he wishes to remain silent, the interrogation must cease. . . . Without the right to cut off questioning, the setting of in-custody interrogation operates on the individual to overcome free choice in producing a statement after the privilege has been once invoked. If the individual states that he wants an attorney, the interrogation must cease until an attorney is present. . . . If the individual cannot obtain an attorney and he indicates that he wants one before speaking to police, they must respect his decision to remain silent. . . . If authorities conclude that they will not provide counsel during a reasonable period of time in which investigation in the field is carried out, they may refrain from doing so without violating the person's Fifth Amendment privilege so long as they do not question him during that time. (pp. 473–474)

However, there is at least one circumstance where the police can question a suspect after he or she asserts the *Miranda* rights. In *Michigan v. Mosley* (1975) the Supreme Court permitted questioning after an assertion of *Miranda*. In that case, two hours after the defendant stated that he did not want to talk, a different police officer confronted him in a different room about another crime and read him his *Miranda* rights for a second time. After this, the man made incriminating statements. In a 7–2 decision the Court held that the suspect's *Miranda* rights were "scrupulously honored." The Court said that the second officer's actions were acceptable because "the police here immediately ceased the interrogation, resumed questioning only after the passage of a significant period of time and the provision of a fresh set of warnings, and restricted the second interrogation to a crime that had not been a subject of the earlier interrogation" (p. 106). The key to this case was that the second set of questions concerned a separate crime. Had the police questioned Mosley about the first crime—which he did not want to discuss—any inculpatory statements would have been obtained in violation of the Fifth Amendment.

Due process acts as a fall-back and is always relevant. The Sixth and Fifth Amendments, by contrast, apply in specific circumstances. And it is possible (albeit rare) for all three provisions to come into play.

The Role of the Exclusionary Rule in the Confession Analysis

We believe it is important to focus on the role of the exclusionary rule in the confession analysis. Generally speaking, a confession obtained in violation of *Miranda* or some constitutional provision will be excluded. Important, however, is the fact that just because a confession is obtained illegally does not mean that any evidence thereby obtained will be automatically excluded. Indeed, illegally obtained statements themselves are considered admissible in certain circumstances. We focus here on three lines of cases involving confessions and the exclusionary rule. These are based on standing, impeachment, and the fruit of the poisonous tree doctrine.

Confessions and standing. For a confession (or evidence thereby obtained) to be excluded, the person arguing as such must have standing. That is, one person cannot exclude the confession of another, even if that confession was obtained in violation of *Miranda*. This is because, as noted in *Couch v. United States* (1973), *Miranda* is considered a "personal" right. Thus, a person arguing for exclusion of an (unconstitutionally obtained) incriminating statement must have standing; otherwise the statement and subsequent evidence will be deemed admissible.

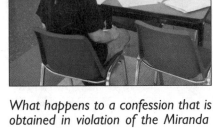

What happens to a confession that is obtained in violation of the Miranda warnings?

Confessions and impeachment. Another situation in which incriminating statements obtained in violation of *Miranda* are admissible is when such statements are used for purposes of impeachment. A key restriction on this rule, however, is that the statement(s) be obtained voluntarily in the due process sense (discussed earlier in this chapter). An illustrative case in this regard is *Harris v. New York* (1971). In that case, the prosecution sought to introduce an out-of-court statement that was inconsistent with Harris' in-court testimony, even though the out-of-court statement was obtained in violation of *Miranda*. The Supreme Court held that Harris' out-of-court statements, obtained in violation of *Miranda*, were admissible. The Court noted further that the statements must be obtained voluntarily, which they were in Harris' case (see also *Oregon v. Hass*, 1975; *New Jersey v. Portash*, 1978).

Note that to be admissible for impeachment purposes the statements obtained in violation of *Miranda* must be oral communications. The prosecution cannot introduce evidence of an accused's out-of-court silence for impeachment purposes. This issue arose in the case of *Doyle v. Ohio* (1976), where, following the defendant's in-court exculpatory story, the prosecution sought to introduce evidence that the defendant did not offer the same explanation to the police. The

Supreme Court held that the defendant's silence was not admissible for purposes of impeachment (see also *Wainwright v. Greenfield*, 1986).

Confessions and fruit of the poisonous tree. As we have seen, evidence obtained in flagrant violation of the Fourth Amendment is not admissible under the so-called fruit of the poisonous tree, or derivative evidence doctrine. However, the Supreme Court has not been so quick to apply the rule in the case of illegally obtained confessions. Instead, the Court has held that (physical) evidence obtained in violation of *Miranda* is admissible as long as the information supplied by the accused was voluntary—that is, in line with the Fourteenth Amendment's due process clause.

The first case of note concerning the derivative evidence doctrine in the confession context was *United States v. Bayer* (1947), a case decided well before the *Miranda* decision was handed down. In that case the Court held that the Fourth Amendment fruit of the poisonous tree doctrine "did not control" the admissibility of improperly obtained confessions. And in *Michigan v. Tucker* (1974), a case decided after *Miranda*, the Court suggested that it had not changed its position. Then, in *Oregon v. Elstad* (1985), the Court made clear that evidence obtained from violations of *Miranda* is admissible, but only if voluntarily obtained.

Identification Procedures

Identification procedures include those procedures allowing witnesses of crime to identify perpetrators. The three most common types of identification procedures are lineups, showups, and photographic arrays. In a lineup, the suspect is placed alongside several other people who resemble the suspect. Then the witness (or victim) picks the suspect out of the lineup. In a showup, the suspect is brought before the witness—alone—so the witness can be asked whether the person being brought before him or her was the perpetrator. Finally, with **photographic arrays** several photographs, including one of the suspect, are shown to a witness or victim so he or she can pick out the perpetrator.

Naturally, it is in the prosecution's interest to introduce evidence that a witness or victim picked the perpetrator out of a lineup. However, it is not as simple as demonstrating that a witness identified the perpetrator. The identification procedure must be fair and in line with constitutional requirements. These constitutional requirements place restrictions on what officials can do in terms of arranging lineups, showups, or photographic arrays. Restrictions are critical, because witnesses to crimes are frequently inaccurate in their descriptions.

Constitutional Restrictions on Identification Procedures

Identification procedures have been challenged on several grounds. These challenges have stemmed from the Fourteenth Amendment's due process clause, the Fifth Amendment's self-incrimination clause, and the Sixth Amendment's right-to-counsel clause. People have also challenged the constitutionality of identification procedures on Fourth Amendment grounds. We consider each of these in turn, then we move into a discussion of the three types of identification procedures.

Right to counsel. In *United States v. Wade* (1967), a defendant was placed in a police lineup, without his attorney present, *after* he had been indicted for a crime. The Supreme Court held that this procedure violated the Sixth Amendment because a postindictment lineup is a "critical stage" in the criminal process. Further, "the presence of counsel [at post-indictment lineups] is necessary to preserve the defendant's basic right to a fair trial" (p. 227).

The key in *Wade* was that the lineup was postindictment—that is, conducted after charges had been filed. Had charges *not* been filed, a different decision would probably have been the result. Another important feature of the *Wade* decision was that it distinguished lineups from "various other preparatory steps, such as systematized or scientific analyzing of the accused's fingerprints, blood sample, clothing, hair and the like" (p. 227). Counsel is not required for these types of activities because

> knowledge of the techniques of science and technology is sufficiently available, and the variables in techniques few enough, that the accused has the opportunity for a meaningful confrontation of the Government's case at trial through the ordinary processes of cross-examination of the Government's expert witnesses and the presentation of the evidence of his own experts. (pp. 227–228)

Due process. The Supreme Court has also clearly stated that the Fourteenth Amendment's due process clause bears on the constitutionality of identification procedures. For example, in *Stovall v. Denno* (1967) the Court held that the accused is entitled to protection against procedures "so unnecessarily suggestive and conducive to irreparable mistaken identification" (p. 302) as to amount to a due process violation. In general, for an identification procedure to comport with the due process clause it must be (1) reliable and (2) minimally suggestive.

Whether an identification procedure is reliable is determined in light of the facts and circumstances surrounding the case. The following factors are used in determining whether an identification procedure is reliable:

> The opportunity of the witness to view the criminal at the time of the crime, the witness' degree of attention, the accuracy of the wit-

ness' prior description of the criminal, the level of certainty demonstrated by the witness at the confrontation, and the length of time between the crime and the confrontation. (*Neil v. Biggers,* 1972, p. 199)

Indeed, the Supreme Court stated in *Biggers* that reliability is more important than suggestiveness. In the Court's words, it is "the likelihood of misidentification which violates a defendant's right to due process" (p. 198). This position was reaffirmed in the case of *Manson v. Braithwaite* (1977), in which the Court held that "the totality of circumstances" determines whether an identification procedure is unreliable.

Suggestiveness has also been important in determining whether an identification procedure is violative of the due process clause. If the procedure is set up such that the witness or victim is all but guaranteed to pick the perpetrator, it is unnecessarily suggestive. If, for example, an offender is 6 feet tall but is placed in a lineup with several others who are considerably shorter, such a lineup will be considered suggestive. The main case in this regard is *Moore v. Illinois* (1977) in which it was noted

> It is difficult to imagine a more suggestive manner in which to present a suspect to a witness for their critical first confrontation than was employed in this case. The victim, who had seen her assailant for only 10 to 15 seconds, was asked to make her identification after she was told that she was going to view a suspect, after she was told his name and heard it called as he was led before the bench, and after she heard the prosecutor recite the evidence believed to implicate petitioner. Had petitioner been represented by counsel, some or all of this suggestiveness could have been avoided. (pp. 229–230)

The Fifth Amendment. The Fifth Amendment's self-incrimination clause has been invoked with regard to identification procedures. In particular, some defendants have argued that being forced to participate in a lineup or photographic lineup is itself incriminating and, as such, violates the Fifth Amendment. However, in *United States v. Wade* (1967) the Court stated that the privilege against self-incrimination does not limit the use of identification procedures. The reason the Court offered is that even though incriminating information can result from identification procedures, such evidence is physical or real as opposed to testimonial. In *Wade,* the Court decided on the constitutionality of an identification procedure in which the accused was required to utter words that were presumably uttered by the perpetrator. The Court concluded that this type of identification procedure was constitutional because, in *Wade,* his voice was used as an identifying characteristic, not to speak his guilt, but to identify him. Thus, the Fifth Amendment does not apply to identification procedures.

The Fourth Amendment. Finally, identification procedures have been challenged on Fourth Amendment grounds. As with the Fifth Amendment, the Fourth Amendment has yet to be successfully invoked with regard to identification procedures. This is because, according to the Supreme Court, no one enjoys a "reasonable expectation of privacy" in characteristics that are exposed to the public. For example, if an offender is viewed by a witness, the witness' identification of the offender will be admissible in court even though the identification is incriminating. The offender-now-defendant may argue that the act of being viewed by the witness is incriminating, but the courts view this sort of knowing exposure as beyond constitutional protection.

One of the leading cases in this area is *Schmerber v. California* (1966). There, a sample of Schmerber's blood was taken by a doctor in a hospital following his arrest. The sample was used as evidence in Schmerber's trial for drunk driving. The defendant argued that the blood sample was incriminating and should be excluded from trial. The Supreme Court disagreed, noting,

> Particularly in a case such as this, where time had to be taken to bring the accused to a hospital and to investigate the scene of the accident, there was no time to seek out a magistrate and secure a warrant. Given these special facts, we conclude that the attempt to secure evidence of blood-alcohol content in this case was an appropriate incident to petitioner's arrest. (pp. 770–771)

Obviously, if the police want to "seize" a person so as to obtain fingerprints or a voice exemplar (or some other form of evidence), they are bound by Fourth Amendment restrictions. As we have seen elsewhere in this book, probable cause is required before the police can seize a person. Assuming a seizure is justified, any real or physical evidence obtained from the arrestee will be admissible under the reasonable expectation of privacy argument advanced in the preceding paragraph.

There is at least one exception to the Fourth Amendment's probable cause requirement as it pertains to identification procedures. In *Hayes v. Florida* (1985), the Court stated:

> There is . . . support in our cases for the view that the Fourth Amendment would permit seizures for the purpose of fingerprinting, if there is reasonable suspicion that the suspect has committed a criminal act, if there is a reasonable basis for believing that fingerprinting will establish or negate the suspect's connection with that crime, and if the procedure is carried out with dispatch. (p. 817)

However, such seizures, if conducted in the home, must be preceded by judicial authorization.

To summarize, only two constitutional provisions actually place restrictions on identification procedures. These two are the Fourteenth Amendment's due process clause and the Sixth Amendment's right to counsel clause. The Fifth Amendment, while important to confession law, does not come into play when identification procedures are at issue. Similarly, the Fourth Amendment does not apply to identification procedures directly, but it does apply indirectly insofar as probable cause is required if law enforcement officials plan to seize somebody for purposes of identifying them. We now turn to a brief discussion of the three most common identification procedures: lineups, showups, and photographic identifications.

Lineups

As we have seen, suspects can be forced to participate in lineups because **lineups** exhibit physical characteristics, not testimonial evidence. Indeed, suspects placed in lineups can also be required to supply voice exemplars, but the suspect's use of his or her voice in this context is solely for identification purposes, not as a confession. If a suspect refuses to participate in a lineup, he or she can be cited with contempt (*Doss v. United States*, 1970), and the prosecutor can comment at trial about the suspect's refusal to cooperate (*United States v. Parhms*, 1970).

As we have indicated, the due process clause restricts identification procedures. In particular, an overly suggestive lineup violates due process. In *United States v. Wade*, the Supreme Court noted that lineups become suggestive when, for instance,

> all in the lineup but the suspect were known to the identifying witness, . . . the other participants in a lineup were grossly dissimilar in appearance to the suspect, . . . only the suspect was required to wear distinctive clothing which the culprit allegedly wore, . . . the suspect is pointed out before or during a lineup, and . . . the participants in the lineup are asked to try on an article of clothing which fits only the suspect. (p. 233)

The *Model Rules for Law Enforcement* (1974) propose several steps to minimize suggestiveness in police lineups:

1. Lineups should consist of at least five people, including the suspect.

2. Persons in the lineup should have similar physical characteristics.

3. The suspect should be permitted to choose his or her place in line.

4. *All* persons in the lineup should be required to take whatever specialized action is required (e.g., uttering certain words).

5. Persons in the lineup should be warned to conduct themselves such that the suspect does not stand out.

6. Lineups should be photographed or videotaped.

The International Association of Chiefs of Police (1975) Legal Center has recommended similar guidelines:

1. All lineups should consist of five to six people.

2. All participants in the lineup must sign the appropriate waiver form, unless counsel is present.

3. All persons in the lineup should be of the same sex and race and approximately the same age. They should also be of approximately the same height, weight, coloring, build, etc.

4. All participants in the lineup should wear approximately the same clothing.

5. The accused should be placed in the lineup at random, so as to not stand out.

6. Persons known to the witness should not be placed in the lineup.

7. Private citizens participating in the lineup (if insufficient numbers of prisoners are available) should sign a written consent form indicating they are aware that no charges are filed against them, that they are free to leave at any time, and so on.

8. Each witness should view the lineup separately so one witness does not unduly influence another in his or her identification of the perpetrator.

9. Each participant in the lineup should be given the same instructions and should perform the same acts (e.g., supplying a voice exemplar).

10. Participants in the lineup should be instructed not to make any statements or comments unless ordered to do so.

11. Frontal and side-profile photographs of the lineup should be taken.

12. A single officer should oversee the lineup procedure.

13. A written waiver of counsel should be obtained if the suspect waives his or her Sixth Amendment right to have counsel present at postindictment lineups.

Showups

Showups are defined as one-on-one victim-offender confrontations, usually conducted outside the courtroom setting. Lineups are always preferable to showups (because lineups consist of several potential suspects); however, showups are necessary under certain circumstances. For example, when a witness is immobile and cannot be present at a lineup, a showup is an effective alternative. In *Stovall v. Denno* (1967) the Supreme Court noted, "Faced with the responsibility for identifying the attacker, with the need for immediate action and with the knowledge that [the victim] could not visit the jail, the police followed the only feasible procedure and took [the accused] to the hospital room" (p. 295). In a similar vein, showups are preferable when the *suspect* is immobile.

Showups are sometimes desirable to facilitate prompt identification when time is of the essence; if the witness is required to wait for a lineup, it is more likely that misidentification will result. A showup conducted more than 60 minutes after the crime, however, will usually not be upheld (see *United States v. Perry,* 1971). But, in at least one case, the Supreme Court upheld a stationhouse showup in which no emergency existed. In *Neil v. Biggers* (1972), the Court sanctioned an arranged one-on-one showup even though it took place well after the point at which the crime in question was committed. The Court noted, given the facts, that there was "no substantial likelihood of misidentification" (p. 201). This was because the witness had an opportunity to view the suspect for almost 30 minutes, under good lighting, prior to the showup.

The same constitutional rules that govern lineups also govern showups. Specifically, the Sixth Amendment right to counsel applies, but only after adversarial proceedings have commenced (see *Moore v. Illinois,* 1977). Due process protections also exist. If the showup is unnecessarily suggestive under a "totality of circumstances" analysis, any identification that flows from it will not be admissible in court.

Practice Pointer 8-2

Whenever possible, lineups should be used in lieu of showups. The reason is that showups can be highly suggestive and possibly violate the Fourteenth Amendment. A carefully constructed lineup is constitutionally defensible.

Photographic Identifications

Photographic identifications involves displaying a picture of the suspect along with several other people to a victim or witness for the purpose of identification. Photographic identification procedures approximate real-life lineups by including several people, but they are not subjected to the same constitutional restrictions that lineups are. In particular, there is no Sixth Amendment right to counsel during photographic identifications. However, due process protections *do* apply. Several photographs of like individuals should be shown to minimize unnecessary suggestiveness.

Summary

This chapter addresses two main issues: confessions and identification procedures. Several of the same constitutional provisions govern police actions in both areas. Two of the more commonly raised constitutional concerns with regard to confessions and identifications stem from the Fifth and Fourteenth Amendments. The Fifth Amendment's self-incrimination clause offers accused individuals protection from implicating themselves in criminal activity. The Fourteenth Amendment's due process clause requires that confessions be obtained and identification procedures conducted in a fair manner.

The Fifth Amendment's self-incrimination clause is frequently relied upon when challenging the constitutionality of confessions. However, several requirements must be met for it to be successfully invoked. First, the police must "compel" a statement that is incriminating as well as testimonial. And, of course, the accused individual is the only one who can assert Fifth Amendment protection against unconstitutionally obtained confessions. Further, a confession will be thrown out if a suspect's incriminating statement is a result of custodial interrogation without the presence of counsel.

Confessions are also governed by the Sixth Amendment's right-to-counsel clause, but only when formal charges have been filed. Due process protections also exist, especially when an incriminating statement is obtained involuntarily. Confessions are afforded more protection than any other form of evidence. Whereas searches and seizures are governed by only one amendment (the Fourth), law enforcement officials must abide by the Fifth, Sixth, and Fourteenth Amendments when seeking to obtain confessions. The Fourteenth Amendment voluntariness requirement *always* applies, but the Fifth Amendment applies only when custodial interrogation takes place. The Sixth Amendment only applies once formal charges have been filed.

Identification procedures are of three types: lineups, showups, and photographic identifications. These three procedures are each bound by the Fourteenth Amendment's due process clause. That is, if they are too suggestive, they will be declared unconstitutional. Lineups and showups are restricted by the Sixth Amendment's right-to-counsel clause, but this clause does not apply to photographic identifications. Identification procedures are not protected by the Fifth and Fourth

Amendments because identifications are not considered testimony or "seizures."

Discussion Questions

1. Discuss *Miranda v. Arizona* (1966). What has been the impact of this case on law enforcement?

2. When is a police officer justified in questioning a suspect in custody before he has been made aware of his *Miranda* rights? Please cite the appropriate case.

3. Which three constitutional amendments govern confessions and admissions? Why?

4. When is it permissible to legally question people without making them aware of their *Miranda* rights?

5. What two requirements must be satisfied before a waiver of *Miranda* rights is considered valid? Explain.

6. What is the role of the exclusionary rule in obtaining confessions?

7. What is the "fruit of the poisonous tree" doctrine?

8. Explain the difference between lineups and showups.

9. Give some suggestions that may help minimize suggestiveness in police lineups. State where the suggestions came from.

10. Explain why suspects are entitled to counsel during postindictment lineups but not during preindictment lineups.

Further Reading

Alito, S. (1986). "Documents and the Privilege Against Self-Incrimination." *U. Pitt. L. Rev.* 48:27.

Amar, A. R., and R. Lettow. (1995). "Fifth Amendment First Principles: The Self-Incrimination Clause." *Mich. L. Rev.* 98:857.

Dressler, T., and G. C Thomas III. (2001). *Criminal Procedure: Principles, Policies, and Perspectives.* Eagan, MN: West Group.

International Association of Chiefs of Police. (1975). "Eyewitness Identification," *Legal Points.* Gaithersburg, MD: IACP Legal Center.

Langbein, J. H. (1994). "The Historical Origins of the Privilege Against Self-Incrimination at Common Law." *Mich. L. Rev.* 92:1047.

Leo, R. A. (1992). "From Coercion to Deception: The Changing Nature of Police Interrogation in America." *Crime, Law and Soc. Change* 18:35.

Model Rules for Law Enforcement. (1974). Arizona State University and Police Foundation, "Model Rules for Law Enforcement," *Eyewitness Identification,* 52.

Stuntz, W. (1988). "Self-Incrimination and Excuse." *Colum. L. Rev.* 88:1227.

White, W. S. (1979). "Police Trickery in Inducing Confessions." *U. Pa. L. Rev.* 127:581.

Whitebread, C. H., and C. Slobogin. (2000). *Criminal Procedure:An Analysis of Cases and Concepts* (4th edition). New York, NY: Foundation Press.

Worrall, J. L. (2004). *Criminal Procedure: From First Contact to Appeal.* Boston: Allyn and Bacon.

Cases Cited

Albertson v. Subversive Activities Control Board, 382 U.S. 70 (1965)

Allen v. Illinois, 478 U.S. 364 (1986)

Arizona v. Fulminante, 499 U.S. 279 (1991)

Ashcraft v. Tennessee, 322 U.S. 143 (1944)

Beckwith v. United States, 425 U.S. 341 (1976)

Beecher v. Alabama, 408 U.S. 234 (1972)

Berkemer v. McCarty, 468 U.S. 420 (1984)

Blackburn v. Alabama, 361 U.S. 199 (1960)

Brogan v. United States, 522 U.S. 398 (1998)

Brown v. Mississippi, 297 U.S. 278 (1936)

Brown v. United States, 356 U.S. 148 (1958)

California v. Beheler, 463 U.S. 1121 (1983)

California v. Byers, 402 U.S. 424 (1971)

California v. Prysock, 453 U.S. 355 (1981)

Chambers v. Florida, 309 U.S. 227 (1940)

Colorado v. Connelly, 479 U.S. 157 (1986)

Colorado v. Spring, 479 U.S. 564 (1987)

Connecticut v. Barrett, 479 U.S. 523 (1987)

Couch v. United States, 409 U.S. 322 (1973)

Crooker v. California, 357 U.S. 433 (1958)

Doss v. United States, 431 F.2d 601 (9th Cir. 1970)

Doyle v. Ohio, 426 U.S. 610 (1976)

Duckworth v. Eagan, 492 U.S. 195 (1989)

Escobedo v. Illinois, 378 U.S. 478 (1964)

Estelle v. Smith, 451 U.S. 454 (1981)

Fare v. Michael C., 442 U.S. 707 (1979)

Fikes v. Alabama, 352 U.S. 191 (1957)

Fisher v. United States, 425 U.S. 391 (1976)

Frazier v. Cupp, 394 U.S. 731 (1969)

Garner v. United States, 424 U.S. 648 (1976)

Garrity v. New Jersey, 385 U.S. 493 (1967)

Gilbert v. California, 388 U.S. 263 (1967)

Grosso v. United States, 390 U.S. 62 (1968)

Haley v. Ohio, 332 U.S. 596 (1948)

Harris v. New York, 401 U.S. 222 (1971)
Hayes v. Florida, 470 U.S. 811 (1985)
Haynes v. United States, 390 U.S. 85 (1968)
Holt v. United States, 218 U.S. 245 (1910)
In re Gault, 387 U.S. 1 (1967)
Lefkowitz v. Turley, 414 U.S. 70 (1973)
Leyra v. Denno, 347 U.S. 556 (1954)
Lynumm v. Illinois, 372 U.S. 528 (1963)
Malloy v. Hogan, 378 U.S. 1 (1964)
Manson v. Braithwaite, 432 U.S. 98 (1977)
Marchetti v. United States, 390 U.S. 39 (1968)
Massiah v. United States, 377 U.S. 201 (1964)
Michigan v. Mosley, 423 U.S. 96 (1975)
Michigan v. Tucker, 417 U.S. 433 (1974)
Mincey v. Arizona, 437 U.S. 385 (1978)
Minnesota v. Murphy, 465 U.S. 420 (1984)
Miranda v. Arizona, 384 U.S. 436 (1966)
Moore v. Illinois, 434 U.S. 220 (1977)
Moran v. Burbine, 475 U.S. 412 (1986)
Neil v. Biggers, 409 U.S. 188 (1972)
New Jersey v. Portash, 437 U.S. 385 (1978)
New York v. Quarles, 467 U.S. 649 (1984)
North Carolina v. Butler, 441 U.S. 369 (1979)
Oregon v. Elstad, 470 U.S. 298 (1985)
Oregon v. Hass, 420 U.S. 714 (1975)
Oregon v. Mathiason, 429 U.S. 492 (1977)
Orozco v. Texas, 394 U.S. 324 (1969)
Pennsylvania v. Muniz, 496 U.S. 582 (1990)
Rhode Island v. Innis, 446 U.S. 291 (1980)
Rogers v. Richmond, 365 U.S. 534 (1963)
Rogers v. United States, 340 U.S. 367 (1951)
Schmerber v. California, 384 U.S. 757 (1966)
Shapiro v. United States, 335 U.S. 1 (1948)
South Dakota v. Neville, 459 U.S. 553 (1983)
Spano v. New York, 360 U.S. 315 (1959)
Stovall v. Denno, 388 U.S. 293 (1967)
United States v. Bayer, 331 U.S. 532 (1947)
United States v. Dionisio, 410 U.S. 1 (1973)
United States v. Mandujano, 425 U.S. 564 (1976)
United States v. Mara, 410 U.S. 19 (1973)
United States v. Monia, 317 U.S. 424 (1943)
United States v. Parhms, 424 F.2d 152 (9th Cir. 1970)
United States v. Perry, 449 F.2d 1026 (D.C. Cir. 1971)
United States v. Sullivan, 274 U.S. 259 (1927)
United States v. Wade, 388 U.S. 218 (1967)
United States v. Washington, 431 U.S. 181 (1977)
United States v. Wong, 431 U.S. 174 (1977)
Wainwright v. Greenfield, 474 U.S. 284 (1986)

Westover v. United States, 384 U.S. 436 (1966)
Williams v. United States, 341 U.S. 97 (1951)
Wilson v. O'Leary, 895 F.2d 378 (7th Cir. 1990)
Wyrick v. Fields, 459 U.S. 42 (1982) ✦

Section III

Criminal Evidence

Chapter Nine

Witness Competency, Credibility, and Impeachment

Key Terms

- Accredit
- Competency
- Corrobative evidence
- Credibilty
- Cumulative evidence
- Discrediting

- Impeachment
- Perjury
- Rehabilitation
- Spousal privilege
- Testimony
- Witness

Introduction

A **witness** is a person who has knowledge about the facts of a case. For example, if a person witnesses a fight in a bar, naturally the person may have important information to supply when the case goes to trial. Similarly, if a gas-station patron observes a robber flee from the station in a car, the patron-now-witness has important information that may be needed if the robber is caught, arrested, charged, and tried in court.

Witnesses are essential in criminal trials. They present evidence in the form of testimony to the judge or a jury. **Testimony** is an oral or verbal description of a person's present recollection of some past event or set of facts.

It is not the case that all witnesses supply information intended to prove guilt. Witnesses can testify on behalf of the defendant in order to absolve the defendant of guilt. For example, a witness can give testimony to confirm a defendant's alibi. If a murder defendant states that he was out with a friend on the night that the murder took place and argues that his friend can confirm that he was not at the scene of the crime, the defendant's friend may testify in that regard. Thus, witnesses in the U.S. court system serve one of two purposes: They can testify for either the prosecution *or* the defense. For obvious reasons, though, a witness will not testify for the prosecution and defense in the same trial.

Without witnesses, it can be exceedingly difficult to prove guilt. Consider the following hypothetical situation: A motorist runs a stop sign and hits a pedestrian while she is crossing the street, killing her. The only witness to the incident is another motorist who happened to be waiting at the stop sign on the cross street. If the first motorist is charged criminally for vehicular homicide, the testimony of the second motorist will be very helpful to the prosecution. This witness would be especially improtant if no physical evidence was found to link the first driver to the pedestrian's death.

Not just anyone can be a witness. First and foremost, a witness must have something meaningful to contribute to the trial; the witness needs to be witness *to* something. If someone lacks personal knowledge concerning the case, he or she cannot be considered a witness. Stated differently, a witness may not testify to a matter unless evidence is introduced sufficient to support a finding that the witness has personal knowledge concerning the facts at issue in the trial.

A court of appeals judge recently stated that lay testimony—that is, testimony by ordinary persons—not based on personal information is useless because a witness cannot supply information about a matter he or she knows nothing about (*United States v. Allen*, 1993). Therefore, witnesses—as a form of evidence—must satisfy the criterion of relevance introduced in Chapter 4. If a witness communicates information unrelated to the case at hand, the witness's "testimony" will be deemed irrelevant. In such a situation, the witness will probably not be called to testify.

This chapter focuses on who can be a witness. First, it covers the topic of witness competency. Second, it covers the various means of challenging witness competency. The next section considers witness credibility and impeachment, while the last section discusses witness rehabilitation. Additional sections of this chapter consider such topics as witness oaths, the importance of corroboration, and the duty to tell the truth and narrate events. In short, this chapter pours the foundation for discussions in subsequent chapters of expert versus lay witnesses and the privileges associated with witness communication.

Competency

Competency, as defined in *Donovan v. Sears Roebuck and Company* (1994), is the presence of particular characteristics and the absence of particular disabilities that render the witness legally qualified to testify in court. The "particular characteristics" referred to in this definition include such things as the potential witness's age, role in the trial, and relationship to the defendant. Age, for example, can be a relevant factor in determining competency. Naturally, a three-year-old's testimony would need to be viewed cautiously when compared to that of an adult. "Disabilities" concerns a person's understanding of the duty to tell the truth. If a person cannot understand the duty to tell the truth, then under this definition the person cannot be a witness.

Judges are responsible for assessing a witness's competency. Often judges will decide on competency outside the presence of the jury so the jury does not confuse competency with credibility. This task is usually accomplished in a separate hearing designed to determine competency. Indeed, in *United States v. Gates* (1993), the 11th Circuit Court of Appeals stated that courts have a *duty* to hold separate hearings to determine witness competency. The procedures for judging the competency of witnesses are found in Rule 601 of the Federal Rules of Evidence.

The party seeking to call a witness bears the burden of convincing the judge that the person is competent. If the prosecutor wants to call a witness, he or she bears the burden of demonstrating the witness's competency. Alternatively, if the defense attorney wants to call a witness, he or she bears the same burden. The judge then decides whether the witness can be considered competent. Note, however, that competency is assumed at the outset, unless the opposition objects to the witness. For example, if the prosecution objects to a defense witness, it is at that point that the defense attorney must convince the judge that the witness is competent to testify.

We should distinguish at this point between the competency of witnesses and the competency of evidence. A witness may be competent to give testimony but cannot because the rules of evidence preclude the witness's testimony. For example, assume a witness hears two suspects conversing about a crime they "got away with." Because of the hearsay rule, which we will discuss in Chapter 12, the witness will probably not be able to introduce what he or she heard in trial. Thus, even though this witness has something meaningful to communicate, and even though he or she is competent, the rules of evidence may preclude the witness from reporting what he or she heard when the case goes to trial.

Grounds for Challenging Witness Competency

At common law, many people were barred from testifying because they fit into specific categories. For example, people who failed to believe in God, people convicted of crimes, and children were frequently declared incompetent to be witnesses. See Table 9-1 for the so-called "Five I's" of incompetence under English Common Law.

Table 9-1	The Five I's of Incompetency Under English Common Law
Interest:	Witnesses with an interest in the outcome of the case (such as spouses) may be motivated to lie and should be disqualified.
Infants:	Young children should be disqualified because of their inability to understand the obligation to tell the truth.
Insane:	Insane persons were thought incapable of recalling events and understanding the duty to tell the truth.
Idolatry:	The idolatry of adherents to nonmainstream religions was thought to make the oath not binding on their consciences.
Infamy:	Infamous criminals were deemed civilly dead and thereby incapable to serve as witnesses.

Nowadays, the competency requirement has nothing to do with "categories" of persons. Rather, it focuses on a person's ability to narrate the events in question and understand the duty to tell the truth. Some of the "I's" in Table 9-1 (e.g., insanity) are therefore relevant today, because of the contemporary focus on the duty to narrate and tell the truth. An "insane" person, in other words, may be considered incompetent because of an inability to describe what he or she witnessed.

The Federal Rules of Evidence explicitly state that "every person is competent to be a witness except as otherwise provided in these rules" (Rule 601). Similarly, California's general competency rule states that "except as otherwise provided by statute, every person, irrespective of age, is qualified to be a witness and no person is disqualified to testify to any matter" (Ca. Evidence Code, Section 700). On the other hand, Alabama's Evidence Code (Section 12–21–165) defines as incompetent "persons who have not the use of reason, such as idiots, lunatics during lunacy and children who do not understand the nature of an oath . . . "

It is actually more meaningful to speak in terms of witness "qualification" rather than witness competency. This is because nearly anyone can be a witness if he or she possesses the qualifications already discussed. A more appropriate question would seem to be if the person is *qualified* to be a witness. Nevertheless, courts still refer to witness competency at trial and in their opinions.

At least six categories of people have been challenged on competency/qualification grounds throughout history: (1) those whose mental capacity is called into question, (2) children, (3) spouses, (4) people previously convicted of crimes, (5) people who have certain religious beliefs, and (6) judges and jury members.

Before addressing each witness category, it is critical that we point out that these six types of people are not objectionable as witnesses because of who they are. That is, they are not undesirable witnesses for reasons tied to discrimination, narrow mindedness, or bigotry. Rather, their ability to narrate events and understand the duty to tell the truth are what is generally questioned. It should also be emphasized that just because persons are mentally infirm or underage does not mean they cannot be witnesses. We are merely providing a historical overview of the categories of individuals who have proven to be the most problematic as witnesses. Keep in mind that *anyone* can be a witness, as long as he or she can communicate adequately and understand the duty to tell the truth.

Mental incapacity. As early as 1882, the Supreme Court developed a rule aimed at assessing the mental capacity of witnesses. In *District of Columbia v. Armes* (1882) the Court held:

> [The general rule is that] a lunatic or a person affected with insanity is admissible as a witness if he has sufficient understanding to apprehend the obligation of an oath, and to be capable of giving a correct account of the matters which he has seen or heard in reference to the questions at issue; and whether he has that understanding is a question to be determined by the court, upon examination of the party himself, and any competent witnesses who can speak to the nature and extent of his insanity. (p. 521–522)

Significantly, the Supreme Court has observed that "the existence of partial insanity does not prevent individuals so affected . . . from giving a perfectly accurate and lucid statement of what they have seen or heard" (p. 521). In *Armes,* the Supreme Court actually admitted the testimony of a person who was confined to an asylum and who had attempted suicide a number of times by sticking a fork into his neck.

Other courts have relied on the Supreme Court's standard set forth in *Armes.* For example, the Ninth Circuit Court of Appeals in *Shibley v. United States* (1956) ruled that the trial court was correct in admitting the testimony of a person who had previously been deemed insane. Accordingly, just because a witness is determined to be insane, even by a court of law, such a determination is generally not enough to declare the witness incompetent to give testimony in a criminal trial.

Indeed, given rule 601 of the Federal Rules of Evidence, it is exceedingly difficult for a person to be declared incompetent because of a mental condition. In *United States v. Roach* (1979), the court held that because the rule that "every person" can be a witness, provided he or she is competent, means that it is doubtful that a mental condition can be enough to disqualify someone as a potential witness. Similarly, one court ruled that the lower court was wrong to declare a witness incompetent "because he had been found to be criminally insane and incompetent to stand trial, and was subject to hallucinations" (*United States v. Lighty*, 1982). In another case (*United States v. Bloome*, 1991) the court ruled that, even though a government witness suffered traumatic effects from a bullet wound to the head, he was competent to testify because there were no observable long-term effects or prolonged mental illness.

The question that courts need to address in determining competency is if the witness is *currently* competent to testify. Just because a person was declared insane in the past, committed to a facility, or otherwise mentally challenged in some fashion does not necessarily mean that person cannot give testimony. The only time that a witness will not be competent to testify because of a mental condition is if the witness does not have the capacity to recall the events in question or does not fully understand the duty to testify truthfully during criminal trial.

Regardless of mental condition, any witness is competent to testify unless evidence is introduced to the contrary. The burden of persuading the court that a witness is incompetent because of a mental condition falls on the party alleging that the witness is incompetent. The challenging party needs to demonstrate one of three things: (1) the witness does not understand the oath and the obligation to give truthful testimony; (2) the witness does not understand the consequences of giving false testimony; or (3) the witness cannot perceive or recall enough to give an accurate account of the events for which he or she was presumably a witness.

Childhood. Another common ground for challenging witness competency is youth. The reason that people have been opposed to children giving testimony is that young children may not understand their role as witness or be able to recall important events. Just as the judge determines the competency of a witness who has a mental condition, so too is the judge responsible for determining the competency of a child. It is not essential that a child understand the full meaning of the "oath" to give truthful testimony, but the child should be able to distinguish truth from falsehood.

To illustrate, consider the case of *Idaho v. Wright* (1990). In that case, Laura Lee Wright and Robert Giles were charged on two counts of lewd conduct with a minor under the age of 16. The victims were Wright's daughters, ages 5½ and 2½. The court ruled that the younger daughter was not capable of communicating to the jury and could not serve as a witness. This decision was upheld by the U.S. Supreme Court. Arguably, a child under age three cannot be expected to give meaningful testimony at trial.

In *White v. Illinois* (1992), on the other hand, a 4-year-old child's statements to her mother and her doctor were admitted as evidence in a case where the defendant was accused of sexual assault against the child. The *White* case dealt with the hearsay rule for children (discussed in Chapter 12), but at issue here is the child's age. Similarly, in another case the court permitted a 5-year-old rape victim and her 7-year-old sister to testify even though their competency was challenged by the defense (*Pocatello v. United States*, 1968).

Some statutes expressly prohibit children from being witnesses. For example, Ohio law provides that "children under ten years of age, who appear incapable of receiving just impressions of the facts respecting which they are examined, or of relating them truly" (Ohio R. Evid. 601A) cannot be considered competent. Generally, though, there are no age restrictions. In one case, the Supreme Court offered clarification:

> That the boy was not by reason of his youth [5½ years], as a matter of law, absolutely disqualified as a witness is clear. While no one would think of calling as a witness an infant only two or three years old, there is no precise age which determines the question of competency. This depends on the capacity and intelligence of the child, his appreciation of the difference between truth and falsehood, as well as of his duty to tell the former . . . (*Wheeler v. United States*, 1895, p. 524)

Problems are posed when a witness is of sufficient age at the time of trial but was significantly younger at the time the crime was committed. In one case, the witness was 10 at the time of the trial but was asked to narrate events that occurred when he was 4. In light of just this type of situation, some courts have ruled that competency needs to be determined at essentially two points in time, at the time of the crime and at trial (*Huprich v. Paul W. Varga and Sons, Inc.*, 1965; *Cross v. Commonwealth*, 1953). In other words, the child must be able to narrate the events as they occurred in the past but also remain competent as a trial witness.

What exactly are the rules for determining the competency of a child? There are no clear answers, but the courts have offered a number of guidelines in several important cases. For example, in *Kelluem v. State* (1978, p. 5), the Supreme Court of Delaware ruled that four factors must be considered: (1) the child's ability to perceive accurate impressions of fact or capacity to observe the acts about which he is to testify; (2) the child's ability or capacity to recollect these impressions or observations; (3) the child's ability to recall and his capacity to communicate what was observed; and (4) the child's understanding of truth and falsity and his capacity to appreciate the moral responsibility to be truthful.

Similarly, in *State v. Cabral* (1980, pp. 628–629), a Rhode Island court ruled that a competent witness who is a child must possess four criteria: The child must be able to (1) observe, (2) recollect, (3) communicate, and (4) appreciate the necessity of telling the truth.

In an important study, McCord (1986) found that while adults are naturally more capable of recalling and communicating events, it is not necessarily the case that children are more vulnerable to suggestion or less capable of recalling and communicating events than adults. McCord pointed out that "there is some intriguing evidence that young children sometimes notice potentially interesting things that older children and adults miss" (p. 48).

To ensure that child testimony is accurate, McCord offers a number of suggestions: (1) children should be able to testify out of court—that is, by closed-circuit television or some other medium; (2) children should be allowed to meet courtroom officials, including the judge, before trial if they are to be required to testify in court; (3) judges should caution the prosecution or the defense if the questions asked of a child are too advanced or difficult to understand; and (4) tired and traumatized children should be allowed to rest or take a break during testimony, if it is determined that such would improve the child's ability to accurately narrate the events.

Spousal relationships. In the past, husbands and wives were considered incompetent to testify for or against each other. The reason should be clear: self-interest. For example, if the husband is accused of rape, the wife may wish to testify on behalf of her husband, arguing that he could not have committed the crime. Assuming the wife believes in her husband's innocence, she has a strong self-interest in seeing that he is found not guilty. On the other hand, if the wife were to testify *against* her husband, consensus was that such testimony would be impermissible. The Fifth Amendment, as we have seen, prohibits self-incrimination, and it was believed that husbands and wives were "one person" in essence, so to have one partner testify against the other would violate the Fifth Amendment.

Not surprisingly, the courts have created a number of exceptions to the rule of **spousal privilege**, which holds that wives cannot testify against their husbands and vise versa. In *Stein v. Bowman* (1837), the U.S. Supreme Court held that the rule barring spousal testimony does not apply in cases where the husband commits a crime against the wife (or, by extension, where the wife commits a crime against the husband). Other courts have subsequently reaffirmed this ruling, holding that the self-interested motives of one party should not prevent his or her testimony (*Fund v. United States*, 1933). Because defendants are permitted to testify on their own behalf, it does not make sense to prevent spouses from testifying.

As early as 1887, Congress permitted spouses to testify in prosecutions for bigamy, polygamy, and unlawful cohabitation. Congress then expanded this rule to permit spousal testimony in cases involving the importation of aliens for immoral purposes (18 U.S.C. Section 1328). The law also permits spousal testimony in cases where marriages are premised on fraud. For example, in *Lutwak v. United States* (1953), three illegal aliens married war veterans who were prosecuted for conspiracy to defraud the United States because it was believed their marriages were designed solely for the purpose of allowing the women to obtain U.S. citizenship. The court ruled that the women were competent to testify against their "husbands" because they had no intention to live together as husband and wife once they were safely inside the U.S. border.

A number of restrictions continue to govern spousal testimony, but the restrictions depend on the laws in specific states. Many states permit spouses to testify against each another, but only for certain offenses. For example, under Ohio state law spouses can testify on behalf of each other without restrictions but are only allowed to testify *against* each other in (1) prosecutions for personal injury in which one partner inflicts harm on the other; (2) prosecutions for bigamy; and (3) prosecutions for failure to provide for, neglect of, or cruelty to their children (Ohio Rev. Code Ann., Section 2945.42, 1994). Some states leave the decision to testify in the hands of the husband and wife. For example, Georgia law holds that spouses are competent to testify against each other, but courts cannot compel testimony by the husband or the wife (OCGA, Section 24–9–23, 1994).

California's Evidence Code (Article 4, Section 970) provides that "a married person has a privilege not to testify against his spouse in any proceeding." The rationale behind California's rule is that a requirement of spousal testimony, particularly incriminating spousal testimony, would seriously disrupt or disturb the marital relationship. California's Evidence Code also grants a privilege not to be *called* as a witness against a spouse (Article 4, Section 971). The only exception to this second rule is if the party calling the spouse does so in good faith without the knowledge of the marital relationships.

Interestingly, California's Evidence Code (Article 4, Section 972) outlines a number of exceptions in which a married person does not have a privilege to decline to testify or be called to testify. The exceptions are proceedings (1) brought by or on behalf of one spouse against the other; (2) to commit or place a spouse or his or the spouse's property, or both, under the control of another because of the spouse's alleged mental or physical condition; (3) brought by or on behalf of a spouse to establish his or her competence; (4) under Juvenile Court Law; and (5) in which one spouse is charged with a specific crime. California's Evidence Code refers to several "specific crimes." Two examples are crimes against the person or property of the other spouse and bigamy.

An interesting issue related to spousal testimony concerns the ability of the prosecution to compel such testimony. Even though many evidence codes seem to grant a privilege to spouses who decline to testify against their partners, can prosecutors nevertheless "threaten" potential witnesses with charges if they refuse to testify? There is little if any proof that this situation occurs, but it is possible for the prosecution to demand that a spouse testify, despite rules of evidence to the contrary threatening the partner with criminal charges. This is something of a deceptive, manipulative tactic, but one that has certainly happened from time to time.

As we have seen, the privilege of a spouse to decline to testify against his or her partner is based on the logic that such testimony would disrupt marital harmony. But what if the marriage is on shaky ground prior to the trial? Alternatively, what if the marriage is based on a whirlwind courtship and at the time of testimony the partners have known each other for less than three months? In both situations the rationale for the spousal privilege against giving adverse testimony is called into question. Unfortunately, there have not been any cases addressing such issues.

Another interesting issue concerning the spousal privilege to not testify adversely against a partner has to do with the distinction between actual and common law marriages. An "actual" marriage is one in which a formal ceremony takes place in the presence of a judge, priest, or other person authorized to perform such events. A "common law" marriage, on the other hand, is one in which a couple lives together for a long period of time and such cohabitation can be considered a marriage for all practical purposes. In one case, a couple had lived together for four years and the court ruled that the legislature should determine whether the privilege should apply to such relationships (*People v. Delph*, 1979). The lack of case law with regard to this issue is important, especially in light of the current debate over "domestic partnership." One controversial question that has yet to be answered is if the privilege should apply to same sex domestic-partnerships.

The privilege granted to a spouse to not give adverse testimony against a marital partner does not survive the termination of marriage. In *United States v. Bolzer* (1977) the Ninth Circuit Court of Appeals held that the privilege no longer applies, even during divorce judgments under appeal by the husband or wife (see also *United States v. Fisher,* 1975). The same rule seems to apply to some marriages that, while still intact, are no longer viable. In *United States v. Cameron* (1977) the court disallowed the privilege in a damaged marriage where both partners had no desire for reconciliation.

It is appropriate to mention at this juncture that the privilege discussed in this section applies only to testimonial or communicative evidence from the spousal witness. It does not include the use of the spousal witness's fingerprints where such evidence tends to incriminate the partner (*United States v. Thomann*, 1979). Handwriting samples can also be required by one partner if such samples tend to incriminate the other partner (e.g., *In re Rovner*, 1974). It also appears that the privilege is not extended to protect a spouse from being called to testify before a grand jury (*In re Lochiatto*, 1974).

Prior convictions. The Supreme Court decided in 1918 that "the dead hand of the common law rule," disqualifying witnesses because they had previously been convicted of a crime, should no longer be applied in criminal cases in federal court (*Rosen v. United States*, 1918). Many states have followed suit and have begun to permit the testimony of people previously convicted of crimes. In one federal case, for example, the court ruled that "the government cannot be expected to depend exclusively upon the virtuous in enforcing the law, and so long as a reasonable jury could believe an informant's testimony, after hearing relevant impeachment evidence regarding his or her reliability, the government may rely upon such testimony" (*United States v. Richardson*, 1985, p. 1521), even if the witness has been previously convicted. In another case involving a witness who had been treated for alcoholism and had an extensive criminal record, a Connecticut court ruled that such a background could not render the witness incompetent to testify (*State v. Valeriano*, 1983).

While prior convictions may be immaterial as far as competency is concerned, prior convictions can be of profound significance with regard to witness *credibility*. The general rule is that a witness's prior convictions damage the witness's credibility but do not "disqualify" or render the witness incompetent to testify. There are several exceptions to this general rule, however. We consider the credibility issue—in reference to prior convictions as well as several other issues—later on in this chapter.

Religious beliefs. Religious beliefs cannot be considered grounds to declare a witness incompetent. In other words, if a person has an objectionable religious belief or opinion, that person cannot be declared incompetent. The issue, instead, is "whether or not the individual has the ability to observe, recollect and communicate, and some sort of moral responsibility" (*State v. Phipps*, 1982, p. 131). In the past, a *lack* of religious background was also used to declare some witnesses incompetent. Nowadays, though, if the witness is able to understand the obligation to tell the truth, the witness can be considered competent even if he or she has no religious background (e.g.,*Chapell v. State*, 1986).

There are at least two situations in which a person's religious beliefs and opinions may be brought up in court. First, religious opinions can be grounds for impeachment. It is possible for the prosecution or defense to argue that a witness cannot be considered credible because of a belief he or she holds. Second, religious beliefs can be cause for concern during the jury selection process. For example, if a potential juror is fundamentally opposed to the death penalty for capital crimes, that person will probably not serve on the jury in a capital case. Generally, religion cannot factor into the competency determination.

Judges and jurors as witnesses. A final—though certainly not the last—reason for challenging competency occurs when judges and jurors become witnesses. Controversy exists, in particular, over the role of judges and jurors as witnesses in their own trials. Admittedly, the occasions where judges or jurors are called to testify are rare, but they deserve some attention nonetheless.

There has been some debate over the rule of judges as witnesses in the trials over which they preside, but rule 605 of the Federal Rules of Evidence now states, "The judge presiding at the trial may not testify in that trial as a witness . . . " Indeed, federal law requires that judges excuse themselves from cases in which they are or have been witness to the events in question (28 U.S.C. Section 455). Many states have adopted similar rules in their evidence codes. For example, Nebraska law holds that a judge presiding at a trial may not testify as a witness in that trial.

With regard to jurors, the generally accepted rule is that jurors may not testify as witnesses in the trials of which they are a part. The reasoning for this rule is clear: A juror who testifies for either the prosecution or the defense is likely to have an undue influence on the outcome of the case. For example, if a juror testifies to the effect that the defendant's friends threatened her while she was serving on the jury, her testimony would probably influence not only her decision during deliberations but also the opinions of the other members of the jury. Therefore, as rule 606(a) of the Federal Rules of Evidence dictates, "A member of the jury may not testify as a witness before that jury in the trial of the case in which the juror is sitting . . . "

Jurors are also granted protection from being compelled to testify about their deliberations. The federal courts have recognized (and rule 606(b) serves as the basis for such recognition) that permitting people to attack jury verdicts would be unduly burdensome on jury members. However, rule 606(b) does hold that jurors can be compelled to testify as to extraneous information or outside influences concerning the verdict. An example of extraneous information would be if a newspaper article that is prejudicial to the defendant found its way into jury deliberations. An example of outside influence would be threats against a particular jury member to vote a certain way. In either case, the court will explore the extent and consequences of extraneous or outside information and attempt to decide whether such information influenced the jury's decision, calling on specific jury members only as a last resort (*Owen v. Duckworth*, 1984; *United States ex rel. Buckhaha v. Lane*, 1986).

An interesting case with regard to juror testimony is *Fulgham v. Ford* (1988). In that case, two jurors, well after the trial, communicated to the defendant's counsel that they thought the defendant had been insane at the time of the murder but decided not to return a verdict of not guilty by reason of insanity because for fear that the defendant would be released into society. The defense challenged the verdict on these grounds, but the Eleventh Circuit Court of Appeals ruled that the jurors' statements could not be used to challenge the verdict. In one case to the contrary (*Isaacs v. Kemp*, 1985), the court held that a jury member's testimony that she attended the trials of other persons involved in the same case could be admitted, as it was considered an outside influence within the meaning of rule 606(b).

To summarize, we have briefly introduced six grounds for challenging witness competency. Most modern evidence codes, including the Federal Rules of Evidence, have done away with the past practice of declaring certain witnesses incompetent because they fall into a certain category (such as that they possess a strange religious belief or are of a fixed age). The rules of evidence vary a great deal across states, but the general rule concerning witness competency is (1) if a person has something relevant to say, (2) understands the obligation to tell the truth *and* (3) is capable of narrating the events in question, the person will almost certainly be permitted to serve as a witness. (see Table 9-2 for a different way of thinking about these three requirements of witness competency.)

Table 9-2	Essential Requirements of a Competent Witness
Requirement	**Description**
Perception	The person must be capable of perceiving events (usually by seeing them).
Recollection	The person must be able to recall the events.
Narration	The person must be able to narrate the events.
Sincerity	The person must be sincere in his or her testimony. Sincerity is generally assumed but is nonetheless sought by administering an oath.

We give careful consideration in the following subsections to the duty to tell the truth as well as to what it means to narrate the events in question, both of which are essential witness requirements. Then, before getting to our discussion of witness credibility, impeachment, and examination, we briefly comment on the so-called dead man's statutes as well as the occasional requirement that witness testimony be corroborated.

The Duty to Tell the Truth

The duty of witnesses to tell the truth is traced to the oath they are required to take before providing testimony. The most common oath administered to witnesses nowadays is one in which the witness promises to "tell the truth, the whole truth, and nothing but the truth, so help me God." It is not necessary that a witness swear on the Bible or even that God be mentioned in the oath. This is because atheists and agnostics may not see any value in an oath with religious language. Sometimes, instead of an oath an "affirmation," or promise to tell the truth, will be preferred. Regardless of the actual terminology in the oath, the witness must understand the duty to tell the truth.

The purpose of an oath or affirmation is to communicate to a witness that he or she will be testifying under penalty of perjury. That is, if the witness lies on the stand, he or she can be prosecuted for **perjury,** the offense of lying under oath (or following an affirmation). The mere threat of being charged with perjury would seem to be enough to ensure that witnesses will always tell the truth, but in reality, perjury charges are rarely filed.

For illustration, let us consider California. California's Evidence Code (Section 710) provides that "Every witness before testifying shall take an oath or make an affirmation or declaration in the form provided by law," but this requirement alone does not require a moral obligation to tell the truth. It is conceivable that a would-be witness would swear or affirm to tell the truth but have no intention to do so. What, if anything, can be done to disqualify such a witness? Fortunately, Section 701(a)(2) of California's Evidence Code states that "A person is disqualified to be a witness if he or she is . . . incapable of understanding the duty of a witness to tell the truth." Thus, at least in California, witnesses must swear to tell the truth as well as understand the duty to do so.

The form of the oath has received some scrutiny in recent trials. Consider the case of *United States v. Ward* (1992). Ward was the president of I & O Publishing Company, a mail-order house and publisher in Boulder City, Nevada. He was prosecuted for failure to pay income taxes for the years 1983, 1984, and 1985. Ward chose to represent himself at trial, and on July 9, 1990, he filed a "Motion to Challenge the Oath." In his motion he proposed an alternative oath that replaced the word "truth" with the phrase "fully integrated honesty." He believed that the word "honesty" was preferable to "truth."

The court in the *Ward* case ruled that "the oath or affirmation which has been administered in courts of law throughout the United States to millions of witnesses for hundreds of years should not be required to give way to the defendant's idiosyncratic distinctions between truth and honesty." The district court then overruled Ward's objections to the magistrate's ruling. As a result, Ward did not testify in his own trial and was convicted. He then appealed his case to the United States Court of Appeals for the Ninth Circuit, arguing that because the district court did not allow him to swear to an oath of his own creation, he was precluded from testifying in his own defense. The Court of Appeals reversed the lower court decision and remanded the case for a new trial. This case illustrates that the *form* of the oath does not matter so much as what the oath stands for. As long as witnesses swear in one form or another to tell the truth, the precise terminology they use prior to doing so would seem to be immaterial.

The situation is considerably more complicated with regard to children. Because young children may not understand the meaning of "oath," "affirmation," or "under penalty of perjury," they are often sworn in a different, somewhat simplistic fashion. Young children who serve as witnesses are often asked whether they know that it is wrong to tell a lie, or some other question that can be easily understood. It would not be fair to exclude child testimony just because a child cannot understand the meaning of the term "perjury." Instead, other methods should be taken to swear in child witnesses when it is necessary.

What of expert witnesses? We turn attention to expert witnesses in the next chapter, but their oaths/affirmations are worthy of consideration in this section. It is well known that expert witnesses are frequently *paid* for testifying. Moreover, they are not called unless the calling party (a defense attorney, for instance) has good reason to believe they will testify in the party's favor. Consider a hypothetical murder case: A woman's body was dumped on a rural dirt road and the only trace of evidence left behind was a set of tire tracks. At trial an expert witness for the prosecution testifies that the tire tracks matched the tires on the defendant's vehicle. An expert witness for the defense, on the other hand, testifies that the tire tracks could not possibly match those on the defendant's vehicle. Who is telling the truth? Is it that each side honestly believes that his/her testimony is accurate? These are difficult questions, but it is certainly possible that one or the other (or both) of these hypothetical expert witnesses is not telling the truth.

In summary, witnesses are duty-bound to tell the truth. Of course, it would be naive to assume that every witness is truthful. One need only consider recent litigation involving "big tobacco." The CEOs of several leading cigarette manufacturers were lambasted for flagrant lies during the course of their testimony in civil trials and before Congress.

If the "penalty of perjury" is not enough to deter dishonesty, little recourse is available. Fortunately, most people are truthful in their testimony and legitimately fear the potential consequences they may face for being dishonest. The main message of this section is that "truth," the hopeful end result of witness testimony is what is important, not the procedure for ensuring that the witness swears to be truthful.

The Ability to Observe and Remember

To be a witness, a person must be able to communicate with the judge and jury about what happened. In other words, the witness will be required to narrate the events in question. Witnesses may have trouble communicating about what happened for any number of reasons. A witness may not understand the question, either because of a mental condition or a language barrier. Alternatively, the witness may not be able to remember and recall what happened, particularly if the crime was committed some time in the past.

There is a great deal of controversy as to witnesses' ability to observe and remember important events. There is also controversy over witnesses giving their "opinions" as to what they reportedly saw. We give more detailed treatment to the subject of opinions in the next chapter, but opinions are worth considering here as well. For example, in the case of *Gladden v. State* (1951) a police officer testified that he believed the defendant, who was charged with drunk driving, was drunk at the time of his arrest. The defendant attempted to exclude the officer's testimony but was unsuccessful, and he was ultimately convicted. On appeal, the Court of Appeals of Alabama stated

> Where in a proper case a non-expert is permitted to give opinion evidence, and cross examination discloses that his opportunity for observation was insufficient to afford any reasonable basis for the conclusion expressed, his opinion testimony should be excluded on motion. Where however an opportunity for observation is shown, even though slight, a witness should be considered competent to testify as to what he did observe. Certainly we know of no way to measure a witness's capacity for observation, other than as it may be determined by a jury which hears the testimony tending to show its strength or weakness on the facts developed from examination of the witness. (p. 199)

The last sentence of this case excerpt is telling. The appellate court basically suggested that it is impossible to measure witness's ability to observe and remember important events. The question as to the accuracy of their testimony should be left up to the jury.

Another illustrative case is *State v. Ranieri* (1991). This case involved a prosecution for burglary and assault. Someone broke into Elsie's apartment during the night and assaulted her. Hearing the commotion in Elsie's apartment, a neighbor, Picard, entered the apartment and attempted to remove the assailant from Elsie. Picard was also assaulted while attempting to intervene. For many months after the incident Elsie said she could not identify the assailant; however, on the eve of the trial, she stated that she could identify him. Before the trial she picked the defendant's picture out of a photographic lineup and also identified him at trial. The question before the Supreme Court of Rhode Island was if Elsie had sufficient opportunity to view the defendant to be considered a competent witness. Despite her identification of the defendant during and immediately preceding the trial, the court ruled that she was incompetent as a witness because she "had an insufficient opportunity to view the assailant."

The court further stated,

> We think it unmistakenly clear that Elsie has a history of making unwarranted and unfair accusations against defendant. Elsie had absolutely no factual basis to make two prior serious allegations against defendant and we see nothing to indicate a factual basis . . . to consider her competent as a witness.

The message from the court was basically that witnesses, though afforded a great deal of latitude in their testimony, must be able to communicate a certain minimal amount of information to be considered competent and have their testimony included at trial.

In another case (*State v. Singh*, 1979) the question of a child's ability to recall and narrate events was raised. In that case, the Missouri Court of Appeals heard an appeal from a defendant who was convicted in a lower court of manslaughter of his wife. The defendant testified at trial that in the course of an argument with his wife, which became violent, that she had gone to a closet and obtained a revolver, which the defendant had taken from her and put in his pocket. The defendant also testified that the wife hit him with a stick and that a struggle then occurred, first inside the house then outside, at which point the gun "went off." The government offered as a witness the nearly six-year-old daughter who had been present. She testified that she was awakened by the quarrel, that she observed her mother lying down outside the house, and that the mother had been shot. The defense moved to declare the child witness incompetent; however, the Court of Appeals permitted the testimony, stating that "this child appears to have been candid, alert and intelligent." Moreover, according to the court, "There is no fixed age at which a child may be a competent witness."

In support of its decision the court noted that the time interval between the crime and daughter's testimony was relatively short, which served to reinforce the belief that her testimony was accurate and believable. By way of contrast, another court ruled that it is wrong to find competent a girl who was four at the time of the incident and eleven at the time of trial. "The evidence does not support a finding that Jane had a reasonable ability to recall . . . , in 1991, events that occurred in 1983. She was unable to recall even basic aspects of her life as it was in 1983 other than the detailed description of the events of the one day on which she was allegedly assaulted" (*State v. Rippy*, 1993, pp. 337–338).

A case involving residents in a nursing home raises interesting issues concerning witnesses' ability to recall and narrate events. In *People v. White* (1968), the Supreme Court of Illinois had occasion to decide whether an elderly person who could not communicate verbally could be declared a competent witness. In that case, Mrs. Idelle Broday shared a room in a nursing home with Mrs. Mickey Kallick. Broday was robbed of a ring that was taken from her with sufficient force to cause a cut on her finger. The defendant, a nurse's aid, was accused of the crime. Broday was incompetent to testify because she was apparently not conscious at the time of the crime. The only witness, Mrs. Kallick, was not permitted by her doctors to be moved. As a result, a portion of the trial was held in the nursing home. Also, the only way Mrs. Kallick could communicate was to raise her right knee if her answer was "yes" and remain still if her answer was no. The trial judge declared Kallick competent as a witness, and the defendant was convicted based on her testimony. The Supreme Court of Illinois disagreed with his decision, "While the record may not establish total incompetency of the eyewitness, we are of the opinion that her condition was such that defendant could not get a fair trial. The witness had no means of originally communicating an accusation."

In summary, the ability of witnesses to observe, remember, and communicate important events is usually assumed. As we showed earlier, with few exceptions any witness can be considered competent unless he or she is unable to understand questions or communicate about the events in question. The cases just reviewed suggest that certain conditions such as youth, old age, and mental conditions can impair a witness's ability to remember, thus rendering him or her incompetent.

Dead Man's Statutes

Some states have "dead man's statutes" that prohibit witnesses from testifying about transactions with a person involved in a case if the person died prior to the trial. Such laws are based on the assumption that a survivor of a deceased person should be looked with suspicion as someone who may, on the first opportunity, make false claims against the deceased because he or she is unable to contest or affirm them.

Basically, dead man's statutes are intended to prevent fraud against those people who are unable to testify on their own behalf because they are dead. Such laws owe their origins to the common law rule of "disqualification by interest." Early common law courts concluded that witnesses with an "interest" in the outcome of the case were prevented from giving testimony (e.g., *Vastbinder v. Spinks*, 1849, p. 387).

According to one source:

> The existence of the dead man statutes represents the judgment of legislative bodies that the general honesty and truthfulness of people in modern society is at a pretty low ebb and that all it takes is the motive of interest plus a good chance created by death of one of the parties to cause the majority of people to concoct false claims to plunder the estates of dead persons. (Weinstein, Mansfield, Abrams, and Berger 1997, p. 272)

Many states have rejected dead man's statutes. For one thing, it is unreasonable to assume that people who stand to benefit from the death of a person will necessarily testify in a fraudulent fashion. In fact, the Federal Rules of Evidence (rule 601) contain no rules concerning testimony within the meaning of dead man's statutes. Also, to the extent that dead man's statutes still exist in certain states, they are almost exclusively limited to civil matters, particularly cases involving wills and estates.

An example of a case dealing with dead man's statutes is *Mathews v. Hines* (1978). This case concerned a dispute over more than $10,000 between the widow and daughter of a deceased man. The plaintiff, the daughter, alleged that prior to his death the man (known as a *decedent* in legal terms) transferred real and personal property to his wife, which presumably reduced the daughter's share that she would have received after his death had he not transferred funds before he died. The daughter alleged that the widow breached her promise to the decedent, her dead husband, to ensure that his estate was distributed according to his will. On two occasions the daughter deposed the widow to ask her about communications made to the husband prior to his death in which, presumably, arrangements were made to hide some of his assets from other family members besides the wife. The United States District Court for the Middle District of Florida ruled in favor of the plaintiff and ordered the widow to testify.

Why did we choose to focus on a civil case? The fact is that there are few, if any, published *criminal* cases focusing on dead man's statutes. Dead man's statutes, again, are designed to protect against false witness statements against a decedent—a dead person who cannot challenge such statements. In criminal cases, however, there are no decedents—that is, no dead people who stand to be "harmed" in some fashion by statements offered by a witness. The only person who stands to lose something in a criminal action is the defendant, and the defendant clearly needs to be "alive" for the trial to commence.

When Corroboration Is Required

The credibility of a witness is stronger if there is information to corroborate the witness's story. Supporting evidence is called corroboration. Do not confuse **corroborative evidence** with cumulative evidence. **Cumulative evidence** is evidence that repeats what is already known. For example, several witnesses testifying that they saw an event can be considered cumulative. Corroborative evidence is supportive, not duplicative.

Corroboration can be presented by another witness or as physical evidence. For example, if two witnesses observe a crime, then if both witnesses testify at trial, one's testimony corroborates the other's. Similarly, if a witness to a domestic assault observes that a husband hit his wife, physical evidence of injury corroborates the witness's testimony. The witness's testimony in such a case is an improvement on the mere presence of a physical injury because such an injury may or may not be tied to the husband's criminal act. The wife could have received the injury as a result of a fall rather than at the hands of her husband.

For the most part, witnesses can give their testimony without corroboration. That is, a witness usually does not need another person or other evidence to support the statements he or she makes in court. There are exceptions, however. In fact, Article III, Section 3 of the U.S. Constitution states that "No Person shall be convicted of treason unless on the testimony of two Witnesses to the same overt Act, or on Confession in open Court." Other statutes, some of which we now consider, also require corroboration.

For example, many jurisdictions require corroboration for a conviction of perjury. In *Weiler v. United States* (1945) the Supreme Court upheld the requirement that federal law requires corroboration in federal perjury cases on the ground that "the rules of law must be so fashioned as to protect honest witnesses from hasty and spiteful retaliation in the form of unfounded perjury prosecutions." The court's ruling seems sensible; to prove that someone is lying (the essence of perjury), some "evidence" would be necessary to support the charge.

Corroboration is also considered mandatory in some cases involving accomplices. The logic is simple: When one party testifies against the other, it is generally assumed that he or she is doing so in an effort to reduce his or her culpability or gain favors with the prosecution. For example, unless two men suspected of robbery are the best of friends, it is reasonable to assume that the first man may say something during an interrogation to implicate the second man and make himself look less culpable. Because of the motive to falsify testimony, corroboration is required for a conviction based on the testimony of an accomplice regardless of the nature of the crime.

It is generally accepted in the U.S. criminal justice system that a defendant cannot be convicted on his or her confession alone. Instead, confessions almost always have to be corroborated by other evidence (e.g., *Warszower v. United States,* 1941; *Opper v. United States,* 1954). One reason offered for this rule is that police coercion may be enough to compel a person to confess to a crime he or she did not commit. In the wake of important Supreme Court decisions such as *Miranda,* however, the reasoning for requiring corroboration is now simply that "physically uncoerced false confessions occur with sufficient regularity to justify prophylactic measures" (*Government of Virgin Islands v. Harris,* 1966, p. 409). Corroboration is necessary, therefore, to ensure that wrongful convictions are minimized.

Somewhat controversially, certain jurisdictions require that rape victims' testimony be corroborated by additional information. This requirement has been abandoned in several areas, but the Model Penal

Code continues to retain the corroboration requirement. A comment to Section 213.6(5) of the Model Penal Code states, however, that retaining the corroboration requirement is "only a particular implementation of the general policy that uncertainty should be resolved in favor of the accused." In other words, corroboration should be viewed as a means of improving the government's case against the defendant in a rape trial for which witness corroboration is required.

In those jurisdictions that retain corroboration requirements, it is not always clear to which elements of an offense the corroboration requirement attaches. In *Smith v. United States* (1954), the Supreme Court stated that all elements of the offense must be corroborated. However, in *Wong Sun v. United States* (1963, p. 490, n. 15) the Court stated that when a crime involves physical damage to a person or property, corroboration is necessary only for the *corpus delecti*—damage that is criminally caused. Corroboration was not considered essential in that case to show that the defendant was the cause of the physical damage. The decision as to the defendant's guilt or innocence was to be left to the jury.

We introduce corroboration in this chapter simply because additional information is sometimes necessary (even required) when the veracity of a witness's testimony is questionable. However, any good attorney will do whatever possible to corroborate witnesses' testimony. Even though the rules of evidence may not require it, both sides to a criminal case, if they are reasonable competent, will always try to introduce as much evidence as possible to corroborate the testimony of their witnesses as well as to improve their chances to "win the case."

To conclude, witness testimony can regularly stand alone —that is, it does not need corroboration most of the time. Corroboration is necessary only in specific situations depending on state law. The Federal Rules of Evidence give no mention to corroboration, so the extent that corroboration is necessary is left up to the states to decide.

Witness Credibility

We now turn our attention to the topics of credibility and impeachment. Credibility, first off, should be distinguished from competency. Competency, as we saw have seen, pertains to a witness's ability to remember events, communicate effectively, and understand the importance of (1) telling the truth and (2) the consequences for not doing so. **Credibility** asks if the witness's testimony should be believed. In other words, are the witness's statements such that they can be judged as truthful? If the witness is able to remember events, communicate clearly to the jury, and come across as convincing, he or she will probably be regarded as credible.

When discussing competency courts often refer to the processes of "accrediting" and "discrediting." **Discrediting** occurs when the prosecution or defense challenges the witness's credibility. **Accrediting** is the opposite: It occurs when the prosecution or defense attempts to support, bolster, or improve a witness's credibility.

There are specific rules governing the processes of accrediting and discrediting. First, it is universally agreed that in absence of an attack on a witness's credibility, no evidence may be introduced to support or bolster credibility. According to one court (*United States v. Price*, 1983, p. 90), "[T]here is no reason why time should be spent in proving that which may be assumed to exist. Every witness must be assumed to be of normal moral character for veracity, just as he is assumed to be of normal sanity . . . Good character, therefore, in his support is excluded *until his character is brought into question* and it thus becomes worthwhile to deny that his character is bad." Simply put, a witness generally cannot be accredited until someone (prosecution or defense) attempts to *discredit* the witness.

Consider the situation in which a witness is asked to introduce himself or herself and describe his or her background. The prosecution or defense may ask direct questions about the witness's familiarity with the case or, in the case of expert witnesses, questions about the witness's occupation, background, and professional accomplishments. This type of questioning would appear to be accrediting, but a certain amount of background information can be supplied by introductory witness questioning without it being considered accreditation. However, there is a point at which accrediting must stop, absent an attack on the witness's credibility. Unfortunately, there are few answers as to what amount of accrediting "background" information is permissible. According to one court (*Government of Virgin Islands v. Grant*, 1985, p. 513):

> The jurisprudence of "background" evidence is essentially undeveloped. "Background" or "preliminary" evidence is not mentioned in the evidence codes, nor has it received attention in the treatises. One justification for its admission, at least in terms of the background of a witness *qua* witness, is that it may establish absence of bias or motive by showing the witness's relationship (or nonrelationship) to the parties or to the case . . .

It is safe to conclude, though, that when the introduction process turns aggrandizing—that is, into more than an introduction—the accrediting of a witness must stop.

In one interesting case (*Pointer v. State*, 1954) the prosecutor, during his closing statements, stated that if the prosecution witness had been of bad character, the defense would have raised the issue. The court reversed the ensuing conviction, holding that because the witness's credibility was not attacked during trial, the prosecutor was not permitted to bolster the witness's credibility (see also *Poole v. Commonwealth*, 1970).

A controversial issue with regard to accrediting concerns what can be done to bolster a witness's credibility when he or she cannot remember important events. If, for example, a witness testifies to a series of events but states that she is unable to remember everything, can another witness be called to offer reasons for the woman's memory lapse? A similar question was raised in *United States v. Awkward* (1979). In that case, the Ninth Circuit Court of Appeals ruled that it was wrong for a prosecution witness to testify that he had been hypnotized and to permit a prosecution expert who had hypnotized the first witness to testify about the effects of hypnosis on the first witness. As the court observed

> unless an adverse party attacks the witness's ability to recall by bringing out or exploring the fact of hypnosis, the use of expert testimony to support the efficacy of hypnosis is improper. The party calling a witness should not be permitted to inquire in any way into the witness's ability to recall, or methods of pretrial memory refreshment, until such questions have been raised by the adversary. (p. 679)

In sum, witness accrediting is permissible but usually "only after the character of the witness for truthfulness has been attacked by opinion or reputation evidence or otherwise" (*Blake v. Cich*, 1978, p. 403). In legal parlance, accrediting of this sort is also known as witness rehabilitation, which we address following our discussion of impeachment. Note, however, that this restriction on accrediting rule is not recognized in most modern evidence statutes, except with regard to character evidence. That is, most modern statutes do not allow accrediting of a witness's character, but are silent as to other types of accrediting (see rule 608(a)(2) of the Federal Rules of Evidence).

Impeachment

Impeachment is the formal term for attacking a witness's credibility. The prosecution or defense may decide, when faced with a witness who is not believed to be telling the truth, to challenge the witness's believability before the jury. The jury will then draw its own conclusions as to the witness's truthfulness and believability.

How does impeachment occur? Generally, the process begins on cross examination. There are several established and well-founded reasons for attacking witness credibility. However, there is little value in attempting to impeach a witness if the witness's testimony does not carry much weight or is unpersuasive to the jury. Alternatively, if there is no basis for an attack on a witness's credibility but the opposing side attempts to attack the witness's credibility anyway, an impeachment effort could backfire.

Almost without exception, impeachment occurs when the prosecution attacks the credibility of a defense witness or vise versa. However, there are certain situations in which the prosecution or the defense may wish to impeach its own witness. Indeed, Federal Rule of Evidence 607 states, "The credibility of a witness may be attacked by any party, including the party calling the witness."

Why might a party wish to impeach its own witness? The primary and perhaps only reason is surprise. (*Hickory v. United States*, 1894). "Surprise" occurs when the witness's testimony is contrary to that which is anticipated by the party calling the witness (*United States v. Miles*, 1969).

To illustrate the notion of surprise, consider the case of *Sullivan v. United States* (1928), in which three persons pled guilty to participation in a mail robbery. All three men then served as prosecution witnesses against the defendant, a fourth man who had not pled guilty. To the surprise of the prosecution, though, one of the three men gave testimony that exculpated the defendant. Accordingly, the prosecution could have impeached the witness because of the surprise.

In another case (*People v. Spinosa*, 1953), the witness at first stated prior to trial that he had not committed the offense but then later stated that he *had* committed the offense. At trial, the witness testified that he had not commited the crime. The court held that the prosecution was surprised because the prosecution had the right to assume that the witness would testify in accordance with his latest story. A second reason for one party to impeach its own witness is to lessen the blow imposed by cross examination (see *United States v. Shields*, 1993).

Despite rule 607's statement to the effect that a party may impeach its own witness, there are significant restrictions on impeaching one's own witness. For example, the government or the prosecution cannot impeach its own witnesses by presenting what would otherwise be considered impermissible hearsay (*United States v. Ince*, 1994). Nigel D. Ince was convicted by a jury for assault with a dangerous weapon. The Fourth Circuit Court of Appeals reversed Ince's conviction because the government's only purpose for impeaching one of its own witnesses was to circumvent the hearsay rule and expose the jury to otherwise inadmissible evidence.

Impeachment is most often used by one party against another. The prosecution or the defense can attack a witness's credibility for a number of well-established reasons, including (1) bias or prejudice, (2) prior convictions, (3) uncharged crimes and immoral acts, (4) prior inconsistent statements, (5) inability to observe, and (6) reputation. See Table 9-3 for a summary.

Bias or prejudice. Perhaps the most effective way of calling into question a witness's credibility is to introduce evidence of bias or preju-

Table 9-3	Common Grounds for Challenging Witness Credibility
Grounds	**Description**
Bias or prejudice	If a witness is inclined to favor or oppose one party for any reason (such as interest, corruption, or intimidation), the witness is said to be biased. Witnesses can also be biased because of friendship, family ties, animosity, or prejudice.
Prior convictions	With some exceptions, convictions for felonies and crimes involving deception can be used to discredit a witness.
Uncharged crimes and immoral acts	A witness's uncharged crimes can be called attention to in order to impeach the witness, but the crimes (1) must have probative value in the eyes of the judge; (2) must be limited to the witness's character for telling the truth; and (3) cannot be proved by extrinsic evidence.
Contradictions and prior inconsistent statements	These can be called attention to at trial.
Inability to observe	Defects in a witness's ability to perceive, recollect, or narrate events can be used to discredit the witness.
Reputation	The witnesses reputation can be called into question but is limited to the witness's propensity for telling the truth.

dice. If, for example, a witness for the defense is a close personal relative of the defendant, there would seem to be strong bias in *favor* of the defendant (that is, assuming the defendant and witness are on good terms). Any motive for the witness to falsify his or her testimony or to testify in an untruthful fashion so as to benefit or harm the defendant can be raised by the opposing side as evidence of bias or prejudice.

One especially well-known example of a witness's credibility being attacked for prejudice was in the famous O.J. Simpson case. Recall that Detective Mark Fuhrman was cross examined regarding his prejudice against blacks. The prosecution fought to avoid the questioning of F. Lee Bailey (one of Simpson's defense attorneys) to this effect, but Judge Ito permitted it. As a result, Bailey was able to introduce evidence supporting Detective Fuhrman's racially prejudicial sentiments.

In another case (*McKnight v. State,* 1994), the court held that the examination of the defendant's wife concerning her withdrawal of previous complaints against the defendant was permissible in order to impeach her as to her bias.

One important reason to impeach a witness for evidence of bias is if a prosecution witness is offered promises of leniency. The bias motive is clear: If the witness knows that his or her testimony will garner favor with the prosecution, the witness may be inclined to tell the prosecution what it wants to hear. In one case, a Tennessee court ruled that the defendant had the right to attack a prosecution witness's credibility because of promises of favorable treatment made by the prosecution (*State v. Spurlock*, 1993).

In an interesting Supreme Court case, *United States v. Abel* (1984), the issue of cross examining for bias was raised. John Abel was charged in federal court with robbery. Two of his accomplices had pled guilty to the crime, and one, Kurt Ehle, agreed to testify against Abel. At trial, Ehle implicated Abel in the robbery. However, Abel called a witness, Robert Mills, to testify that Ehle had planned to implicate Abel falsely. Mills and Ehle had both spent time together in prison. Under cross examination the prosecution asked Mills if he was, like Ehle, a member of prison gang, the Aryan Brotherhood. Mills denied that he was. The prosecution then called Ehle back to the stand, who testified that Mills was a member of the prison gang and that the gang's tenets required its members to "lie, cheat, steal [and] kill" to protect each other. The jury convicted Abel, and the Supreme Court upheld the conviction. In the Court's words, "We hold that the evidence showing Mills' and respondent's membership in the prison gang was sufficiently probative of Mills' possible bias towards respondent [Abel] to warrant its admission into evidence."

Prior convictions. Federal Rule of Evidence 609 provides,

> For the purpose of attacking the credibility of a witness, evidence that the witness has been convicted of a crime shall be admitted if elicited from the witness or established by public record during cross-examination, but only if the crime (1) was punishable by death or imprisonment in excess of one year under the law under which the witness was convicted, *and* the court determines that the probative value of admitting this evidence outweighs its prejudicial effect to the defendant, or (2) involved dishonesty or false statement, regardless of the punishment.

Under the first limitation, a prior felony conviction can be introduced, but only if the court (through the eyes of the judge) determines that testimony to this effect is not prejudicial to the defendant. Under the second limitation, any conviction can be introduced assuming it was for a crime involving dishonesty or some variation thereof. With regard to the second limitation, the Supreme Court of California has stated that "The case law is clear: The only relevant consideration is whether the prior conviction contains as a necessary element the intent to deceive, defraud, lie, cheat, steal, etc." (*People v. Spearman*, 1979).

Rule 609 of the Federal Rules of Evidence goes on to outline other limitations on what evidence of prior convictions can be introduced to impeach a witness. First, evidence of prior conviction is not admissible if a period of more than ten years elapsed between the trial for which the person is to be a witness and the prior conviction or from confinement for that conviction, whichever is the later date. If, however, the court sees that value in such evidence outweighs prejudice to the defendant, it will be permissible. Second, evidence of a prior conviction will not be admissible if the conviction has been the subject of a pardon, annulment, or certificate of rehabilitation. Third, evidence of prior convictions is generally not permissible with regard to juvenile witnesses. Finally, it does not matter whether a convicted person has an appeal pending; the conviction would still be admissible to impeach the witness, assuming there is substantial probative value in doing so.

Practice Pointer 9-1

Evidence of the defendant's past convictions can be used to discredit him or her only if the judge decides that it is not prejudicial. Otherwise, evidence of past convictions cannot be brought to the attention of the jurors.

If a defendant takes the stand in his or her own defense, the prosecution may seek to impeach the defendant on the grounds of having previously been convicted of a crime, but not if the prosecution's motive is to prove that the defendant committed the crime. Rather, evidence of prior convictions can be used only to cast doubt on the defendant's credibility. Clearly it must be difficult for jury members to separate one motive from the other, but the prosecutions motive *should* nevertheless be aimed at impeachment. Judges will generally be cautious about admitting into evidence the defendant's prior conviction(s) because of the potentially prejudicial effect doing so may have.

Nondefendant witnesses who have been convicted of crimes, on the other hand, are more likely to see their prior records introduced at trial for impeachment purposes. The ordinary witness will probably be asked a question along the lines of, "Have you ever been convicted of a felony?" or "Have you ever been convicted of a misdemeanor involving moral turpitude?" If the answer is yes, evidence of the witness's prior convictions has been introduced. However, the judge can restrict the questions asked by the prosecution, assuming the defense objects. Alternatively, the prosecution can object to defense questioning of state witnesses concerning prior convictions. Separate hearings (out of earshot of the jury) can be held in which the judge determines whether evidence of witnesses' prior convictions can be introduced at trial.

A conviction for a trivial offense, as shoplifting, may be introduced for the purpose of impeaching a witness, because such an offense involves a significant degree of dishonesty that may cast doubt on his or her credibility. Other examples of crimes of dishonesty and false statements include forgery and embezzlement because both are classic examples of offenses that call into question a witness's ability to be honest.

Even bank robbery (a felony) has been considered one of the offenses within the meaning of Federal Rule of Evidence 609; however, some courts have been hesitant to admit evidence of bank robbery convictions because bank robbery is less deceptive than less serious crimes involving illegitimate means of obtaining money. A bank robber simply communicates something along the lines of "Give me the money or I'll shoot you," a statement that is rather direct and confrontational. Convictions for offenses such as smuggling and tax evasion can usually be admitted, however, because they involve surreptitious activity and deception.

Convictions for serious offenses are not admitted for the purpose of impeaching a witness as often as less serious offenses are. The logic is that most serious offenses, with rare exceptions, do not shed light on a witness's motive to give false or misleading testimony. One could argue, for instance, that a witness previously convicted of robbery has such contempt for the laws of a civilized society that he could not possibly be inclined to tell the truth on the stand, but this is a risky assumption. Just because a person has been convicted of a serious crime does not mean that the person will necessarily lie on the stand (even if such a person is the defendant). Instead, the only way that evidence of a serious conviction can be admitted for impeachment purposes is if it passes a balancing test comparing its probative value to certain risks of misuse, particularly prejudice that could influence the jury negatively.

Consider a hypothetical example involving a conviction for a serious offense: The defense calls a witness to testify on the defendant's behalf. On cross examination the prosecution asks the witness, "Have you ever been convicted of a felony?" The witness answers, "Yes, for grand theft auto." Assuming this questioning passes muster with the judge, it is not difficult to see how the jury could be influenced by this evidence. Not only is the witness's credibility now damaged, but the jury may assume that "birds of a feather flock together." In other words, because the witness is affiliated with the defendant and the witness is a convicted criminal, then the defendant must be a criminal too. It is quite likely that the judge would not permit such evidence to be presented to the jury; however, if the evidence of the prior conviction has substantial probative value, as it would appear to (because grand theft auto is clearly a crime involving deception), the judge may allow it.

Uncharged crimes and immoral acts. Evidence about uncharged crimes or prior immoral acts is generally *not* admissible for the purpose of impeachment. If it turns out that a witness is a habitual shoplifter but has never been convicted of one such offense, this information would seem to bear substantially on the witness's credibility, but such evidence would probably not be admissible at trial.

There is one exception to this general rule though. Rule 608 provides that "Specific instances of the conduct of a witness . . . [may] . . . in the discretion of the court, if probative of truthfulness and untruthfulness, be inquired into on cross-examination of the witness (1) concerning the witness' character for truthfulness, or (2) concerning the character for truthfulness or untruthfulness of another witness as to which character the witness being cross-examined has testified." These exceptions may seem convoluted, but they are actually quite straightforward. For example, if the prosecution wishes to impeach a defense witness and wants to introduce evidence of prior acts of deception that did not result in convictions, the prosecutor may do so assuming the judge believes the line of questioning to have probative value. Similarly, if a witness testifies to another witness's character, evidence of untruthfulness may be admitted.

Two significant restrictions are placed on questions of witnesses concerning prior immoral or deceptive acts for which there was no conviction. First, there must be a basis in fact in such questioning. Second, the party seeking to impeach a witness cannot (1) call other witnesses to refute the witness's testimony or (2) produce other evidence to prove that such acts were committed. In essence, prosecutors and defense attorneys should not go on "fishing expeditions" to find evidence of witnesses' prior immoral or deceptive acts that did not result in convictions. There needs to be a factual basis for the questions, and any evidence as to the witness's prior acts is strictly limited to what the witness says in response to questions concerning such acts.

An interesting case that illustrates these limitations is *People v. Sorge* (1950). This case involved a prosecution for abortion (note that the date is prior to the landmark *Roe v. Wade* decision). The Court of Appeals of New York had occasion to determine whether prejudicial error was committed by the district attorney in conducting his cross examination of the defendant. The defendant, the woman charged with the crime of performing abortion, was questioned by the prosecutor about abortions that she *had* allegedly performed on four other women. She testified that she did not perform the abortions, but the prosecutor pressed further in an effort to get her to testify that she had performed the abortions. The court affirmed the woman's conviction because, even though the prosecutor questioned the woman extensively about performing previous abortions, he did not seek to call other witness or to introduce other evidence to this effect. The court stated that negative answers to the prosecutor's questions should not bar subsequent questioning because, if it did, "the witness would have it within his power to render futile most cross-examination."

Contradictions and prior inconsistent statements. For any number of reasons, witnesses may forget or may misinterpret important facts surrounding a case. At the other extreme, some witnesses may intentionally offer contradictory testimony. In either case, the party cross examining the witness may seek to call the jury's attention to the statement it believes to be contradictory. In other words, contradictory statements made by witnesses can be introduced for the purpose of impeachment. This is another way of saying that when witnesses make statements that appear contradictory, the opposition may take steps to attack the witness's credibility. This type of impeachment is dealt with in Rule 613 of the Federal Rules of Evidence.

It is not permissible for the party cross examining the witness to point to *any* mistake or false statement made by the witness. It would take too much of the court's time if the opposition spent a great deal of time pointing to trivial inconsistencies or contradictions in a witness's testimony. For example, assume a witness testifies that "I was at the corner of Main and Broadway, and I saw the defendant run out of the National Bank carrying a gun and a bag of money." What if the bank on the corner is actually First National Bank? Would the jury benefit from being informed of this contradiction? Probably not, especially if the witness is able to accurately recall the other facts.

If, on the other hand, a contradictory statement is significant, the jury would clearly benefit from learning of it. For example, assume a defense witness testifies that "I saw the robber the afternoon of the robbery and he had a full beard." If it turns out that the robber did not have a beard, this is information the jury should probably hear. Accordingly, the prosecution would probably call eyewitnesses to testify that that robber did not have a beard. The prosecution's witnesses would be contradicting the defense witness's statements. Moreover, the evidence of the robber's physical appearance would be of significant value to the jury, because the evidence bears directly on the defendant's guilt or innocence.

What happens when a witness is hesitant or evasive when it comes to admitting to a contradictory statement? In this situation, the party cross examining the witness will be permitted to press the issue by asking detailed questions. Assume that a wife testifies at her husband's criminal trial for assault and says "He did not hit me." Assume also that prior to trial when being questioned by the police that she said, "He hit me." If the prosecution points out this contradiction but the woman refuses to admit it, the prosecution will be permitted to press the issue in order to get the witness to admit that she made a contradictory statement. The prosecutor may ask, "Did you not state during questioning that your husband *did* hit you?" If the woman still refuses to admit to the contradiction, the prosecutor may be entitled to admit additional evidence to prove that the contradictory statement was made (assuming all other requirements for the admissibility of evidence are met). For example, the prosecutor may call one of the police officers who questioned the woman prior to trial to testify that he or she heard the prosecution's witness make the contradictory statement.

A witness's prior inconsistent statements can also be introduced for the purpose of impeachment. When is a statement inconsistent as compared to contradictory? In *United States v. Barrett* (1976), a witness testified that after the defendant's arrest he said "[I]t was a shame that Bucky [the defendant] got arrested on this matter . . . Bucky didn't have anything to do with it." The witness was testifying for the prosecution, but when his prior statement came to light at trial, there was evidence of an inconsistency. How could he testify for the prosecution given his earlier statement that he believed the defendant to be innocent?

So far we have pointed out that contradictions and inconsistencies can be based on mistakes and deliberate falsehoods, but what if a witness has been entirely silent regarding an issue that he or she later testifies about at trial? This issue has been raised in a number of significant cases. For example, in *United States v. Hale* (1975), the defendant was pointed out to the police by a robbery victim. The defendant was arrested, taken to the police station, and advised of his right to remain silent. He was searched and found in possession of $158. When asked where the money came from, he did not reply. At trial, the defendant took the stand and testified that the money the police recovered was money that his wife had given him after she cashed her welfare check. On cross examination the prosecution got the defendant to admit that he had not offered this explanation to the police at the time of his arrest. The Supreme Court held that this cross examination was impermissible. The Court offered several reasons for its finding, including the observation that the defendant had been advised that he had a right not to speak and that anything he said could be used against him.

Inability to observe. Another method of impeaching a witness relates closely to our earlier discussion of competency. As we indicated, a witness can be declared incompetent because of an inability to observe or recall the events under question. Witnesses can also be impeached based on the argument that they were unable to observe or recall the events in question. If a witness whose eyesight is poor testified that she saw the defendant fleeing the scene of the crime, the defense may wish to call attention to the woman's vision problem.

As indicated in the previous section, witnesses do not need to have a perfect ability to recall events. Insignificant "holes" in a witness's testimony may not be relevant to the determination of the defendant's guilt or innocence. Nevertheless, on cross examination the opposition may wish to call attention to a witness's inability to observe or remember if it is believed that the witness's shortcomings will influence the jury.

A witness's inability to observe can also be hampered by physical obstructions at the scene of the crime. Assume a witness reports that he saw the defendant flee the scene of a car-jacking in the victim's vehicle, but the victim's vehicle had darkly tinted windows. If the witness had not seen the defendant prior to his entering the vehicle, the defense on cross examination may wish to question the witness's ability to observe the defendant given that the windows of the vehicle made it difficult to see inside.

The party cross examining a witness cannot challenge the witness's ability to observe if it is not relevant. For example, a witness's hearing problem is not relevant if the witness's testimony concerns something she saw. Obviously the witness's hearing problem has nothing to do with her ability to observe, because her testimony is not based on what she heard.

Reputation. Generally speaking, the defendant's reputation cannot be called into question at trial. However, when the defendant calls a character witness to testify as to the defendant's upstanding character, the witness can be subject to an attack by the prosecution. The prosecution can seek to impeach the witness based on the witness's reputation. Likewise, character witnesses for the prosecution can be subject to impeachment by the defense during cross examination.

Rule 608 of the Federal Rules of Evidence places significant restrictions on character-based impeachment. Rule 608(a) states that

> The credibility of a witness may be attacked or supported by evidence in the form of opinion or reputation, but subject to these limitations: (1) the evidence may refer only to character for truthfulness or untruthfulness, and (2) evidence of truthful character is admissible only after the character of the witness for truthfulness has been attacked by opinion or reputation or otherwise.

With regard to the first limitation, the rule is much like the earlier rule we discussed concerning witnesses' prior convictions. Opinion or reputation evidence needs to be restricted to the witness's propensity for telling the truth. The second limitation provides that witness character cannot be bolstered unless it is attacked.

How is a witness's credibility attacked? Typically the side seeking to impeach the witness will call its own witness to testify to the other witness's propensity for telling the truth. For example, assume a murder defendant takes the stand in his own defense. The prosecution may elect to call its own witnesses to challenge the defendant's propensity for telling the truth. Indeed, if a friend of the defendant took the stand to testify on his behalf (to support the defendant's alibi, for instance),

---

Practice Pointer 9-2

It is risky for the defense or prosecution to call a witness to testify to another witness's reputation. Doing so opens the reputation witness's testimony to challenge by the opposing party. For example, if the defense calls a witness to testify that the defendant has a solid reputation, the prosecution can challenge the witness's testimony.

the prosecution could call its witnesses to attack the character of the defense witness. Except in rare circumstances deemed appropriate by the court, the questioning should be limited to the general reputation of the witness for honesty, not specific acts of misconduct.

Rehabilitation

When the credibility of a witness is attacked, the side that produced the witness can take steps to bolster the witness's credibility, either by calling other witnesses or introducing other evidence. This process is known as **rehabilitation.** Rehabilitation occurs during redirect examination following cross examination. For example, assume the defense calls a witness. The defense attorney will question the witness in an effort to absolve the defendant of guilt. If the prosecution sees fit to impeach the defense witness and succeeds in doing so, the defense attorney will work to rehabilitate its witness during the redirect examination stage.

In discussing the importance of rehabilitation, one court observed that "it is well recognized that once a witness's credibility has been attacked, whether it be by the introduction of evidence of bad reputation, conviction of crime, inconsistent statements, evidence of misconduct, or by incisive cross-examination, the party calling the witness has a right to present evidence designed to rehabilitate the witness's credibility" (*State v. Bowden*, 1982).

There are three common approaches used to rehabilitate witnesses. The first is to argue that the witness was untruthful in the past but is telling the truth now. Perhaps the witness was once a deceptive miscreant but has seen the error of his ways and has changed his life to the extent that he can now be trusted. Alternatively, if a witness lies in order to avoid prosecution, it is possible that evidence could be admitted to show that the witness has a reputation for telling the truth (*United States v. Lechoco*, 1976).

Second, the party seeking to rehabilitate its own witness may argue that a contradictory or inconsistent statement alluded to by the other side was taken out of context. For example, if part of a police report is used to impeach the officer who is giving testimony, the party seeking to rehabilitate the officer may introduce other portions of the police report that shed light on the part of the report used to impeach the officer (see *Short v. United States*, 1959).

Another way to rehabilitate a witness is to introduce other evidence to bolster the witness's credibility. For example, if a witness makes a statement prior to trial that contradicts her statement at trial, the other side may elect to introduce additional pretrial statements supportive of her statements at trial. Referring back to the infamous O.J. Simpson case, recall that Mark Fuhrman was impeached by the defense because of his prior racially discriminatory statements. Had the prosecution called other police witnesses to testify as to Fuhrman's objectivity with regard to race (if there were any), their testimony may have rehabilitated Fuhrman as a witness.

Summary

This chapter has been divided into two primary sections. First, we discussed the topic of witness competency. Nowadays, almost anyone can be considered a competent witness. However, competency can still be challenged on a number of grounds. Mental incapacity can render a potential witness incompetent. Young children are sometimes considered incompetent. Spouses are generally incompetent to give testimony against their partners, although there are a number of exceptions to this rule. Certain prior convictions can render a witness incompetent. Finally, judges and jurors are usually considered incompetent as witnesses at their own trials. Religious beliefs, however, cannot render a witness incompetent.

To be a competent witness, one must also be able to understand the duty to tell the truth and have the ability to observe and remember the events in question. Accordingly, we devoted special attention to witness oaths and affirmations and the duty to tell the truth. We also discussed certain conditions under which witnesses' ability to observe and remember have been hampered, such as being too young at the time of the crime or not having had enough time to observe the perpetrator.

We also discussed dead man's statutes, which, while quickly disappearing in this day and age, prevent witnesses from giving harmful testimony on behalf of a decedent—a dead person who is unable to defend himself or herself in court. We also discussed the topic of corroboration, the extent to which additional evidence can be permitted or required in order to "back up" a witness's testimony.

The second major section of this chapter dealt with witness credibility. Credibility pertains to whether a witness should be believed. When the prosecution or defense has reason to believe a witness cannot be considered credible, it may seek to impeach the witness. Common grounds for impeachment include bias or prejudice, prior convictions, uncharged crimes and immoral acts, contradictions and inconsistent statements, the inability to observe events, and reputation. Once a witness is impeached on cross examination, the party that called the witness can seek to rehabilitate the witness by introducing additional testimony that seeks to bolster the witness's credibility. It is important to note, though, that a witness's credibility cannot be supported or "rehabilitated" unless it is first challenged.

Discussion Questions

1. Explain the criteria for finding a witness competent.

2. Assuming that a man and woman are or were married, explain the circumstances under which the spousal privilege will not apply.

3. What are the six grounds for challenging witness competency?

4. What is the reason for an oath or affirmation? What is the difference between the two?

5. Explain "dead man's statutes." What was this original purpose and are these rules still in use?

6. What may taint the credibility of a witness?

7. After a witness has been impeached, what methods may be used to rehabilitate him?

8. Explain the Federal Rule of Evidence 609.

9. What are the common grounds for impeaching a witness?

Further Reading

Blumenthal, J. A. (1993). "A Wipe of the Hands, A Lick of the Lips: The Validity of Demeanor Evidence in Assessing Witness Credibility." *Neb. L. Rev.* 72:1157.

Caine, M. L. (2001). "Using Prior Convictions to Impeach the Credibility of a Defendant-Witness in Massachusetts—Do We Go Too Far?" *Suffolk J. Trial and App. Adv.* 6:121.

Fishman, C. S. (1992). *Jones on Evidence, Civil and Criminal* (7th ed.). Eagon, MN: West.

Graham, M. H. (1992). *Federal Practice and Procedure: Evidence* (interim ed.). Eagon, MN: West Group.

Jackson, J. W. (1996). "Commentary: Impeachment of a Witness by Prior Convictions Under Alabama Rule of Evidence 609: Everything Remains the Same, or Does it?" *Ala. L. Rev.* 48:253.

Lilly, G. C. (1996). *An Introduction to the Law of Evidence* (3rd ed.). Eagon, MN: West.

McCord, David. (1986). "Expert Psychological Testimony About Child Complainants in Sexual Abuse Prosecutions: A Foray Into the Admissibility of Novel Psychological Evidence." *Journal of Criminal Law and Criminology* 77:1–68.

Morris, M. L. (2001). "Comment: Li'l People, Little Justice: The Effect of the Witness Competency Standard in California on Children Sexual Abuse Cases." *J. Juv. L.* 22:113.

Mueller, C. B, and L. C. Kirkpatrick (1999). *Evidence* (2nd ed.). New York: Aspen Publishing Inc.

Strong, J. W. (1992). *McCormick on Evidence* (4th ed.). Eagon, MN: West Group.

Weinstein, J. B., J. H. Mansfield, N. Abrams, and M. A. Berger. *Evidence: Cases and Materials* (9th ed.). Westbury, NY: Foundation Press.

Cases Cited

Blake v. Cich, 79 F.R.D. 398, 403 (D. Minn. 1978)

Chapell v. State, 710 S.W.2d 214 (Ark. 1986)

Cross v. Commonwealth, 195 Vs. 62 (1953)

District of Columbia v. Armes, 107 U.S. 519 (1882)

Donovan v. Sears Roebuck and Company, 849 F. Supp. 86 (D. Mass. 1994)

Fulgham v. Ford, 850 F.2d 1529 (11th Cir. 1988)

Fund v. United States, 290 U.S. 371 (1933)

Gladden v. State, 36 Ala. App. 197 (1951)

Government of Virgin Islands v. Grant, 775 F.2d 508 (3rd Cir. 1985)

Government of Virgin Islands v. Harris, 938 F.2d 401 (1966)

Hickory v. United States, 151 U.S. 303 (1894)

Huprich v. Paul W. Varga and Sons, Inc., 3 Ohio St. 2d 87 (1965)

Idaho v. Wright, 497 U.S. 805 (1990)

In re Lochiatto, 497 F.2d 803, 805, n. 3, 1st Cir. (1974)

In re Rovner, 377 F.Supp. 954, E.D.Pa., aff'd, 500 F.2d 1400, 3d Cir. (1974)

Isaacs v. Kemp, 778 F.2d 1482 (11th Cir. 1985)

Kelluem v. State, Del. Lexis 652 (1978)

Lutwak v. United States, 344 U.S. 604 (1953)

Mathews v. Hines, 444 F. Supp. 1201 (1978)

McKnight v. State, 874 S.W.2d 745 (Tex. 1994)

Opper v. United States, 348 U.S. 84 (1954)

Owen v. Duckworth, 727 F.2d 643 (7th Cir. 1984)

People v. Delph, 94 Cal.App.3d 411 (1979)

People v. Sorge, 301 N.Y. 198 (1950)

People v. Spearman, 157 Cal. 883 (1979)

People v. Spinosa, 252 P.2d 409 (Cal. Ct. App. 1953)

People v. White, 40 Ill.2d 137 (1968)

Pocatello v. United States, 394 F.2d 115 (9th Cir. 1968)

Pointer v. State, 74 So.2d 615 (Ala. Ct. App. 1954)

Poole v. Commonwealth, 176 S.E.2d 917 (Va.1970)

Rosen v. United States, 245 U.S. 467 (1918)

Shibley v. United States, 237 F.2d 327 (9th Cir. 1956)

Short v. United States, 271 F.2d 73 (9th Cir. 1959)

Smith v. United States, 348 U.S. 147 (1954)

State v. Bowden, 439 A.2d 263 (R.I. 1982)

State v. Cabral, 122 R.I. 623 (1980)

State v. Phipps, 318 N.W.2d 128 (S.D. 1982)

State v. Ranieri, 586 A.2d 1094 (1991)

State v. Rippy, 626 A.2d 334, (Me. 1993)

State v. Singh, 586 S.W.2d 410 (1979)

State v. Spurlock, 874 S.W.2d 602 (Tenn. 1993)

State v. Valeriano, 468 A.2d 936 (Conn. 1983)

Stein v. Bowman, 10 L.Ed. 129 (1837)

Sullivan v. United States, 28 F.2d 147 (9th Cir. 1928)

United States ex rel. Buckhaha v. Lane, 787 F.2d 239 (7th Cir. 1986)

United States v. Abel, 469 U.S 45 (1984)

United States v. Allen, 10 F.3d 405 (7th Cir. 1993)

United States v. Awkward, 597 F.2d 667, cert. denied, 444 U.S. 885 (9th Cir. 1979)

United States v. Barrett, 539 F.2d 244 (1st Cir. 1976)

United States v. Bloome, 773 F. Supp. 545 (E.D.N.Y. 1991)

United States v. Bolzer, 556 F.2d 948 (9th Cir. 1977)

United States v. Cameron, 556 F.2d 752 (5th Cir. 1977)

United States v. Fisher, 518 F.2nd 836, 2d. Cir., cert. den., 423 U.S. 1033 (2nd Cir. 1975)

United States v. Gates, 10 F.3d 765 (11th Cir. 1993)

United States v. Hale, 422 U.S. 171 (1975)

United States v. Ince, 21 F.3d 576 (4th Cir. 1994)

United States v. Lechoco, 542 F.2d 84 (D.C. Cir. 1976)

United States v. Lighty, 677 F.2d 1027 (4th Cir. 1982)

United States v. Miles, 413 F.2d 34 (3rd Cir. 1969)

United States v. Price, 722 F.2d 88 (5th Cir. 1983)

United States v. Richardson, 764 F.2d 1514 (11th Cir. 1985)

United States v. Roach, 590 F.2d 181 (5th Cir. 1979)

United States v. Shields, 999 F.2d 1990 (7th Cir. 1993)

United States v. Thomann, 609 F.2d 560 (1st Cir. 1979)

United States v. Van Meerbeke, 548 F.2d 415, cert. denied, 430 U.S. 974(2nd. Cir 1977)

United States v. Ward, 989 F.2d 1015 (1992)

United States v. Abel, 469 U.S. 45 (1984)

Vastbinder v. Spinks, 16 Ala. 385 (1849)

Warszower v. United States, 312 U.S. 342 (1941)

Weiler v. United States, 323 U.S. 606 (1945)

Wheeler v. United States, 159 U.S. 523 (1895)

White v. Illinois, 502 U.S. 346 (1992)

Wong Sun v. United States, 371 U.S. 471 (1963) ✦

Chapter Ten

Examining Witnesses

Key Terms

- Affidavits
- Collective facts doctrine
- Compulsory process clause
- Confrontation clause
- Daubert test
- Declarations
- Depositions
- Frye test
- Hostile witness
- Lay opinion
- Leading question
- Opinion evidence
- Past recollection recorded
- Present memory revived
- Subpoena
- Supoena duces tecum
- Substantive objections
- Ultimate issue rule
- Voir dire
- Witness exclusion
- Witness sequestration

Introduction

In a criminal trial in the United States, the witness (or witnesses) must appear in front of the defendant. This requirement stems from the Sixth Amendment to the Constitution, which states in relevant part that, "In all criminal prosecutions, the accused . . . shall be confronted with the witnesses against him." This is known as the **confrontation clause.** There are a few exceptions, but witnesses are generally required to appear in the courtroom.

The confrontation clause imposes important restrictions on the role witnesses play in criminal trials. For example, witness statements in the form of affidavits, declarations, or depositions are often frowned upon because they are made out of the presence of the defendant. **Affi-**

davits and **declarations** are sworn statements; **depositions** are sworn testimony given prior to trial, usually in an office outside the courtroom in the presence of attorneys. All three are common in civil trials but not in criminal trials because of the Sixth Amendment's confrontation clause.

Witnesses are not afforded much privacy in criminal proceedings because of the confrontation clause. They are almost always required, when called upon to testify in court, in the presence of the defendant. Of course, witnesses may be hesitant (and even resistant) to testify in sensitive criminal trials, but the Sixth Amendment usually requires them to be present and "in the open."

Because of the confrontational nature of criminal trials, witnesses are provided with a number of protections. Most important, witnesses in criminal trials enjoy the Fifth Amendment's protection against self-incrimination. That is, even though witnesses provide testimony designed to prove the defendant's guilt (or, if they act on behalf of the defense, to exculpate the defendant), they cannot be compelled to answer questions that incriminate themselves. The Fifth Amendment's protection against self incrimination is not limitless, however. Witnesses can be compelled to answer questions about the case at hand. Witnesses can "plead the Fifth" only when their statements are self-incriminating—that is, when they implicate themselves in a crime different from that for which the defendant is being tried.

Securing the Attendance of Witnesses

The Sixth Amendment also contains what is known as the **compulsory process clause.** Stated simply, this clause provides that individuals can be compelled, or forced, to serve as a witness. To ensure that a witness appears at trial, the prosecution or defense will often issue a subpoena. A **subpoena** is an official court document issued by a judge, the clerk of a court, or an attorney. It is delivered to, or "served upon," the witness, who must then appear at trial. A variation on a subpoena is a **subpoena duces tecum**, which requires the witness to bring certain documents or material to the trial. Failure to appear after being subpoenaed can result in a number of serious sanctions.

Many witnesses are asked to testify and do so voluntarily. In such instances, subpoenas are obviously not required. And, if a witness fails to appear after a simple request to testify (as opposed to a subpoena), no sanctions can be imposed. However, the prosecution or defense has the leverage of compulsory process in such a situation. See Figure 10-1 for a sample witness subpoena.

Figure 10-1 Sample Subpoena

SAMPLE SUBPOENA

NAME OF ATTORNEY
1234 EAST 5678 SOUTH
SALT LAKE CITY, UT 84121
PHONE: 456-7890

BEFORE THE DIVISION OF OCCUPATIONAL AND PROFESSIONAL LICENSING
DEPARTMENT OF COMMERCE, STATE OF UTAH

JOHN DOE,   )
)
            Petitioner,   )   **SUBPOENA DUCES TECUM**
)
vs.   )
)
RICHARD ROE, M.D.   )
)
            Respondent.   )   Case No. _____
)

    TO: Richard Roe, M.D.
          000 Medical Plaza
          Anytown, U.S.A. 84100

    RE: John Doe
          Date of Birth: 8/28/48

    YOU ARE COMMANDED to produce at the offices of (Name), (Address), on or before (Date), a complete copy of your medical records, pertaining to the above-referenced individual who has requested the Division of Occupational and Professional Licensing, to conduct a prelitigation panel review of a claim of medical malpractice. Attendance is not required if records are timely forwarded to the indicated address.

    DATED this _____ day of _____, 2000.

                              DEPARTMENT OF COMMERCE

          By: _____
                 W. Ray Walker, Regulatory & Compliance Officer
                 Division of Occupational & Professional Licensing

Source: www.dopl.utah.gov/programs/prelitigation/sample_subpoena.doc

Types of Witnesses

It is useful to distinguish between three types of witnesses. The first type is an expert witness. The second type is a lay witness. Expert and lay witnesses are people other than the defendant. It is also possible, however, for the accused to serve as a witness. As such, we devote a brief section to the role of the defendant as a witness. The accused never has to testify, but once the decision to testify is made, several important issues arise.

Expert Witnesses

Modern statutes do not actually define what it means to be an expert; nevertheless, an expert witness can be defined as anyone who knows more about the subject testimony than the average juror would. The Federal Rules of Evidence (Rule 702) state that a witness is an "expert" if he or she is "qualified" to help the jury "understand the evidence" or "determine a fact in issue" by virtue of his or her "knowledge, skill, experience, training, or education." Similarly, the California Evidence Code (Section 720) describes an expert as one who "has special knowledge, skill, experience, training or education sufficient to qualify him as an expert on the subject to which his testimony relates."

Types of experts. There are two types of expert witnesses: (1) degree-bearing experts and (2) nondegree-bearing experts. Degree-bearing experts are those individuals conjured up in most people's minds when they think of the term "expert." There are persons who have been certified by some educational institution as knowledgeable in some subject. The educational institution does not necessarily have to be a university or college. Nondegree-experts include individuals who through education or *experience* know something that jurors do not.

The prerequisites for expert testimony. For an expert witness to be used, three prerequisites must be in place. First, there must be a *need* for expert testimony. If the facts can be understood by lay jurors, there is no need for an expert. For example, common knowledge (e.g., that objects fall toward earth when dropped) does not need expert testimony. However, specific knowledge—say, what type of track a certain tire will leave behind— often requires expert interpretation.

The second prerequisite for expert testimony is that a sufficiently established body of knowledge exist on the subject about which the expert will testify. In other words, the expert's field must be one requiring specific scientific or technical knowledge. There are several tests in place to determine whether a relevant knowledge base exists. In *Daubert v. Merrell Dow Pharmaceuticals, Inc.* (1993) the Supreme Court created a test for determining whether the expert's field has reached the level of "scientific knowledge." The so-called **Daubert test** requires that the trial judge make the determination based on two primary factors: (1) The science must be valid, and (2) the evidence must "fit" the case. Prior to the Daubert test, the Supreme Court relied on the **Frye test,** which required that expert testimony be based on scientific knowledge "generally accepted as reliable in the relevant scientific community."

Often the courts will deem a certain body of knowledge, for lack of a better word, "unscientific." A good example is polygraphs. Many people believe that a well-trained polygraph operator can tell when a person is lying, but the courts have been very reluctant to rely on polygraph evidence. In a similar vein, courts do not rely on psychic testimony or astrology because both fields lack a scientific base.

The third prerequisite is that the witness must be shown to have a background necessary to qualify as an expert in the field. Because the process can be somewhat complicated and arduous, we reserve the next subsection for a discussion of what it takes to qualify as an expert witness.

The third prerequisite in depth: deciding who is an expert. Once it is clear that an expert is needed and that a sufficient body of scientific knowledge exists, the decision as to who will be considered an expert is left to the judge. However, before the judge can make his or her decision as to whether a person will be allowed to testify as an expert, a voir dire process must take place. **Voir dire** in this context is a questioning process in which the expert's "expertise" is established or refuted.

The party calling the supposed expert must begin by qualifying the witness as an expert. Usually the calling party does so without reservation because qualifying the expert lends credibility to the witness's testimony. This qualification process takes place when the witness answers questions posed by the calling party. The calling party will ask questions about the witness's education, experience, training, and work in order to establish that he or she is an expert. Indeed, the calling party may go to great lengths in questioning the witness (above and beyond education and experience) in order to convince the trial judge that the witness is in fact an expert in his or her field.

After this preliminary questioning, many jurisdictions require that the calling party *formally tender* the witness. This means that (1) the qualification process has been concluded and (2) that the calling party is asking the court to recognize this witness as an expert. The opposing attorney can then conduct his or her on voir dire examination of the witness. The opposing side's questions are usually asked *before* the witness offers opinions as we will see later. This procedure allows the opposing attorney to convince the judge that the supposed expert is not actually an "expert" in the field. For example, opposing counsel may attempt to show that the witness lacks the necessary education and qualification to serve as an expert witness. It is advisable, therefore, that the party seeking to qualify an expert go to lengths to ensure that the witness's expertise cannot be refuted by the opposing side.

An expert witness need not be renowned in his or her field (e.g., *United States v. Rose*, 1984, p. 1346). On the other hand, minimal preparation or experience should not be viewed as sufficient to qualify one as an expert. Unfortunately, there are no hard and fast rules as to what level of experience and training is sufficient. In the end, the trial judge will make the determination as to whether a witness can be considered an expert. Once the decision is made to recognize a witness as an expert, the jury then decides what amount of weight will be given to the witness's testimony.

Court-appointed experts. It is easy for jury members to become confused when experts for opposing sides testify as to the same issue. For example, the prosecution's expert may argue that an automobile accident was caused by the defendant. The defense attorney's expert may argue, on the contrary, that the defendant could not possibly have been responsible. Who is the jury to believe? This quandary can be especially significant if the prosecution and defense both call several expert witnesses. One solution to this problem is a court-appointed expert.

The Federal Rules of Evidence (Rule 706) state, in part, that "The court may on its own motion or on the motion of any party enter an order to show cause why expert witnesses should not be appointed, and may request the parties to submit nominations." Further, "The court may appoint any expert witnesses agreed upon by the parties, and may appoint expert witnesses of its own selection." A court-appointed expert is supposedly one who is neutral and objective and so inclined not to side, *a priori*, with either the prosecution or the defense.

The decision of whether to select a court-appointed expert (as opposed to one or several called by the parties to the case) is entirely discretionary; courts are not under any obligation to do so. However, in situations in which the prosecution and defense experts fail to produce evidence of clear probity, a court-appointed expert may be desirable (e.g., *Students of California School for Blind v. Honig*, 1984, pp. 548–549).

As a general rule, court-appointed experts should be relied upon only when absolutely necessary because the prosecution and the defense bear the main responsibility for presenting their sides of the case. Courts decide matters of law and usually know less about the evidence and issues than the lawyers representing the government and the accused. However, when court-appointed experts *are* used, it is best if the wheels are set in motion long before trial. Stopping a trial for the purpose of selecting a court-appointed expert can be quite disruptive.

The procedure for selecting court-appointed experts established by Rule 706 contains five elements:

1. The trial judge has broad discretion in deciding whether and whom to appoint, but both parties to the case should be able to be heard on the matter if they so desire. Actions by the court in accordance with this rule do not affect the rights of the opposing parties to call their own experts.

2. Court-appointed experts must consent to testify. In other words, courts should avoid compelling witnesses to serve as court-appointed experts. However, the court's (like the opposing side's) subpoena power can ensure that a witness

serve as a court-appointed expert (see *Kaufman v. Edelstein,* 1976, pp. 820–821).

3. The court-appointed expert must be notified of his or her duties in advance of testimony. This notice is to be provided in writing.

4. The court-appointed expert is to advise the parties of his or her findings. Either party may take the expert's deposition. The witness may also be called to testify by the court or by either party to the case.

5. Finally, the court-appointed expert shall be subject to cross examination by both parties to the case.

Subjects of expert witness testimony. Experts can testify to countless subjects, but we briefly consider several common subjects here.

1. *Automobile accidents.* For example, a police officer with several years of experience investigating accidents and who is extensively trained in accident investigation may serve as an expert (see *Bonner v. Polacari,* 1965).

2. *Physical and mental condition.* Experts often testify to the defendant's mental condition (such as after ingesting drugs), but courts usually do not allow experts to render opinions in such situations. For example, an expert in the effects of drugs on a person's mental condition could testify as to the likely effect that a certain amount of drugs will have on a person generally. However, such a witness will probably not be allowed to offer an opinion as to whether the defendant was affected in the same way (see, for example, *People v. Cronin,* 1983).

3. *Handwriting comparisons.* Experts will occasionally testify that a piece of handwriting was written by a certain person. For example, in a prosecution for conspiracy to import marijuana, the trial court allowed a handwriting expert to testify that he had a "high degree of belief" that the handwriting on a motel bill was that of one of the defendants. Of course, it is up to the jury in such situations to decide whether the expert's testimony should carry weight.

4. *Typewriter comparisons.* Prior to the advent of computers, experts would testify that a typewritten documents came from a specific typewriter. Experts could even determine that a document came from a specific model of typewriter without actually having to see or handle the particular typewriter responsible for the document. In some cases, courts have even allowed typewriter comparison experts to draw

opinions about the identity of the operator of the typewriter (see, for example, *Thomas v. State,* 1946).

5. *Voice print identification.* Some states authorize the use of spectrographic voice print evidence. Devices are used to compare the defendant's voice with a voice print recorded from an earlier conversation (such as during a telephone call). In *United States v. Williams* (1978), the Second Circuit noted that "spectrographic voice analysis evidence is not so inherently unreliable or misleading as to require its exclusion from the jury's consideration in every case." Understand, however, that voice print identification is not permissible in every (or even most) jurisdiction throughout the country.

6. *Neutron activation analysis.* On some occasions suspects in shootings have their hands swabbed with a nitric acid solution. Then a neutron activation analysis is used to determine whether the suspect fired a gun recently. In one case, *State v. Spencer* (1974), the Minnesota Supreme Court upheld an expert's testimony as to the results of neutron activation analysis. In that case, a suspect was accused of shooting a police officer. After the suspect was taken into custody, his hands were swabbed with the solution. The swabs were then sent to the Treasury Department laboratory in Washington D.C. The court concluded

> We believe that neutron activation analysis is a useful law enforcement technique and that the increasing use of technology in criminal investigation should not be inhibited but encouraged where consistent with the rights of the accused. (pp. 461–462)

The court also expressed concern, however, about unrestricted use of neutron activation analysis:

> An expert witness could be permitted to testify that in his opinion the chemicals present on the defendant's hand may have resulted from the firing of a gun. He should not have been permitted to state, as he did, that this defendant had definitely fired a gun. To allow this testimony to stand without a cautionary instruction to the jury was technical error. (p. 461)

7. *Fingerprint identification.* To show that fingerprints lifted from a crime scene are that of the defendant usually requires expert testimony. In an illustrative case, one court found that a police officer, who was a veteran of the sheriff's department and who had extensive training in footprints and latent

prints, was qualified to testify as an expert (*State v. Oliver,* 1987). Not just any law enforcement officer will be permitted to testify as an expert for the purpose of fingerprint identification; special training and expertise are usually required.

8. *Insanity.* Experts are required when mental disorders are raised as defenses to criminal liability. Perhaps the best example of a mental disorder raised at trial (albeit rarely) is insanity. The expert, usually a trained psychiatrist, will explain to the jury the effect of the condition on the personality and likely behavior of the accused. The defense expert will argue that the defendant could not form the requisite mens rea required for criminal liability; the prosecution's expert, on the other hand, will argue that the defendant should be found guilty of the crime with which he or she is charged.

9. *Ballistics.* When a bullet slug is recovered from the scene of a crime, an expert is necessary to convince the jury that the slug came from a particular gun. The pattern of marks and grooves in the barrel of a gun leaves a particular pattern on the bullet fired. If the gun is recovered, a ballistics expert can test-fire the gun then conduct a microscopic comparison of the two bullets in order to find a positive match.

10. *Testimony concerning drug operations.* Expert witnesses are often called on to testify about the price of narcotics, the language used by drug dealers, and the nuances of complex drug manufacturing operations. In several cases, the courts have permitted expert opinions as to the meaning of "drug lingo" (e.g., *United States v. Nunez,* 1987). In another case, a trial court properly admitted a police officer's expert testimony regarding the countersurveillance techniques used by a drug dealer to avoid apprehension (*United States v. deSoto,* 1989).

11. *Others.* Experts are relied for a wide variety of other determinations. Some of these include the modus operandi of offenders, such as in serial killing cases (e.g., *Johninson v. State,* 1994); cause of death (e.g., *State v. Vining,* 1994); blood and tissue matching; and polygraph examinations, where permissible (e.g., *United States v. Miller,* 1989).

Lay Witnesses

A lay witness is an ordinary person who has personal knowledge about the facts of the case at hand. The Federal Rules of Evidence define a lay witness as any witness who "is not testifying as an expert"

(Rule 701). Lay witnesses run the gamut from mere observers of criminal activity to police officers. Lay witnesses are called to testify as to the facts only. Lay witness opinions are severely restricted. Accordingly, we devote a later section of this chapter to lay witness opinion.

Most people testify as lay witnesses. These are people who state that the crime occurred, who talked to the suspect before or after the crime, or who observed what happened or supplied information to law enforcement officials. Even a person who regularly testifies as an expert can also testify as a lay witness. If, for example, a ballistics expert observed an assault while driving home, he or she would be allowed to testify as a lay witness, assuming that a ballistic analysis is not required.

Lay and Expert Witness Protection Under the Fifth Amendment

Any witness, other than the accused, has the privilege to refuse to disclose any information that may "tend to incriminate" him or her. The reason is that the witness is not on trial. The witness is only on the stand to provide information about what happened. Thus, witnesses cannot "plead the Fifth" simply because they are nervous about answering questions (perhaps out of fear of retaliation by the defendant or his or her cronies). Only if the answer to a question tends to incriminate the witness may he or she assert Fifth Amendment protection. For example, if the prosecution asks a witness, "Did you, Mr. Smith, sell narcotics with the defendant?" Smith would be within his rights to refuse to answer such a question. Indeed, the question need not be so explicit. For the Fifth Amendment privilege against self-incrimination to apply, the answer need only furnish a link in the chain of evidence needed to prosecute.

The Accused as a Witness

The Fifth Amendment expressly provides that "no person . . . shall be compelled in any criminal case to be a witness against himself." As seen in Chapter 8, this guarantee is designed to restrain the government from using force, coercion, or other controversial methods to obtain statements from criminal suspects.

As we also saw in Chapter 8, the Fifth Amendment's self-incrimination clause only applies to testimonial evidence. As such, real or physical evidence (or things knowingly exposed to the public) does not enjoy constitutional protection. Also, several restrictions exist concerning the procedures law enforcement officials can rely upon for the purpose of eliciting confessions.

What about Fifth Amendment protection at trial? The defendant in a criminal case has a privilege of the accused *not* to take the stand and not to testify. Thus, the Fifth Amendment ensures that an accused is not required to act as a witness against himself or herself. Additionally, prosecutors cannot comment on the accused's refusal to testify. That is, the jury cannot infer guilt from mere silence on the defendant's part.

The Supreme Court has recognized a fair response rule, which allows the prosecutor to comment, during closing arguments, on the defenden's refusal to take the stand. Such a comment is only allowed, however, if the defense argues that the government did not allow the defendant to explain his or her side of the story (*United States v. Robinson*, 1988).

It is critical to note, however, that once an accused makes the decision to testify—that is, to take the stand—he or she waives Fifth Amendment protection. This means that the accused must answer *all* inquiries (from the prosecution and the defense) about the crime for which he or she is charged. A defendant who decides to testify cannot claim "immunity from cross examination on the matters he has himself put in dispute" because this would make the Fifth Amendment "a positive invitation to mutilate the truth" (*Brown v. United States*, 1958). For this reason, many defense attorneys do not encourage their clients to take the stand. To do so opens up any number of potentially damaging questions. For example, if the accused has a spotty past, the prosecution may bring this up (see Chapter 8).

In summary, even though many evidence texts discuss only two types of witnesses (lay and expert), it is possible for the accused to serve as a witness for or against himself or herself. The decision is solely the defendant's, and the Fifth Amendment guarantees that an accused need not take the stand.

How Witnesses Are Examined

By custom, the plaintiff in a civil case has the burden of persuasion, so he or she goes first. That is, the plaintiff calls all witnesses and presents the evidence required to build the case. When the plaintiff rests, the defense has its turn. Criminal cases are similarly choreographed; first the prosecutor presents the state's case, then the defendant has an opportunity to present his or her case. The process of examining witnesses, however, is much more complicated than this simple description. The following sections are designed to shed light on this often confusing aspect of evidentiary procedure. The discussion draws heavily from Rule 611 of the Federal Rules of Evidence, which describes how testimony is to be presented in federal court.

Order and Scope of Questions

Witness testimony proceeds in a set of stages. Each examination is conducted by a particular party to the case (state/defendant, plaintiff/defendant), and each is subject to limitations in terms of scope. In other words, the stages must occur sequentially, and there are limitations as to what types of questions are permissible.

The four stages of witness examination are (1) direct, (2) cross, (3) redirect, and (4) recross. Thus, every witness called to the stand in either a criminal or civil case may be questioned four separate times. To see how these stages of witness examination fit into the typical criminal case, see Table 10-1.

Direct examination. The first examination of a witness is called *direct examination*. Direct examination is usually conducted by the party calling the witness. The scope of direct examination is broad. In general, questions about any consequential facts that may prove or disprove a certain point are permissible.

Why are leading questions allowed only during cross-examination?

Table 10-1 Phases of a Case
1. Plaintiff or prosecutor presents his or her case then rests.
2. Defendant presents his or her case then rests.
3. Plaintiff or prosecutor presents his or her case in rebuttal.
4. Defendant presents his or her case-in-rejoinder, also known as case-in-rebuttal.
5. Each side may then present further cases-in-rebuttal or rejoinder.

Cross examination. The next step in examining witnesses is cross examination. *Cross examination* is conducted by a party other than the party who called the witness. For example, the state may call a witness in a criminal trial. Once direct examination concludes, the defense will have an opportunity to cross examine the state's witness.

Whereas the scope of questioning in a direct examination is broad, the scope of questioning on cross is restricted. In particular, cross examination is limited to matters covered on direct examination. Inquiries into the credibility of the witness are also permissible. Together, these two restrictions constitute the *scope of direct rule*. The scope of direct rule helps ensure that the opposing party (the party conducting the cross examination) cannot use cross-examination of the witness to direct the jury's attention to issues not raised by the party calling the witness.

Perhaps an example will bring the scope of direct rule into clear focus. Assume that in a robbery trial a defense witness testifies about the defendant's whereabouts on the day of the robbery. Assume further that on cross examination the prosecutor asks whether the defendant expressed the desire to rob a bank on the day before the robbery. The prosecutor's question is not permissible because it is beyond the scope of the defense's direct questioning (assuming, of course, that the defense did not ask its witness about the defendant's feelings the day before the robbery).

Redirect examination. Redirect examination is conducted by the party calling the witness *after* cross examination. Redirect examination is subsequent to the first cross examination. The scope of questioning on redirect is limited to the scope of questioning on cross examination.

Let us consider another example. Let's say that on cross examination a burglary victim is asked about persons who have permission to enter his residence while he is away. Assume further that on redirect the prosecutor asks the burglary victim about an incident that occurred several days prior to the burglary in which he saw the defendant "casing" the neighborhood. The prosecutor's question is not permissible because it is beyond the scope of the cross examination (assuming, again, that the prior incident did not come to light during the defense cross examination).

Recross examination. The last stage in witness questioning is known as recross examination. Recross includes any subsequent examination of a witness by a party who has previously cross examined the witness. Recross examination is also limited in scope to the subject matter of the examination that preceded it. That is, the party engaged in recross examination cannot probe into issues not raised during redirect examination.

Assume that an eyewitness to an accident who is testifying for the plaintiff is asked on cross examination whether she was wearing her prescription glasses. If during redirect examination it is determined that the witness could see fine *without* her glasses, the defense cannot question the witness on recross examination about her relation to the plaintiff.

The four stages of witness examination follow a pattern of "progressive narrowing." That is, subsequent examination should become narrower and narrower such that there is little left to ask the witness. In other words, the four stages of examination should clarify rather than confuse. See Table 10-2 for a summary of the order and scope of witness questioning.

Table 10-2 Order and Scope of Witness Examination
1. Direct examination by the party calling the witness.
2. Cross examination by adverse party.
3. Redirect examination by the calling party.
4. Recross by adverse parties.

The Form of Questioning

As a general rule, on direct examination, the questions must be *specific* but not *leading*. First, a **specific question** is one that does not call for a narrative. If the party calling the witness says, "Tell us what happened on the day of the incident," the opposing side will probably object. Instead, it is proper to ask something along the lines of, "Were you the victim of a burglary on August 6th of this year?"

At the other extreme, it is possible to be too specific such that a question becomes leading. A **leading question** is, according to the California Evidence Code (Section 764), one "that suggests to the witness the answer that the examining party desires." Leading questions are generally impermissible on direct examination (subject to some exceptions described below) but are permissible on cross examination. Further, leading questions are permissible on redirect examination but not on recross examination.

Identifying a leading question. Determining whether a question is leading is not an easy task. Whether a question is leading is, according to some commentators, a matter of degree. For example, a request of a witness to "tell us anything about anything" is not specific and not leading. At the other extreme, a question such as "You drank one beer per hole when you were golfing, didn't you?" is clearly leading. So, what of the gray area in between? Courts have tried to devise tests to determine when questions are leading, but these tests have proven ineffective.

A safe rule, however, is that a question is leading when it suggests an answer. For example, the question "Is it true that you locked your door when you left the house?" would be leading because it suggests a particular answer—namely, that the door was locked. This question can be rephrased, however, so that it is not leading, "What, if anything, did you do as you left the house?" Another example of a leading question is "You wouldn't say you're in favor of abortion, would you?" This question can also be restated so that it is no longer leading, "What is your position on abortion, for or against?"

Leading questions during direct examination. As we have seen, leading questions are generally not permissible on direct examination. However, there are a few exceptions. As the California Evidence Code attests, leading questions on direct examination are permissible "where the interests of justice" require (C.E.C. Section 767). Similarly, the Federal Rules of Evidence [Rule 611(c)] permit leading questions on direct examination when it is "necessary to develop testimony."

Leading questions are permissible on direct examination under the following circumstances: (1) in questioning on preliminary or undisputed matters for which accuracy of the witness's response is more important than efficiency; (2) when the witness is difficult to control without the use of leading questions (e.g., children, people with mental problems, experts, and so on); (3) for the purpose of refreshing the recollection of a forgetful witness (see below for further discussion of the refreshing process); and (4) when eliciting testimony from hostile witnesses.

The fourth exception requires that we define the term *hostile witness*. A **hostile witness** need not be (and rarely is) a person who is physically hostile. Instead, witnesses of this type are considered either "hostile in fact" or "hostile in law." The former is what we think of when a person is resistant or uncooperative. A witness is hostile in fact when he or she exhibits hostility toward the examiner. For example, a witness who acts as though she does not understand a simple question may be considered hostile in fact. A witness who is hostile in law, by contrast, is one who identifies with an adverse party. For example, the widow of a deceased partner is "identified with" the plaintiff-estate and thus is considered hostile in law to the defense (e.g., surviving children, as in a dispute over the deceased's estate).

Leading questions on cross examination. Cross examination is commonly characterized by leading questions. As the Federal Rules of Evidence put it, "Ordinarily leadings questions should be permitted on cross examination" (Rule 611c). Further, as the FRE attest, the use of leading questions on cross examinations "conforms to tradition in making the use of leading questions on cross examination a matter of right."

Leading questions during cross examination serve a number of important purposes. First, leading questions appeal to the conscience and awaken the witness's memory. The hope is to get the witness to tell the truth. Second, leading questions expose inaccuracies or falsehoods expressed during direct examination. Finally, leading questions help the witness focus attention on what is important.

There are a few circumstances in which leading questions are viewed as improper on cross examination. First, if the questioner goes beyond the scope of direct examination, he or she should not ask leading questions (see, e.g., *MDU Resources Group v. W.R. Grace & Co.*, 1994). Second, when a party in a civil case calls an adverse party as a witness, the usual method of questioning is reversed. Say, for example, that in a civil asset forfeiture case the government calls the defendant's wife, an adverse witness, to the stand to testify concerning her husband's marijuana grow room. In this instance, the direct examination proceeds by leading questions (because the questioner is counsel for the adversary), then cross examination proceeds by nonleading questions. Third, if the calling party is allowed for some reason to lead on direct examination (see exceptions in previous subsection), it is likely that cross examination will be limited to nonleading questions. What if a witness is hostile to both parties? In such a situation, leading questions will probably be permitted on both direct and cross examination.

Refreshing a witness's memory. Witnesses frequently forget the facts to which they are supposed to testify, particularly if a great deal of time has elapsed between the event witnessed and the witness's in-court testimony. To remedy this problem, the Federal Rules of Evidence (Rule 612) provide that a witness's prior experience may be "revived" by referral to the witness's prior statements. Of course, a witness who has no memory whatsoever of the event to which he or she is to testify, is an incompetent witness. But if a "refresher" is all the witness needs, then the examining party should be able to remind the witness of what he or she said in the past.

The process of refreshing a witness's memory involves two important concepts: (1) present memory revived and (2) past recollection recorded. With regard to **present memory revived,** the testimony of the witness is the evidence. By contrast, **past recollection recorded** results in writing being the evidence, not the witness's in-court testimony.

Let us first consider present memory revived. Stated simply, a witness's present memory is revived when, for example, the witness is asked to refer to records or other written documents. After the witness views the document and has his or her memory refreshed, the witness's statement to this effect is admitted as evidence. The document(s) shown to the witness is not read or shown to the jury because the document is not evidence, only the witness's testimony. Assume, for example, that a witness to a car accident is asked whether she remembers the license plate number of the car that sped away from the scene. She replies that she is uncertain but may be able to recall the number if she can consult some notes she had written on the day she witnessed the car leaving the scene. If the witness is permitted to rely on her notes and she then remembers the license plate number, she will be permitted to testify to this effect under a theory of present memory revived.

Somewhat controversial method of refreshing a witness's present memory is hypnosis. In the case of *State v. Beachum* (1967), a court in New Mexico developed a six-prong test for determining whether the results of a hypnosis session can be used to refresh a witness's memory. The six prongs are as follows:

1. The session must be conducted by a qualified professional.

2. The professional conducting the session should be independent and not regularly employed by the prosecution or
   defense.

3. Any information given to the hypnotist before the hypnotic
   session should be recorded.

4. Before inducing hypnosis, the hypnotist should obtain a detailed description of the facts as the witness remembers
   them.

5. All contacts between the hypnotist and the person hypnotized should be recorded.

6. Only the hypnotist and the person hypnotized should be
   present during any stage of the hypnotic session.

When a document is introduced to refresh a witness's present
memory, it is usually required that the opposing side have an opportunity to view it. Under the Federal Rules of Evidence, in fact, the adverse
party is entitled to see and ask questions about the document used to
refresh the witness's memory. What about a writing that is consulted
by a witness *in advance* of trial? In such an instance, the document
does not necessarily need to be disclosed to the opposing side (see, for
example, *United States v. Blas,* 1991, pp. 1326–1328); *United States v.
Williams,* 1989). There are exceptions, however. In the case of *United
States v. Sheffield* (1995, pp. 343–344), a detective returned a file to the
office because he "had trouble keeping up with it on breaks and did not
want to carry it with him to the stand" and did not need it to refresh on
any point to which he testified. The defense in that case was not
allowed to view the file. Generally, it is within the discretion of the
court to decide whether documents viewed prior to trial should be disclosed to the other side.

With the second theory of refreshing a witness's memory past recollection recorded, it is the recording itself that is admitted as evidence.
That is, the jury considers the document as opposed to the witness's
testimony. The written document essentially becomes a substitute for
the witness's memory.

There are certain requirements before a past recollection recorded
will be admitted into evidence. First, the witness must testify that he or
she had personal knowledge of the facts at one point in time. Second,
the witness must testify that the recording was accurate. Finally, the
witness must testify that he or she does not have adequate recollection
of the facts such that he or she could testify to them in court. The trial
judge must then be satisfied with the document for it to be admissible
into evidence. Finally, once a past recollection recorded is admissible

into evidence, the opposing side should have the opportunity to view the document (see *United States v. Kelly*, 1965; *People v. Banks*, 1974).

Objections to Questions

Notwithstanding what we have discussed so far, the court has the discretion to control the types of questions posed by both parties to a case. However, the court will only exercise its discretion to exclude a question if an objection is raised. For ease of exposition it is useful to distinguish between two categories of objections: substantive and formal.

Before considering them, it is important to recall that objections are either sustained or overruled. An objection is *sustained* when the judge prohibits the witness from answering the specific question posed. By contrast, an objection is overruled, when the judge permits the witness to answer the question.

Substantive objections. **Substantive objections** are those relying on particular rules of evidence. They are raised for the purpose of excluding evidence when its admission does not conform to established rules. For example, assuming no exceptions apply, a hearsay objection is a substantive one because it is based on a rule of evidence that excludes hearsay in the courtroom.

Most forms of evidence are admissible unless a substantive objection is raised by either party to the case. There are as many substantive objections as there are rules of evidence, so we will not delve further into the varieties of substantive objections in the interest of keeping this chapter as brief and introductory as possible.

Other objections. Most objections apart from substantive ones are objections to form. That is, the objecting party believes there is a problem with the way its adversary posed the question to a witness. There are eight fairly common objections of this nature.

1. *Asked and answered.* The question simply asks the witness to repeat testimony previously offered in response to a question. Often the examining party will pose the same question over and over in order to force the desired response. In such a situation, the opposition will probably have his or her "asked and answered" objection sustained, and the examining party will be ordered to move on.

2. *Assumption of facts not in evidence.* If a witness is questioned concerning some fact not in evidence, a successful objection can be raised. For example, if the examiner asks a witness, "Where was Mr. Smith when he signed the contract?" the question would be objectionable if no evidence has been introduced that Mr. Smith signed the contract.

3. *Argumentative.* Argumentative questions are those designed to win over the jury rather than elicit critical information. Questions such as, "You expect the jury to believe that cockamamie story?" are clearly argumentative. Sarcastic, patronizing questions and attorney "grandstanding" commonly lead to objections on argumentative grounds.

4. *Compound.* Compound questions compromise more than one question followed by a single question mark. "Did you leave your house and were you drunk?" is a compound question. Another example is, "Did you read the instructions and use the hairdryer properly?" If the witness responds "Yes" to such a question, the answer may obscure the truth. This is especially true if both "yes" and "no" answers would have been offered if the compound questions had been separated.

5. *Misleading.* Questions based on mistakes of evidence or misinterpretation are considered misleading. For example, if a witness testifies on direct examination that while driving he had rolled through a stop sign, a misleading question on cross-examination would be, "Why did you speed through the stop sign without stopping?" The examining party would likely have an objection to this question sustained.

6. *Speculation and conjecture.* Witnesses, especially lay witnesses, are supposed to answer questions with what they know, not with a guess or expectation. For example, questions that ask witnesses what they "would have done" if the opportunity to share an experience had presented itself would be objectionable.

7. *Uncertain, ambiguous, and unintelligible.* Questions that have either many meanings or none at all fall within the scope of this type of objection. Such a question might be, "After you stopped the suspects, you searched some suspects and not others, and arrested some and not others, and your decisions were based on the suspects' race, were they not?" Clearly, this is an awkward and nearly unintelligible question that should be rephrased.

8. *Nonresponsive to the question.* If, when asked a yes/no question, the witness responds evasively or vaguely, an objection can be raised. Assume that when asked whether he was under the influence of alcohol while driving the witness responds, "Maybe, but I wasn't drunk, and your client is at fault for the accident." Opposing counsel will raise an objection to the effect that the witness was nonresponsive. Further, opposing counsel will ask that the witness's response be stricken from the record.

Countless other objections exist. One important category left untouched in this section concerns questions that call for opinions. Because opinion testimony is a fairly complex topic, we revisit it toward the end of this chapter. Now we turn our attention to methods for protecting witnesses from abuse and humiliation.

Preventing Abuse of Witnesses During Examination

As noted in *Alford v. United States*(1931, p. 694), courts have a duty "to protect [witnesses] from questions which go beyond the bounds of proper cross-examination merely to harass, annoy, or humiliate." It is not *essential* but still desirable to ensure that witnesses not be unduly harassed or embarrassed. This is because witnesses are not on trial; there is little need to "beat them down," only to elicit factual responses. Of course, it is useful on occasion to discredit a witness, but impeachment can occur in a tactful manner.

One way that witnesses are protected during examination is to place restrictions on evidence of prior acts (such as criminal acts) engaged in by the witness. As a general rule, when prior acts have no bearing on the witness's truthfulness, they should not be exposed through the witness's testimony. In fact, rape shield laws (and FRE Rule 412) completely prohibit opposing counsel from delving into a witness's sexual history.

If the cross examining party appears to bully the witness, the court may step in and order that such questioning be halted. If, for example, the cross examiner leans close to the witness and speaks in a condescending and sarcastic manner, the judge may interrupt the questioning in the interest of preserving the witness's dignity. If the humiliation is such that the witness "caves" and answers the question falsely just to get off the stand, the court will almost certainly intervene. Of course, there is a fine line between unnecessary humiliation and "uncomfortable" testimony. In questioning a hostile witness, the examining party may have to resort to intimidation and fear-mongering in order to elicit a truthful response from the uncooperative witness. Questions that expose falsehood, deception, uncertainty, or bias are perfectly acceptable, as long as they are not "over the top."

Finally, witnesses are protected by the court—sometimes—when the answers to questions bear on especially sensitive topics. Questions about sexual abuse, mental disorders, and so on require special care. A good cross examiner knows that to badger and harass a witness about something sensitive may not curry favor with the jury. Consider an extreme example: Assume a witness reported on direct examination that he stopped a car with the license plate "GETAWAY" fleeing the scene of a crime. If the cross examiner asks, "You couldn't possibly have noted the correct license plate number because you are so totally and hopelessly dyslexic, right?" the jury may be less than impressed.

Calling and Questioning by the Court

Rule 614 of FRE provides that "The court may, on its own motion or at the suggestion of a party, call witnesses. . . ." Further, "The court may interrogate witnesses, whether called by itself or by a party." Judges frequently question witnesses, although they rarely call witnesses. Nevertheless, both occur.

Questioning of witnesses by the court is a common practice because it helps with the clarification of testimony. One illustrative case is *Logue v. Dore* (1997, pp. 1045–1047), in which it was noted that a lower court's decision to question a witness was "little more than the judge's [effort] to clarify testimony, expedite the trial, and maintain courtroom decorum." Judge-initiated questioning is not constrained in the same fashion that the typical witness examination process is—that is, judges are not confined by the fact that their questions were not put by counsel. They have freedom to pursue matters already discussed as well as explore new ones. In questioning a witness, the court will usually notify the jury that the question is for clarification and not designed to belittle or weaken either party's case. It is critical that a judge maintain the image of neutrality and impartiality during questioning, otherwise his or her role may become compromised in the eyes of the jury and the judge may be seen as arguing in favor of one side's case to the detriment of the other's.

Judges may also call their own witness, wholly on their own initiative. There are several reasons doing so. First, if one party to the case is hesitant to call a witness and fails to do so (perhaps because of fears that the witness will be loathed by the jury) but the witness has important information to contribute, the judge may call the witness anyway. Second, the judge may be more concerned with the "truth" than with facts that either party chooses to present. As such, he or she may call a witness not called by either counsel in the interest of ensuring that the truth comes out at trial.

Witness Sequestration and Exclusion

Rule 615 of the Federal Rules of Evidence states, "At the request of a party the court shall order witnesses excluded so that they cannot hear the testimony of other witnesses, and may make the order of its own motion." This situation is known as **witness exclusion.** Witnesses are excluded so they cannot hear other witnesses, not so the accused is denied the constitutional right to witness confrontation. The purpose for excluding witnesses from the courtroom is to encourage honest testimony, uninfluenced by others. Because humans can be susceptible creatures, witnesses are occasionally influenced—even on a subconscious level—by the testimony of others.

Witness sequestration is the process of separating witnesses while they are outside the courtroom. Sequestration is sometimes done to discourage witnesses from speaking to one another and unduly influencing one another's testimony. Often, witnesses will be excluded *and* sequestered as opposed to sequestered *or* separated. The reason should be clear; just because a witness is excluded from the courtroom out of fears that he or she will influence other witnesses does not ensure that the witness will not be in contact with other witnesses outside the courtroom. When witnesses are excluded or sequestered, the court will usually order them not to talk with other witnesses.

What happens when a witness is excluded but in contact with counsel? Further, what if counsel conveys to the witness the substance of another witness's testimony? The answer to the first question is that this action is perfectly valid. The answer to the second question, however, is that Rule 615 will be violated. Counsel should not defeat an order of exclusion (or sequestration) by conveying to a witness the testimony of others. This includes reading court transcripts to a witness (see, for example, *United States v. Friedman*, 1988, p. 568).

What happens when a witness violates an order of exclusion? Several remedies are available. First, the witness could be held in contempt. Another remedy is to let counsel question the witness about the violation and make arguments during the trial about the witness's out-of-court behavior. Finally, courts can exclude the testimony of witnesses who are in violation of exclusion/sequestration orders (see *Holder v. United States*, 1893, pp. 92–93). This last remedy is rarely invoked because it punishes one of the parties to the case, not so much the witness who violates the exclusion order.

It should be pointed out that certain witnesses are exempt from orders of exclusion and sequestration. Under the first exemption, specified in Rule 615, the court should not exclude "a party who is a natural person" and a party to the case. Doing so raises questions about confrontation and effective assistance of counsel.

Second, the court cannot exclude "an officer or employee" of either party who is designated as its representative by its attorney. Government agents, law enforcement officers, officers and employees of corporations, partnerships, and other associations all fall within this exemption.

The third exemption is open ended: The court cannot exclude a person whose presence is shown "to be essential to the presentation." Experts frequently fall within this exemption; it makes little sense to exclude two experts for fear that they are collaborating outside the courtroom. This does not mean that such witnesses are always exempt, only that in most situations orders of exclusion and sequestration are issued for them (for an exception see *Opus 3 Ltd. v. Heritage Park, Inc.*, 1996, pp. 629–630).

Finally, exemption four includes any person "authorized by statute to be present." Victims of crimes occasionally fall within this fourth exemption. In the past, there were few statutes that formally authorized victim attendance at a criminal trial; they were permitted regardless. One recently passed federal statute, however, provides that a crime victim has the right "to be present at all public court proceedings related to the offense, unless the court determines that testimony by the victim would be materially affected if the victim heard other testimony at trial" [42 U.S.C. Section 10606(b)]. A similar statute states that in noncapital cases, federal courts "shall not order any victim of an offense excluded from the trial" because such victim may later "make a statement or present any information" during sentencing; in capital cases, federal courts shall not exclude victims because they may testify during sentencing on "the effect of the offense" on the victim and her family or on "any other factor for which notice is required" (18 U.S.C. Section 3510).

Opinion Testimony

When a witness takes the stand and testifies, his or her testimony is usually limited to the facts within the witness's personal knowledge. For example, a witness may testify that she observed the defendant fleeing the scene of the crime. Here, the witness is communicating to the jury what she observed, not what she believed. However, there are occasions in which witnesses can testify as to what they believe, in essence by offering an opinion. If no better evidence can be obtained, a witness's opinion may aid the jury in reaching its decision. In other words, opinion evidence is not *desirable*, but it may have to suffice from time to time in order to avoid a miscarriage of justice.

Why are expert witnesses allowed to give their opinions in court?

Opinion evidence, as defined in *Black's Law Dictionary,* is "evidence of what the witness thinks, believes, or infers in regard to facts in dispute, as distinguished from his personal knowledge of the facts themselves." The term *opinion evidence* refers to opinions offered by in-court witnesses and is to be distinguished from opinions offered by people outside of a courtroom setting.

The rules regarding opinion evidence differ depend-

Practice Pointer 10-1

Witnesses, both lay and expert, should not be allowed to testify concerning the defendant's mens rea. The jury must make this determination based on all of the evidence presented by the defense and prosecution.

---

ing on the type of witness giving the opinion. Generally, lay witnesses are not allowed to offer opinions, except in rare circumstances. Expert witnesses, on the other hand, frequently testify as to their opinions. We will focus on lay and expert opinions, but first we consider the so-called "opinion rule." It guides the discussion throughout the remainder of this chapter.

The Opinion Rule

At common law, opinion evidence was governed by a "rule of exclusion." Opinions were excluded because they usurped the role of the jury to draw its own inferences from the facts. The modern approach to opinions is a "rule of preference." A rule of preference differs from a rule of exclusion because it focuses on priorities, not absolute rules (the "best evidence" rule is another rule of preference). In a way, the opinion rule is not really a rule at all. Instead, what is presented to the jury should be the most concrete form of evidence possible. If "facts" are not available, opinion evidence can suffice. Rule 701 of the Federal Rules of Evidence permits opinion evidence, particularly lay opinion, if it is helpful to the trier of fact.

Facts and opinions. There is often a fine line between opinion and fact. The distinction is usually a matter of degree. For example, if a person testifies that he smelled burning marijuana, is he offering an opinion or factual testimony? On the one hand, the smell of burning marijuana is distinct and unmistakable. On the other hand, since marijuana is an illegal substance, not everyone has had occasion to smell it. What if, furthermore, the witness testifies, "I think I smelled burning marijuana"—is this an opinion? The short answer is no, but one can clearly see the fine line to be drawn. In the end, it is up to the court to decide when opinions will be admissible.

Consider another example: A witness testifies that she saw a blue car speed away from the scene. This seems like factual testimony, but opposing counsel may argue that what one person calls blue another may call blue-green, or greenish-blue, or even green. Clearly the testimony in this example is more likely than not to be considered factual, but it is impossible to say that no opinion is associated with the identification of colors. However, because the distinction between fact and opinion is a matter of degree, the testimony in this example will almost certainly be admissible.

Personal knowledge and opinion.The so-called "personal knowledge" rule is at the heart of the opinion rule. Witnesses should, in general, state facts based on personal knowledge rather than their inferences or conclusions drawn from such facts. For example, the witness to a robbery can testify that the robber brandished a handgun. Such testimony is based on personal knowledge. The witness probably cannot testify as to the caliber of the gun, because it is difficult (unless one is very familiar with guns) to know the caliber of a handgun without careful examination.

Lay Witness Opinions

Lay opinion is evidence given by a witness who has not been presented as and is not qualified to be an expert. In the past (and even today), witnesses were not supposed to give their opinions or draw conclusions about the facts (e.g., that the defendant is guilty). Under modern statutes, however, witnesses are allowed to offer opinions if the opinion is helpful to the trier of fact.

As indicated earlier, police officers often serve as lay witnesses. Thus, if Officer X testifies that the substance she found on the defendant felt, and looked like cocaine, she will most likely be permitted to testify that the substance was cocaine. She begins by presenting facts then draws a conclusion from those facts. Of course, the opposing side may question the officer as to her conclusions. And because of this likelihood, the prosecution will probably have the substance tested in a laboratory to determine that it is in fact cocaine.

The collective facts doctrine. Some common law courts allowed witnesses to draw conclusions when they are difficult to separate from the facts. In other words, the **collective facts doctrine** allowed witnesses to offer an opinion when recitation of factual perceptions would not convey to the jury what the witness heard or observed. For example, a witness testifying that he heard a woman sing "The Itsy, Bitsy Spider" is basing his testimony on collective facts. The witness would not be required to recite every word in the song.

In a similar vein, a witness could have testified that the defendant was drunk. If the witness were required to testify that she observed a person whose speech was slurred, who had bloodshot eyes, and who staggered around, the jury may not have understood that the person was drunk (maybe the person had a speech disorder and happened to just get out of bed). The collective facts doctrine survives to this day but is not necessarily referred to as such.

The basis for lay opinions. Notwithstanding the collective facts doctrine, the opinions of lay witnesses must be based on facts of which the witness has personal knowledge. This means that lay opinions based on hearsay are impermissible. Furthermore, some courts have required that opinion based on personal knowledge must be "rationally" based, but this requirement is not embodied in evidence law.

Subjects of lay opinion. Lay opinion, when permissible, can consist of several subjects. For example, lay witnesses have been permitted to testify concerning a person's age. "The opinion of a lay witness concerning the age of an accused is admissible into evidence when the witness has had adequate opportunity to observe the accused" (*State v. Cobb*, 1978). Lay witnesses can also testify to people's appearances. In one illustrative case, the court accepted a lay person's opinion that the teller who handed the money over to a bank robber was "distraught and upset" (*Cole v. United States*, 1964). A third subject of lay opinion involves conduct. That is, lay witnesses can sometimes offer opinion about the nature of people's conduct. For example, testimony that the defendant was "trying to get away" has been allowed (*Lewis v. State*, 1871).

Lay opinion as to distance and space is permissible as well. However, if the jury can draw an inference as to distance, the lay opinion will not be required (again, because lay opinion is preferred only where needed; see *Alabama Power Co. v. Brown*, 1921). Lay opinion concerning time and duration is also permissible, subject to the same restrictions. Similarly, lay witnesses can offer opinion as to speed. Testimony, for example, that the car was traveling at an excessive speed will probably be allowed, where as testimony that the car was traveling at 45 miles per hour will not.

In some situations, lay witnesses can even offer opinions about handwriting. In particular, if the handwriting in question belongs to an acquaintance of the witness, conclusions regarding the author of the handwriting may be allowed. In one Seventh Circuit Court of Appeals case, lay testimony concerning the identity of the defendant's testimony was admissible because the witness had become familiar with the defendant's handwriting on several previous occasions (*United States v. Tipton*, 1992).

Practice Pointer 10-2

Prosecutors should avoid asking lay witnesses for their opinions, unless doing so is absolutely necessary. This statement is particularly true regarding lay opinions of guilt and innocence.

Finally, lay witnesses have been permitted to offer opinions about sanity and mental condition. In most situations, lay witnesses cannot opine about such topics, but when a witness clearly demonstrates an acquaintance with the person whose mental condition is in question, such opinion may be permitted. Some courts also require that the witness's conclusion be based on specific instances of behavior or conduct. Indeed, one court required that *three* factors be considered in determining whether lay opinion about mental disorders and sanity will be admissible: (1) the witness's acquaintance with the person, if any; (2) the time during which the observation occurred; and (3) the nature of the behavior observed (*State v. Walls*, 1994).

The Ultimate Issue Rule

Our discussion of opinion evidence would not be complete without some attention to the common law **ultimate issue rule.** Though it is largely abandoned nowadays, the ultimate issue rule prohibited experts from expressing opinions on final issues of which the judge or jury was charged with deciding. Rule 704(a) is testament to the disliked ultimate issue rule, " . . . testimony in the form of an opinion or inference otherwise admissible is not objectionable because it embraces an ultimate issue to be decided by the trier of fact."

The logic behind Rule 704(a) is simple: Witnesses should not be able to testify that "the defendant is guilty" or that the "defendant should lose," but to exclude all opinions as to ultimate issues seemed unfair to the authors of the Federal Rules of Evidence. It is helpful, for instance, to occasionally allow witnesses to testify to such issues as "the defendant was drunk" or "the car was traveling too fast." A blanket rule prohibiting *all* conclusions as to ultimate issues seemed a bit excessive.

Rule 704(b), however, does prohibit witnesses from drawing conclusions on ultimate issues, but only with regard to mental condition:

> No expert witness testifying with respect to the mental state or condition of a defendant in a criminal case may state an opinion or inference as to whether the defendant did or did not have the mental state or condition constituting an element of the crime charged or of a defense thereto.

What this means is that an expert witness in a criminal case cannot testify that the defendant was insane. This exception to Rule 704(a) was revived in light of the highly public trial of John Hinckley, Jr. who was charged with attempting to assassinate President Ronald Reagan. In 1984, Congress reinstated the M'Naghten rule, which states that a criminal defendant will succeed with an insanity plea if he or she is "unable to appreciate the nature and quality or the wrongfulness of his acts." The *jury,* not the expert witness, should make such a determination.

There are also reasons for Rule 704(b). First, it is designed to eliminate conflicting expert testimony, at least as far as sanity is concerned. At common law, jurors could become confused by expert testimony for the defense and the prosecution in a trial in which insanity defense was raised; one side could conclude that the defendant was sane, the other that the defendant was insane. Allowing the jury to decide this issue supposedly makes the guilty/not guilty decision an easier one. Second, rule 704(b) also helps ensure that the jury hears full information concerning an expert's diagnosis, not just an uninformative statement that, for instance, "the defendant is insane." Finally, Rule 704(b) ensures that the expert witnesses do not overstep their bounds and take the decision-making function away from the trier of fact.

Recently, Rule 704(b) has been interpreted to include not just insanity but all mental conditions. It now applies to all mental conditions that constitute elements of the charged offense. For example, in *United States v. DiDomenico* (1993, pp. 1164–1165), the Second Circuit barred testimony that the defendant suffered a condition that would prevent her from knowing equipment was stolen. Indeed, the rule prohibits any expert testimony that the defendant could (or could not) form the requisite mens rea of the offense charged. The rule also prohibits expert testimony as to the mental state required to succeed with criminal defenses such as duress, intoxication, and entrapment. Even so, Rule 704(b) does not apply to lay testimony, and it only restricts expert testimony on the mental state of criminal defendants, not third parties or the parties to any civil action.

Expert Witness Opinions

As indicated earlier, an expert is anyone who knows more about the subject of his or her testimony than the typical juror would. Of great importance in criminal cases are the opinions of expert witnesses. Because expert testimony can be instrumental in the jury's decision, special rules apply to their opinions. For example, Rules 702 through 706 of the Federal Rules of Evidence all govern the testimony of expert witnesses.

The rules governing expert witness opinions arise, in part, from fears that expert witnesses may unfairly influence the jury. For one thing, experts (unlike lay witnesses) are not required to have personal knowledge of what they testify about (e.g., experts do not need to be insane to testify about a party's supposed insanity). This means that the potential exists for nearly unlimited numbers of expert witnesses in a given trial, taking up valuable time. Second, because experts are generally paid for their testimony, their "opinion" may be motivated by the payment. Lay witnesses do not enjoy the same compensation, so judges occasionally fear the potential influence of expert opinions on jurors. Experts can also serve as channels for a great deal of hearsay evidence—again, because their testimony does not have to be based on personal knowledge.

As a result of these and other fears, courts have placed great restrictions on expert opinions. This does not mean that courts restrict the "substance" of expert testimony. Rather, courts are especially cautious about the "techniques" experts have at their disposal to win over the jury. For example, a prosecution expert in a criminal case may have the knowledge to testify that the likelihood of the defendant being insane is one in 300 million (numbers may exist to back this or a similar claim), but it has been held that an expert witness, especially one who specializes in probability theory, cannot explain to jurors how they may go about calculating the probability of the defendant's guilt (see *People v. Collins*, 1968). The courts prefer that there be a "valid scientific connection" between X and Y, not a mere probability.

Bases for expert opinions. Lay witness testimony generally requires personal knowledge. With experts, this is not the case. The basis of expert opinion can be of several forms. Under Rule 703, an expert's opinion can be based on one or more of the following:

1. *Personal knowledge acquired prior to trial.* F.R.E. 703 provides that an expert may rely on "facts or data perceived or made known to the expert before the hearing." This information includes, for example, that gained from physical inspection of a person or thing. A physician who conducted the autopsy prior to a criminal trial may testify as to the supposed cause of death.

2. *Personal knowledge acquired at trial.* Rule 703 provides furthermore that experts may rely on "facts or data perceived by the expert at the hearing." For example, the expert may watch the conduct of the accused at trial and opine that the defendant was insane. Or, the examining party may ask the expert a hypothetical question based on knowledge acquired at trial. This approach involves asking the expert to assume the truth of a prior witness's (or witnesses') opinion, then offer an opinion.

3. *Hearsay statements of others/secondhand information.* An expert might read scientific literature and testify as to research findings, read police reports, examine records, depositions, or engage in any number of similar activities to gain knowledge. If the secondhand information is unpersuasive, however, the court may restrict expert opinion testimony based on such information. Allowing hearsay as a basis for expert opinion raises questions about confrontation rights. In particular, expert testimony relying on out-of-court statements can invite challenge, particularly in criminal trials, under the confrontation clause discussed earlier. To date, however, the Supreme Court has not decided on this matter. Finally, an expert who relies on a scholarly publication, when expressing his or her opinion can be cross examined concerning statements in the publication that are inconsistent with the

expert's opinion. For example, if an expert opines that based on his reading of X's treatise on automotive repair that trans-missions should be serviced every 30,000 miles, he or she can be confronted on cross concerning X's recommendation that engine oil be changed every 100,000 miles, which is ob-viously wrong. The intent of this form of cross examination is to cast doubt on the credibility of the information supplied in the source, thereby weakening the persuasiveness of the expert's opinion.

4. *Testimony at trial.* A person may testify at trial to a particular fact, and the expert could formulate an opinion based on such testimony. For example, a witness may testify that she saw the defendant exchange small baggies for cash with an-other person. The expert may testify that her opinion is that the other witness observed an illicit drug transaction.

5. *Exception.* None of the four bases for expert opinion just in-troduced can serve as the basis for an expert opinion if it cannot be reasonably relied upon (i.e., if there is no scientific basis for such opinion). For example, a defense expert can-not testify that she read a study indicating that the "stars de-termine one's destiny," because there is no scientific basis for astrology.

Disclosing facts and data. Assume that an expert for the plaintiff in a civil rights action argues that "the majority of law enforcement agencies in the United States are dependent on the monies generated from civil asset forfeiture in the war on drugs." Assume further that this expert's opinion is based on a survey he conducted of several hun-dred law enforcement agencies across the country. Should he be required to make available to the court the data used to support his opinion? The short answer to this question is no, but it is within the discretion of the court to decide whether such information should be required.

Rule 705 provides that "The expert may testify in terms of opinion or inference and give reasons therefore without first testifying to the underlying facts or data, unless the court requires otherwise." The rea-son that experts are rarely *required* to disclose the facts and/or data responsible for their opinions is that it would take to long (and be too confusing to the jury, perhaps) to require the details. Also, this "short-hand" approach to expert testimony provides the party calling the wit-ness with some flexibility. That is, the expert is given a measure of cre-ative license with regard to an opinion when he or she is not required to spell out all the details forming the basis of the opinion.

This does not mean that the expert can offer an opinion that is unsupported. As in other areas of evidence law, a fine line exists here.

This line weighs the benefits of efficiency, expediency, and clarity against the costs of sacrificing the details of potential interest to the trier of fact.

In which situations would the court require disclosure? First, disclosure is needed if the expert's opinion is based on "cutting edge" research—that is, research that is on the frontier of scientific understanding. If the knowledge base is relatively new and undeveloped, some attention to the details underlying an expert's opinion may be desirable. Second, it may be essential that underlying facts and/or data be supplied in order to understand the expert's opinion. For example, if the expert testifies as to a person's mental condition, the jury would probably want to hear some of the reasons for a such a diagnosis. Either way, underlying facts and data can be required at trial or at a pretrial hearing of some sort.

Summary

There are two types of witnesses: expert and lay. Experts are relied on when (1) there is need, (2) there is a sufficient scientific basis for their testimony, and (3) they are sufficiently educated or qualified to offer testimony. Experts can also be appointed by the court if the need arises. Lay witnesses are nonexperts, individuals who have personal knowledge concerning the facts at issue. In a criminal trial there can be a third type of witness: If the accused chooses to do so, he or she can testify.

Witnesses in criminal trials enjoy a number of important protections. Lay and expert witnesses enjoy privilege against self-incrimination. That is, they are under no obligation to answer questions that implicate themselves in criminal activity. The accused also enjoys protection. In fact, the accused is not required to testify. However, once he or she decides to take the stand, questions posed by the prosecution must be answered.

Witness questioning is a carefully choreographed event. First, questions proceed through four stages: (1) direct, (2) cross, (3) redirect, and (4) recross. The scope of questions that can be asked at each stage varies. Next, the form of questions is restricted. In general, leading questions are impermissible on direct examination but acceptable on cross. There are exceptions, however. Finally, a number of objections can be raised to questions posed. Substantive objections are based on the rules of evidence. Other objections often relate to the form of the questioning and include "argumentative," "misleading," and the like.

A controversial issue surrounding witness testimony concerns the role of opinions. Expert witnesses are given the greatest latitude in offering opinion. Lay witnesses, by contrast, are not permitted to offer opinions unless necessary. If, for example, no factual testimony is possible, or if additional facts are not available, lay witnesses will be permitted to offer their opinions.

Discussion Questions

1. What are the prerequisites for expert testimony before it may be accepted by the court?

2. What is a court-appointed expert? When are such experts used? Why?

3. What protection does the Fifth Amendment give to witnesses?

4. In what circumstance during trial will the defendant be required to answer the questions put to him by the prosecution?

5. When are leading questions allowed?

6. Explain the concepts of "present memory revived" and "past recollection recorded."

7. Give three substantive objections and explain each one.

8. What is abuse of a witness and how is it prevented?

9. When and by whom is opinion evidence admissible?

10. Name the four stages of questioning and explain each.

Further Reading

Fishman, C. S. (1992). *Jones on Evidence, Civil and Criminal* (7th ed.). Eagan, MN: Lawyers Coop.

Graham, M. H. (1992). *Federal Practice and Procedure: Evidence*(interim ed.). Eagan, MN: West Group.

Lilly, G. C. (1996). *An Introduction to the Law of Evidence* (3rd ed.). Eagan, MN: West Group.

Mueller, C. B. and , L. C., Kirkpatrick. (1999). *Evidence* (2nd ed.). New York: Aspen.

Strong, J. W. (1992). *McCormick on Evidence* (4th ed.). Eagan, MN: West Group.

Weinstein, J. B., J. H., Mansfield, N., Abrams, and M. A, Berger. (1997). *Evidence: Cases and Materials* (9th edition). Westbury, NY: Foundation Press.

Cases Cited

Alabama Power Co. v. Brown, 250 Ala. 167 (1921)

Alford v. United States, 282 U.S. 687 (1931)

Bonner v. Polacari, 350 F.2d 493 (10th Cir. 1965)

Brown v. United States, 356 U.S. 148 (1958)

Cole v. United States, 327 F.2d 360 (9th Cir. 1964)

Daubert v. Merrell Dow Pharmaceuticals, Inc., 509 U.S. 579 (1993)

Holder v. United States, 150 U.S. 91 (1893)

Johninson v. State, 878 S.W. 2d 727 (Ark. 1994)

Kaufman v. Edelstein, 539 F.2d 811 (2nd Cir. 1976)

Lewis v. State, 49 Ala. 1 (1871)

Logue v. Dore, 103 F.3d 1040 (1st. Cir. 1997)

MDU Resources Group v. W.R. Grace & Co., 14 F.3d 1274, 1282 (8th Cir. 1994)

Opus 3 Ltd. v. Heritage Park, Inc., 91 F.3d 625 (4th Cir. 1996)

People v. Banks, 50 Mich. App. 622 (1974)

People v. Collins, 68 Cal. 2d 319 (1968)

People v. Cronin, 60 N.Y.2d 430 (1983)

State v. Beachum, N.M Lexis 2746 (1967)

State v. Cobb, 295 N.C. 1 (1978)

State v. Oliver, 742 P.2d 999 (Mont. 1987)

State v. Spencer, 216 N.W.2d 131 (Minn. 1974)

State v. Vining, 645 A.2d 20 (Me. 1994)

State v. Walls, 445 S.E.2d 515 (W.Va. 1994)

Students of California School for Blind v. Honig, 736 F.2d 538 (9th Cir. 1984)

Thomas v. State, 197 Okla. 450 (1946)

United States v. Blas, 947 F.2d 1320 (7th Cir. 1991)

United States v. deSoto, 885 F.2d 354 (7th Cir. 1989)

United States v. DiDomenico 985 F.2d 1159 (2nd Cir. 1993)

United States v. Friedman, 854 F.2d 535 (2nd Cir. 1988)

United States v. Kelly, 349 F.2d 720 (2nd Cir. 1965)

United States v. Miller, 874 F.2d 1255 (9th Cir. 1989)

United States v. Nunez, 658 F.Supp. 828 (D.Colo. 1987)

United States v. Robinson, 485 U.S. 25 (1988)

United States v. Rose, 731 F.2d 1337 (8th Cir. 1984)

United States v. Sheffield, 55 F.3d 341 (8th Cir. 1995)

United States v. Tipton, 964 F.2d 650 (7th Cir. 1992)

United States v. Williams, 583 F.2d 1194 (2nd Cir. 1978)

United States v. Williams, 875 F.2d 846, 854 (11th Cir. 1989) ✦

Chapter Eleven

Testimonial Privileges

Key Terms

- Adverse testimony
- Beneficial testimony
- Defendant's privilege
- Derivative use immunity
- Freedom of Information Act
- Holder of the privilege
- In camera
- Marital communications privilege

- Marital testimony privilege
- News reporter source privilege
- Privilege
- Privileged communication
- Testimonial privilege
- Transactional immunity
- Use immunity
- Witness privilege

Introduction

The general rule, both at common law and in today's courts, is that it is the duty of every witness called to testify to provide a complete and accurate accounting of the events of which he or she has personal knowledge. As an esteemed evidence scholar put it long ago, the courts have "a right to every man's evidence" (Younger, Goldsmith, and Sonenshein 2000). However, there are occasions when persons with extremely relevant knowledge about a case may not be required or permitted to testify. A criminal defendant has the right, guaranteed under the Fifth Amendment, not to incriminate himself or herself and that includes the right to choose not to testify. Other witnesses may also have a right to refrain from testifying or they may be prohibited from testifying.

When a witness is either shielded or barred from testifying, this is referred to as a **testimonial privilege.** A testimonial privilege excludes evidence (usually testimony about a communication between two parties) without regard for the trustworthiness, reliability, or importance to the trial outcome. When the law protects certain communications from being revealed in court, this is referred to as **privileged communication.** Several types of testimonial privileges have been created by either court decision or statutory enactment. Some testimonial privileges have existed for many years, while others are of relatively recent origin.

A privilege is a rule that gives a witness the option not to testify or that gives another person the option to prevent the witness from testifying. The person who has the right to keep certain information from being revealed is the **holder of the privilege.** It may be the witness or another person, usually the person with whom the witness has spoken. The holder of the privilege may exercise the privilege by requesting the court to prevent the testimony. This request may occur at trial or in pretrial proceedings. The privilege is not limited to trial, it applies to any judicial proceeding in which the witness is under oath. A failure to exercise the privilege at the appropriate time constitutes a waiver of the privilege.

Rules of evidence generally apply only in court proceedings, such as the trial. Privileges, however, are an exception to this general rule. They are recognized in all judicial proceedings, including grand jury hearings and preliminary hearings.

Privileges and Witness Competency

There is some overlap between privileges and incompetency. *Incompetency,* discussed in detail in Chapter 9, relates to classes of persons and is absolute. Incompetent persons are those considered unable, by virtue of who they are, to give reliable evidence and are not allowed to testify. A **privilege,** on the other hand, is a right held by a person who was a party to a confidential relationship, the sanctity of which the law values above even the search for truth. A person deemed incompetent by the court is not allowed to testify at all, while a holder of testimonial privilege may simply be restricted on what he or she can testify about. A privilege may be qualified, meaning it is not absolute.

Waiver

A privilege may be waived by its holder, expressly or by implication, intentionally or inadvertently. Failing to assert a privilege when the holder is able to do so constitutes a waiver of the privilege. Waiver of the privilege for any purpose waives the privilege for all purposes. Consenting to the disclosure of the contents of the communication to a third party is a waiver of the privilege. In many instances the privilege rests with only one member of the relationship, and that person has the sole authority to waive the privilege. The other party may have an obligation to assert the privilege on behalf of the other party however.

Disclosure of a significant portion of the conversation to a third party is generally treated as a waiver, although there is some debate as to what constitutes a "significant" portion of the conversation. An involuntary disclosure (when overheard by an unknown third party or compelled by the court) is generally not treated as a waiver. At common law, if an eavesdropper overheard an otherwise privileged communication, this would destroy the privilege, even if the parties were unaware of the eavesdropper and took reasonable precautions to prevent disclosure. The modern trend is to continue the privilege.

History of Testimonial Privileges

Testimonial privileges have existed in some form since Roman times. A number of the privileges used today were developed at common law, as courts struggled to balance the competing interests of protecting valued relationships (such as husband and wife or priest and penitent) and encouraging the efficient administration of justice in the courts. As states began in the mid-eighteenth century to codify the common law, many of the common law testimonial privileges were written into evidence codes or court rules.

The original draft of the Federal Rules of Evidence, presented to Congress by the Supreme Court in 1972, contained a comprehensive set of nine types of privileged communications, including attorney-client, husband-wife, doctor-patient, psychotherapist-patient, clergy-penitent, and state secrets. These privileges were largely derived from privileges that existed at common law.

Congress chose not to adopt specific testimonial privileges, however, and instead and adopted FRE Rule 501, which states that testimonial privileges "shall be governed by the principles of the common law as they may be interpreted by the courts of the United States in the light of reason and experience." This means that the only testimonial privileges recognized under the Federal Rules of Evidence are those that existed in the federal common law at the time of the passage of FRE 501, along with any privileges later recognized by federal courts. Since the passage of the Federal Rules of Evidence, the Supreme Court has adopted one new privilege, that of psychotherapist-patient (*Jaffe v. Redmond*, 1996). The Court has also altered the husband-wife privilege (*Trammel v. United States*, 1980).

Purpose of Testimonial Privileges

There are several rationales for creating a testimonial privilege. The first is that doing so protects the confidentiality of communications that take place in certain relationships—relationships that society so values that we are willing to hinder the fact-finding process at trial in order to protect that relationship. The absence of a privilege would hinder open and honest communication within the relationship. Common examples include communication between attorney and client, husband and wife, and doctor and patient.

A second reason for creating a testimonial privilege is that the courts realize that the law cannot force certain individuals to disclose confidences which they became privy to as part of their vocation. Thus, where a member of the clergy has taken a vow to maintain the confidentiality of the confessional, the law early on recognized that it could not, and should not, force the clergy to violate that pledge. To force persons to reveal such information would force them to make a difficult choice between the dictates of the law and the moral and ethical obligations of their professions; it would also place the courts in the position of appearing to force people to renounce their promises to others.

Testimonial privileges are sources of much controversy because they operate to exclude often important, relevant evidence. In the words of then-Chief Justice Burger, "These exceptions to the demand for everyman's evidence are not lightly created nor expansively construed, for they are in derogation of the search for truth" *(United States v. Nixon,* 1974). This situation is particularly problematic in criminal cases, where the exclusion of statements by the defendant may result in a factually guilty person being found not guilty. Testimonial privileges generally do not receive as much public attention as the defendant's privilege against self-incrimination, but they have a significant impact on both civil and criminal trials.

The positive aspect of testimonial privileges is that they encourage open and honest communication in relationships where such communication is essential. If the substance of such conversations could be revealed by either person in the relationship, it is reasoned, people would be less likely to speak openly and forthrightly, which would in turn damage the relationship. Spouses would hide their thoughts from each other, creating suspicion and mistrust in what should be the closest of relationships. Clients would not tell their attorney everything, thus hindering the attorney's ability to adequately represent them. According to the Supreme Court, a privilege is warranted only for "public good transcending the normally predominant principle of utilizing all rational means for ascertaining the truth" (*Elkins v. United States,* 1980). Supporters of testimonial privileges argue that the "public good" is well served by promoting open communication in certain relationships.

Testimonial privileges keep some otherwise admissible evidence from the jury because the courts and legislatures have determined that protection of particular relationships is more important than making all relevant evidence admissible. This is clearly a policy decision—the competing interests have been weighed and a value judgement has been made. As you read about the various privileges, think about whether a particular privilege is a good idea or whether that privilege should be eliminated. Also ask yourself if there are other relationships that deserve protection but do not receive it.

The Privilege Against Self-Incrimination

The Fifth Amendment to the Constitution includes the *privilege against self-incrimination,* commonly referred to as the *right to remain silent.* Every state constitution recognizes a privilege against self-incrimination, and the Supreme Court has held that the Fifth Amendment applies to both the state and federal governments. This privilege protects both criminal defendants and any witness in a court proceeding who is testifying under oath. Court proceedings include the trial, grand jury proceedings, and pretrial depositions. The privilege applies only to criminal trials; civil defendants have no right not to testify and can be called to the witness stand by the plaintiff.

The United States Supreme Court has interpreted the privilege against self-incrimination to mean that a criminal suspect has the right not to speak to the police during the investigation or to testify at trial. Additionally, the prosecution is barred from calling the defendant as a witness or commenting adversely on the defendant's decision not to testify (*Griffin v. California*, 1965). This is sometimes referred to as the **defendant's privilege.** Supreme Court has determined that a criminal defendant cannot be forced to assert the privilege, because doing so is likely to cause the jury to assume that he is guilty. The defendant waives the privilege, however, if he or she takes the stand during the trial and testifies. A person who is not the defendant but who is called to testify must take the stand and either testify or assert the privilege against self-incrimination. This is known as the **witness privilege.** Failure to assert the privilege results in a waiver.

The privilege against self-incrimination is not total however. It applies only to testimonial self-incrimination, which means being compelled to speak one's guilt. The Supreme Court has made it clear that the privilege does not apply to nontestimonial acts, such as the police taking fingerprints, conducting lineups, drawing blood, or using breathalyzer machines, as the evidence obtained via these methods, while potentially incriminating, is nontestimonial. Additionally, the compelled production of tangible items, such as documents or personal property, is not included within the privilege.

Immunity

The privilege against self-incrimination is waived if the court grants the witness immunity from prosecution. Typically, a witness called to the stand, when asked a question, will assert his or her right not to incriminate himself or herself. This is often referred to as "taking the Fifth." The prosecutor may then request the court to grant the witness immunity from prosecution and order the witness to either answer the question or be held in contempt of court. If the court grants immunity, the witness cannot refuse to accept the immunity. He or she must testify or risk being held in contempt.

There are three types of immunity; *use immunity, derivative use immunity,* and *transactional immunity.*

Use immunity means that anything the witness says on the stand cannot be used against him or her in a criminal proceeding. This is the most limited form of immunity, as it applies only to specific criminal acts mentioned by the witness on the witness stand.

Derivative use immunity means that the state cannot use any evidence derived from the immunized testimony against the witness. This form of immunity is slightly broader than use immunity because it applies to both specific criminal acts mentioned by the witness and other criminal acts that the police are able to uncover as a result of the testimony.

Transactional immunity means that the witness cannot be prosecuted for any activities about which the witness testifies. This is the broadest form of immunity. It applies to any criminal acts the witness mentions and any criminal acts that are in any way related to the testimony.

Privileged Communications

At early common law, there were no testimonial privileges, but courts soon began to create them as they saw a need to protect certain special relationships. Because excluding privileged communications from trial obviously impedes the fact-finding process, courts have historically been reluctant to extend the privileged communication rule to many relationships. According to Younger, Goldsmith, and Sonenshein 2000, the rule was that courts "start with the primary assumption that there is a general duty to give what testimony one is capable of giving, and that any exemptions which may exist are distinctly exceptional."

Four conditions must be established before a court will determine that a testimonial privilege exists:

1. The parties to a conversation must intend that the conversation be confidential.

2. Confidentiality must be essential to the maintenance of the relationship between the parties.

3. The relationship must be one that society believes should be promoted and protected.

4. The injury that would be caused by disclosure of the confidential communication must be greater than the value of the conversation to the resolution of the trial.

Major Forms of Testimonial Privileges

The development of testimonial privileges, like other evidence rules, has been inconsistent among the states. Different states have different testimonial privileges. And since the Federal Rules of Evidence are largely silent on the matter, there has not been the wholesale adoption of privileges and move toward consolidation that occurred with other evidence rules spelled out by the FRE. Nonetheless, while the privileges contained in the proposed Rule 501 were not adopted by Congress, a number of states did adopt these privileges in whole or in part. Thus, there now exists greater uniformity among the states than existed prior to 1972.

There are several generally accepted testimonial privileges. Some occur primarily in criminal cases, while others occur more frequently in civil cases. We focus our attention on the privileges that are most frequently asserted in criminal cases and that are most frequently recognized by state courts. They include the following: (1) husband and wife, (2) attorney and client, (3) doctor and patient (including psychotherapist and patient), (4) clergy and penitent, (5) government secrets (including informants), and (6) news reporter and source.

Husband and Wife Privilege

It is axiomatic that family relationships are highly valued in American society. Cultural institutions such as the church and schools reaffirm this principle daily. Courts have long acknowledged the primacy of the family, in particular the marital relationship. In *Griswold v. Connecticut* (1965), the Supreme Court held that within the marital relationship is a right to privacy that the government cannot violate.

The husband-wife privilege has a long history. It is actually two distinct privileges. The first privilege involves testimony by one spouse against the other and is often referred to as the **marital testimony privilege.** The second privilege, which protects confidential marital communications from disclosure, is commonly referred to as the **marital communications privilege.** These two are often inaccurately lumped together, but they are in fact different privileges, applicable to different circumstances.

Marital testimony privilege. At common law, a party to a lawsuit was deemed *incompetent* and barred from testifying. This was based on the assumption that an interested party could not give unbiased, accurate testimony. Similarly, courts initially held that neither spouse was a competent witness either for or against the other spouse. This rule was based on the premise that a husband and wife were essentially one person. Consequently, if one spouse was a defendant in a criminal case, the other spouse was treated as an interested and therefore incompetent party.

The rule that a spouse was generally incompetent to testify was gradually replaced in some jurisdictions by one stating that a spouse could choose to testify *for* the other in a criminal trial but could not testify *against* the other spouse if either spouse objected. This created a testimonial privilege that either spouse could assert. Thus, a woman called to testify against her husband could refuse to testify or her husband could refuse to allow her to testify. This became known as the *marital testimony privilege,* or the *husband-wife privilege.*

The justification for this privilege was the need to protect marital harmony. It was assumed that allowing one spouse to give testimony against the other would damage the marital relationship. The marital testimony privilege thus excludes from trial testimony by one spouse *against* the other spouse. The privilege covers only testimony that would be against the interests of the party spouse, or **adverse testimony.** It does not cover **beneficial testimony.**

This restriction originally allowed either spouse to claim the privilege, even in cases in which one spouse was charged with a crime against the other spouse, as when a husband was charged with assaulting his wife. The courts struggled with the perception of unfairness created by allowing a defendant spouse to assert a privilege to prevent the victim spouse from testifying against the defendant spouse.

The marital testimony privilege was adopted by many early American courts. In many states, the privilege was modified to permit only the spouse called as a witness to assert the privilege. This change allowed spouses who were the victims of criminal acts by their spouses to testify against that spouse, if they were willing to do so. This seemed a logical modification of the rule; otherwise a husband who assaulted his wife could prevent his wife from testifying against him by asserting a privilege intended to protect the marital relationship. Courts reasoned that there was likely no marital relationship to salvage at this point, so the privilege was not necessary in such instances.

The Supreme Court, in *Trammel v. United States* (1980), adopted the majority rule and held that the spousal privilege is held only by the spouse acting as a witness and not by the other spouse. This ruling permits one spouse to choose to testify against the other in a criminal trial but does not mandate it. The Court reasoned that allowing the nontestifying spouse to exercise the privilege did not serve a valid purpose because if a spouse is willing to testify against the other, there is no need to protect the marital relationship as it "is almost certainly in disrepair."

Some states still hold that a spouse is incompetent to testify for or against the other spouse. Most states have done away with spousal incompetency and have implemented spousal privilege in some form.

Originally, the marital testimony privilege applied to communications that occurred both before and during the marriage. This situation allowed a person to marry a person into silence. The modern trend is to not extend privilege to premarital communications. Additionally, persons must be married when privilege is exercised. If the persons are no longer married, there is no marriage to protect and so there is no need for the privilege. Most jurisdictions limit this privilege to criminal cases or cases in which the nonwitness spouse is a party (such as a civil damage claim).

Marital communications privilege The *marital communications privilege* protects against the disclosure of confidential communications between the spouses. The rationale for this privilege, like that for the marital testimony privilege, is the protection of the marital relationship, as well as the promotion of open and honest marital conversations. Some courts have also noted that forcing a spouse to give testimony about a confidential marital communication places the court in an unfavorable light. There may also exist a constitutional right to privacy regarding marital communications following the decision in *Griswold v. Connecticut*, (1965) although the Supreme Court has never explicitly addressed this issue.

The privilege covers both verbal and nonverbal communications. Most courts require that the verbal conduct be intended as a substitute for verbal communication. Some jurisdictions do not protect nonverbal communication and hold strictly to the verbal requirement.

The marital communications privilege covers only confidential communications made during the marriage. The privilege does not apply to nonmarital relationships that fail to meet common law marriage requirements. As such, the privilege does not cover same-sex relationships.

The privilege does not apply to communications made prior to a marriage. Thus, if a man says something in confidence to a woman to whom he is not married and later marries the woman, neither person may claim the privilege. Additionally, the privilege does not apply to communications made after the spouses are divorced.

In most states, the privilege applies to communications made during the marriage, even if the spouses later divorce. Thus, a confidential communication made by a wife to her husband during their marriage is privileged both during the course of the marriage and afterward. The minority rule is that divorce destroys the privilege, and a handful of courts have held that the privilege does not apply if the spouses are separated.

The modern rule is that the communicating spouse is the holder of the privilege. If the communicating spouse wishes to reveal what he or she said, the rationale does not apply. Most states allow a witness spouse to assert the privilege on behalf of the communicating spouse, unless the communicating spouse waives the privilege. The minority rule gives the privilege to both spouses.

Generally, any communication between a husband and wife is privileged, as long as there is evidence that the spouses intended for the communication to be private. Thus, the privilege is limited to confidential communications. Courts are split on whether the presence of an eavesdropper who overhears a marital communication destroys the privilege. At common law, an eavesdropper could testify as to what he or she heard, even if the spouses attempted to keep their conversation confidential. A number of states still follow the common law, but a significant number of states hold that the presence of an eavesdropper does not destroy the privilege. If the spouses were unaware that a third party could hear their conversation, the communication remains privileged.

The presence of third parties, even children, destroys the privilege. If spouses speak to each other in front of other family members, there is no privilege. There is no "family privilege," although many people have mistakenly thought otherwise. Communications between a parent and child are not covered under the privilege either.

Another important limitation on the privilege involves marital communications regarding criminal acts. A number of states do not allow the exercise of the privilege when the husband and wife are charged with engaging in a criminal conspiracy and the communication involves the conspiracy. This is because the privilege is an attempt to balance the competing interests of protection of the marital relationship with the smooth administration of justice, and in this instance, courts have determined that the privilege should not apply if it will serve to allow a person to hide criminal conduct.

As with the marital testimony privilege, the modern rule is that the marital communications privilege does not extend to proceedings between the spouses or to cases in which one spouse is charged with crime against the other.

Attorney and Client Privilege

The attorney-client privilege is the oldest testimonial privilege (*Upjohn Company v. United States*, 1981). It was recognized in early Roman law. The privilege is designed to protect the confidentiality of communications between an attorney and a client. The general rule is that confidential communications made in the course of professional employment between an attorney and a client cannot be revealed by the attorney without the consent or waiver of the privilege by the client. Additionally, the client cannot be compelled to testify as to what was said in the course of the attorney-client relationship.

There are several justifications for the privilege. The primary justification is that the privilege will encourage clients to be honest with and to trust their attorney, if they know that whatever they tell the attorney will remain confidential. This protection, it is assumed, will lead to more orderly and efficient litigation, as clients will be willing to tell the truth, thus allowing their attorney to prepare the best possible representation, based on the facts of the case. If it were otherwise, persons might be reluctant to tell the entire story, impairing the attorney's ability to represent his or her client. Also, persons might be reluctant to hire an attorney and might attempt to represent themselves. This was the case at early common law. Courts believed trials would be more efficient if trained specialists conducted them and so created the privilege to encourage individuals to hire attorneys.

Today, the Supreme Court has held that a defendant has the right to self-representation at trial, but only if the court is convinced the defendant can do an adequate job. Incidentally, while the Supreme Court has held that the Sixth Amendment includes the right to represent oneself at trial, the Court has recently held that this right does not extend to an appeal of a criminal conviction. Only licensed attorneys can represent someone; the one exception to this rule allows inmates to assist other inmates in the preparation of legal documents.

The attorney-client privilege applies not only to any communications made during the business relationship but also to any preliminary discussions about hiring the attorney. The privilege applies even to communications in which a client seeks to employ the attorney but the attorney decides not to take the case or the client decides not to hire the attorney. The privilege is created as soon as a person consults with an attorney about legal matters. The privilege applies to both criminal and civil matters.

The privilege includes not only oral communications but also any written communications or physical actions. Thus, it applies to documents such as letters passed between the attorney and the client discussing the case. The privilege does not apply, however, to tangible evidence of a crime transferred to the attorney by the client. An attorney cannot be used to conceal evidence.

The privilege does not apply to the fact that a communication occurred. Thus, an attorney may properly be asked to reveal who his client is or to reveal his fee for services rendered, if the issue is relevant.

The privilege also applies to communications made to agents of the attorney whose presence is necessary, such as a secretary, paralegal, or investigator. If third parties who do not work for the attorney are present, however, the privilege is destroyed. Thus, if a friend accompanies the client to a meeting with an attorney, the communications between the attorney and client at that meeting would not be privileged if the friend overheard the conversation.

The attorney-client privilege rests with the client. As with other privileges, only the holder of the privilege (i.e., the client) can waive it. They may do so by discussing the confidential communication, either outside of court with a third party, or in court during testimony. The attorney may assert the privilege on behalf of the client, unless instructed by the client not to do so. However, if the client waives the privilege, the attorney cannot reassert it.

Crime fraud exception. As mentioned above, an important limitation on the attorney-client privilege is that it does not cover criminal evidence turned over to the attorney by the client. Thus, if a client gives the attorney evidence, such as a murder weapon, the privilege does not apply. The attorney has an obligation as an officer of the court to turn that evidence over to the court. The attorney does not have to reveal how he or she obtained the evidence, however—that is protected by the privilege.

A related exception exists when a defendant consults with an attorney about a possible future crime or about concealing a crime. Recall that the purpose of the attorney-client privilege is to promote the efficient administration of justice. Providing a client with information on how to commit or conceal a crime does not promote justice, and hence this sort of communication is not protected. If an attorney provides advice about how to commit a crime, he or she may also be charged with conspiracy.

Client perjury. Relatedly, a criminal defendant may confess his guilt to his attorney. Such a confession is protected by the attorney-client privilege, and the attorney is barred from disclosing the contents of that conversation. The client cannot be compelled to testify because he is protected by the privilege against self-incrimination. But what if a client attempts to take the witness stand and deny his involvement in the crime charged? The attorney is barred from revealing to the court what he knows, but at the same time, he is aware that his client is about to commit perjury. The attorney is obligated, as an officer of the court, to not knowingly permit his client to commit perjury. Thus he must either convince the defendant not to lie or inform the court that he is ethically unable to continue to represent the defendant. The court will likely allow him to withdraw at this point.

There is nothing wrong, on the other hand, with an attorney allowing a defendant to plead not guilty and then trying to get the client a lesser sentence through a plea bargain or have the client found not guilty at trial. While the attorney knows the client is guilty, he or she has an ethical obligation to zealously represent the client, within the rules of court and the rules of evidence. It is not considered a breach of legal ethics to represent someone who has committed a crime. If an attorney is unwilling to represent a client he or she knows committed a crime, the attorney is free to refuse to do so.

There are several exceptions to the attorney-client privilege. The privilege does not cover the attorney's statements regarding client's mental or physical condition, and if the attorney is accused of wrongdoing by the client, the privilege does not prevent the attorney from disclosing information necessary to defend himself or herself.

Doctor and Patient Privilege

Doctor-patient privilege did not exist at common law. The privilege was not recognized until 1828, when the New York legislature adopted a statutory privilege. While the privilege was slow to be created, it eventually gained widespread acceptance, either by statute or court decision. Only a handful of states, mostly in the South, have refused to adopt the privilege. Some federal courts recognize the privilege, while others do not. Interestingly, the proposed Rules of Evidence did not include a doctor-patient privilege, although they did include a psychotherapist-patient privilege.

The privilege prevents a doctor from testifying about confidential communications made by a patient in the course of the professional relationship. The purpose of the privilege is to protect the doctor-patient relationship and encourage the patient to be truthful in seeking treatment so as to aid the doctor in making an informed diagnosis. The assumption is that a patient is more likely to be open and forthcoming when discussing his or her condition if he or she knows that the doctor cannot reveal any information that would embarrass the patient.

The doctor-patient privilege has been harshly criticized by some commentators and courts (including the Supreme Court in *Jaffee v. Redmond,* 1996). Critics of the privilege assert that there is no compelling reason for the privilege, as adequate treatment may often be provided by the doctor without discussion of the problem with the patient.

A number of modern courts have acknowledged that there is another justification for the doctor-patient privilege: the protection of the patient's privacy. This justification may prove more compelling than the original justification for the privilege.

While most states recognize the doctor-patient privilege, there are significant limitations and exceptions. Many states do not recognize the privilege in criminal cases for instance. The privilege is asserted more frequently in civil cases, particularly ones involving personal injury claims.

Also, the privilege applies only to communications made for the purpose of, and relevant to, obtaining treatment of a disease or injury. The privilege does not extend to communication unrelated to treatment or diagnosis. Many states limit the privilege to communications, while some extend it to observations by the doctor and other material, such as test results.

The identity of the patient and the fact that a doctor was consulted are generally not considered privileged, unless revelation would reveal the nature of the communication regarding treatment (for instance, if the doctor was a specialist in treating a particular disease). Privilege survives the death of the patient.

For the privilege to apply, the communication must have been intended to be confidential. The presence of third parties destroys the privilege, unless these third parties are office staff assisting the doctor or are close family members of the patient.

The privilege is for the protection of the patient, not the doctor. Thus, the patient is the holder of the privilege. The patient may waive the privilege by testifying concerning the consultation, by calling the doctor to testify, or by consent. The doctor may assert the privilege on behalf of the patient until the patient waives it. If the patient waives the privilege, the doctor cannot assert it on behalf of the patient.

The most common exception to the privilege occurs when the patient sues his or her doctor and any part of the claim or defense to the claim places the medical condition at issue. This makes sense, as it would be unfair to allow a patient to sue a doctor and allege the doctor mistreated him but not allow the doctor to prove that his or her treatment was based on what the patient told him or her.

Other common exceptions include statutes that require the doctor to report suspected child abuse or to report to the police the treatment of any wounds inflicted by a deadly weapon. In both instances, courts have determined that the justification for the doctor-patient privilege does not extend to allow patients to prevent doctors from revealing information that is necessary for the protection of society generally.

A majority of states hold that the patient does not waive the privilege by bringing a lawsuit in which his or her physical condition is at issue or by testifying to his or her physical condition. Some states, however, hold that putting one's medical condition at issue constitutes a waiver of the privilege. This is often the case in criminal cases, when the defense to the crime charged is insanity. Some states hold that a plea of not guilty by reason of insanity is an automatic waiver of the doctor-patient privilege, while some other states hold that the privilege is not waived until the defense actually puts on evidence of insanity.

Psychotherapist-Patient Privilege

A 1996 Supreme Court case (*Jaffee v. Redmond*) extended the doctor-patient privilege to psychotherapists. This decision conforms with the original draft of the Federal Rules of Evidence, which included such a privilege, and with the rules of evidence in the states. This is the only instance in which the Supreme Court has created a privilege since the adoption of the Federal Rules of Evidence. While this privilege is of more recent origin than the doctor-patient privilege, it was recognized in all 50 states prior to the Supreme Court decision.

The privilege applies to communications between a psychotherapist and patient, similar to the doctor-patient privilege. The more difficult aspect of the privilege is determining who is a psychotherapist and who is a patient. A *patient* is anyone who consults with a psychotherapist for the treatment and/or diagnosis of a mental or emotional condition. A psychotherapist is generally defined as (1) a person who is authorized and licensed to practice medicine and who devotes a significant portion of his or her time to the practice of psychiatry; or (2) a person licensed as a psychologist. Additionally, many jurisdictions extend the privilege to other licensed professionals who engage in psychotherapy or counseling, such as social workers and counselors.

There is a greater justification for this privilege than the doctor-patient privilege, as a communication between a psychotherapist and a patient is more likely to involve the transmittal of embarrassing or damaging information than a communication between a doctor and a patient. Those with psychological problems are often shunned by the public, so revealing communications at trial would likely deter visits to a doctor. Thus, an absence of the privilege is seen as more likely to deter patients from seeking assistance from psychotherapists than from doctors.

Additionally, total candor between a patient and psychotherapist is thought to be more necessary than between a doctor and patient, as a doctor can often make an adequate diagnosis without discussion with the patient, while such is not the case with mental problems.

An important aspect of the privilege is that it covers confessions of criminal misconduct, as long as the confession occurs in the course of treatment. This means that if a person admits to a psychotherapist that he or she committed a crime, the psychotherapist is barred from revealing that information unless the patient waives the privilege.

However, if a psychotherapist reasonably believes a patient may be a danger to himself or herself or to others, the privilege does not apply and the psychotherapist has a duty to disclose this information to the proper authorities. Obviously, this situation requires the psychotherapist to make a difficult judgment.

Clergy and Penitent Privilege

The early common law did not recognize a privilege for communications between a member of the clergy and a parishioner. Nonetheless, clergy routinely refused to break the sanctity of the confessional. Clergy of many faith are required to keep confidential the matters discussed in confession or in any private communication with a member of the faith. Thus, the development of the privilege was merely a recognition that the law cannot always force people to act according to its wishes and that other forces, such as religion/morality, have a greater impact on people.

This privilege developed in Ireland during the later part of the common law period and was originally intended to protect the confessional of the Catholic Church. England never adopted the privilege. It was recognized very early on in American courts. Today, the privilege is recognized either by statute or judicial decision in all 50 states, as well as by the federal courts. The privilege today applies much more broadly than at common law and is applicable to spiritual advisors of any recognized religious organization.

The clergy-penitent privilege protects against the disclosure of confidential communications made to a member of the clergy or a similar religious person in that person's capacity as a spiritual advisor. Also known as *priest-penitent privilege,* and *religious privilege,* the purpose of the privilege is to allow a person to openly confess his or her sins and misdeeds and seek spiritual guidance and redemption without fear of the confessions being revealed. Were it otherwise, clergy would be hauled into court and forced to act as government agents, and the confessional atmosphere would be chilled.

Originally, the privilege applied only to statements made in confession. Today, however, most jurisdictions extend the privilege to cover any statements made for the purpose of spiritual guidance. The privilege thus covers any communications made in pursuance of a recognized church procedure that creates a confessional-like relationship.

A difficulty sometimes arises in defining what constitutes an effort to receive spiritual guidance. Asking a priest to hide evidence of a crime would not be included in the privilege, but a confession that the penitent had committed a crime would be privileged. The clergy-penitent privilege is similar in this respect to the attorney-client privilege. The privilege does not apply if the clergy person is speaking as a friend or if the communication involves matters unrelated to seeking spiritual guidance.

The privilege applies to any bona fide religion. Courts are generally liberal in defining the term *clergy.* It includes priests, ministers, or anyone who has been ordained by a recognized religious denomination. Statutes codifying the privilege often use the term *religious advisor* or *spiritual advisor* to cover all possible persons.

The majority rule is that the privilege belongs to the penitent, not the clergy. The penitent has the privilege to refuse to disclose and to keep a clergyman from disclosing confidential communications made by that person to the clergyman. The priest may assert the privilege on behalf of the penitent, until the penitent waives the privilege. A minority of states extend the privilege to the clergy as well and allow a clergyman to refuse to waive it even if the penitent waives it. This policy is a recognition that some religions bar the priest from revealing confession even if the penitent reveals it. The privilege generally survives the death of the penitent.

State Secrets Privilege

Courts have long recognized a privilege for state secrets. This privilege originally allowed the government to prevent the disclosure of military and diplomatic secrets and thus was often referred to as the *military and diplomatic secrets privilege*. The purpose of the privilege is to prevent the disclosure of information that might damage the security of the state and to encourage full and honest communication within government agencies.

The privilege exists today and applies to both the federal government and state governments. Additionally, the privilege has been extended to cover not only state secrets but claims of *executive privilege, agency privilege,* and *law enforcement privilege.*

The privilege must be asserted by the government, not a private party. When the government asserts the privilege, the court holds an *in camera* hearing to determine whether application of the privilege is necessary. This means the court will examine the documents in question and uphold the privilege if there is a "reasonable danger" that disclosure would compromise national security. The state secrets privilege was discussed by the Supreme Court in *United States v. Reynolds* (1953).

While this privilege may seem rare, it has been used in recent years. Examples include the Pentagon Papers case, the Watergate cover-up, and the Oliver North case. More important for our purposes, it is the basis for a related privilege, the confidential informant privilege (discussed below).

A number of state and federal agencies require employees to file reports of events. An example is a police report of a crime. Such reports may be privileged by statute under the *privilege for required reports*. If such reports are designated as public information, however, then they are not privileged. This exception typically applies to police reports.

The policy deliberations of state and federal agencies are often privileged to promote full and open disclosure. The **Freedom of Information Act** (FOIA) grants the public access to most, but not all government documents. Information available to the public is not subject to claims of privilege in court. Material not available under the FOIA may still be available, if the litigant can convince the court of the need for the information.

The states secret privilege differs in several important respects from other privileges. First, it is not limited to communications—it also applies to documents and acts. Second, the privilege may be qualified, requiring the court to make a determination of whether privilege should be allowed in a particular case. Additionally, the executive privilege is not just an evidentiary privilege—the Supreme Court has held that it is constitutionally based (*United States v. Nixon,* 1974).

Confidential Informant Privilege

The confidential informant privilege is related to the state secrets privilege. It is sometimes referred to as the *informant's privilege,* as it permits law enforcement agencies to refuse to disclose the identity of an informant in a criminal investigation. The privilege applies only to the identity of the informant. Contents of the communication between informant and police must be revealed if doing so can be accomplished without revealing the identity of the informant. This aspect makes it different from other privileges, which are intended primarily to prevent the disclosure of communications. The purpose of the privilege is to promote efficient law enforcement and encourage people to come forward, by removing the fear of reprisal by the defendant.

While it was a crime to fail to report a crime at common law (this was known as "misprision of a felony"), today there is no legal obligation to report knowledge of a crime, except in some limited circumstances where a duty is imposed (as when a special relationship exists between the parties). Nonetheless, courts recognize a need to encourage reporting, especially when a person is otherwise willing to do so except for fear of reprisal.

The confidential informant privilege is qualified, meaning the court will weigh the effect of permitting the privilege against the need to reveal the information in the particular case. Also, there is an exception to the privilege if disclosure of the informant's identity is necessary for the defendant to receive a fair trial. If the court determines that revealing the identity of the informant is necessary to ensure a fair trial, the identity will be revealed. This rarely happens however.

The most common situation occurs when an informant has provided information used to develop probable cause to justify a search or an arrest. The identity of informants used to develop probable cause generally need not be revealed, as police officers corroborate the information obtained from the informant and thus can testify in place of the informant. The Supreme Court held, in *McCray v. Illinois* (1967), that when a police officer testifies as to the underlying information provided by an informant supporting a probable cause determination, the officer need not identify the informant because he or she is under oath and has provided the same set of facts that the informant would have provided. See also *Roviaro v. United States* (1957).

If it is determined that the informant is an integral part of a transaction for which the defendant is being prosecuted, his or her identity may be revealed, but only if the court determines it is necessary for an adequate defense.

News Reporter and Source Privilege

Some states today recognize a **news reporter source privilege,** also referred to as a *journalist's privilege,* or *shield law.* This privilege is similar to the informant's privilege; it allows news media to refuse to reveal their sources of information. News reporters were not protected from being required to reveal their sources of information at common law. The First Amendment, however, provides for freedom of the press, and it has long been argued that forcing news gatherers to reveal their sources would have a chilling effect on the press.

The Supreme Court in *Branzburg v. Hayes* (1972) rejected the First Amendment contentions of the news media, holding that journalists could be compelled to appear before a grand jury or to testify and to reveal the identity of their sources. The Court determined that news reporters were no different from other citizens and that the concerns that justified protection of a police informant's identity did not apply to news media sources. In response to this decision, a number of states have either enacted or adopted by judicial decision so-called *shield laws.*

Under shield laws, a news reporter may refuse to reveal the identity of his or her source if the source spoke to the reporter with the expectation of remaining anonymous. The privilege includes the identity of the source, not the information itself. The privilege means that a news media person cannot be held in contempt of court for refusing to reveal his or her source. The privilege does not apply to cases in which the news reporter is a party, as when he or she is being sued for libel. The privilege applies to criminal cases in which the news reporter has a confidential informant.

The privilege generally covers reporters from a wide range of news media, including newspaper reporters, magazine writers, television and radio journalists, as well as editors, publishers, and other persons connected with a news media outlet.

The privilege is not absolute but qualified. This means the court will weigh the news media claim of privilege against the need for the information for a criminal prosecution. If the court determines the need for the information outweighs the claim of privilege, the reporter must provide the information or is subject to being held in contempt.

Privileges in Civil Cases

Some privileges occur more frequently in civil cases, such as the *dead man's act.* In about half the states, dead man's acts allow the estate of a deceased person to keep a party, who is contesting the distribution of the estate's assets, from testifying about a transaction with the deceased. Some states allow the estate to bar other interested witnesses as well.

A number of other evidentiary privileges apply only in civil cases. These include offers of settlement and statements made during settlement negotiations. These items are privileged in an effort to promote the efficient settlement of disputes and promote settlement before trial.

If offers to settle or statements made during settlement negotiations were not privileged, parties to a civil lawsuit would be reluctant to discuss the particulars of a case, as anything they said could be used against them to show they were liable for whatever injuries had occurred. Thus FRE Rule 408 provides that evidence of conduct or statements made in compromise negotiations is not admissible to prove liability or nonliability. Furthermore, the involvement of third persons in the offer to compromise or negotiation does not destroy the privilege. However, offers of settlement and statements made during negotiations are admissible for purposes other than proving liability or nonliability.

In criminal cases, offers to plead guilty and withdrawn guilty pleas are not admissible against the defendant, for a similar reason—a failure to provide these statements with a privilege would reduce the willingness of defendants to enter into plea negotiations and would hamper the efficient administration of justice.

Summary

In this chapter, we have reviewed the history and purposes of testimonial privileges as well as the major testimonial privileges. Privileges are like so much of evidence law in that they represent a compromise between the search for absolute truth and society's needs. In the case of privileges, "truth" may at times be made more difficult to discover at trial because testimonial privileges reduce the ability of some witnesses to testify as to what they know about a crime or other event. On the other hand, valued relationships are protected—such as the relationship between husband and wife and the relationship between an attorney and client. Without the ability to trust that what is said in the course of these relationships will remain between the parties, these relationships will be weakened—or so the thinking goes.

Testimonial privileges are controversial precisely because at times they serve to make the search for truth more difficult. This controversy has led to the restricting of some privileges, while others have been created as the need has arisen to protect the sanctity of a particular relationship (such as the relationship between psychotherapist and patient).

Comment at trial on the invocation of a testimonial privilege is allowed for some privileges but not others. Jurisdictions are split on this, but the trend is to bar comment on assertion of all testimonial privileges. The Supreme Court has limited the ability of prosecutors to comment on a defendant's invocation of his right to remain silent, as such commentary would affect the privilege against self-incrimination. This is in line with the general rule that when there is a clash between a nonconstitutional privilege and a constitutional right, a court will treat the privilege as qualified or will overrule the privilege completely.

Discussion Questions

1. Explain the difference between witness incompetency and witness privilege.

2. What are the ways in which privilege may be waived?

3. What are some of the rationales behind the creation of testimonial privileges? Name a source of controversy.

4. Explain the three types of immunity.

5. When are communications covered by the marital communications privilege? When are they not?

6. What communications or actions between an attorney and his or her client are not protected by the attorney-client privilege?

7. Explain shield laws. Who generally invokes them and why?

8. What is the purpose of the confidential informant privilege?

9. What rule governs the conversation between parents if a child hears it? Explain.

10. Explain what is meant by "the holder of the privilege."

11. In what ways has the Supreme Court's interpretation of the privilege against self-incrimination affected different kinds of evidence?

12. What is the purpose of the doctor-patient privilege? What are criticisms of this privilege?

13. What is the purpose of the psychotherapist-patient privilege? What are criticisms of this privilege?

14. How has the Supreme Court altered the husband-wife privilege since the passage of the Federal Rules of Evidence?

15. What conditions must be established before a court will determine that testimonial privilege exists?

16. What are the two separate parts of the husband and wife privilege? What different circumstances are the two parts applicable to?

17. What are some justifications for the attorney-client privilege?

18. What is the purpose of the state secrets privilege and who may assert it? In what ways does it differ from other privileges?

19. What are some evidentiary privileges that apply in civil cases?

20. Can overheard communications between an attorney and client be used as evidence? Support your answer.

Further Reading

Imwinkelried, Edward J. (1980). *Evidentiary Foundations*. Charlottesville, VA: The Michie Company.

Mauet, Thomas A., and Warren D. Wolfson. (1997). *Trial Evidence*. New York: Aspen Publishers.

Rice, Paul. (2001). *Best-Kept Secrets of Evidence Law*. Cincinnati, OH: Anderson Publishing.

Younger, Irving, Michael Goldsmith, and David S. Sonenshein. (2000). *Principles of Evidence*, 4th ed. Cincinnati, OH: Anderson Publishing.

Cases Cited

Branzburg v. Hayes, 408 U.S. 665 (1972)

Elkins v. United States, 445 U.S. 40, 45 (1980)

Griffin v. California, 380 U.S. 609 (1965)

Griswold v. Connecticut, 381 U.S. 479 (1965)

Jaffee v. Redmond, 518 U.S. 1 (1996)

McCray v. Illinois, 386 U.S. 300 (1967)

Roviaro v. United States, 353 U.S. 53 (1957)

Schmerber v. California 384 U.S. 757 (1966)

Trammel v. United States, 445 U.S. 40, 47 (1980)

United States v. Nixon, 418 U.S. 683 (1974)

United States v. Reynolds, 345 U.S. 1 (1953)

United States v. Wade, 388 U.S. 218 (1967)

Upjohn Company v. United States, 449 U.S. 383 (1981) ✦

Chapter Twelve

The Hearsay Rule and Its Exceptions

Key Terms

- Admission by conduct
- Centrality theory
- Declarant
- Excited utterances
- Hearsay
- Intentional nonliteral statement
- Minimalist theory

- Present sense impression
- Procedural rights theory
- Production theory
- Reliability theory
- Reputation
- Statement

Introduction

The hearsay rule is one of the most commonly discussed rules in evidence law. Unfortunately, there is a great deal of confusion surrounding the meaning of hearsay. Many people assume that anything that is "heard" then "said" at trial (usually by a witness who is testifying) is not admissible. Actually, the hearsay rule is far more complicated than that. In fact, many people argue that more hearsay evidence is actually admitted at trial than is excluded because of the many exceptions to the rule.

Hearsay is defined as an *out-of-court statement,* made by a *speaker* other than the in-court witness, *offered in evidence to prove the truth of the matter asserted.* Let us break this definition down:

(1) To be hearsay, the statement must have been offered "out of court." Modern statutes do not define "out of court." Instead, they define "in-court" statements and treat anything outside that definition as hearsay. "In-court statements" are defined as statements made by a witness while testifying at the current trial. If a statement is made by someone other than the

Do you think the hearsay promotes a fair trial?

witness, not under oath, and prior to the current trial (either at an earlier hearing or out of court), it will almost certainly be considered hearsay.

(2) A **statement** is either a verbal assertion or a nonverbal act intended to be an assertion. *Verbal* means consisting of words, whether written or oral. The Federal Rules of Evidence Advisory committee stated, "It can scarcely be doubted that an assertion made in words is intended by the declarant to be an assertion. Hence verbal assertions readily fall into the category of 'statement.'" The only confusion centers around nonverbal "statements" and their role in the hearsay determination.

(3) "Speakers" are commonly referred to as **declarants.** Technically, a "declarant" is anyone who makes a statement (whether in or out of court), but for the sake of simplicity we will refer to witnesses (those who testify at trial) and "declarants" or "speakers" (those whose statements witnesses seek to introduce at trial to prove a particular fact).

(4) Finally, when a statement is "offered in evidence to prove the truth of the matter asserted," the in-court witness is "repeating" what another person said for the purpose of supporting his or her position. Two questions need to answered in determining whether a statement is offered in evidence to prove the truth of the matter asserted. First, what is the content of the statement? Second, what was the statement intended to assert? Because there are no easy answers to these two questions, we devote two full sections below to answering them.

Simply put, hearsay is an attempt to get the jury to believe that something was said outside its presence, prior to the present trial. There is no easier way to understand the meaning of hearsay than with an example. Assume that John is on trial for assault with a deadly weapon. Witness Craig testifies that while he did not actually see the assault, his friend Andy did. Specifically, Craig asserts at trial that Andy said, "I saw John assault the victim." This quoted statement, having been made by a person other than Craig, the witness, is hearsay. Craig will attempt to get the jury to believe that a statement was made even though the statement was not made in the presence of the jury.

Consider another hypothetical example, this time involving a statement that *is not* considered hearsay. Assume Bill sues Hillary for hitting him with her car. Witness Monica testifies that her friend Linda said, "Bill hit Hillary." Assume further that Hillary never did hit Bill with her car and that the lawsuit is fraudulent. Witness Monica is now on trial for perjury, but she maintains that she told the truth when she testified that "Linda told me that Bill hit Hillary." Monica calls Chelsea to the stand to testify that Chelsea also heard Linda say that Bill hit Hillary. Chelsea's statement at Monica's perjury trial is not hearsay because, even though she testified the same as Monica, her statement is not offered to prove that Linda told the truth but rather to prove that Linda stated that Bill hit Hillary. In other words, Chelsea's testimony is being offered to exculpate Monica, not to prove that Bill hit Hillary. Therefore, Chelsea's statement is not hearsay.

Origins of the Hearsay Rule

The hearsay rule traces its origins to Anglo-American evidence law. Prior to the development of the hearsay rule, cases were often decided based on statements made out of court. As Rakos and Landsman (1992) observed

Why was the hearsay rule created?

Medieval English jury adjudication was, in essence, based upon hearsay. Juries in the thirteenth and fourteenth centuries decided cases on the basis of rumor, gossip, and community opinion to which they were exposed before the trial commenced. While reservations about hearsay were articulated as early as 1202, it was not until the latter half of the 1500s that serious concerns were voiced about its use in litigation.

The trial of Sir Walter Raleigh in 1603 is illustrative of the role hearsay played in early English courts. Raleigh was on trial for conspiracy to overthrow the King of England. The prosecution relied almost exclusively on a witness who testified that another man, Lord Cobham, spoke of Raleigh's guilt. Raleigh objected to this evidence and argued that Lord Cobham should appear in court. Unfortunately, he did not succeed with his hearsay objection and was convicted of high treason. He was ultimately executed.

In 1813, Chief Justice Marshall explained the adoption of the hearsay rule when he stated that "Our lives, our liberty, and our property, are all concerned in the support of these rules, which have been matured by the wisdom of ages, and are now revered from their antiquity and the good sense in which they are founded. One of these rules is that hearsay evidence is by its own nature inadmissible." Furthermore, hearsay's "intrinsic weakness, its incompetency to satisfy the mind of the existence of the fact, and the frauds which might be practiced under its cover, combine to support the rule that hearsay is totally inadmissible" (*Mima Queen and Child v. Heburn,* 1813).

Hearsay and the Sixth Amendment

The modern-day hearsay rule also finds support in the confrontation clause of the Sixth Amendment, which states that in criminal cases the defendant is entitled to be "confronted with the witnesses against him." This means that the accused is entitled to be present at his or her trial and to see and hear the witness(es) against him or her. Indeed, in 1988 the Supreme Court held that the Sixth Amendment entitles the accused not only to see and hear adverse witnesses but to personally view such witnesses (*Coy v. Iowa,* 1988). There are some exceptions to the confrontation clause that the Supreme Court has carved out, such as allowing youthful victims of assault to testify via closed circuit television (*Maryland v. Craig,* 1990); however, such exceptions are comparatively rare.

As to the issue of hearsay, a strict interpretation of the Sixth Amendment's confrontation clause would lead one to believe that any statement intended to prove guilt that is not made in the presence of the defendant would not be admissible. The question is if a person's out-of-court statement "against" the accused, but is introduced at trial by a third-party, should be considered hearsay. In other words, does the confrontation clause entitle the accused to exclude hearsay? The short answer to the second question is "no." There are some 30 exceptions to the hearsay rule that permit the use of hearsay at trial against the accused. Nevertheless, the relationship between hearsay and the confrontation clause is still debated at great length by legal scholars. We briefly outline the contours of this debate.

One perspective on the hearsay-confrontation relationship is that the confrontation clause entitles the accused to be present at trial and to face adverse witnesses but that it also permits the prosecution to take protective measures on the behalf of witnesses. An example of this perspective would be a court permitting a witness against the mob to conceal his or her identity because of the risk of retaliation.

Another view on the hearsay-confrontation relationship is that as long as the defendant has had a chance to cross examine adverse witnesses prior to the current trial, the Sixth Amendment is not violated. This was the point raised by the Supreme Court in *Pointer v. Texas* (1965), regarding an armed robbery trial in which the Court condemned the use of testimony at a preliminary hearing where the defendant was not provided with counsel. Justice Black said that the case would be "quite a different one" if the defendant had been represented by counsel and "given a complete and adequate opportunity to cross examine." Reading between the lines, it seems that the Court was suggesting that prior cross examination (if it had occurred in Pointer) would have satisfied the Sixth Amendment's confrontation requirement.

At the other extreme, some commentators believe that even limited use of out-of-court statements at a trial violates the confrontation clause. The logic is that since such statements cannot be proven or disproven by cross examination, they should not be admissible as evidence against the accused. This point was raised in *Douglas v. Alabama* (1965). In that case, the prosecution desired to "refresh the recollection" of a convicted co-offender by the name of Loyd by reading his previous confession that implicated the defendant, Douglas. Loyd, however, refused to be cross examined. As such, the Court ruled that the use of the out-of-court confession violated that confrontation clause. In a similar case, *Bruton v. United States* (1968), the Supreme Court held that the introduction of a confession by defendant Evans implicating defendant Bruton violated Bruton's confrontation rights where Evans could not be cross examined.

A fourth perspective on the hearsay-confrontation relationship is that the confrontation clause requires, whenever possible, that the state produce at trial the person whose out-of-court statement is introduced against the accused. This issue was raised in *Barber v. Page* (1968), in which the Court held that the prosecutor who offered testimony from a preliminary hearing should have tried to produce the witness who made the statement, even though the man was in a federal prison in a neighboring state and could not be easily subpoenaed to appear before the court.

Finally, some people believe that certain types of hearsay should be admissible while other types should be excluded. For example, in *Cali-*

fornia v. Green (1970), the Supreme Court rejected challenges to the use of statements by a witness who appeared forgetful and evasive at trial and who had previously implicated the defendant while speaking with the police and in testimony at the defendant's preliminary hearing.

Mueller and Kirkpatrick (1999, pp. 1084–1087) describe five theories concerning the relationship between hearsay and the Sixth Amendment's confrontation clause. **Minimalist theory** "entitles the defendant to be present and cross examine witnesses who testify but does not stop the prosecutor from offering testimonial accounts of what others said or from freely using prior statements by those who do testify." **Production theory** holds that the confrontation clause requires the prosecutor to produce the "speaker" at trial wherever possible. **Reliability theory** holds that hearsay is permissible as long as it is reliable. By contrast, unreliable or questionable statements should not be admissible. The view underlying **centrality theory** is that hearsay should be permissible insofar as it corroborates or serves as circumstantial proof of guilt, but not as direct and critical evidence. Finally, **procedural rights theory** holds that the state should gather and present as much live testimony as possible. In other words, the state should be prevented from building its case against the accused primarily with out-of-court statements by people who cannot be cross-examined.

Clearly, there is little agreement among courts and legal scholars as to the relationship between the Sixth Amendment's confrontation clause and the hearsay rule. This lack of agreement is responsible in large part for the complexity of modern-day hearsay law. The many exceptions we will discuss, for example, are in response to some of the aforementioned views that some out-of-court statements are more reliable than others and, as such, should be allowed into evidence against the accused.

Problems with Hearsay

Testimonial evidence is relevant if four conditions are satisfied: (1) the witness accurately perceived the event he or she is testifying about; (2) the witness now correctly recalls that perception; (3) the witness now wishes to communicate that recollection accurately and honestly; and (4) the witness has the verbal skills to effectively narrate the events he or she is testifying about. Several trial safeguards are commonly taken to ensure that these four requirements are met: (1) taking an oath so the witness feels compelled to tell the truth; (2) subjecting witnesses to cross examination so their perceptions, ability to recollect, and sincerity can be called into question by the opposition; and (3) displaying the witness before the whole court so the judge and jury can observe the witness's demeanor and behavior.

The problem with hearsay is that it defeats all four safeguards. When a witness testifies about a statement that was made out of court, the court does not have the benefit of swearing in the person who made the statement, overseeing cross examination, or displaying that person before the judge and jury. In essence, the trier of fact is asked to assume that the out-of-court statement was true and, in fact, uttered by an honest and credible person.

Courts typically frown on hearsay evidence for several reasons. Mueller and Kirkpatrick (1999) offer four such reasons. The first and most obvious is that the speaker may misperceive or misunderstand what was said out of court. The second reason is faulty memory. The third is the risk of uncertainty. Finally, hearsay introduces the potential for narrative ambiguity. Collectively, these problems are referred to as errors of perception, errors of memory, and errors of narration. It is immaterial whether the errors are intentional or unintentional.

Misperception and misunderstanding. The first risk concerning hearsay is that the speaker may misperceive or misunderstand what took place. For example, if Speaker tells Witness that she saw Defendant flee the scene of the crime, Speaker may have mistaken Defendant for someone else. Speaker may have had poor vision, may not have been able to hear well, or may have only briefly observed who he *thought* was the perpetrator. Indeed, there are countless reasons that speakers or declarants can misperceive the events in question. Anything from deficient sensory capacities to deficient mental capacity to physical circumstances (such as poor lighting or distractions) can cause someone to mistakenly perceive a series of events.

Faulty memory. The second risk, faulty memory, is another reason that hearsay is viewed with caution. As Mueller and Kirkpatrick observe (1999, p. 784), "The acuity of memory is affected by factors operating both at the time of observation, such as attentiveness, interest, emotional involvement, and nature of the experience . . . [however,] . . . [i]t is also affected by factors that come into play when the event is later called to mind, including the type of information, the attitude of the observer, and the suggestivity of the situation." Clearly, in-court witnesses can have faulty memory as well, but the problem with hearsay is that the speaker is not present in court to be questioned as to his or her ability to remember the events in question. In other words, without confrontation, there can be no clarification (see, e.g., *Krist v. Eli Lilly & Co.* 1990).

The risk of uncertainty. A third reason for viewing hearsay statements with caution is the risk of uncertainty. It is possible that, for whatever reason, a declarant has a motivation to shade or distort the truth to ensure that the defendant is the one convicted for the crime. Unfortunately, if such a motivation exists, there is no way for it to be revealed in court. For example, assume Witness Brian testifies in court that his friend Jay stated, "I saw Dan commit the crime." Assume further that Jay was insincere in his statement and, in fact, wanted to see Dan convicted of a crime. This deceptive tactic could not be revealed in court because, unless Jay is actually called to testify, the defense will not be able to question the veracity of Jay's claim.

Narrative ambiguity. The final reason that hearsay is problematic concerns the potential for narrative ambiguity. In other words, the declarant may have misspoke or been misunderstood. Because he or she will not be present at the hearing, the opposing side will not be able to seek clarification. Narrative ambiguity can occur for several reasons. First, the declarant may have meant one thing but said another. We discuss this problem later in the section titled, "Determining the Matter Asserted." The second reason is that the declarant may have communicated clearly and unequivocally, but the witness still misunderstood him or her. Finally, narrative ambiguity can be introduced by virtue of hearsay evidence because the declarant's statement may not be sufficiently specific—or clarified—to the point that the witness understands its true and intended meaning. Figure 12-1 shows the relationship between these problems with hearsay vis-à-vis the hearsay process.

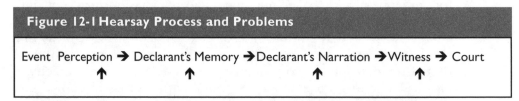

Figure 12-1 Hearsay Process and Problems

Event Perception ➔ Declarant's Memory ➔Declarant's Narration ➔Witness ➔ Court

Practice Pointer 12-1

Hearsay statements should always be avoided. The main reason is that hearsay statements are not made under oath and may therefore be inaccurate or untruthful.

For the Truth of the Matter Asserted

As indicated in the definition of hearsay set forth at the beginning of this chapter, two questions must be answered when determining whether a statement is offered in evidence to prove the truth of the matter asserted. These questions focus on (1) the content of the statement and (2) the purpose of the statement.

In many situations, the content and the purpose of a statement are the same. For example, if the witness wants to prove that the light was red and offers an out-of-court statement that "the light was red," the content of the statement is that the light was red and the statement is offered to prove that the light was red. More problematic is the situation in which the intent of a statement differs from the content. What if the same statement is offered by a witness, but only to prove there was a light at the intersection? The answer to this question requires further analysis. We begin by focusing on the "purpose" of the statement, then we move to the "content."

No other topic in hearsay law is more difficult to understand than the relevance of the "purpose" of an out-of-court statement. Formally, a statement is offered "for the truth of the matter asserted" when its relevance requires the jury (or judge) to infer that the statement is true. If the jury is not being asked to determine whether an out-of-court statement is true, the statement is not hearsay. Put a different way, an out-of-court statement is not hearsay if it is relevant to prove the fact that it is offered to prove, regardless of whether it is true or false. For example, to prove that Dale was still alive after his car crashed into a wall, a witness testifies that as the paramedics approached the scene of the crash, one called out, "Are you alive?" and Dale called back, "No, I'm dead." Dale's statement is not hearsay because it does not require the jury to determine whether his statement was true or false (he was obviously alive because he responded to the paramedic's question).

Consider another example. Assume that Husband has motive to kill Wife because she has a large life insurance policy. At Husband's trial for murder, Witness testifies that Husband told Witness (out of court and prior to the murder), "I am sick and tired of my wife's infidelity." This statement is not hearsay because, if true, demonstrates motive. If false, it still suggests that Husband may eventually have murdered Wife. Because the jury does not need to focus on the truthfulness (or untruthfulness) of Husband's statement, Husband's statement is not hearsay. A twist on this example is this: If Husband told Witness, "I am going to kill my wife," his statement, if offered in court by Witness, *would be* considered hearsay because the jury will have to determine whether or not Husband's statement was true.

Four commonly recognized types of statements are not offered for the truth of the matter asserted. They are (1) legally operative conduct, (2) effect on hearer, (3) circumstantial evidence of declarant's state of mind, and (4) prior statements.

Legally operative conduct. An out-of-court statement is not offered for the truth of the matter asserted when the (substantive) law makes uttering the statement a consequential fact. In the criminal context, whenever the making of some statement is an element of the crime, the statement—even if made out of court—will not be considered hearsay. For example, assume that the crime of kidnapping requires a ransom demand. Kidnapper X demands $10,000 dollars from Victim Y for the return of his daughter, Z. X's out-of-court ransom demand, if introduced by a witness at trial (most likely Y), is not hearsay. Returning to our definition concerning the truth of the matter asserted, the jury will not need to determine whether the ransom demand was legitimate or merely an empty threat. The only thing that matters is that the statement was made. Therefore, it is not hearsay.

Effect on hearer. An out-of-court statement is not for the truth of the matter asserted (and therefore not hearsay) when it is offered to prove that it had an effect on the person who heard it. The most common type of "effect on hearer" statement is an out-of-court notice. For example, assume that Mechanic tells Driver, "Your brake pads need to be replaced." Driver ignores Mechanic's advice, leaves the shop, and crashes into a pedestrian because of brake failure. Pedestrian's surviving spouse sues Driver, and Witness is called to testify that she (who happened to be in the shop at the same time as Driver) heard Mechanic tell Driver that Driver's brake pads needed to be replaced. Witness's testimony is not hearsay because the jury does not have to determine whether it was true, only that it was said. In other words, Mechanic gave Driver "notice" that her car had a problem, which demonstrates knowledge as to the problems with Driver's vehicle. A key limitation of the "effect on hearer" doctrine, however, is that it only covers statements of others (Mechanic) to the person whose state of mind is supposed to have been affected (Driver).

Circumstantial evidence of a declarant's state of mind. Circumstantial evidence of a declarant's state of mind is another situation in which a statement is offered for a reason other than to prove the truth of the matter asserted. To understand this idea, it is important to remember the definition of circumstantial evidence (see Chapter 4). Assume the prosecutor wants to prove that the defendant had the knowledge and ability to rob an armored car. Witness testifies that the defendant said, "I am going to rob Acme Armored's number 1 car when it stops in the Thriftway parking lot on December 10." Ordinarily, this statement would be hearsay; however, if the prosecutor introduces evidence that the defendant had a written record of Acme's delivery and armor-piercing explosives, the defendant's statement will not be considered hearsay. The key is that the statement is offered to prove the defendant's state of mind, not to prove whether his statement was true or false.

Indeed, this example suggests there is a fine line between hearsay and nonhearsay. The thing to remember is that in certain situations, the declarant's statement alone (without additional corroborating evidence) can be admissible and not considered hearsay, but not to prove whether or not it was true.

Prior statements. A fourth type of out-of-court statement not offered for the truth of the matter asserted is a prior statement. Evidence that an in-court witness made an out-of-court statement not consistent with his in-court testimony is not hearsay. If the witness testified out of court (possibly during a grand jury investigation or while being interrogated at the police station) "I was drunk," but testifies in court "I was sober," this is an example of an inconsistent statement.

Prior consistent statements can also be offered, but not for the truth of the matter asserted. In other words, the jury does not need to determine whether the statement was true or false. For example, assume that Doctor Expert testifies that Victim was raped. On cross-examination, Prosecutor asks, "Dr. Expert, are you being paid for your services today?" Dr. Expert replies, "Yes, I am." On re-direct, the defense attorney introduces an out-of-court statement, made by Dr. Expert prior to his being retained as an expert witness, that "It is my opinion that this girl was raped." Such a statement can be offered to prove the truthfulness of Dr. Expert's in-court testimony, even though the jury will not have to determine the veracity of Dr. Expert's prior out-of-court statement. For a summary of this section, see Table 12-1.

Table 12-1 When Prior Statements are Admissible
Prior *Consistent* Statements Made *Under Oath*
Admissable to rebut claims of improper influence or fabrication
Prior *Consistent* Statements *Not Made Under Oath*
Admissible to rebut claims of improper influence or fabrication
Prior *Inconsistent* Statements Made *Under Oath*
Always admissable
Prior *Inconsistent* Statements *Not Made Under Oath*
Not admissible

Determining the Matter Asserted

The hearsay doctrine generally assumes that a statement is hearsay or not. For example, saying "It is cold outside" (an assertion) and putting on a coat (a nonverbal act) are clearly two different acts. The statement "It is cold outside" is hearsay if offered in court to prove temperature. The act of putting on a coat is not hearsay if it is not intended to show—nonverbally—that it is cold outside. In reality, though, there are situations in which nonverbal acts and explicit assertions can be both hearsay and nonhearsay when offered for one purpose. To the extent that this occurs, it becomes difficult to discern what the "matter asserted" is. In other words, what is the person trying to communicate?

Determining the "matter asserted" is sometimes more difficult than the hearsay rule assumes. Three types of statements pose problems. First, statements offered intentionally but not literally cause confusion. An example of an **intentional, nonliteral statement** is the response "Nice move!" to a person who trips. The statement is made intentionally, but its literal meaning is opposite from what is said. Usually, if the declarant consciously intends to assert something other than the literal truth of the statement, the courts will consider it hearsay. Sarcasm, code words, and slang, therefore, will usually be considered hearsay.

Implicit assertions are the second type of confusing statement. For example, Husband is annoyed that Wife likes to keep the heat down in their house and complains, "It's freezing in here!" Clearly, Husband believes it is cold, but his statement is an implicit assertion insofar as it is really a statement of belief or opinion. In other words, the truthfulness of Husband's statement is wholly subjective.

The hearsay analysis becomes particularly complicated with regard to statements that look simple but are actually complex. In evidence parlance, several *subassertions* can be uttered in a single statement. Assume Stacy makes the following out-of-court statement: "Rod hit a water-skier with his boat yesterday." This main assertion contains several subassertions. These could include (1) I know a person named Rod; (2) I saw Rod yesterday; (3) Rod was operating a boat yesterday; (4) Rod was going too fast; (5) Rod intended to hit the water-skier; (6) my eyes are capable of determining who was operating the boat; (7) there was a water-skier in the boat's path, and so on. On the one hand, these subassertions can be considered hearsay because they may be what was *intended* by the main assertion, "Rod hit a water-skier with his boat yesterday." On the other hand, these subassertions may not be considered hearsay if they were not what Stacy intended to communicate.

Yet another way of understanding hearsay is to think of an assertion that the declarant wants the witness to believe is true but that in fact may not be true. Assume, for example, that a person gives false testimony to a police officer during an investigation. In one view, this statement cannot be considered hearsay because it would appear that the intent of the statement is simply to mislead the officer. However, the statement *can* be considered hearsay because the speaker wants the listener to believe what is being said.

One of the most confusing situations concerning determining the matter asserted is when hearsay is disguised as acts. Some courts allow parties to get around the hearsay requirement by disguising oral or written statements as an act. For example, if a doctor is allowed to testify that "the patient complained of pain," this statement would appear to be hearsay. However, if the intent with this statement is to report on an act (pain) and not to determine whether the patient actually felt pain, it may be admissible as nonhearsay.

A court case should help clarify. In *United States v. Singer* (1982), the Eighth Circuit concluded that an eviction notice sent to "Carlos Almaden" at 600 Wilshire Drive in Minnetonka, Minnesota, was *not* hearsay when offered to prove that Almaden lived at the residence. Two actions supported the contention that Almaden lived at 600 Wilshire Drive: (1) the landlord's act of *sending* the eviction notice and (2) the actual written contents of the notice. The court said that one can rely on "the landlord's behavior" in mailing the letter rather than "the implied truth of its written contents." Had the witness referred to the written contents of the eviction notice as opposed to the landlord's act of sending the notice, the court would have decided differently.

Another example concerns drug orders and bets. Frequently, during raids and searches of drug houses or gambling operations, the police intercept calls from people seeking to place orders or make bets. Such calls can be viewed in two ways. On the one hand, the calls can be viewed in terms of their content. If an officer testifies in court by saying, "I heard Defendant X state that he would like to order one pound of marijuana," this would be considered hearsay. However, if the officer-now-witness merely wishes to demonstrate a pattern of conduct (that drug orders where taking place at the house) instead of demonstrating that what the person on the other end of the phone said was true, it would not be considered hearsay.

The point of this section is, simply, to illustrate that the question of whether a statement is hearsay is not "black and white." In many situations, determining what the "matter asserted" is depends on why and how the out-of-court statement is introduced in court. A sense of proportionality is essential. Consider the *Singer* case again. The eviction notice is clearly more of a "formal" indicator that Almaden lived at the residence. Yet, the court relied on the landlord's act of mailing the notice in order to circumvent the hearsay rule. Had the court focused on the formal indicator (the eviction notice) and given it more weight, the outcome probably would have been different.

Multiple Hearsay and Nonverbal Statements

In most situations the answer to the question, "Is a statement hearsay?" is relatively simple. However, there are occasions where the answer is far from self-evident. It is more difficult to distinguish between hearsay and nonhearsay in two common situations: (1) when multiple people are involved in making a statement (i.e., one person says something, another hears it, who in turn repeats it yet another person) or (2) when a person makes a nonverbal statement.

The hearsay analysis can be more complicated than our earlier examples attest. Multiple hearsay, or hearsay within hearsay, is occasionally encountered. For instance, assume that Jack is on trial for raping Jill. Witness Bill testifies in court that he was told by his friend Will that he in turn was told by his friend Gill that Jack raped Jill. Bill's testimony would contain (Will's) hearsay within (Gill's) hearsay. In such a situation, every level of hearsay must be considered carefully. Naturally, hearsay within hearsay will be viewed with more caution than outright hearsay.

Another troubling situation arises when a "statement" offered by a witness is nonverbal. FRE Rule 801 suggests that a statement can be *nonverbal* conduct of a person *if it is intended by the person as an asser-tion.* An example will help clarify this rule. Assume that a defendant wishes to prove that it was unseasonably hot one day in August. Wit-ness Pamela testifies that although she did not know how hot it was that day (she was inside her comfortable, air-conditioned office), she did see Dale emerge from *his* office and promptly remove his sweater. As such, Dale must have thought it was hot outside. In other words, Dale was nonverbally asserting to Pamela that it was hot outside. Dale's conduct, then, seems to be an out-of-court statement that is being offered to prove the truth of the matter asserted (that it was hot out-side), but such a nonverbal act is not hearsay, at least in this example.

Had Dale stopped by Pamela's office on his way out, looked at her, and wiped his brow as though to suggest it was sweltering outside, this nonverbal statement would be intentional. Assuming Pamela testifies to the effect that Dale wiped his brow, such a nonverbal act can be con-sidered hearsay because (1) it is intended to prove the matter asserted, namely that it was hot outside, and (2) it has an *intentional* effort on the part of Dale to suggest, albeit nonverbally, that it was in fact hot outside (see *United States v. Abou-Saada,* 1986, and *United States v. Ross,* 1963, for further examples).

Exemptions and Exceptions Distinguished

There are two ways that an out-of-court statement can be admitted over a hearsay objection. First, one must ask if the statement falls within the definition of hearsay. If the answer is no, the statement is not hearsay. Because it is not hearsay, it is exempt from the hearsay rule. If the statement is hearsay, then one must ask, does the statement fall within one of the established hearsay exceptions? We introduce hearsay exemptions and exceptions throughout the remainder of this chapter.

Statements Not Considered Hearsay: Hearsay Exemptions

Two categories of statements are not considered hearsay. These are also known as hearsay *exemptions,* as opposed to hearsay *exceptions.* They correspond to FRE Rule 801(d)(1) and (d)(2)—namely, prior statements by the witness and admissions by party opponents. Each category in turn has several subcategories (three for prior statements and five for admissions by party opponents). Hearsay exemptions used to be considered hearsay exceptions (and, to an extent, still are). For simplicity's sake, we distinguish between exemptions and exceptions. Statements not considered hearsay are *exempt* from the hearsay requirement. Statements that are considered hearsay can be admissi-ble by way of an *exception* to the hearsay rule.

Prior statements. Three types of prior statements made by a testi-fying witness cannot be considered hearsay. First, if a witness makes an out-of-court statement that contradicts his or her in-court testi-mony, the out-of-court statement is not considered hearsay. For exam-ple, assume that prior to trial, Witness tells Officer that "Defendant committed the crime." In court, however, Witness testifies that Defen-dant did not commit the crime. The out-of-court statement can proba-bly be introduced as evidence (*United States v. Matlock*, 1997). We say "probably" because the Federal Rules of Evidence state that in order for the prior statement to be considered exempt from the hearsay rule, it must have been made under oath or subjected to the penalty of per-jury. In our example, had Witness signed a sworn statement prior to trial to the effect that Defendant committed the crime, the court would be correct in admitting it into evidence.

Certain types of prior *consistent* statements are also exempt from the hearsay rule. However, such statements are only admissible in order to rebut a charge of fabrication, improper influence, or motive. For example, assume that Bill is on trial for murder. Witness Pat testi-fies that he saw Bill commit the murder. In rebuttal, Bill's attorney calls Police Officer Jones to the stand to testify that Pat told him after the murder that Hank, not Bill, had committed the murder. This is an example of an inconsistent statement. Assume further, that following Police Officer Jones' testimony the prosecution calls witness Wilma, who states that Pat told her directly after the murder that Bill was responsible. This is an example of a prior consistent statement being introduced for the purpose of rebutting Police Officer Jones' charge that Pat's testimony was fraudulent.

A third type of statement exempt from the hearsay requirement is a prior statement of identification. Statements of prior identification are simply out-of-court statements identifying a person after the declarant has seen the person. For example, assume Henry testifies that he saw someone steal Lewis' car but that he cannot remember who committed the crime because his memory has faded. The prosecutor then intro-duces evidence that, directly following the crime, Henry accompanied Police Officer Harris on a ride-along during which Henry pointed to a person and said, "That's the person who stole Lewis' car." Henry later picked the Defendant's photo out of a photographic lineup. This is an example of a third-party identification. In general, any out-of-court identification of a suspect in a photographic lineup, actual lineup, or showup is admissible under this hearsay exemption (e.g., *United States v. Evans*, 1971; *United States v. Hallman*, 1971; *United States v. Simmons*, 1991). Note, however, that Sixth Amendment counsel requirements (if any) need to be satisfied (see Chapter 8).

In summary, each of the "prior statements" hearsay exemptions has two common and critical requirements. First, for a prior statement to be exempt from the hearsay rule, the declarant must take the stand

and testify at the hearing wherein the statement is offered. Second, the declarant must be subject to cross examination. This means that the declarant must be subjected to cross examination as to the prior statement at the *current hearing,* not some previous hearing.

Admissions by party opponents. Admissions by party opponents are generally statements attributed to criminal defendants or the party named in a civil lawsuit. Statements by party opponents are not considered hearsay because such statements are not made by an unavailable out-of-court witness. The are five such admissions: (1) the party's own statement; (2) the party's admission by adoption or conduct; (3) an admission by a person authorized by a party to speak; (4) a statement by the party's agent, servant, or employee; and (5) an admission by a co-conspirator of the party. Admissions can be written, spoken, or in the form of nonverbal assertions (*Tamez v. City of San Marcos, Texas,* 1997; *United States v. Seelig,* 1980).

The *party opponent's own statements* can be introduced at trial and are not considered hearsay. For example, assume that Sally sues Officer Rush for negligence, following a high-speed collision between their cars. Sally offers evidence that before the accident her friend Officer Slow (who happens to work with Rush and is disgusted with Rush's reckless driving habits) told Sally that Officer Rush said to him, "I can drive as fast as I want—I'm a cop." Although this statement fits the general definition of hearsay, it is not hearsay because the statement is made by a party opponent, namely Officer Slow. Even if Slow's statement does not have any real guarantee of trustworthiness (the problem with hearsay generally), it is admissible because it is offered *against* the party who presumably made it (Officer Rush).

A party opponent's **admission by conduct** is also exempt from the hearsay rule. Assume Shady is on trial for narcotics offenses. Officer Vigilant testifies that Shady fled from her when she attempted to effect an arrest. Vigilant can testify that Shady fled. This is an example of admission by conduct. It resembles hearsay; however, it is not because Vigilant is testifying *against* Shady. In our example, then, flight from a police officer is considered an admission of guilt.

Other types of admissions by conduct are not admissible for policy reasons. If the conduct is one that society generally encourages, it would be detrimental to admit such evidence into trial. For example, if a defendant offers to pay the victim's medical bills (an implied admission of guilt), such evidence will not be admissible under a hearsay exemption because it is generally desirable—from a policy standpoint—for guilty parties to take responsibility for their actions. If evidence such as this *were* admissible, it would discourage future defendants from paying medical bills.

Admissions by conduct are similar to adoptive admissions. Adoptive admissions occur when silence serves as an admission of guilt. For example, assume that X and Y approach each other on a crowded street. X points to Y and says, "That's the man who murdered my wife!" Y says nothing in response and remains silent. Witness Z testifies at trial as to Y's silence. This evidence is admissible because it is offered by a party opponent. Had Y said, "No I didn't," his statement would not be admissible. The rationale for this exemption is that it is reasonable to expect someone who is not guilty of a crime (or responsible for some other act) to make a statement to that effect.

One significant exception to the adoptive admission exemption concerns *Miranda*. If police officers advise a suspect of her *Miranda* right to remain silent and she stands mute, this type of silence cannot be admitted into evidence as an implied admission of guilt. As the Supreme Court stated in *Miranda*, a defendant cannot be penalized for exercising Fifth Amendment privilege during custodial interrogation; prosecutors may not "use at trial the fact that [defendant] stood mute or claimed his privilege in the face of accusation" (*Doyle v. Ohio*, 1976, p. 627).

Admissions not by party opponents but *by individuals authorized to speak for party opponents* are also exempt from the hearsay rule. Such admissions are referred to as either "representative admissions," "vicarious admissions," or "authorized admissions." Virtually anyone can act as an authorized speaker. That includes spouses, attorneys, children, business partners, and so forth. Assume, for example, that Chris sues Larry for injuries Chris suffered while shopping in Larry's store. Keith, an employee of Larry's, approached Chris and said, "My boss, Larry, sent me to apologize for your injury." If Keith's statement is authorized by Larry and is attributed to Larry, it is an authorized admission. As such, it will not be considered hearsay. Again, the reason is that the statement in our example was made by a party opponent, namely an authorized speaker for the defendant, Larry.

Statements made by a *party's agent, servant, or employee* are also exempt from the hearsay rule. Note, however, that the difference between this exemption and the "authorized admission" exemption discussed in the previous paragraph is that speaking authority is not necessary. In other words, the speaker does not have to be given "authority" to speak for his or her employer for the statement to be admissible against the party opponent. One important qualifier, though, is that the speaker be to blame—if only in part—for the injury or crime. Assume, for example, that Jerri works for a babysitter service and is hired by the Smiths. While babysitting, she falls asleep and the Smiths' toddler wanders outside into the street and is struck by a car. When Jerri wakes up, she calls the Smiths' cell phone and says, "There's been an accident. I'm sorry, it's all my fault." The Smiths then sue Madeline, the owner of the babysitter service. Jerri's statement would be admissible against Madeline as though Madeline had made the statement herself. It is immaterial whether Jerri was authorized to speak. Moreover, her statement will not be considered hearsay because it is provided by a party opponent, the person (or persons) named in the Smiths' lawsuit.

Finally, *statements made by a party opponent's co-consipirator* are not considered hearsay. This hearsay exemption is frequently raised in criminal trials. However, two additional requirements must be satistified for a co-conspirator's statement to be exempt from the hearsay rule. Not only must the statement be made by a co-conspirator, it also must be made (1) *during* the conspiracy and (2) in furtherance of the conspiracy (e.g., *United States v. Nixon,* 1974; *Anderson v. United States,* 1974). Assume Susan is on trial for the murder of Sara. Witness Clyde testifies for the prosecution that he overheard a conversation between Fred and Barney in which Barney stated, "Susan has agreed to help us kill Sara." According to the general definition of hearsay, Barney's statement is hearsay if offered by Witness Clyde. However, Barney's statement will be admissible under the co-conspirator exemption because the statement was made by a co-conspirator (Barney) both prior to the murder and in furtherance of the conspiracy to commit murder. Were it not for this exemption, it is unlikely that secretive conversations made in furtherance of a conspiracy would ever be disclosed in a courtroom setting.

In summary, for a statement by a party opponent to be exempt from the hearsay rule, it must be offered against the party who made the statement or is otherwise responsible for the statement. A party statement is not admissible on behalf of the party who made it or did not make it. A full understanding and grasp of this hearsay exemption requires a correct answer to this important question: *Who is offering the statement?* If the opposing party offers the statement, it is not hearsay.

Hearsay Exceptions

Before considering whether a hearsay exception applies, it is important that three questions be answered. First, is the statement relevant? If the answer is no, it does not matter whether the statement is subject to a hearsay exception or, for that matter, is hearsay at all; it will not be admissible. Second, who is the declarant? If the declarant is someone other than the witness, it is more likely that the statement will be considered hearsay. Third, is the statement offered for the truth of the matter asserted? If the answer is no, the statement is not hearsay. If the answer is yes, the statement is hearsay. At this point, when it is clear that the statement is relevant, was made out of court, and is hearsay, the exceptions come into play.

There are so many hearsay exceptions that students of evidence law can get easily mired in the possibilities. A common approach used to determine if a hearsay exception applies is to scrutinize the facts of a case then decide which hearsay exception is most likely to apply. This approach makes for more work than is necessary. Instead, it is useful to think in terms of *categories* of exceptions to the hearsay rule. The best way to do it is to ask if the declarant is available to testify? If the answer is yes, there are several hearsay exceptions that apply. These are known as "unrestricted" hearsay exceptions, insofar as they do not require that the declarant be inaccessible. If the answer is no, there is another specific category of hearsay exceptions that apply only when the declarant is unavailable. We organize the remainder of this chapter around both categories of hearsay exceptions: (1) unrestricted hearsay exceptions and (2) exceptions requiring the unavailability of the declarant.

Notwithstanding the many varieties of hearsay exceptions, a *hearsay exception* can be defined as a rule that for policy reasons permits an out-of-court statement to be used as substantive evidence of the matter it asserts. There are two reasons that justify the use of hearsay as evidence under certain circumstances. The first is *reliability*. Statements falling within established hearsay rule exceptions are thought to have the highest degrees of trustworthiness and believability. For example, a statement by a patient made to his or her doctor about symptoms of an illness are likely to have a high degree of reliability because of the patient's vested interest in being truthful (few people elect to lie to their doctors about symptoms of illness). The second reason for certain hearsay exceptions is *necessity*. In some situations hearsay is the only evidence available. In other words, hearsay is better than no evidence at all. However, with regard to necessity, it is also desirable that necessary hearsay statements be reliable. It would be unfair to convict a defendant solely on hearsay evidence with few indiciations of reliability.

Keep in mind the fact that hearsay statements can fall within many hearsay exceptions at the same time. For example, a *present sense impression* [FRE Rule 803(1)] that is *made for the purpose of securing medical treatment* [Rule 803(4)] is admissible under two specific provisions of the Federal Rules of Evidence. Also, be reminded that we are discussing *exceptions* throughout the remainder of this chapter, not *exemptions*. Exemptions fell into the categories of prior statements and admissions by party opponents discussed earlier in this chapter.

Unrestricted Hearsay Exceptions

There are at least nine categories of hearsay exceptions not requiring that the declarant be unavailable. We approach each of these in the order they are covered in the Federal Rules of Evidence. Our introduction to each exception will consist of approximately three paragraphs. The first will describe the exception, the second will offer the rationale for the exception, and the third will describe restrictions and modifications (if any) to the exception. Some of the more complex hearsay exceptions will be discussed in more detail.

Present sense impressions. A declarant's statement, whether or not he or she is available is admissible if (1) the contents of the declarant's statement describes or explains an event or condition, and (2) the timing of the statement places it within the period when the declarant was observing the matter in question (Rule 803[1]). For example, Lisa sues Nicole for negligence following an automobile accident, alleging that Nicole ran a stop sign. Witness Brian testifies for Lisa that he was standing next to Jay just before the collision and heard Jay say, "Wow! That car blew through the stop sign!" Jay's statement is hearsay, but it is admissible because it was a **present sense impression,** a description of the event that sparked the lawsuit.

The rationale for this exception is reliability. First, courts tend to believe that there is no problem of recollection when the statement was made at the time of the perception (see *Dutton v. Evans,* 1970; *Nuttall v. Reading Co.,* 1956). In our example, Jay's statement is likely to be reliable because he both observed and commented on Nicole's driving at nearly the same point in time. Second, it is likely that statements of present sense impressions are sincere, again because they are uttered at the same point in time as the event in question (in our example, Nicole's act of running the stop sign).

Importantly, the present sense impression hearsay exception does not require that the declarant be a participant in the event described by the statement (in our example, Jay was merely an observer). Also, the declarant does not have to have direct, personal knowledge of the matter in question. Assume a witness testifies that while speaking on the phone with a murder victim he heard the victim say, "Let me call you back—my neighbor just walked in . . . no, Jim, don't shoot . . . " (BANG! BANG! BANG!). This statement is hearsay, but it is admissible as a present sense impression, even though the declarant had no direct, personal knowledge of the event (i.e., he did not technically *observe* what happened). Next, the present sense impression exception does not require that the statement be precisely contemporaneous with the event. A "slight lapse" between the event and the statement is permissible, but too much time weakens reliability. Finally, the present sense impression exception applies to statements made by *identified* (though not necessarily "available") and unidentified declarants; however, statements by unidentified declarants are somewhat less reliable because the declarant's statement can not be challenged as unreliable.

Excited utterances. A statement is admissible whether or not the declarant is available as a witness if (1) the content of the statement relates to a startling event or condition, and (2) the statement was made while the declarant was under the stress or excitement caused by the event or condition (Rule 803[2]). For example, assume Steve was severely injured by a hit-and-run driver. While he was being treated in the hospital emergency room he saw Mary walk in. He started to shake, then he shouted, "That's the woman who ran me down and nearly killed me!" Assume further that the nurse who was treating Steve testifies at trial as to Steve's emergency room statement. Steve's statement is admissible (through the nurse) as an **excited utterance** because the statement relates to a startling event and was made while the declarant, Steve, was under stress and excitement.

The rationale for the excited utterance exception is reliability. In other words, when a person is under stress and excited about a recent event, it is less likely that he or she will fabricate the statement (*Ferrier v. Duckworth*, 1990). The excitement presumably increases the accuracy of the declarant's recollection of what happened. Also, because excited utterances are usually made in close temporal proximity to the event in question (the hit-and-run in our example), they are also less likely to be fabricated.

In the past, courts required that excited utterances "narrate, describe, or explain" the traumatic event; however, Rule 803(2) specifies that the statement merely "relate to" the event. What is an "exciting" event that can give rise to an excited utterance? The courts have not defined "exciting" qualities, but accidents and crimes usually qualify as exciting events. The excited utterance exception is two dimensional, meaning that it requires (1) that the exciting event caused the statement and (2) that the statement must have been made while the excitement from the event persisted. Finally, like the present sense impression exception, the excited utterance exception to the hearsay rule requires that the excited utterance be made in close temporal proximity to the event in question. In some cases, however, courts allow several hours to pass between the event and the excited utterance. The logic is that excitement can persist for a relatively long period of time after a traumatic event. Such statements, if not admissible under the excited utterance exception, will be admissible under the present sense impressions exception (see, for example, *United States v. Sowas*, 1994; *United States v. Golden*, 1982).

Then-existing mental, emotional, or physical condition. A statement of the declarant's then-existing state of mind is admissible to prove that state of mind regardless of whether the declarant is now available (rule 803[3]). In other words, statements that describe the declarant's mental, emotional, or physical condition at the time of the statement are admissible. For example, assume Sally testifies that she heard Lewis say, "John looks really tired," just before John fell asleep at the wheel of his eighteen-wheeler and jumped the median, killing a motorist traveling in the opposite direction. Sally's testimony is admissible because it is in reference to John's state of mind at the time of the crash (he was tired). The same applies to statements concerning physical condition. If Lewis had said, "Look, John is wearing a cast. I don't know how he thinks he can drive," this statement would also be admissible. In short, the "then existing mental, emotional, or physical condition" exception covers statements *about what a person was feeling at the time he or she spoke.*

The rationale for this exception to the hearsay rule is not only reliability, but necessity. Because such statements are made at or near the time of the event, there is little chance for inaccurate recollection. Also, because such statements are often made in situations where witnesses don't know that a crime has occurred, there is little incentive to fabricate a statement or to lie in order to ensure that the perpetrator will be convicted. Finally, because mental state is a requirement for most criminal offenses, unless the testifying witness knows of the defendant's mental state, it is often necessary to rely on the statements of third-party declarants to prove *mens rea.*

There are three exceptions to the hearsay rule that often get confused with the "then-existing mental, emotional, or physical condition" exception. First, do not confuse "then existing" with "past state of mind." The past state of mind exception requires unavailability of the declarant, which we cover later in this chapter. Second, do not confuse the "then-existing mental, emotional, or physical condition" exception with the use of the statement of one person to prove the state of mind of another who heard the statement (see "Effect on Hearer" above). Such exceptions are admissible because they are not offered for the truth of the matter asserted. Finally, this exception should not be confused with the nonhearsay use of the statement of the declarant together with extrinsic evidence as circumstantial evidence of the defendant's state of mind (see "Circumstantial Evidence of a Declarant's State of Mind" above).

A key restriction on the "then-existing mental, emotional, or physical condition" hearsay exception is that it does not permit statements of memory or belief. A statement of the declarant's memory or belief concerning if something is admissible is used only to prove that the declarant remembered or believed something; it cannot be used to prove the declarant's memory or belief. For example, to prove that the declarant went to the movies on a Friday, an out-of-court statement on Saturday by the declarant that "I went to the movies yesterday" would be excluded as hearsay to *prove* that the declarant went to the movies on Friday. This is because the statement amounts to the declarant's "past memory." Declarant's statement is admissible to prove that he or she believes that he or she went to the movie but not to *prove* that he or she went to the movie. However, had the declarant stated on Friday that "I will go to the movies on Saturday," the statement would be admissible because it does not speak to belief or memory of something that happened in the past. It is strange indeed that statements about what the declarant did or actually saw have less probative value that statements about what might occur (i.e., what a person's plans are), but the drafters of the Federal Rules of Evidence apparently believed that statements about past belief/memory are less reliable than statements about planned events.

What value is there in a statement of past belief to prove that the declarant believed something, not that what he or she believed was true? Consider one of the oft-cited hearsay dilemmas, a statement that "I am the king of Mars." A declarant's statement that "I am the king of Mars" is admissible under the "then existing mental, emotional, or physical condition" exception to the hearsay rule to prove that the declarant *believed* he was the king of Mars. Obviously, it is impossible (and unnecessary) to prove that the declarant is in fact the king of Mars.

Statements for medical diagnosis/treatment. A statement made for the purpose of medical diagnosis of the declarant or some other person is admissible, regardless of whether the declarant is available as a witness (Rule 803[4]). This exception to the hearsay rule recognizes two types of "medical diagnosis" statements. The first concerns medical history, symptoms, pains, and other sensations. The second concerns "pertinent causes," the sources of the patient's condition that are reasonably pertinent to the diagnosis or treatment. In other words, the exception's coverage extends to descriptions of what caused the patient's problems—not just the problems themselves—as long as the descriptions are relevant.

The primary rationale for this exception is reliability. The theory is that people have a high degree of self-interest in ensuring that they speak truthfully with their health-care practitioners concerning illness and injury; people desire to be cured. However, another rationale for the medical diagnosis exception is need. In some cases, such statements are necessary to provide a basis for a medical expert's testimony or to impeach that testimony.

Statements of medical diagnosis need not be made by the patient to fall within the exception. For example, if a parent or a guardian describes a child's condition to the doctor, the parent or guardian's statement will probably be admissible. This is true despite the fact that a parent's statement may be multiple hearsay (e.g., the parent tells a doctor that the child complained of a "stomach ache"). Another point of clarification concerning the medical diagnosis exception is that such statements can be made to intermediaries, including hospital attendants, ambulance drivers, nurses, and others, not just doctors. The exception can also apply to nontreating physicians. For example, if a plaintiff in a medical malpractice lawsuit describes a condition to a doctor hired to testify on her behalf, anything she says to the doctor concerning her medical condition will be admissible under the medical diagnosis exception.

Past recollection recorded. A recorded (written or recorded on audio) statement of a declarant may be read into evidence or played for the trier of fact, provided that a number of conditions are met (Rule

803[5]). First, the declarant has to be a witness in the case. Second, the statement has to concern a matter of which the declarant would have had personal knowledge. Third, this exception applies only if the declarant cannot remember the matter such that he or she can testify accurately (see *Vicksburg & Meridian Railroad Co. V. O'Brien*, 1886; *United States v. Felix-Jerez*, 1982). Fourth, the statement had to be made or "adopted" by the declarant when the event he or she was making a statement about was still fresh in his or her memory. Finally, the statement must be an accurate reflection of the knowledge of the witness/declarant at the time that it was made. Assume, for example, that Professor Paula witnessed a mugging at a bus stop. At the time of the crime, she jotted some notes down to herself concerning the description of the perpetrator (she knew, after all, that her profession renders her "absent-minded"). Paula testifies at trial that she cannot remember what the perpetrator looks like but that she has written notes describing the defendant. Her written statements are admissible, subject to the above restrictions.

The rationale for the "past recollection recorded" exception is necessity. If the witness can no longer remember the events in sufficient detail, it makes sense to admit a "recording" of the incident when no other evidence is available. To an extent, this exception is also justified by reliability. Even though the declarant does not remember the event in order to testify sufficiently at trial, his or her recollection of the event through a "recording" is probably better than any such "recording" provided by a third party.

A thorough understanding of this exception requires that one distinguish between past recollection recorded and past recollection *refreshed*. The distinction is a subtle, but important one. A past recollection refreshed occurs when a testifying witness examines something in court that refreshes his or her memory. For example, assume that Witness Forgetful looks at a police report and says, "Now I remember. The license plate on the hit-and-run truck was BADGUY." This is past recollection refreshed and is (1) not considered hearsay and (2) not subjected to the hearsay rule or any of its exceptions. Past recollection refreshed was discussed in Chapter 10. Only past recollections *recorded* constitute exceptions to the hearsay rule.

Another important restriction concerning the past recollections recorded exception is that such past statements are not introduced into evidence as exhibits. Past recordings cannot be introduced into evidence by the proponent. For example, if the plaintiff in a lawsuit wishes to introduce evidence of a past recording in order to support his testimony, he may not do so. The rationale for this restriction is that allowing proponents to introduce evidence of past recordings may result in them simply using this exception as a method of getting a record of important testimony before the jury. In other words, the jury may give more weight to the written words than to the oral testimony of the witness. Thus, the opponent is the only party that can introduce evidence of a past recollection recorded.

The business records exception. Statements recorded (again, in writing or by audio) as a matter of routine in the records of a regularly conducted business (or businesslike) activity are admissible, without regard to the availability of the declarant (Rule 803[6]). Four important restrictions govern this hearsay exception. The statement must have been recorded (1) during the regular course of business, (2) as a record of some event or condition, (3) at or near the time of the event or condition, and (4) by someone with personal knowledge of the event or condition. In addition to these four restrictions, the custodian of the record or other authorized witness must testify to or provide an affidavit showing that these four restrictions were met. Also, it needs to be shown that the sources of information and/or the method of preparation of the recording are trustworthy.

The justification for this exception includes both reliability and necessity. Businesses rely on their records for their operation, so it is highly likely that such records are reliable. Aside from being essential to the operation of a business, business records are also kept so that *people* do not need to remember every transaction or important occurrence. Without records being available, businesses would not be able to prove that transactions or events took place. In this sense, then, it is occasionally *necessary* for courts to rely on business records, even though they are considered hearsay.

There are several restrictions concerning the business records exception. First, such records must be in writing, although the Federal Rules of Evidence remain silent on the definition of "writing." Most modern statutes construe "writing" to include not just written documents, but audio and video recordings as well as photographs, movies, and computerized business records. Second, records associated with the "regular course" of business include those books and records that are regularly relied on in the operation of a business. These include records of receipts, orders, and so on. For example, assume that Harry Homicidal reserved a wood chipper at Acme Rentals. The record of his reservation would be admissible under the business records exception, assuming Acme regularly documents reservations in writing. Third, the definition of "business" in the business records exception is expansive. "Business" is not limited to commercial enterprises but includes government agencies, nonprofit organizations, and even criminal organizations. Virtually any record that is not purely personal falls within the business records exception. Fourth, the business record must be of an "act, condition, or event," otherwise it will not be admissible under the business records exception. However, Rule 803(6) now provides that even "opinions" and "diagnoses" are admissible under the business records exception.

Still other restrictions on the business records exception require elaboration. Fifth, the record must be made "at or near" the time of the event or act. For example, a receipt documenting a purchase at the time of the purchase would be admissible. A doctor's documented opinion about a patient's condition she diagnosed 10 years ago would probably not be admissible because the record was not made at the time of the diagnosis. Sixth, we stated that the exception applies only to people with personal knowledge of the event or condition. To clarify, the information recorded must first come from someone with personal knowledge, but his or her perception can be transmitted to and recorded by any employee authorized as part of a "business duty" to transmit such information. Unfortunately, in complex business operations, records are often transmitted through multiple parties, raising problems of multiple hearsay. To keep things as simple as possible, remember that "business duty" means that the statement must be part of a the person's job to make or record such statements. Statements that fall outside of a "business duty" (such as reports of witnesses at crime scenes) are not admissible under the business records exception.

Keep in mind the fact that business records can be admitted into evidence through other channels besides the business records exception. If, for example, a statement in a business record is offered not for the truth of the matter asserted but for another person (such as to show that the statement had an effect on the "hearer"), the record would be admissible. Such a statement would be *exempt* from the hearsay rule.

The official (public) records exception. A writing, statement, report, data compilation, or other record by a government agency (known as either "official" or "public") is admissible if it records (1) acts of the agency, (2) matters the agency is required to observe and report, and/or (3) factual findings of investigations (Rule 803[8]). Such writings are not admissible, however, if they include matters observed by police officers or are offered against the defendant. Also, such writings are not admissible if it turns out that the source of the information is not reliable and trustworthy. The official records exception bears striking resemblance to the business records exception previously discussed, but it operates differently and is easier to use. Official records need not be routinely maintained, and no custodian of the records or other witness is usually required to testify as to their authenticity.

Official records are not admissible in criminal proceedings against the defendant. Few people think prosecutors should use police reports prepared after the crime was committed as evidence against a defendant, because such reports are often based on outsider statements and are provided by people who themselves are implicated or involved in any number of ways in the crime. This is not to say that police reports are inaccurate—they probably are in most situations—but the material they contain, if offered alone to prove guilt, threaten the Sixth Amendment's confrontation clause. In other words, if people were convicted based on evidence supplied in a police officer's report, they would be denied their Sixth Amendment right to confront adverse witnesses and cross examine them as to the truthfulness of their statements.

Notwithstanding the problems associated with official records used to prove guilt, the rationale for the official records exception is generally reliability and necessity. By virtue of being in an official position or working in a public capacity, official/public records are assumed to be kept accurately. Also, because of the desire to allow public employees to continue working, it is often necessary to rely on the reports they prepare. For example, assume Passenger's surviving spouse sues Airline for negligence following a crash that occurred because of faulty maintenance. Investigator, who works for the NTSB, prepared a report, which was offered at trial. The official records exception ensures that Investigator can continue to go about her investigative duties while her report can be admitted at trial.

A source of controversy surrounding the official records exceptions concerns the extent to which prosecutors and others can evade the restrictions and limitations on the use of official records and instead rely on the business records exception. Many courts have said no, this cannot be done. However, given that there are several other exceptions (e.g., past recollection recorded), prosecutors have other possible channels through which they may be able to admit otherwise restricted official records. See Table 12-2 for a summary of this discussion.

Table 12-2 Admissibility of Public Records	
Type of Report	**Admissible By**
Activities of public office	Civil plaintiff & defendant; criminal prosecutor & defendant
Non-law enforcement reports/observations	Civil plaintiff & defendant; criminal prosecutor & defendant
Findings from official investigations	Civil plaintiff & defendant; criminal defendant only
Law enforcement observations/reports	Civil plaintiff & and defendant only

The vital statistics exception. Public records of vital statistics, including births, deaths, and marriages, are the subject of two separate hearsay exceptions in the Federal Rules of Evidence [Rule 803(9) and Rule 803(12)]. Such documents are usually made by people with an obligation to report and with no motive to lie. Thus, the rationale for exempting such records from the hearsay rule is reliability. Also, it would be difficult to obtain such records from other sources, so they are often necessary. As with the official records exception, the custodian of the records does not have to testify as to their authenticity; however, certified copies of vital statistics and similar records are usually required.

The "silent hound" exceptions. Rule 803(7) and 803(10) are known collectively as the "silent hound" exceptions. They are the mirror images of the business records and official records exceptions, respectively. Rule 803(7) says that the *absence* of records kept in accordance with the business records exception is admissible to prove the nonoccurrence or nonexistence of the matter. Similarly, rule 803(10) says that *absence* of records kept in accordance with the official records exception is admissible to prove the nonoccurrence or nonexistence of the matter. In one view, the absence of records can be considered nonhearsay, which does not fall within any particular hearsay exception. Even so, the framers of the Federal Rules of Evidence saw fit to state that the absence of records is exempt from the hearsay rule. Assume, for example, that Carol sues the local police department for negligently failing to respond to citizen complaints that were phoned in via the department's 800 number for complaint filing. She introduces evidence at trial that no records of complaints were kept by the agency. This failure to document complaints would fall under rule 803(10).

Miscellaneous hearsay exceptions. Several other less "popular" hearsay exceptions that do not require that the declarant be unavailable as a witness deserve a brief description.

Records of religious organizations, including statements of births, marriages, divorces, deaths, legitimacy, ancestry, relationship by blood or marriage, or other similar facts of personal or family history, are not bound by the hearsay rule (rule 803[11]). In certain proceedings, such as probate hearings or litigation, it is occasionally necessary to rely on church records. Church records are viewed with a high degree of reliability because the aura of "God" (or a similar deity) is thought to discourage fabrication. This exception also holds that the use of sacramental certificates issued by a person with ecclesiastical or governmental authority to administer the sacrament are admissible to prove facts contained in the certificate regarding the ritual and its participants.

Certain *family records and memorabilia* are also exempt from the hearsay rule (Rule 803 [12–13]). These include statements of fact concerning personal or family history contained in family Bibles, genealogies, charts, engravings on rings, inscriptions on family portraits, and engravings on urns, crypts, or tombstones and other items. The rationale for this exception is reliability. It is thought that statements concerning family history are likely to be accurate when they are made in places that are subject to inspection and are viewed as important. California law limits this exception to facts about family history of members of the family, but the Federal Rules of Evidence are silent on this issue.

Records of and statements in *documents affecting an interest in property* are admissible under yet another exception to the hearsay rule

(Rule 803 [14–15]). The most common type of record of an interest in property is a title (such as a car title). Additional documents such as deeds, mortgages, and wills also affect the ownership of property. The rationale for relying on such documents is reliability; given their "official" nature, they are given a high degree of deference. Also, it is frequently *necessary* to rely on such documents because the original may not be available. Instead, it is useful to prove transfer of title or ownership by the record of title documents filed with the appropriate public official. There are three requirements to this exception. First, the instrument must purport to establish or affect an interest in property. Second, the statement must be relevant to the purpose of the document. Finally, later dealings with the property cannot be inconsistent with the truth of the statement or purport of the document.

Another hearsay exception pertains to *statements in ancient documents* (Rule 803[16]). According to the Federal Rules of Evidence, statements in a document in existence for 20 years, the authenticity of which is established, are not bound by the hearsay rule. The rationale for this exception is twofold. First, it is occasionally necessary to rely on ancient documents because of the unlikelihood of finding a witness who recalls appropriate facts because of the passage of time. In some cases it may even be difficult to find any witness at all. The Federal Rules permit authentication of an ancient document by proof that it was found in a place and in such condition as would suggest its authenticity.

Market reports and commercial publications, including business publications, are exempt from the hearsay rule as well (Rule 803[17]). For example, a statement in a published document, such as stock market quotations, phone directories, real estate listings, or compilations of commodity sales, are admissible. A key restriction on this exception is that such documents must be relied upon by the public or by members of the same occupation. Thus, the rationale for permitting such documents is reliability; they are thought to be compiled by people with no motive to lie. Also, such documents are used by the public (or other members of the same occupation), so errors are likely to be discouraged and infrequent. Certain states place additional restrictions on this exception, including limiting reliance on business publication to other business, not the public, and excluding statements of opinion in such compilations.

Learned treatises are the subject of another hearsay exception (Rule 803[18]). This exception covers statements published in books, magazines, pamphlets and other such documents. However, the Federal Rules of Evidence require that (1) the reliability of the text be shown by the testimony of experts or judicial notice and (2) the statement(s) be called to the attention of an expert witness either on cross examination or relied on by the expert in direct examination. Statements falling within this exception can be introduced into evidence, but the publications in which they are found cannot. Furthermore, the rationale for this exception is the need to rely on an accumulated body of knowledge rather than "reinvent" knowledge whenever a particular fact is in dispute. Assume, for example, that Coffee Addict cannot afford to hire an expert witness to prove that when coffee is too hot, it burns. When Coffee Executive testifies that it is careless people who burn themselves, not the coffee, Addict reads an excerpt from a book called *The Perils of Hot Coffee* (a highly respected and reliable treatise) to the effect that coffee, when served too hot, burns people. The statement from the book is admissible under an exception to the hearsay rule.

There are also three hearsay exceptions concerning reputation. **Reputation** refers to what people think about someone. Three types of reputation evidence are admissible under the Federal Rules of Evidence.

First, *reputation evidence concerning personal or family history* is admissible (Rule 803[19]). This includes reputation among members of a person's family or among a person's associates or in the community as to a person's birth, adoption, marriage, divorce, death, legitimacy, or other similar fact of personal or family history. The reason for this is exception is that, in some cases, it is necessary to rely on the hearsay statements of others (besides in-court witnesses) to establish reputation.

Second, *reputation concerning character* can be admitted into evidence without regard to the declarant's availability (Rule 803[21]). However, character hearsay is limited to character in one's community or in a group of which he or she is a member. Moreover, hearsay statements concerning character are also bound by the rules governing the use of character evidence (see Chapter 10).

Third, *reputation evidence about boundaries* (community history) is also admissible without regard to the declarant's availability (Rule 803[20]). This exception is limited to statements about community history, geographic boundaries, and customs.

These three exceptions to the hearsay rule have in common the fact that they allow evidence of common repute (what people say about someone) to be offered as proof that things are just as people think, and it is not a necessary precondition that the declarant be unavailable to testify as a witness.

Finally, *evidence of past judgments* is not bound by the hearsay rule, (Rule 803[22–23]). These include criminal and civil judgments. With regard to past criminal convictions, evidence of past *felony* convictions is admissible to prove any consequential fact if (1) the judgment results from a trial or guilty plea (but not a plea of *nolo contendere)* and (2) if offered by the prosecution in a criminal case, the judgment involves the accused. Do not confuse this rule with what we discussed in Chapter 9 about witness credibility. Next, evidence from civil judgments is admissible to prove personal, family, or general history or boundaries if (1) the fact was a consequential fact essential to the judgment and (2) the fact is one of those described in the exceptions for reputation evidence of such history or boundaries.

Hearsay Exceptions Requiring 'Unavailability' of the Declarant

We now move into the second category of hearsay exceptions. The exceptions that follow can be used only if the declarant is dead or is otherwise "unavailable" to act as a witness. The reason for having a category of exception requiring the "unavailability" of the declarant is that necessity dictates the few exceptions that require it. These exceptions stem from FRE Rule 804(a).

The Federal Rules of Evidence go to great lengths to define "unavailable." Eight types of people are considered unavailable. The first includes *"privileged declarants."* According to Rule 804(a)(1), "a declarant is unavailable as a witness if a privilege could be asserted to prevent her from testifying about the facts asserted in her statement."

Second, a declarant is unavailable as a witness if he or she is ordered to testify about his or her out-of-court statements but refuses to do so (a so-called *contemptuous declarant*). Obviously, a declarant who refuses to testify cannot be considered available.

Third, *"forgetful declarants"* are considered unavailable. The forgetful person must actually testify that he or she cannot remember the facts of his or her out-of-court statement. People state that they have no memory in many instances, sometimes truthfully and sometimes to avoid testifying.

Fourth, *"defunct or infirm declarants"* are considered unavailable. This means that the person is dead or unable to appear because of a physical illness or infirmity. Death is, of course, the ultimate form of unavailability and is responsible in large part for the "dying declaration" exception discussed below.

Fifth, the Federal Rules consider unavailable "distant declarants." Distant declarants are those who are absent, beyond subpoena, and undeposable. An important requirement concerning distant declarants is that the proponent take reasonable steps to procure the witness's appearance and act diligently in so doing.

Sixth, *"incompetent declarants"* are considered unavailable. If a witness is not competent (see Chapter 9) with regard to an out-of-court statement, he or she will be considered unavailable. Recall that if a person cannot understand the duty to tell the truth and cannot narrate the events in question (or, in the case of hearsay, narrate his or her out-of-court statement), the person will be considered incompetent to act as a witness.

Seventh, *"vulnerable declarants,"* such as those who would likely suffer severe harm or trauma from testifying, can be considered unavailable. A problem with considering vulnerable declarants unavailable is that the Sixth Amendment's confrontation clause is compromised if the defendant does not have the opportunity to cross-examine the declarant.

Finally, the Federal Rules provide for a *"proponent procurement proviso."* This proviso states that a declarant is unavailable if (1) the grounds for the declarant's unavailability were caused by the proponent of the declarant's statement and (2) the causative act was intended to prevent the declarant from testifying. In other words, the hearsay exceptions that follow may not be used by a party who intentionally prevents the declarant from being present.

The former testimony exception. When a person is unavailable as a witness, his or her previous testimony can be admitted into evidence in the present trial subject to the following restrictions: (1) it was made under oath and subject to direct or cross examination, and (2) the former testimony was given in a prior trial, deposition, or similar judicial hearing (Rule 804[b][1]). And unless expressly required by law, the former testimony need not be proven by a transcript of the former proceeding.

An important restriction is the direct or cross-examination requirement. Assume that Jack has sued his insurance company to collect the insurance owed on his car that was stolen. Assume also that Jill testified at Jack's earlier trial for auto theft that Jack said, "I'm going to make it look like my car was stolen so I can collect the insurance money." If Jill is "unavailable" to testify in the civil trial, her testimony will be admissible, but only because Jack (through Jack's attorney) had an opportunity to cross examine Jill at the previous criminal trial. Had Jack not been able to cross examine Jill at the previous trial, her past testimony would not be admissible in the civil trial. Note that only the *opportunity* to cross examine (or directly examine) is required. Had Jack's attorney not cross examined Jill at Jack's criminal trial, her testimony would still be admissible in the civil trial because Jack had the opportunity to cross examine her.

Dying declarations. At common law, a dying declaration of a homicide victim was admissible against the murderer in a criminal prosecution. The rationale for the present-day version of this exception is reliability (there is no motive to lie right before one is about to die; see *Mattox v. United States,* 1892; *United Services Auto. Assn. v. Wharton,* 1965). Federal Rule of Evidence 804(b)(2) makes a dying declaration admissible as evidence if (1) the declarant is unavailable; (2) the declarant believed his or her death was imminent when the statement was made; (3) the statement concerns the cause and circumstances of the declarant's anticipated death; and (4) the statement is offered in a civil action or prosecution for homicide.

These four requirements may seem restrictive, but not when compared to California's evidence code. Section 1242 of the California Evidence Code makes a dying declaration admissible if (1) the declarant is dead; (2) the declarant was actually dying when the statement was made; (3) the declarant was under a sense of immediately impending death when the statement was made; (4) the statement concerned the cause and circumstances of the declarant's death; and (5) the declarant had personal knowledge of the matters stated. Unlike the Federal Rules of Evidence, California's dying declaration exception to the hearsay rule requires that the declarant actually be dead and was actually dying when the statement was made. The Federal Rules contain no such restrictions. Technically, under the federal rules a declarant can still be alive, but unavailable, for the dying declaration exception to apply. Note, however, that neither the Federal Rules or the California Evidence Code permit dying declarations to be admitted into evidence in any type of criminal proceeding other than a homicide trial.

Declarations against interest. A statement by an unavailable person (whether or not a party to the current proceedings) that, at the time it was made, would have been harmful to some interest of the declarant is admissible under another exception to the hearsay rule (Rule 804[b][3]). For example, assume Dealer is on trial for selling drugs to high school students. When a witness testified at trial that she had seen Dealer sell drugs in the cafeteria, Dealer cried out in the courtroom, "You liar! It was in the gym!" Assume further that the gym teacher is fired for having failed to intervene. If the gym teacher sues to challenge the firing, Dealer's statement would be admissible in the civil trial. The rationale for permitting this staement is, not surprisingly, reliability. A reasonable person would not make such a statement unless he or she believed it was true. Of course, for this exception to apply, the person making the statement knows that the statement is against his or her interest (see *Roberts v. Troy,* 1985).

A major source of confusion concerning this exception lies in its relationship to the exemption for party admissions. An admission must be a statement by a party, whereas a *declaration* can be made by any unavailable witness. Also, an admission does not require that the declarant be unavailable; a declaration against interest does. Moreover, an admission need not be against one's interest (it can be *in* one's interest), but a declaration against interest is always *against* the declarant's interest. Finally, an admission does not need to be based on personal knowledge; however, a declaration against interest must.

Determining whether a statement is against one's interest is not always easy (see Table 12-3 for some assistance in this regard). Some statements may "on their face" seem to be against interest when in fact they are not. Assume that the statement of a declarant places him at the scene of a misdemeanor. This may seem to be against the declarant's interest, but not if the declarant is also a suspect in a more serious crime. Some statements may be against one's interest but also in one's interest at the same time. For example, if a declarant says, "I have paid half the mortgage on my house," this statement is self-serving as far as payment goes but is against the declarant's interest as to the unpaid portion of the loan.

Table 12-3 **Admissions and Statements Against Interest Compared**	
Admission	**Statement Against Interest**
Can only be made by party in present case	Can be made by anyone
Declarant can be available or unavailable	Declarant must be unavailable
Is adverse to party's interest at trial	Is adverse to party's interest at or beyond trial
Is admissible against declarant or coconspirator	Is admissible against any party

An important restriction on the declaration against interest exception arises when the confession of an unavailable third person is used to exculpate a criminal defendant. The Federal Rules require that, in this situation, additional corroboration be offered to establish innocence. Assume that at his trial for first degree murder, Mike introduces an out-of-court statement from Henrietta, who is now unavailable, that she murdered the victim. This statement alone would not be enough for Mike to be found not guilty; additional evidence would be required. According to Rule 804(b)(3), "A statement tending to expose the declarant to criminal liability and offered to exculpate the accused is not admissible unless corroborating circumstances clearly indicate the trustworthiness of the statement."

Statements of family history. Statements of family history are admissible if (1) the declarant is unavailable and (2) the statement concerns the declarant's own family history (Rule 804[b][4]). "Family history" refers to the declarant's birth, adoption, marriage, ancestry, or other similar fact. For example, Susan claims that her late father Don was the son of Claude. Margie testifies that she was once told by Don that he was Claude's son. Don's statement, though hearsay, is admissible for the truth of its assertion. The rationale for this exception is reliability; one is unlikely to be mistaken about one's own history or about that of persons or families with whom one is associated.

Forfeiture by wrongdoing. A party forfeits the right to exclude hearsay if the party was involved in an act that wrongfully kept the declarant from being a witness at trial (Rule 804[b][6]). In other words, if a party wrongly prevents a person from testifying by bribing, intimidation, or killing, any statement that person ever made can be introduced against the party. Assume, for example, that Jean has the "dirt" on Larry, who has been charged with multiple counts of burglary. She has told her friend Cody all the details of Larry's criminal activities. She plans to testify against Larry at his criminal trial, but Larry promptly has her killed when he learns of her intent to testify. Unfortunately for Larry, Cody can testify about everything that Jean told him. Her statements are admissible not only because she is unavailable but because her death was a result of Larry's wrongdoing.

Past state of mind. Some states recognize a hearsay exception for statements of a prior mental or physical state if (1) the declarant is unavailable and (2) the physical or mental state involved in the statement is the consequential fact it is offered to prove. This exception should not be confused with the *then-existing* mental state exception discussed in the section on unrestricted hearsay exceptions. That exception prohibited statements of *past* mental state, but when the declarant is unavailable, statements concerning his or her past state of mind are admissible. The statement must, however, be trustworthy. Note also that the Federal Rules of Evidence do not recognize this exception.

The Residual (Catchall) Hearsay Exception

Another hearsay exception exists in the Federal Rules for statements that do not fit any of the aforementioned exceptions (see Rule 807). There are six requirements for applying the catchall exception. The statement must (1) not be covered by one of the existing, enumerated exceptions; (2) have equivalent circumstantial guarantees of trustworthiness to the enumerated exceptions; (3) be offered as evidence of a material fact; (4) be more probative than other evidence its proponent can with reasonable diligence procure; and (5) serve the general purposes of the rules and the interests of justice. Additionally, proper advance notice and opportunity to meet must also be provided.

Assume that an investigative reporter wrote a series of articles exposing abuse of force in the local police department. The articles gave hypothetical names for the officers involved, but the stories were based on observations the writer made after having been hired to work as a janitor at the stationhouse. An alleged victim of excessive force sues the department for damages. To bolster his case, the victim seeks to introduce one of the newspaper articles, along with the notes the writer made that gave the real names of the officers involved. Assume also that (1) the writer has died of natural causes since writing the articles, (2) that the articles were written only two years prior to the lawsuit (so the ancient documents exception doesn't apply), and (3) that a period of several months had elapsed between the abuse of force and the reporter's note-taking (so the business records exception doesn't apply). What exception, if any, applies?

Rule 807, the residual exception, may apply in our example. The proponent (the plaintiff in our example) would have to give notice to the defendant of the intention to introduce the notes and article and would have to establish that they are trustworthy. With regard to trustworthiness, it is reasonable to assume that reporters have an obligation to report the truth, so their notes are probably reliable. Next, the evidence in the notes and the articles would have to be more probative in terms of revealing excessive force than other evidence that could be procured through reasonable effort. Assuming that notes and articles are all that is available, they may be admissible under the residual exception.

Hearsay Procedure

It is easy to get caught up in the complexity of hearsay definitions, exemptions, and exceptions. Hearsay, however, is subject to all the usual metarules of evidence. First, if no objection is made, the hearsay statement(s) may be admitted and given the same weight by the jury as testimony by an in-court witness. Hearsay, though perhaps relevant, may be excluded if its probative value is substantially outweighed by the danger of prejudice. Also, if the statement is confusing or a waste of time, the judge has the discretion to exclude it.

When hearsay is admitted, the declarant is basically treated as a witness for the purpose of impeachment. This means that evidence of felony convictions and evidence of character can be used to impeach the declarant. Also, it means that the opposing party can call the declarant to the stand and cross examine, provided that he or she is available. Of course, the declarant can also be "rehabilitated" by the proponent.

Practice Pointer 12-2

Hearsay statements are generally considered inadmissible at trial, except for the various exemptions and exceptions discussed throughout the this chapter. But if there is no objection to a hearsay statement, the statement could be admitted. Therefore, prosecutors and defense attorneys should be on the lookout for hearsay statements.

Summary

The general rule is that hearsay is not admissible in court. In some situations, however, hearsay is admissible. If a statement is made out of court and is offered for the truth of the matter asserted, it may be admissible, provided that the statement is trustworthy and comes from a reliable declarant.

To recap, there are three specific steps that should be taken when analyzing a potential hearsay problem. First, identify the "statement." While this may seem easy, it often is not. The statement may not be an actual quotation, or even a declarative sentence. Instead, the statement may actually consist of some nonverbal act. When a nonverbal act is the statement, convert the nonverbal act into a statement. For example, if Harry swung a baseball bat at his lawnmower, one can safely conclude that his "statement" was, "I've had it with this lawnmower!"

The next step in the hearsay analysis is to identify the declarant as well as the time or place he or she made the statement. In our example from the previous paragraph, the declarant is obviously Harry. The determination may be considerably more complicated, however, if several people were present and engaged in similar nonverbal acts (or were making similar statements). The time frame of the statement is important, too. If the statement was made at a prior trial or a similar hearing, it is not hearsay because it was not made "out of court."

The third step is to analyze the content of the statement—that is, to identify the consequential fact it is offered to prove. If the statement is not offered for the truth of the matter asserted, then it is not hearsay. A hearsay statement to the effect that "I will take great pleasure in seeing you die from the gunshot wound I will inflict" would obviously be offered for the truth of the matter it asserts (that one person killed or planned to kill another), but a statement to the effect that "little green men are going to kill me" would not be offered for the truth it asserts but perhaps to demonstrate that the declarant was not of sound mind when the statement was made.

Discussion Questions

1. In what way does the Sixth Amendment govern the hearsay rule?

2. What are the four requirements that must be satisfied for testimonial evidence to be relevant?

3. What are the risks concerning hearsay? Briefly explain each one.

4. Explain and give an example of a nonverbal statement. Why are these statements troublesome?

5. What is the difference between hearsay exceptions and hearsay exemptions?

6. What is an admission by conduct?

7. Explain how a statement made by an agent, servant, or employee of a person may be exempt from the hearsay rule. What is the one qualifier that must be in place in order for the statement to be accepted by the court?

8. What is a "dying declaration"? What do the Federal Rules of Evidence say about dying declarations? What does California say?

9. Explain "present sense impressions."

10. What is the rationale for the "excited utterances" exception?

Further Reading

Choo, A. L. T. (1996). *Hearsay and Confrontation in Criminal Trials*. NY, Oxford University Press.

Coady, C. A. J. (1992). *Testimony: A Philosophical Study*. NY, Oxford University Press.

Friedman, R. D. (2002). "The Conundrum of Children, Confrontation, and Hearsay." *Law and Contemp. Problems* 65:243.

Holland, B. (2002). "Using Excited Utterances to Prosecute Domestic Violence in New York: The Door Opens Wide, or Just a Crack?" *Cardozo Women's L.J.* 8:171.

Kirgis, P. F. (2001). "Meaning, Intention, and the Hearsay Rule." *Wm. And Mary L. Rev.* 43:275.

Mueller, C. B. and L. C Kirkpatrick. (1999). *Evidence* (2nd ed.). New York: Aspen.

Rakos, R. F. and S. Landsman. (1992). "The Hearsay Rule as the Focus of Empirical Investigation." *Minn. L. Rev.* 76:655.

Cases Cited

Anderson v. United States, 417 U.S. 211 (1974)

Barber v. Page, 390 U.S 719 (1968)

Bruton v. United States, 391 U.S 123 (1968)

California v. Green, 399 U.S 149 (1970)

Coy v. Iowa, 487 U.S 1012 (1988)

Douglas v. Alabama, 380 U.S. 415 (1965)

Doyle v. Ohio, 426 U.S. 610 (1976)

Dutton v. Evans, 400 U.S. 74 (1970)

Ferrier v. Duckworth, 902 F.2d 545 (7th Cir. 1990)

Krist v. Eli Lilly & Co., 897 F.2d 293 (7th Cir. 1990)

Maryland v. Craig, 497 U.S 836 (1990)

Mattox v. United States, 146 U.S. 140 (1892)

Mima Queen and Child v. Hepburn, 7 U.S. 290 (1813)

Miranda v. Arizona, 384 U.S. 436 (1966)

Nuttal v. Reading Co., 235 F.2d 546 (3rd Cir. 1956)

Pointer v. Texas, 380 U.S 400 (1965)
Roberts v. Troy, 773 F.2d 720 (6th Cir. 1985)
Tamez v. City of San Marcos, Texas, 118 F.3d 1085 (5th Cir. 1997)
United Services Auto. Assn. v. Wharton, 237 F.Supp. (W.D.N.C. 1965)
United States v. Abou-Saada, 785 F.2d 1 (1st Cir. 1986)
United States v. Evans, 438 F.2d 162 (D.C. Cir. 1971)
United States v. Felix-Jerez, 667 F.2d 1297 (9th Cir. 1982)
United States v. Golden, 671 F.2d 369 (10th Cir. 1982)
United States v. Hallman, 439 F.2d 603 (D.C. Cir. 1971)
United States v. Matlock, 109 F.3d 1319 (8th Cir. 1997)
United States v. Nixon, 418 U.S. 683 (1974)
United States v. Ross, 321 F.2d 61 (2nd Cir. 1963)
United States v. Seelig, 622 F.2d 207 (6th Cir. 1980)
United States v. Simmons, 923 F.2d 934 (2nd Cir. 1991)
United States v. Singer, 687 F.2d 1135 (8th Cir. 1982)
United States v. Sowas, 34 F.3d 447 (6th Cir. 1994)
Vicksburg & Meridian Railroad Co. v. O'Brien, 119 U.S. 99 (1886) ✦

Chapter Thirteen

How Different Types of Evidence Are Introduced

Key Terms

- Attestation
- Authentication
- Best evidence rule
- Competent evidence
- Demonstrative evidence
- Documentary evidence
- Duplicate
- Execution
- Inscribed chatells

- Legally operative conduct
- Material evidence
- Original
- Profiles
- Real/physical evidence
- Relevancy
- Secondary evidence
- Syndrome
- Writing

Introduction

There are three broad types of evidence: (1) testimonial evidence, (2) documentary evidence, and (3) real/physical evidence. We have already focused in detail on testimonial evidence; this chapter considers the other two forms of evidence. **Documentary evidence** consists of documents and writings. **Real/physical evidence** (the terms will be used synonymously from here on out) consists of actual tangible items that can be displayed. Think of it this way: anything that is not testimonial or documentary is probably real/physical.

Indeed, there are several types of physical evidence. We will focus on three in this chapter. First, we will focus on the usual types of physical evidence, including displays of items used in crimes, photographs, sound recordings, and so on. Next, we will focus on demonstrative evidence. The term *demonstrative* refers to a demonstration, typically using physical evidence (such as a crime scene reconstruction) to demonstrate a point. The third type of real evidence consists of that resulting from scientific experiments and procedures. These include DNA analysis, mental diagnoses, and the like.

Before we delve into the rules concerning demonstrative, scientific, and real evidence we focus on two important admissibility tests: the authentication test and the best evidence test. For documentary or real evidence to be admissible, it must be authenticated and it must be the best possible evidence (the original, for instance, in the case of documentary evidence).

We do not devote a special section to documentary evidence. Instead our discussion of documentary evidence is woven into the authentication and best evidence rule sections. The reason for doing so is that authentication and the best evidence rule most frequently apply in the documentary context. However, as we will see, real/physical evidence often needs to be authenticated and can be bound by the best evidence rule.

Authentication

Authentication means "the introduction of evidence sufficient to sustain a finding that [an object or document] is the [object or document] that the proponent of the evidence claims it is" (FRE Rule 901[a]). In other words, only authentic evidence, as opposed to a fake or fabrication, is admissible.

At common law the authentication requirement was limited strictly to writings. To this day many evidence texts discuss authentication only as it applies to documentary evidence. Modern evidence statutes, however, have expanded the authentication requirement to include not only all writings but also all evidence related to proving some point. Rule 901(a) attests that authentication is a prerequisite to admissibility to ensure that the "matter in question is what the proponent claims." Similarly, California's Evidence Code defines "writing" to include such things as photographs, comput-

Why must physical evidence be authenticated?

erized records, and similar items.

There are several keys to understanding the authentication process. First, it is important to understand that authentication is required only when the proponent (the person seeking to introduce evidence) wants to prove a point. For example, if a witness testifies that "I called Bob's Automotive and Bob told me that the price to repair my transmission was $1,400," the proponent will be required to prove that Bob spoke to the witness. In other words, the proponent will be required to authenticate the phone call in order to prove that Bob in fact answered the phone. If, however, the witness testifies that the "person on the other end of the phone line told me . . . ," authentication is not required. Thus, it may behoove the proponent to minimize what needs authentication, as doing so could prove difficult.

The second key to understanding authentication is to realize that it is not required when it serves little purpose. For example, if the proponent seeks to introduce a photograph into evidence, the photographer who took the picture is not needed to authenticate the picture. Similarly, other representations such as maps do not require authentication; it makes little sense to call the mapmaker to authenticate the map. However, if something in the photograph or map (or similar item) is in dispute, authentication may be required. If it is argued, for instance, that a photograph is a fabrication, authentication may be required. On that note, the process of authentication sometimes includes nonauthentication. If the proponent (or opponent) seeks to prove that "the photograph is a fake," proof of its "inauthenticity" will be required.

Yet another key to understanding authentication is that it is analogous to conditional relevancy. Items are *conditionally relevant* when they give the jury the responsibility of determining whether a fact has been proven. In other words, authentication is a preliminary fact that is determined by the jury, not the judge. This means that the proponent does not need to satisfy the court that the document (or item) is authentic. Instead, the proponent need only introduce sufficient evidence that a "reasonable juror" could find that the matter is authentic.

That authentication is needed only to appease the jury is sometimes controversial and confusing. This is because it is possible for both parties to a case to authenticate two (perhaps conflicting) items as the true ones. In a contract case, for example, one proponent could seek to authenticate a contract specifying that Ace's Air Conditioning would do the work for free, while the other proponent could seek to authenticate a similar contract specifying that Ace's Air Conditioning would do the work for $200. In such a situation it would be up to the jury to decide which contract was authentic.

Finally, the best way to understand the authentication process is to compare it to the process for establishing relevance. In general, authentication is a higher hurdle to clear than that of relevancy. FRE

Rule 401 provides that evidence is relevant if it has a "tendency" to prove a fact in issue. For example, a letter with what seems to be university letterhead and a professor's signature has a "tendency" to prove that the letter was written by a professor. Authentication, however, will require something more—namely, that the letter was written by a professor. It is entirely possible in this example that someone else (perhaps a student) acquired some university letterhead and forged a professor's signature at the end of the letter.

How, then, is evidence authenticated? Rule 901 lists several examples of how evidence is authenticated. As Rule 901 attests, though, this list is *not exhaustive*.

1. *Testimony of a witness with knowledge.* A witness can testify, for example, "that is my signature on the letter."

2. *Nonexpert opinion on handwriting.* A witness can testify that "I believe the signature on that letter is that of my spouse."

3. *Comparison by trier or expert witness to previously authenticated document.* An expert witness could testify that in her opinion the handwriting exemplar before her was written by the same person who presumably wrote a previously authenticated document (e.g., one authenticated earlier in the trial).

4. *Distinctive characteristics.* A writing can be authenticated by its "[a]ppearance, contents, substance, internal patterns, or other distinctive characteristics."

5. *Voice identification.* A witness may testify that the voice on a certain recording is that of a particular person.

6. *Outgoing telephone conversations.* Authentication may be required if a witness claims that he called a particular business. In one case *United States v. Portsmouth Paving Corp.* (1982), testimony by *R* that he 'called Mr. Saunders' office" was sufficient to "authenticate the occurrence of the telephone call in accordance with the standard illustrated by rule 901 . . . "

7. *Public records or reports.* Certain documents can be authenticated by showing that they are from the public office where items of a similar type are normally kept. For example, in *United States v. Wilson* (1982), a receipt for a federal prisoner "signed by the director" and "identified by her at trial" was properly authenticated.

8. *Ancient documents or data compilations.* The authentication requirement can also be satisfied when, according to Rule 901(b)(8), evidence that a document or data compilation, in

any form, is in such condition as to create no suspicion concerning its authenticity, was in a place where it, if authentic, would likely be, and has been in existence 20 years or more at the time it is offered. A witness could testify, for instance, that he found the document inside an Egyptian pyramid, and the authentication requirement would be satisfied.

9. *Process or system.* This example often applies to tape recordings. The case of *United States v. Lance* (1988) is illustrative. Tapes consisting of voice recordings were "adequately authenticated" by testimony . . . that they "contained accurate recordings of the conversations that occurred."

10. *Methods provided by statute or rule.* This is the residual category. Statutes and/or court decisions providing for other forms of authentication must be recognized.

We now turn to some of these methods of authentication in some more detail. We divide the remainder of our discussion concerning authentication into three categories: authentication of documents; authentication of objects, and authentication of voices. We will conclude with a discussion of self-authentication.

Authentication of Documents

Documents are most often authenticated by direct evidence—that is, by someone who has personal knowledge of the document's authenticity. If a person saw a document written by another, then that person can serve as a witness testifying to the document's authenticity. Documents can also be authenticated by lay or expert witness opinion. A lay witness familiar with the handwriting of the supposed author can testify in his or her opinion that a document was written by the author. Familiarity with the author's handwriting can come from having seen the author write other documents, from having received letters from the author, or by similar means. Experts can also authenticate documents; however, they need not necessarily see the document being written by the supposed author (or even be familiar with the supposed author's handwriting). Instead, experts can testify to a document's authenticity by comparing the document to another document. This method assumes, though, that the document used as a base of comparison has itself been authenticated. Other sophisticated techniques (such as by using computer technology or ink analysis) can also be used to authenticate documents.

Next, documents can be authenticated by circumstantial evidence. First, a document can be authenticated by evidence that it was received in response to a communication sent to its supposed author. Second, a writing can be authenticated by evidence that it states facts that are unlikely to be known to anyone but its supposed author. Third, a document can be authenticated by admission—that is, by evidence that the adversary admitted it was authentic or behaved as if it was such. For example, if in a letter between two co-conspirators X tells Y to run like hell, and Y then runs like hell the letter will be authenticated if evidence is offered that Y ran like hell. Fourth, documents can be authenticated by custody. If the document is filed or recorded in a public office authorized to file such a record and the document is obtained from said office it will be authenticated.

There are countless other ways to authenticate documents. Understand that the methods for authentication discussed in the Federal Rules of Evidence (and in other evidence codes) are not exhaustive. Any relevant evidence that would lead a reasonable juror to conclude that a document is authentic will suffice.

Authentication of Objects

The rules for the authentication of objects are essentially the same as those for documents, except it is important to take into account the differences between objects and writings. An expert in electric guitars, for instance, can testify that the guitar in question is not an 1957 American-made Stratocaster but rather a cheaper imported version of the same guitar. As with documents, the expert may testify that in his or her opinion the guitar is not a '57. The expert would then point to unique features of a '57 Stratocaster, not to writing samples.

There are additional means for authenticating objects besides having to rely on expert opinion. For example, witnesses with knowledge can testify that objects are authentic. Mary's fiancé Craig could testify that Mary's diamond is real because Craig was with her when she bought the stone from a reputable jeweler. Or, a witness could testify that the bicycle the defendant was riding when he was arrested is hers because it has a driver's license number inscribed on the frame that is the same number as on the witness's driver's license.

Authentication of Voices

Voices can be authenticated in ways similar for those of objects or documents. First, a person with knowledge of another's voice can testify concerning that person's voice. For example, if X works for Y and is in regular communication with him, X can testify that the voice on a tape recording making death threats to the president sounds like Y's voice because she has become familiar with Y's voice.

Different rules apply in the case of telephone calls. A telephone conversation with a person can be authenticated if the caller testifies (1) that he or she called the number listed in the phone book for the person called or (2) the person on the other end identified himself or herself as the one called. The same applies to business, with one added exception: If the call is related to business that normally takes place over the phone, testimony that the call took place will authenticate the call.

Self-Authentication

The Federal Rules of Evidence (Rule 902) create a category of self-authenticating documents. Such documents require no extrinsic evidence, such as witness testimony, as to their authenticity. They are deemed authentic on their face, or at first glance. No such rule existed at common law.

Here are some examples of self-authenticating documents.

1. *Sealed writings.* If a document has the apparent seal of a state or federal governmental entity or official, it is self-authenticating. In addition to a seal, however, the document must bear "a signature purporting to be an attestation or execution." **Execution** means that the document was written or adopted by the signer; **attestation** means that the signer examined the document after the fact and found it to be a genuine document or public record. A college diploma, for example, contains at least one signature (usually of the college president) "attesting" that the person named on the diploma satisfied certain requirements and has graduated.

2. *Public documents.* Unsealed public documents are also self-authenticating. However, the document must be signed by an officer or employee of the public agency *and* bear a sealed attestation that the signature is genuine. In other words, there will be one signature followed by a second signature (usually by another individual higher up in the chain of command) verifying that the first individual's signature is genuine.

3. *Diplomatic documents.* A foreign public document is self-authenticating if it satisfies three requirements: (a) it must be executed or attested to by someone authorized to do so; (b) the person's authority is certified; and (c) the validity of the document is then certified by a U.S. diplomatic officer. The last requirement can be abandoned, however, if there is good cause to do so. The court will make this determination.

4. *Certified copies of public records.* A certified copy of a public record or a recorded and filed private document is self-authenticating, but it must (a) be certified as a correct copy by the custodian of the original and (b) comply with applicable rules. Copies are acceptable under certain circumstances

because of the difficulty (or impossibility) of obtaining the original document.

5. *Official publications.* Any publication issued by a public authority is self-authenticating. It is not always clear, however, what constitutes a "public authority." Further, such documents may be excludable on hearsay grounds. Nevertheless, the reason for allowing official publications to be self-authenticating is that forgery or misrepresentation of such publications is unlikely.

6. *Newspapers and periodicals.* Any newspaper or periodical is self-authenticating. The newspaper or periodical need not be popular, well known, or widely circulated. The only requirement is that it appear with some regularity. The reason for the self-authentication of newspapers and periodicals is that falsification or forgery is unlikely. Most such sources have distinctive layouts, logos, and other characteristics, making misrepresentation a difficult task indeed.

7. *Trade inscriptions.* A tag or label on a commercial product is sufficient to authenticate the product as that of its source. The tag or label must appear to have been affixed during the course of business *and* the tag or label must appear to indicate ownership, control, or origin. A painting of a bottle of Coca-Cola would not be self-authenticating because the label indicated in the painting would not have been "affixed" during the normal course of business and, as such, would not be self-authenticating.

8. *Acknowledged documents.* This term applies most frequently to documents bearing the seal of a notary. A writing is self-authenticated if the author of the writing acknowledges it is genuine before an authorized notary public. The reason for allowing notarized documents to be self-authenticating is that notaries are legally obligated to take reasonable steps to ensure the true identity of the person who appears before him or her.

9. *Statutory authenticity.* Finally, a document will be self-authenticating if the provision of the Uniform Commercial Code or similar statute so provides. Several federal statutes provide for the self-authentication of documents, some of which include legislative records, records of judicial proceedings, documents filed with federal agencies, published statutes, tax returns, and so forth.

Best Evidence Rule

The **best evidence rule** is also sometimes called the "documentary originals" rule. It is a rule of preference requiring that when the contents of a writing are at issue, the contents should be proved by the original writing and not by secondary evidence. In other words, the original writing is preferable unless it is not easily obtainable. The best evidence rules actually amounts to several rules listed in the Federal Rules of Evidence, specifically Rules 1001–1008.

What is the purpose of the best evidence rule?

The preference for original documents arises in two circumstances. First, as indicated, an original writing is desirable when the contents of a copy are in dispute. That is, if one party argues that a copy is not the same as an original, it is preferable to obtain the original for purposes of comparison. Second, original documents are preferable when witnesses are asked to recall the contents of such documents.

The logic for the best evidence rule is efficiency. It would be a waste of time to draw on secondary evidence to determine whether the contents of a document are identical to the original or whether a witness adequately recalls the contents of an original document. When the original is obtainable, the question as to recollection or contents can be easily resolved.

The Best Evidence Rule Is Not Authentication

The best evidence rule is separate and distinct from the authentication process. A simple way to distinguish between "best evidence" and authentication is to think in terms of the oft-cited metaphor of the forest and the trees. Authentication concerns the forest: Is the writing an original or is the evidence in question genuine? Or, equivalently, is the evidence what its proponent says it is? The best evidence rule, by contrast, concerns the trees: Are the contents of a writing the same as those found in the original?

It is possible for the best evidence rule to apply in a case and also require authentication. If the concern is with the "forest," not the trees, the best evidence rule will not apply. Alternatively, if the concern is with the trees and not the forest (say, for instance, the document is self-authenticating), authentication will not be required. The forest-trees metaphor may be somewhat crude, but it is designed to emphasize that the distinction between the best evidence rule and authentication is really one of priority and preference; whether both doctrines apply depends on what is at issue in a case.

Another way to understand the difference between authentication and best evidence is to note that the former determines whether a document or writing is an original or a copy, whereas the latter determines whether the document or writing *has to* be an original or a copy. Authentication asks if the evidence is an original or a copy. The best evidence rule asks if the evidence needs to be an original, or if a copy can suffice.

Best Evidence and Hearsay Distinguished

The best evidence rule focuses on the accuracy of the contents of writings submitted to the trier of fact. The hearsay rule, by contrast, concerns the truth or falsity of those contents. Both hearsay and best evidence problems can be raised in the same case. If a writing is offered to prove the truth of its contents, hearsay objections may be raised and the best evidence rule implicated. However, if the truth of a writing's contents are not at issue, only the existence of such contents, then hearsay problems are circumvented. If, for example, a witness testifies that the marriage is invalid because there was never an official marriage certificate and a second witness produces the marriage certificate, hearsay concerns are not raised because the truth or falsity of what is contained in the marriage certificate is not at issue. In all likelihood, the best evidence rule will not apply either. This is because of the "memorialized and recorded transactions" exception discussed below.

Definitions

So far we have been referring to documents as though they are the same as writings. This is not always the case. A **writing,** as far as the best evidence rules is concerned, includes "every means of recording upon any tangible thing any form of communication or representation" (CEC. Section 250).

California's Evidence Code states that the means of recording include handwriting, typewriting, photostating, and photographing. The Federal Rules of Evidence (Rule 1001[1]) extends this list to include "magnetic impulse, mechanical or electronic recording or other forms of data compilation."

The forms of communication or representation listed in modern evidence codes are several. They include "letters, words, numbers or their equivalent," according to the Federal Rules of Evidence. California's Evidence Code adds "pictures, sounds, or symbols, or combinations thereof" to the list of possible communications or representations.

The definition of **original** as it pertains to the best evidence rule is "the writing itself or recording itself or any counterpart intended to have the same effect by a person executing or issuing it" (FRE 1001[3]); CEC Section 255). An "original" of a photograph "includes the negative or any print therefrom." As for computers, any printout or other readable output from a computer is an "original."

As we have seen, originals are preferable in place of "secondary evidence" to prove the contents of a writing. **Secondary evidence** in this case refers to any evidence of the contents of a writing other than the original. If, for instance, a witness testifies as to the terms of a contract, this is secondary evidence. The original contract would of course be the original. The Federal Rules of Evidence mention "other evidence," not "secondary evidence." This seems to indicate that circumstantial evidence could even be used to prove the contents of a writing if the original is unobtainable.

Rule 1001(4) recognizes that a **duplicate** can occasionally serve in place of an original. "A 'duplicate' is a counterpart produced by the same impression as the original, or from the same matrix, or by means of photography, including enlargements and miniatures, or by mechanical or electronic rerecording, or by chemical reproduction, or by other equivalent technique which accurately reproduces the original." An "impression" can be a carbon copy. "Matrix" refers to an impression from, for example, a printing plate, mimeograph stencil, or similar device. Photographs of originals can suffice, as can photographic enlargements (blown up pictures) or miniatures (such as microfilm). "Rerecordings" include, but are not limited to, digital cleaning up of recordings from informants. The rules do not define "chemical" copies, and several other unmentioned techniques can be properly relied upon.

The Rule in Operation

The purpose of the best evidence rule is to prove *content*. This is why the rule does not apply to other *physical* evidence. It does not require, for instance, that a party produce the best physical evidence (e.g., the murder weapon instead of the defendant's hair sample found at the scene of the murder). Only when the contents of writings (which now seems to include photographs and recordings), are in dispute does the rule apply. If the contents of such evidence are *not* in dispute, the rule will not apply.

In the following subsections we briefly describe situations in which the best evidence rule does and does not apply. The rule applies, as indicated, when the content of a writing is at issue. In the remaining situations—legally operative conduct and the like—the rule usually does not apply, although there are exceptions (e.g., for testimony about written rules).

Proving content. If the party seeks to use writings, recordings, or photographs to prove other matters besides content, doing so does not violate the best evidence rule. For example, if a party seeks to prove that John owned a car by introducing a copy of a car title with John's name on it, the rule does not apply. In such an instance the original title is not required because the content of the title is not at issue. If, however, one party argues that the title is in fact a fraud, the original would be required.

The rule also does not apply when writings serve as the basis for expert opinion. If an expert refers to a scholarly study as the basis for her opinion, the best evidence rule is not triggered. However, if the expert dwells considerably on the content of the study and the contents come into dispute, an original may be required. In such a situation a copy of the original will suffice regardless.

These examples notwithstanding, it is often difficult to determine when someone is attempting to "prove the content" of a writing. A safe rule of thumb for making this determination is whenever the jury is required to decide or infer that the writing contains a particular statement, the best evidence rule applies.

Legally operative conduct. The best evidence rule also applies when a writing is **legally operative conduct.** This term applies to words that affect the legal relationship of the parties. Most often, "legally operative conduct" consists of words in written contracts. If, for example, two parties enter into a written contract and one party sues the other for breach of contract, the best evidence rule applies.

Matters incidentally recorded. Sometimes statements asserted in writings, recordings, or photographs are "incidental"—that is, not purposeful. For example, assume two customers in a bank teller's line get in a verbal altercation, which then leads to a physical fight over their position in line. Because banks record virtually every event that takes place inside their premises, a recording capturing the fight would be incidental. In other words, the recording was not set up to capture the fight. Instead, it just so happens that the fight was recorded on videotape.

The rule governing these types of recordings is that an original is not required. Indeed, simple testimony from witnesses that the fight took place (or from the victims) could suffice. The videotape of the fight is not considered "best evidence" because it caught the fight by chance. This does not mean, of course, that the video would not be introduced as evidence in addition to witness testimony, only that the best evidence rule does not apply to matters incidentally recorded.

Memorialized and recorded transactions. A party can prove a nonwritten transaction that is memorialized in writing without producing the original writing. Ownership of property can be shown without having to produce a title. Proof of a person's employment or income level need not be accompanied by written proof of employment. A party can show that he or she is married without having to produce the marriage license. Courts even permit testimony that dealers are licensed without requiring that they always produce their licenses, and proof that goods cost a particular amount can be offered with testimony, not the original receipt. All such transactions (and countless others) are "memorialized" in writing and are not bound by the best evidence rule. As before, however, if the contents of the writings memorializing such transactions are in dispute, originals may have to be produced.

Witnesses can testify to facts or events of which there is a record without producing the record. For example, police officers can testify to a defendant's confession without producing the tape on which the confession was recorded. Witnesses can testify to the former testimony of a person without producing a transcript of the earlier testimony. Witnesses of car accidents, crimes, and other violent events can testify to what they saw without producing photographs taken at the scene. Witnesses can testify as to what occurs in meetings without having to produce the transcripts from such meetings. Recorded transactions are similar to memorialized transactions; however, the former are recorded whereas the latter are often documented in written form.

Testimony about rules. Usually a witness cannot testify about the contents of written rules without producing those rules. For example, in *Conway v. Consolidated Rail Corp.* (1983) a conductor's proposed testimony that he did not "have any authority to stop a passenger from boarding a train with a footlocker" was properly excluded as not best evidence. However, in situations where a writing records preexisting rules, such as with an employee's copy of the rules, the original will not need to be provided. Further, in situations where rules are oral rather than written, originals need not be provided. This was illustrated in the case of *Hood v. Itawamba County, Miss.* (1993). There, testimony concerning a sheriff's policy of dealing with detainees with mental problems was properly admitted where the actual policies were oral instead of written.

Admissibility of duplicates. Duplicates of originals are admissible unless one of two things occur. First, if the authenticity of the duplicate is questioned, the original should be produced if it is obtainable. Second, if it would be unfair to admit a duplicate writing in lieu of the original, then the latter should be produced. If, for example, a duplicate does not bear all of the elements of the original, admission of the duplicate may result on an unfair outcome for a party to the case.

Special problems. Some confusion exists concerning the relationship between the best evidence rule and so-called inscribed chattels. **Inscribed chattels** include badges, logos on automobiles, and the like. What if, for instance, the plaintiff in a civil rights action argues that the person who assaulted her stepped out of an automobile bearing the inscription "to protect and serve" and was wearing a badge with the name Smiley? Should the plaintiff in this instance be required to produce the car or the badge? Most courts would probably say the best evidence rule does not apply, but a literal interpretation of the best evidence rule may lead one to conclude otherwise; the plaintiff in our example is in essence trying to prove the contents of the writing.

The inscription on the car would lead one to believe that the person who stepped out of it was a police officer, so it would seem that the content of the inscription is of particular importance. Understood in a different way, the plaintiff is trying to prove the "contents" of the car by the inscription on the door. However, if a witness testifies that the plaintiff rode her bicycle headlong into the side of a car bearing the inscription "to protect and serve," the car would not need to be produced and the best evidence rule would not apply because the content of the writing is not at issue.

Another best evidence rule problem arises with writings within writings. Many times documents contain excerpts from other documents. Textbooks often contain quotes from other sources; hospital records and the like often contain diagnoses or quotes from other individuals. To what extent should the originals be required in these situations? If the content of the message within a message is in dispute, the best evidence rule will apply.

Finally, is the best evidence rule implicated when it needs to be determined whether the contents of a writing *do not* contain a certain entry or statement? Or, in terms of an example, would the original writing be required if a witness testifies that "I have no record of an appointment for Patient X on September 5th"? In this situation, the best evidence rule would not apply because the purpose of the testimony in this example is not to prove contents but to prove the *absence of contents*.

When the Original Cannot Be Obtained

The best evidence rule is a rule of preference, so original writings are not *required* when, for some reason, they cannot be acquired. Modern evidence statutes describe several circumstances under which secondary evidence of writings (e.g., witness testimony as to contents) can serve in lieu of original writings. The most common circumstances are (1) when the original is lost, (2) when the original is unavailable, (3) when the original is in the possession of an opponent, and (4) when the writing is one characterized as collateral, official, voluminous, or produced.

Lost original. Secondary evidence of the contents of a writing is permissible when the original is lost or when the original has been destroyed without bad faith or "fraudulent intent" (CEC Section 1501) on the part of the proponent. The proponent will need to prove by a preponderance of the evidence that the original was lost. Further, the court may require a fairly intense search for the original if the original is of particular importance or if fraudulent intent is suspected.

Unavailable original or beyond reach of judicial process. If the original cannot be obtained by any available judicial process or procedure and is not lost, secondary evidence is acceptable. Even if the original is obtainable by judicial process, it may not be required if acquiring the original would be too arduous a task. For example, it would be ridiculous for a court to require the proponent to produce a 20-ton statue bearing a plaque with the inscription "All who enter these premises shall never return." If a writing or photograph is in the possession of a third party, a subpoena *duces tecum* may be used to acquire the original, but not if the third party successfully asserts a privilege blocking production of the original.

Original in possession of opponents. The contents of a writing may be proved by secondary evidence when the original is in possession of an opponent and the opponent is given proper notice that the contents would be proven at trial. The logic underlying this exception is that if the opponent is given notice that the contents of a writing will be proved with secondary evidence, the opponent can correct any erroneous testimony by producing the original. This exception only applies when (1) the opponent is given reasonable notice that the contents will be proved with secondary evidence; (2) the opponent is in possession or control of the original at the time of the notice; and (3) the opponent does not produce the original at the hearing. Modern evidence statutes do not define "reasonable notice," and the time period for giving notice is not altogether clear.

Collateral, official, and voluminous writings. Secondary evidence of the contents of a writing is permissible if it is "not closely related to a controlling issue" (Rule 1004[4]). For example, if a witness testifies that the defendant was driving down the road at a high rate of speed speaking into a hand-held tape recorder, the tape recording would be collateral—that is, not a controlling issue—and so would not be required.

Copies of official writings are acceptable if the original is a recorded document. The rationale for this exception is that it would be burdensome for courts to require the originals of official copies, but this is only if the proponent does not have a copy of the original and could not obtain one with reasonable care.

Next, secondary evidence in the form of a chart or a summary is acceptable in lieu of the original when the original is too voluminous to be "conveniently examined." If, for example, the original is a 3,000 page accounting record but only a handful of sections are at issue, a summary will probably suffice. Two key restrictions to this exception are that the original be accessible for inspection by both parties and that the summary be authenticated. Do not confuse this exception with the demonstrative evidence discussion later in this chapter. This exception to the best evidence rule is merely geared toward *summarizing* information. Demonstrative evidence, by contrast, concerns tools and techniques for illustrative or pedagogical purposes.

The Admissions Doctrine

Rule 1007 provides that the "contents of writings, recordings, or photographs may be proved by the testimony or deposition of the party against whom it is offered or by that party's written admission, without accounting for the nonproduction of the original." What this rule means is that production of the original is unnecessary where the opponent admits to the contents of the writing, recording, or photograph. An oral or written admission will suffice under this rule.

Best Evidence Rule Procedure

Procedures surrounding the best evidence rule can be somewhat confusing. This is because a number of preliminary questions must be decided by either the judge or the jury. The Federal Rules of Evidence require that judges decide a number of such preliminary issues. See Table 13-1 for examples.

Table 13-1 Preliminary "Best Evidence" Issues Decided by Judges

Judges Must Decide Whether
1. An item constitutes a writing, recording, or photograph
2. A writing, recording, or photograph is "original"
3. A "duplicate" meets the requirements of Rule 1001(4)
4. A "genuine question" has been raised about authentication of the original
5. It would be "unfair" to rely on a duplication in place of the original
6. The original has been "lost" or "destroyed"
7. The original has been lost or destroyed in "bad faith"
8. The original is unobtainable by judicial process
9. The original is in possession of the opponent and proper notice was given
10. The evidence goes to a "collateral" matter
11. A copy of a public record has been properly certified
12. A copy of a public record cannot be obtained with "reasonable diligence"
13. Writings are too "voluminous" to be examined by the jury

The lines between the role of the judge vis-à-vis the jury become blurry when the best evidence rule and the authentication doctrine collide. In particular, the factual issues that govern admissibility under

What is the difference between testimonial and real evidence?

the best evidence rule, which are usually decided by a judge, can be the same used to determine authentication, which the jury is supposed to decide. As such, juries occasionally decide (1) whether a writing that a party seeks to introduce ever existed, (2) which of two writings introduced at trial is the original, and (3) whether a copy or duplicate "accurately reflects" the original. Suppose, for example, one party argues that its document is the original contract while the opposing party argues that *its* document is the original contract. Here, a question of authentication arises so the jury decides. As a general rule, if the decision goes directly to the matter being litigated, the jury should decide, not the judge. Judges make legal decisions; juries make factual ones.

Real/Physical Evidence

Real evidence and *physical evidence* are forms of evidence that are discernible by the senses without the use of witnesses. From here on we will refer strictly to real evidence. Understand that when we refer to real evidence we are also discussing physical evidence; the terms are used interchangeably.

Real evidence is usually the most persuasive type of evidence. Witness testimony can come across as unbelievable, requiring that the jury decide who and what to believe, but real evidence is often black and white. For example, a murder weapon with the defendant's fingerprints on it is much more believable than a witness's testimony to the effect that the defendant murdered the victim.

Real Evidence and the Fifth Amendment

People who are unfamiliar with the laws of evidence and rules of criminal procedure often get upset when a suspect's testimony is excluded because of a *Miranda* violation or other Fifth Amendment violation. These people often forget that testimonial evidence (that protected by the Fifth Amendment) is not the only type of evidence required to secure criminal convictions. Even if a defendant's confession is thrown out because of a Fifth Amendment violation, he or she can still be convicted with real evidence.

Real evidence is not protected by the Fifth Amendment because of the Supreme Court's decision in *Schmerber v. California* (1966). There the Court decided that the Fifth Amendment's self-incrimination protection applied to evidence of a testimonial or communicative nature but did not apply to real evidence. In the Court's words:

> . . . courts have usually held that it [the Fifth Amendment] offers no protection against compulsion to submit to fingerprinting, photographing, or measurements, to write or speak for identification, to appear in court, to stand, to assume a stance, to walk, or to make a particular gesture.

Furthermore:

> Compulsion which makes a suspect or accused the source of real or physical evidence does not violate it [the Fifth Amendment].

Of course, when it comes to *acquiring* real evidence, law enforcement officials (and the courts) are bound by the Fourth Amendment. Even though the Fifth Amendment does not offer protection to criminal defendants in the case of real evidence, the Fourth Amendment's search and seizure provisions still apply. Probable cause—or a similar level of justification, depending on the conduct in question—is still required for officials to obtain real evidence during a search or seizure. If real evidence is obtained by means *other* than a search or seizure, Fourth Amendment protections do not apply (see Chapter 5).

Admissibility Requirements

In legal parlance, a proper "foundation" must be in place before real evidence can be considered admissible in court. Real evidence must first meet the requirements of relevancy, competency, and materiality.

First, real evidence is **relevant** when it sheds some light on a contested matter. According to a Georgia court, "relevancy is a logical relationship between evidence and a fact in issue or to be established" (*Continental Trust Co. v. Bank of Harrison*, 1926). Understood differently, evidence is relevant when it throws or tends to throw light on guilt or innocence of the accused even though its tendency to do so is minimal.

Second, real evidence is **competent** when, in particular, it is not obtained illegally. If evidence is obtained in violation of the Fourth Amendment, for instance, it cannot be considered competent. If real/physical evidence is not competent, it is not admissible.

Third, real evidence is material when it *significantly* affects that matter at issue in a case. According to one court, **material evidence** is that which is relevant and goes to substantial matters in dispute, or has legitimate influence or bearing on the decision of the case (*Hill v. State,* 1981). Materiality and relevance are not the same; the former refers to the significance of the evidence where the latter suggests that evidence merely relates to the issue in question.

If necessary, real evidence may need to be authenticated. Authentication is particularly relevant in the case of written documents, but as we have seen, real evidence sometimes needs to be authenticated as well. Finally, the evidence must follow a proper chain of custody. In other words, the evidence must have been in constant possession or custody of one or more persons typically charged with handling evidence. If the evidence was tampered with at some point between where the evidence was taken in custody and the trial, authentication may not be possible.

For example, a videotape of an ATM robbery was "misplaced" for a time while it was supposed to be in custody. A strong case could be made that the videotape to be introduced at trial is not authentic because of the potential for tampering. Consider what one federal appeals court stated with regard to the chain of custody:

> As to the chain of custody for the proper admission of a physical exhibit, there must be a showing that the physical exhibit is in substantially the same condition as when the crime was committed . . . When there is no evidence of tampering, a presumption of regularity attends the official acts of public officers in custody of the evidence; the courts presume they did their jobs correctly . . . All the government must show is that reasonable precautions were taken to preserve the original condition of evidence; an adequate chain of custody can be shown even if all possibilities of tampering are excluded . . . Merely raising the *possibility* of tampering is not sufficient to render the evidence inadmissible; the possibility of a break in the chain of custody of evidence goes to the weight of the evidence, not its admissibility. (*United States v. Harrington,* 1991)

What are the types of real evidence?

Types of Real Evidence

There are numerous types of real evidence. It would be impossible to cover all of them completely Instead, we focus on the most common forms of real evidence encountered in criminal cases: (1) the exhibition of a person, (2) items connected to the crime, (3) photographs, (4) sound recordings, (5) videotapes/motion pictures, and (6) the results from x-rays.

Exhibition of a person. In cases involving physical injury to a victim (in either a civil or criminal case), it is useful to present the actual victim to the jury. Of course, if a great deal of time has elapsed between the infliction of the injury and the trial date, photographs may be necessary to document the injury. But if the injury is lasting, allowing the victim to "show" himself or herself to the jury may be of substantial probative value. However, if the injury is too serious or potentially inflammatory, the trial judge may decide that the exhibition of the victim is not acceptable.

The flipside of displaying the victim to the jury is displaying the defendant to the jury. As a general rule, judges should not allow criminal defendants to appear before the jury in leg irons or handcuff unless there is clear justification for doing so. One court stated that the defendant may not be placed in any form of physical restraint while in the presence of the jury unless there is some compelling reason for doing so (see *People v. Duran*, 1976). The reason for this rule is that placing a defendant in shackles, handcuffs, leg irons, or the like makes the defendant *look* guilty.

Items connected to the crime. By far the largest category of physical evidence includes items connected with the crime. Any device or object used to facilitate any crime can fall in this category. These include weapons, items used during the crime other than weapons, clothing, drugs and drug paraphernalia, and so on.

Weapons can range from guns and knives to blunt objects and even simulated explosives. Interestingly, if the specific type of weapon used to commit a homicide is not known, any weapons found in the defendant's possession that could have been used to commit the homicide will be considered admissible. However, if the prosecution argues that a specific type of weapon was used (e.g., a .38 caliber pistol), weapons of other types found in the defendant's possession will not be considered admissible (see *People v. Riser*, 1956).

Items other than weapons used to commit crimes are also admissible, but with special care. Items such as burglary tools fall into this category, but their identification must be certain. If the prosecution argues that the defendant used a crowbar to burglarize the victim's apartment, the mere fact that the defendant possesses a crowbar may not be enough to render it admissible. If no evidence is left behind to connect the specific crowbar with the crime, the prosecution will be hard-pressed to build a case with physical evidence.

Clothing is another form of real evidence. Everyone remembers the famous "bloody glove" in the O. J. Simpson case. In other cases, clothing identified by a witness that was worn by the accused during the commission of a crime can be admitted into evidence. In one case, a hat, jacket, and pants found in a washing machine shortly after a robber had entered a house wearing similar clothing were admissible, and did not violate the Fifth Amendment (*Warden v. Hayden*, 1967). According to an appellate court decision:

> Evidence is relevant and admissible if it tends to logically prove or disprove facts in issue, or if it corroborates other material evidence. . . . The articles were found by the police at the crime scene. The robe and sheets contained seminal stains while the nightgown was torn and bloody. This evidence corroborated the victim's story that she had been raped and that her lip had been cut during the struggle. . . . (*State v. Atkins*, 1985, p.227)

Among the largest varieties of items connected with a crime are narcotics and narcotics paraphernalia. Narcotics seized from suspects, as well as containers, records, scales, packages, chemicals, and similar items, are frequently admitted against defendants in drug cases. In one case, a gun and pager found on the defendant during a search incident to arrest were considered relevant to the drug trafficking charges against the defendant (*United States v. Brown*, 1994).

Photographs. We have seen that photographs frequently need to be authenticated and can be bound by the best evidence rule. In instances where photographs *are* authenticated and constituted best evidence, they can be particularly useful and convey important information to the jury to aid in its decision. Photographs can also be controversial. This is especially the case with gruesome and graphic photographs. In deciding whether, for example, a graphic photograph of a murder victim should be admitted into evidence, courts will make a cost-benefit decision determining if the probative value of the photograph outweighs the potential for prejudice to the defendant. As one court explained it, gruesome photographs are admissible if they assist the jury in any of the following ways:

> . . . by shedding light on some issue; by proving a necessary element of the case; by enabling a witness to testify more effectively, by corroborating testimony, or by enabling the jurors to better understand the testimony. (*Sanders v. State*, 1994)

Sound recordings. The use of sound recordings as evidence raises a number of issues. For example, electronic eavesdropping and similar techniques used to obtain incriminating information are protected by the Fifth Amendment. Indiscriminate sound recording activities can result in the evidence thereby obtained being declared inadmissible. Even if sound recordings are obtained legally, several evidence questions still remain. According to one court, seven steps must be taken before a sound recording will be considered admissible (*State v. Toomer*, 1984):

    1. The recording was legally obtained.

2. The device used was capable of recording statements and was operating properly.

3. The operator of the device was competent and operated it properly.

4. The recorded voices were identified.

5. The accuracy and authenticity of the recording is verified.

6. No changes, additions, or deletions have been made to the recording,

7. Evidence is introduced showing an acceptable chain of custody.

Videotapes/motion pictures. Videotapes and similar "motion pictures" are often admitted into evidence. Bank robbery videotapes, for example, can be of particular value to the prosecution's case. Videotapes of crime scenes have also been properly admitted (e.g., *Seibert v. State*, 1989). However, at least one court has cautioned against the potential damage that can be done with videotape/motion picture evidence:

> Motion pictures should be received as evidence with caution, because the modern art of photography and the devices of an ingenious director frequently produce results which may be quite deceiving. Telescopic lenses, ingenious settings of the stage, the elimination of unfavorable portions of a film, and angle from which a picture is taken, the ability to speed up the reproduction of the picture and the genius of a director may tend to create misleading impressions. (*Harmon v. San Joaquin L. & P. Corp.*, 1940)

X-rays. Photographs can be authenticated with relative ease. Usually witness testimony to the effect that a photograph genuinely depicts a particular event or thing will suffice. X-rays, however, present a special problem. Because x-ray photographs show only shadows of internal parts of the body, they are not as easy to authenticate. In recent years, courts have held that x-ray photographs can be admitted into evidence if a qualified expert testifies that they are genuine.

Viewing the crime scene. As yet another form of real evidence, some jurisdictions actually permit the jury to exit the courtroom and physically view the crime scene. The purpose of doing so is, in part, to surmount some of the problems inherent in other types of real evidence, such as photographs. The argument for these so-called jury views is to enable jurors to more adequately understand the evidence in question as well as the location in which the crime took place. Photographs may not do the scene justice, so an actual visit to the scene may help fill in the gaps. In some criminal cases the accused is allowed to be present; in others he or she is not. Regardless, special care must be taken in facilitating jury views because of their potentially prejudicial and inflammatory effects.

What about scientific evidence? The careful reader is by now asking, what about scientific evidence? This includes the use of blood, hair, DNA, and other samples as well as polygraphs, criminal profiles, spectography, hypnosis, narcoanalysis, statistical analysis, and countless other techniques. Several strict rules govern the admissibility of scientific evidence. As such, we devote a full section later in this chapter to scientific evidence. For now, though, we turn to demonstrative evidence—that is, the use of demonstrations and other exercises to help the jury make its decision.

Demonstrative Evidence

The term *demonstrative evidence* appears nowhere in the rules of evidence. Nevertheless, it is well known that charts, drawings, pictures, and other tools can help jurors sort through a complex matter. Some have called **demonstrative evidence** anything that appeals to the senses. Others have opted for a narrower definition, claiming that demonstrative evidence is that which is conveyed with a "firsthand sense impression" (Strong, 1992). This definition excludes witness testimony because witness testimony is secondhand. Yet another author calls demonstrative evidence "illustrative evidence" (Brain and Broderick 1992).

Even though the Federal Rules make no mention of demonstrative evidence, it is still bound by Rules 401 and 403. In particular, the demonstrative evidence in question must be relevant— that is, it must have a tendency to make the existence of a consequential fact more or less probable than it would be without the evidence. Furthermore, demonstrative evidence can be excluded under Rule 403 if its benefits are substantially outweighed by the potential for unfair prejudice, delay, or confusion. These rules notwithstanding, courts are very cautious when it comes to considering the admissibility of demonstrative evidence because of the potential to mislead jurors or mistakenly convey important information.

Drawings and Diagrams

Drawings, diagrams, and similar devices are perhaps the most common forms of demonstrative evidence. For example, the prosecution may rely on a diagram showing where and how the defendant entered the house for the purpose of committing a murder there. Similarly, a doctor providing expert testimony may rely on a drawing or illustration of a human body in order to point out an important feature. The potential uses for drawings and diagrams is limited only by the imagination.

The only barrier to the admissibility of drawings and diagrams (beyond the Rule 401 and 403 concerns discussed above) is authentication. Drawings and diagrams are required to be authenticated. This is to ensure that a drawing accurately depicts what it is supposed to depict. Authentication of drawings and diagrams is frequently accomplished by testimony from the person who prepared it. Authentication is not *always* required. A doctor's reliance on a commonly used drawing of the interior of the human body rarely needs to be accompanied by witness testimony to the effect that the drawing is accurate.

Displays and Demonstrations

Displays and demonstrations are also commonly used in order to aid the jury with its decision. It would be easier for a jury to understand the severity of a plaintiff's wounds by being able to *see* the wounds as opposed to relying on the plaintiff's testimony. To use a real-world example, one appellate court held that the plaintiff in a civil action should have been allowed to display injuries to her breasts (*Hillman v. Funderburk*, 1986).

Displays and demonstrations are restricted, of course, by standards of decency. It is possible, in other words, to go too far in trying to make a point to the jury. In *Bates v. Newman* (1954), for example, an appellate court held that the trial court properly refused the plaintiff's offer to demonstrate to the jury his ability to hold an erection.

Displays and demonstrations are not limited to physical characteristics of human beings. Demonstrations that depict mechanical processes are also permitted. A witness could use a model of a working engine, for instance, in order to show the jury precisely what goes on *inside* the engine when it is running.

Courts are rightly cautious when it comes to admitting displays and demonstrations. Demonstrations might appeal to the jury's sympathies unfairly. They might distort the facts somewhat and "reenact" important events in a manner different from what originally occurred. Demonstrations can also be fabrications. Either way, one court has stated that demonstrations "should be carefully staged" with "the widest opportunity allowed for cross examination" (*United States v. Skinner*, 1970).

One controversial form of demonstrative evidence is known as a "day-in-the-life film." Plaintiffs in workers compensation cases, for example, may wish to demonstrate the effects of a work-related injury (such as a back injury) on their daily lives. Such films need to be authenticated as accurately depicting the true extent of the injuries in question. Further, day-in-the-life films raise hearsay concerns. This is because the plaintiff may, in the video, make nonverbal "assertions" about his or her injuries (see Chapter 12).

Computer Animations

According to one author, "Computer animation is likely to become the single most powerful evidentiary tool used by trial lawyers in the [twenty-first century]" (D'Angelo 1998). Even so, computer animation requires authentication under FRE Rule 907(b)(9). Computer animations often amount to "assertions" of their creators, so hearsay concerns are raised with their use. Such concerns are often overcome, however, if the creator of the animation is present in the trial and subject to cross examination.

Computer animations have been used to re-create shooting incidents, car accidents, and countless other events. As one example, the Ninth Circuit Court of Appeals held that a lower court did not abuse its discretion by admitting a computer animation of a shooting with all the facial expressions of the participants removed, even though there was an objection that one simulated party looked like a "nutty android" or "somebody who is crazed" (*Byrd v. Guess*, 1998). In another case, the Tenth Circuit Court of Appeals held that there was no abuse of discretion where a video animation of a train-automobile accident was admitted and where an instruction was given to the jury that the animation was not an actual re-creation of the accident (*Robinson v. Missouri Pac. R. Co.*, 1994). Because computer imagery can have a powerful impact on the jury, courts are and should be cautious about its admission.

Experiments

Experiments of various forms are also used to demonstrate important points to the jury. The term *experiments* is used broadly here; it does not necessarily refer to laboratory experiments conducted under strict conditions of control. For example, one court permitted a film showing a car approaching an inclined ramp, becoming airborne, and landing, all in an effort to show the trajectory of the car (*Bannister v. Town of Noble, Okla.*, 1987). Nearly everyone has seen videos on the news of automobile safety experiments. Videos resulting from such experiments could be used for demonstrative purposes.

In another case (*Brandt v. French*, 1981), the court held that it was appropriate to admit a film of a motorcycle passing cars in order to show how the motorcycle leans when it turns. Another videotaped experiment of a driver of a truck traveling 35 miles per hour and taking his foot off the accelerator one-quarter mile from a curve was properly admitted in order to show that the truck would come to a stop before hitting the curve (see *Champeau v. Fruehauf Corp.*, 1987).

In all the experiment examples thus far, the experiments were conducted out of view of the jury and replayed for them via videotape or film. Of course, it is also possible for an experiment to be conducted before the jury's eyes. An example of this technique can be found in the case of *United State v. Rackley* (1984). The court in that case ruled that the lower court acted appropriately by conducting an experiment in front of the jury of how Biff, a narcotics dog, could sniff out cocaine hidden in closed containers.

Courts are also cautious when it comes to the use of experiments. The most important requirement is that the experiment be conducted under circumstances similar to the event in question. The conditions do not have to be identical, but they should be close. Also, the results from experiments may be excluded if they are unfairly prejudicial or misleading. And, of course, the relevancy requirement still attaches.

Scientific Evidence

In Chapter 10 we briefly discussed the important case of *Daubert v. Merrell Dow Pharmaceuticals* (1993). In it the Supreme Court declared that scientific testimony be "supported by appropriate validation" and must have a "valid scientific connection" or "fit" with the issues in the case. The *Daubert* decision did away with the earlier *Frye* decision—namely, that scientific validity was shown if the science had gained "general acceptance."

Practice Pointer 13-1

Scientific evidence standards are rapidly evolving. So are the various types of scientific evidence. Prosecutors should stay carefully attuned to these changes.

There are two critical requirements for meeting the *Daubert* standard. First, the science in question must be "valid." According to the Supreme Court, this means that the evidence is "reliable" or "trustworthy." Actually, it is useful to distinguish validity from reliability. A technique is *valid* when it supports what it intends to show. *Reliability* is concerned with producing consistent results. Validity is not easy to determine. As such, courts rely on several factors. See Table 13-2 for a list of these factors.

"Fit" is the next requirement under the *Daubert* test. This requirement is closely related to relevancy in that the results of the scientific technique should be closely connected to the facts in dispute. As the Supreme Court stated in *Daubert*, the evidence must be "sufficiently tied to the facts of the case that it will aid the jury."

Table 13-2 Factors Considered In Determining Scientific Validity

1. Whether the theory or technique has been tested
2. Whether the theory or technique has been subjected to peer-review
3. The error rate (and types of errors) involved in application of the theory or technique
4. Whether standards are in place that govern use of the technique
5. The degree of the theory or technique's acceptance
6. The "newness," or novelty of the technique
7. The qualifications and stature of the technique or witness
8. Whether a body of professional literature exists concerning the theory or technique

Other considerations should go into determining whether "scientific" evidence is appropriate in a courtroom. If the technique is exceedingly technical or complicated, for example, the jury may become confused. Alternatively, if the technique or theory in question is nascent, undeveloped, and prone to error, special care should be taken in basing important decisions on the resultant evidence.

Several types of scientific evidence have led to much confusion and controversy in the courts (some more than others). Certain techniques probably do not require much validation, but we focus here on the techniques that do. These include the use of statistics, DNA evidence, the results from polygraph examinations, evidence concerning the reliability of eyewitness testimony, and evidence of syndromes and profiles. The admissibility of these types of evidence is essentially controlled by rules 702 and 703 of the Federal Rules of Evidence, even though the FRE contain no direction mention of scientific evidence.

Statistics

The problem of statistical evidence was clearly illustrated in the case of *People v. Collins* (1968). An eyewitness in that case testified that a black man and a blonde woman mugged a woman in an alley in Los Angeles. The prosecutor argued that the statistical probability of two such people being together was so minute that the defendants had to be responsible for the mugging (the witness also pointed out other characteristics of the suspects, but these are beside the point). The California Supreme Court, however, overturned one of the convictions.

There are at least four reasons that statistical evidence is usually not admissible. The first is that it is impossible to state with confidence the odds of an event occurring without knowing how likely the event is. Consider a simple example: We know how likely it is that two heads will result from two flips of a coin because we know that there are only two possible outcomes associated with any given flip of a coin. At the other extreme, though, and to stick with the *Collins* case illustration, no one knows how likely a black man and blonde woman are to associate with each other. We have enough trouble trying to count the number of people in this country, not to mention the odds of different individuals associating with one another!

Another problem with statistical evidence stems from the so-called product rule. Going back to the coin example, we know that in flipping a coin the likelihood of two heads is ¼. This result is calculated by the product of the likelihood of both events occurring in isolation (½ times ½). The product rule becomes problematic when it is used to calculate the probability of *non*independent events. We know that two coin tosses are independent; there is no way that the result of one toss will somehow influence the result of the second toss.

To illustrate nonindependence, assume we have a group of 20 people, of which 5 are black (so the probability of being black is $^5/_{20}$, which reduces to ¼); and 15 are white. Further, 2 are women and 18 are men (the probability of being a woman is $^2/_{20}$, which reduces to $^1/_{10}$). Finally, 3 are wearing red, 7 are wearing yellow, and 10 are wearing blue (probability of wearing red is $^3/_{20}$). It would be wrong to predict the likelihood of selecting a black woman wearing red by multiplying ¼ by $^1/_{10}$ by $^3/_{20}$. The result is $^1/_{800}$, but we know that since there are only 20 people, the odds of any one person being selected cannot possibly be less than $^1/_{20}$. In our example, the qualities of being black or white, male or female, and wearing any of the three colors are not independent, so the product rule is inappropriate. The rule exaggerates the probability of events and would mislead a jury.

There are several other reasons for viewing statistical evidence cautiously, but they can become technical and quite mathematical. Following example of the misuse of the product rule requires careful attention, so it is no wonder that jurors can become confused and overwhelmed when presented with too many numbers.

One of the most important reasons for excluding statistical evidence is that it seems to conflict with the notion of proof beyond a reasonable doubt. As the system currently stands (and students of legal topics are taught), proof beyond a reasonable doubt is not quantifiable. This standard does not mean 99 or 95 percent certainty, or even any level of likelihood below or above these points. To attach specific probabilities raises some ethical dilemmas. Would we be satisfied with 95 percent certainty, or even 99 percent certainty? What is the appropriate cutoff point? It is naive to assume that judges, prosecutors, defense attorneys, and jurors could all agree on the same level of certainty, so it is safe to leave the definition of "proof beyond a reasonable doubt" open ended.

In sum, think of statistics as just another method of drawing inferences. As we have seen earlier in this book, circumstantial evidence is very similar. It requires arriving at the "truth" through inferences of probabilities arising from the association of certain facts. An example of circumstantial evidence is the testimony of a witness in an adultery case that she saw the accused and a woman who was not his wife together in a hotel room. Such testimony should not lead anyone to conclude with 100 percent certainty that adultery was taking place, but most jurors will probably *infer* that it was taking place.

Statistics constitutes a family of sophisticated techniques for making inferences. Statistics, in our view, take "common sense" out of play and try to substitute relatively formal and "objective" tools for making decisions. Unfortunately, statistics can often be confusing as well as manipulated (everyone's heard the homily, "You can prove anything with statistics"), so courts should be especially careful in deciding whether evidence resulting from statistical analysis should be admitted to prove consequential facts.

Practice Pointer 13-2

Statistical evidence should be avoided at trial. Statistical evidence is based on probabilities, which conflicts with the "proof beyond a reasonable doubt" standard, which is itself a probability determination. In other words, statistical evidence often confuses rather than clarifies matters.

DNA Evidence

In recent years, DNA evidence has gained popularity in both criminal trials and paternity cases. The reason is its unsurpassed ability to point to particular individuals. What is interesting, though, is that DNA evidence frequently goes hand in hand with statistics. One often hears about the "probability" of the DNA not belonging to the defendant, or the probability of the DNA match between a parent and child being of a certain level. Despite the language of probability, the use of DNA evidence has been approved by all courts across the country.

DNA evidence is fully acceptable under the *Daubert* standards discussed earlier, but it still raises potential problems. Special care needs to be given to the handling of DNA evidence. Laboratory protocol also needs to be followed with special care. Statistics need to be applied cautiously, and the information needs to be communicated to the jury in clear and understandable terms.

A recent DNA-evidence development of some controversy is that of DNA dragnets. In the wake of a serious crime, all people in the town where the crime was committed and who fit the profile of the offender are asked to voluntarily submit DNA samples. This sampling can be accomplished by swabbing the inside of a person's cheek with a Q-tip. Then, by process of elimination, the suspect is found. Usually, the suspect is one of the few who fail to submit to DNA testing.

DNA dragnets have been used successfully in a handful of European countries. There have been some attempts to "import" them to the United States, but they are highly controversial here because of constitutional concerns. Taking a DNA sample from a person constitutes a search and is therefore protected by the Fourth Amendment. Thus, if DNA dragnets are to gain acceptance within our borders, they need to be voluntary. Just because a person refuses to consent should not mean that that he or she is a suspect. Another reason DNA dragnets face potential problems in the United States is that their success abroad has mostly been in small, isolated towns. It would be nearly impossible to obtain voluntary samples from people fitting the profile of a criminal suspect in a town as big as New York City.

Polygraph Evidence

Another variety of scientific evidence that has been particularly controversial is expert testimony based on the results of polygraph examinations. *Frye v. United States* (1923), one of the leading cases that established the standard for scientific evidence that prevailed for several years, did not consider polygraph testing a science. Most courts have followed suit; today most jurisdictions have rules against permiting polygraph-based testimony. Even in light of the more recent *Daubert* decision, which was more liberal than *Frye* in terms of its test for the admissibility of scientific evidence, most courts avoid polygraph evidence. There are exceptions, however (e.g., *United States v. Cordoba*, 1997; *United States v. Posado*, 1995).

Some courts permit polygraph testimony if both parties agree to it (e.g., *United States v. Gordon*, 1982), but others will still exclude it even if both parties agree because of a perception that such evidence is unreliable (e.g., *People v. Baynes*, 1981). As one court noted, agreement by both parties "neither enhances the uncertain reliability of the polygraph examination nor blunts the prejudicial effect" (*State v. Lyons*, 1987).

In a more recent case (*United States v. Scheffer*, 1998), the Supreme Court held that criminal defendants have no constitutional right to introduce expert testimonial evidence that they passed a polygraph examination. A key feature of this decision was that the Court only considered whether polygraph evidence *must be* admitted. The decision suggests, then, that polygraph evidence *can be* admitted at trial, but it does not need to be. The Court did note, however, that because the scientific community is still in disagreement over the reliability of polygraph evidence that a rule providing for its exclusion is perfectly acceptable, but it is up to the lower courts to decide.

Some commentators believe that even if polygraphy were an infallible truth-seeking technique, admitting such evidence would bypass the role of the judge or jury in determining guilt. As one court noted, criminal defendants should be "treated as persons to be believed or disbelieved by their peers rather than as electrochemical systems to be certified as truthful or mendacious" (*State v. Lyons*, 1987).

In light of the debate over the reliability of polygraph evidence, Congress has even become involved. For example, the Employee Polygraph Protection Act places restrictions on the use of polygraphs in the employee context. It should prove interesting to follow future court decisions and congressional actions concerning the admissibility of polygraph evidence in criminal and civil trials.

The Reliability of Eyewitness Testimony

Psychologists routinely testify (as experts) to the effect that eyewitnesses are notoriously inaccurate in terms of their recollections. This testimony is another variety of "scientific" evidence, and like polygraph evidence, it is viewed with some caution because the research suggesting that eyewitnesses misinterpret and fail to remember events is not conclusive. Experts in this area often testify to such commonly agreed-upon facts (*United States v. Curry*, 1992, pp. 1050–1052):

1. Memory diminishes quickly

2. Stress causes inaccurate recollections

3. Witnesses often include inaccurate information in their testimony

4. Conversations witnesses have following events reinforce flawed perceptions

5. Even accurate descriptions are not necessarily indicative of guilt

6. Cross-racial identifications are frequently inaccurate

Some courts approve testimony concerning the inaccuracy of eyewitness testimony (e.g. *People v. Enis*, 1990). A handful of decisions have even resulted in reversals because of such evidence (*United States v. Stevens*, 1991). Other courts, however, are skeptical and may hold separate hearings on whether such testimony is admissible. Still others exclude altogether expert testimony that eyewitnesses are notoriously inaccurate in what they observe (e.g., *United States v. Larkin*, 1992).

In general, it is up to the judge to decide on the admissibility of expert testimony in this area. If, for example, a witness identifies the defendant after he or she had seen the defendant at great length (or if the witness knew the defendant), the testimony will probably prove reliable. Furthermore, if eyewitness testimony is tangential and not the "whole" of the prosecution's case, there is not really any advantage to allowing an expert to testify that the witness may have been wrong; a guilty verdict could be arrived at regardless. At the other extreme, however, where identity is crucial and a substantial portion of the prosecution's case, expert testimony may be desirable. This is particularly true if the witness caught no more than a fleeting glimpse of the perpetrator.

Syndromes and Profiles

Experts are often called on to testify as to a syndrome shared by a witness or party to the case. The term **syndrome** simply refers to a pattern of behavior or mental attitude exhibited by a particular person. Prosecutors often offer evidence of a syndrome as it relates to a victim. Other times, the defense will argue that the defendant's actions can best be understood in terms of some debilitating condition. Either way, the courts are not surprisingly cautious about such testimony. The question of scientific validity is often raised because many "syndromes" that experts would testify to are not universally recognized. Following are some examples of such syndromes.

Battered woman syndrome. The idea behind this syndrome is that a woman party to an abusive relationship develops a sense of helplessness that keeps her in the relationship. Experts will also testify that women in abusive relationships develop considerable rage that they ultimately "release," resulting in significant injury or death to the abusing partner. This syndrome is often raised in trials involving abused women who have killed their partners. Many courts admit evidence of battered woman syndrome to establish a "social framework" that places the events in context (*Bechtel v. State*, 1992), but other courts suggest that it is difficult to believe testimony concerning what a woman *might* be expected to do in an abusive relationship (e.g., *Hill v. State*, 1986).

Rape trauma syndrome. Rape trauma syndrome exists when women go through specific, identifiable stages after being raped. Experts will testify that rape victims first experience an acute, negative reaction to being raped, then progress through a series of stages akin to posttraumatic stress disorder. Testimony concerning rape trauma syndrome is often presented to refute a defense claim that the victim consented to the sexual encounter. This approach has been accepted by a number of courts (e.g., *Henson v. State*, 1989). A more controversial use of rape trauma syndrome testimony, however occurs when there is no physical evidence linking the defendant to the presumed victim. In such cases, the prosecution may argue that because the "victim" exhibits symptoms consistent with rape trauma, the defendant should be found guilty. Courts are generally quick to reject this approach (e.g., *People v. Taylor*, 1990).

Abused child syndrome. When children are abused or sexually assaulted, they often develop common symptoms, such as nightmares and behavioral problems. Testimony concerning abused child syndrome has been admitted for such purposes as explaining questionable behavior. When the focus shifts from the child to, for example, a parent or guardian, the courts become a bit nervous about allowing expert testimony. This approach essentially asks the jury to infer the guilt or innocence of an adult's alleged abusive actions from the behavior or conditions exhibited by a child. Courts do admit this testimony, but sometimes grudgingly (e.g., *State v. Hester*, 1988).

Criminal profiles. In stark contrast to syndromes are criminal profiles. In general, **profiles** refer to common characteristics shared by certain types of offenders. Whereas syndromes are usually offered to *excuse* questionable conduct on the part of someone (battered spouse, rape victim, etc.), criminal profiles are intended to lead to a conclusion that because someone fits a certain description, he or she is guilty.

For example, because Mr. Smith bought a one-way plane ticket with cash, was traveling to a city known as a "hub" of drug activity, did not carry any luggage, looked nervous, and walked briskly through the terminal he may fit the profile of a "drug courier." Courts do not permit expert testimony that because a person fits a criminal profile, he or she should be found guilty. The courts often consider profiling, but not explicitly. The subject is commonly raised during appellate review of stop and frisk encounters in which the question of whether authorities possessed reasonable suspicion to stop is raised.

Because every person walking through an airport, for example, can realistically be stopped, law enforcement officials are forced to look to specific characteristics of drug couriers. This is because, as the Supreme Court observed in *United States. v. Mendenhall* (1980), "Much . . . drug traffic is highly organized and conducted by sophisticated criminal syndicates . . . And many drugs . . . may be easily concealed. As a result, the obstacles to detection . . . may be unmatched in any other area of law enforcement" (pp.545–546). Further, one of the most significant impediments in the war on drugs is the "extraordinary and well-documented difficulty of identifying drug couriers" (*Florida v. Royer*, 1983).

The drug courier profile is generally attributed to Paul Markonni, a DEA agent who identified a number of suspicious characteristics of likely drug couriers when he was assigned to a drug interdiction unit at the Detroit Airport. The drug courier profile has since been described as an "informally compiled abstract of characteristics thought typical of persons carrying illicit drugs" (*United States. v. Mendenhall*, 1980). There is no single, nationally recognized drug courier profile or set of characteristics indicative of drug courier profiling. Instead, one must look at specific cases to ascertain which types of characteristics fit the drug courier profile.

The first drug courier profile case of note, *United States v. Van Lewis* (1976), listed several characteristics to be used in identifying drug couriers. They include (1) the use of small denominations of currency for ticket purchase; (2) travel to and from major drug import centers; (3) the absence of luggage or use of empty suitcases on trips that normally require extra clothing; and (4) travel under an alias.

In a similar case, the Fifth Circuit in *Elmore v. United States* (1979) described common characteristics of drug couriers: "(1) arrival from or departure to an identified source city; (2) carrying little or no luggage; (3) unusual itinerary, such as rapid turnaround time for a very lengthy airplane trip; (4) use of an alias; (5) carrying unusually large amounts of currency in the many thousands of dollars, usually on their person, or in briefcases or bags; (6) purchasing airline tickets with a large amount of small denomination currency; and (7) unusual nervousness beyond that ordinarily exhibited by passengers" (p.1039, n3).

Some secondary characteristics of drug couriers have also been identified. They include: "(1) the almost exclusive use of public transportation, particularly taxicabs, in departing from the airport; (2) immediately making a phone call after deplaning; (3) leaving a false or fictitious call-back telephone number with the airline being utilized; and (4) excessively frequent travel to source or distribution cities" (*Elmore v. United States*, 1979, p.1039, n.3). See Table 13-3 for a list of common characteristics associated with drug couriers.

Table 13-3 Typical Characteristics of Drug Couriers

1. Use of small denominations of currency for ticket purchase
2. Travel to and from major drug import centers
3. Absence of luggage or use of empty suitcases on trips that normally require extra clothing
4. Travel under an alias
5. Unusual itinerary, such as rapid turnaround time for a very lengthy airplane trip
6. Carrying unusually large amounts of currency in the many thousands of dollars
7. Unusual nervousness beyond that ordinarily exhibited by passengers
8. The almost exclusive use of public transportation upon departing the airport
9. Immediately making a phone call after deplaning
10. Leaving a false or fictitious call-back telephone number with the airline
11. Unusual dress
12. Age between 25 and 35
13. Extreme paleness consistent with being extremely nervous
14. Failure to use identification tags on luggage
15. Purchase of tickets on the day of a flight
16. Exiting first or last from the plane
17. Walking quickly through the terminal while continuously checking over one's shoulder
18. Quickly leaving the airport on arrival

Do not confuse profile evidence with the investigative technique of criminal profiling. Criminal profilers, such as those who "profiled" the individual responsible for mailing anthrax-tainted letters in 2001, seek to narrow the list of potential suspects. In fact, this technique is the exact opposite of expert testimony concerning profiles. Whereas profile testimony starts with a list of characteristics criminals display and concludes that anyone fitting that description is a criminal, investigative profiling seeks to a develop a list of characteristics that can lead authorities to a single individual. If an investigative profile is accurate enough and leads to apprehension of the perpetrator, the criminal trial will proceed as usual, without any testimonial evidence to the effect that the defendant was apprehended because of the work of a criminal profiler.

Summary

Authentication refers to the originality of evidence. Forms of evidence that frequently require authentication are documents, objects, and voice recordings. Some evidence, however, is self-authenticating. The best evidence rule is related to authentication but is not the same. Whereas authentication focuses on whether evidence is an original, the best evidence rule is concerned with whether the original is required. The best evidence rule is a rule of preference; if an original is available, it should be used.

Real evidence must satisfy the requirements of relevancy, competency, and materiality. It must also follow a proper chain of custody. In addition to evidence such as items connected with a crime, demonstrative and scientific evidence are also considered "real." Because of the complexity and potential problems associated with demonstrative and scientific evidence, we devoted special attention to their forms and admissibility requirements.

Discussion Questions

1. What are the ways in which documents can be authenticated?

2. Explain self-authentication. Give examples.

3. Explain the best evidence rule. What is it? What is it not? How does this rule relate to hearsay?

4. Is real evidence protected by the Fifth Amendment? Why or why not?

5. What foundation must be in place before real evidence may be admitted in court? Explain each requirement.

6. Give examples and brief explanations of the six types of real evidence named in the text.

7. Name and explain the types of demonstrative evidence named in the text.

8. Explain "syndromes" and give examples.

9. Explain the difference between criminal profiles and the investigative technique of criminal profiling.

10. According to the text, what are the common characteristics of drug couriers? What type of evidence is this? Is it admissible?

Further Reading

Aitken, C. G. G. (1995). *Statistics and the Evaluation of Evidence for Forensic Scientists.* New York:John Wiley and Sons.

Brain, R. D., and D. J. Broderick. (1992). "The Derivative Relevance of Demonstrative Evidence: Charting Its Proper Evidentiary Status." *U. Cal. Davis L. Rev.* 25:957, 968–969.

D'Angelo, C. (1998). "The Snoop Doggy Dogg Trial: A Look at How Computer Animation Will Impact Litigation in the Next Century." *U.S.F. L. Rev.* 32:561, 585.

Downs, D. A. (1998). *More than Victims: Battered Women, the Syndrome Society, and the Law.* Chicago: University of Chicago Press.

Foster, K. W. and P. W. Huber. (1999). *Judging Science: Scientific Knowledge and the Federal Courts.* Cambridge: MIT Press.

Goldstein, E. (1995). *Visual Evidence: A Practitioner's Manual.* Toronto, ON: Carswell.

Imwinkelried, E. J. (1992). *Methods of Attacking Scientific Evidence* (2nd ed.). Charlottesville, NC: Michie.

Moenssens, A. A. (1995). *Scientific Evidence in Criminal Cases* (4th ed.). Westbury, NY: Foundation Press.

Robertson, B. J. and G. A Vignaux. (1995). *Interpreting Evidence: Evaluating Forensic Science in the Courtroom.* New York: John Wiley and Sons.

Rychlak, R. J. (1995). *Real and Demonstrative Evidence: Application and Theory.* Charlottesville, NC: Michie Butterworth.

Strong, J. W. (1992). *McCormick on Evidence* (4th ed.). Eagan, MN: West.

Cases Cited

Bannister v. Town of Noble, Okla., 812 F.2d 1265 (10th Cir. 1987)

Bates v. Newman, 121 Cal. App. 2d 800 (1954)

Bechtel v. State, 840 P.2d 1 (Okla. Crim. App. 1992)

Brandt v. French, 638 F.2d 209 (10th Cir. 1981)

Byrd v. Guess, 137 F.3d 1126 (9th Cir. 1998)

Champeau v. Fruehauf Corp., 814 F.2d 1271 (8th Cir. 1987)

Continental Trust Co. v. Bank of Harrison, 36 Ga. App. 149 (1926)

Conway v. Consolidated Rail Corp., 720 F.2d 221 (1st Cir. 1983)
Daubert v. Merrell Dow Pharmaceuticals, 509 U.S. 579 (1993)
Elmore v. Untied States, 595 F. 2d 1036 (5th Cir. 1979)
Florida v. Royer, 460 U.S 491, 519 (1983)
Frye v. United States, 54 App D.C 46 (CADC 1923)
Harmon v. San Joaquin L. & P. Corp., 37 Cal. App. 2d 1064 (1940)
Henson v. State, 535 N.E.2d 1189 (Ind. 1989)
Hill v. State, 159 Ga. App. 489 (1981)
Hill v. State, 507 S.2d 554 (Ala. Crim. App. 1986)
Hillman v. Funderburk, 504 A.2d 596 (D.C. App. 1986)
Hood v. Itawamba County, Miss., 819 F. Supp. 556 (N.D. Miss. 1993)
People v. Baynes, 430 N.E.2d 1070 (Ill. 1981)
People v. Collins, 438 Cal.P.2d 33 (Cal. 1968)
*People v. Duran,*16 Cal. 3d 282 (1976)
People v. Enis, 564 N.E.2d 1155 (Ill. 1990)
People v. Riser, 47 Cal. 2d 566 (1956)
People v. Taylor, 552 N.E.2d 131 (N.Y. 1990)
Robinson v. Missouri Pac. R. Co., 16 F.3d 1083 (10th Cir. 1994)
Sanders v. State, 317 Ark. 328 (1994)
Schmerber v. California, 384 U.S. 757 (1966)
Seibert v. State, 555 So. 2d 772 (Ala. 1989)
State v. Atkins, 697 S.W.2d 226 (Mo. App. 1985)
State v. Hester, 760 P.2d 27 (Idaho 1988)
State v. Lyons, 744 P.2d 231 (Or. 1987)
State v. Toomer, 311 N.S. 183 (1984)
United States v. Brown, 16 F.3d 423 (D.C. Cir. 1994)
*United States v. Cordoba,*104 F.3d 225 (9th Cir. 1997)
United States v. Curry, 977 F.2d 1042 (7th Cir. 1992)
United States v. Gordon, 688 F.2d 42 (8th Cir. 1982)
United States v. Harrington, 923 F.2d 1371 (9th Cir. 1991)
United States v. Lance, 853 F.2d 1177 (5th Cir. 1988)
United States v. Larkin, 978 F.2d 964 (7th Cir. 1992)
United States v. Mendenhall, 446 U.S. 544, 547 (1980)
United States v. Portsmouth Paving Corp., 694 F.2d 312 (4th Cir. 1982)
United States v. Posado, 57 F.3d 428 (5th Cir. 1995)
United States v. Rackley, 742 F.2d 1266 (1984)
United States v. Scheffer, 118 S.Ct. 1261 (1998)
United States v. Skinner, 425 F.2d 552 (D.C. Cir. 1970)
United States v. Stevens, 935 F.2d 1380 (3rd Cir. 1991)
United States v. Van Lewis, 409 F.Supp. 535 (E.D Mich. 1976)
United States v. Wilson, 690 F.2d 1267 (9th Cir. 1982)
Warden v. Hayden, 387 U.S. 294 (1967) ✦

Glossary

Accredit When the prosecution or defense attempts to support, bolster, or improve the credibility of a witness.

Actual possession Physically holding or grasping a piece of property.

Actus reus The criminal act itself.

Administrative justification The courts permitting select types of unjustified searches by weighing society's safety interests against individuals' interests in being free from unreasonable searches.

Administrative regulations Rules enacted by state or local agencies, such as regulations affecting food and drugs and occupational safety requirements.

Administrative search warrants Warrants issued in anticipation that the evidence will be at a particular location at some future time.

Admissions by conduct (adoptive admissions) Not conduct, but silence serves as an admission of guilt.

Adverse testimony Testimony that is against the defendant.

Affirmative defense An affirmative defense is raised after the prosecution has established its case and permits the defendant to avoid liability even when the government has met its burden of proof on the elements of the offense.

Affidavits Sworn statements.

Anticipatory Search Warrant A warrant issued based on the expectation that evidence will be present or arrive at a particular location.

Appellate jurisdiction The power of a court to review a decision of a lower court.

Appointed counsel Private attorneys who are paid by the state on a case-by-case basis to represent indigent defendants.

Appointment A method of selecting judges.

Arm span rule Guideline that a search incident to arrest is limited to the area within the immediate control of the person arrested.

Article Three Courts Courts established under the authority of Article Three of the Constitution.

Ascertainable fact A fact that can be determined by looking it up in some source, the accuracy of which cannot be easily disputed.

Attestation Indication that the signer examined the document after the fact and found it to be a genuine document or public record.

Attorney general An administrator who sets prosecution priorities for deputy attorneys general.

Authentication The introduction of evidence sufficient to sustain a finding that an object or document is what it is claimed to be.

B

Beneficial testimony Testimony that is for the defendant.

Best evidence rule A rule of preference. If an original writing is available, it should be used instead of a copy.

Bills of attainder Legislation imposing punishment without trial.

Blank pad rule An assumption that the court and the jury in a criminal case know nothing about the dispute between the two parties involved.

Burden of persuasion The burden placed upon the party to convince the jury with regard to a particular issue. This requires that the prosecution provide enough evidence to secure a conviction. Also called the burden of proof.

Burden of production The obligation placed on one side in a trial to produce evidence, to make a *prima facie* showing on a particular issue. Also called burden of going forward.

C

Centrality theory Holds that hearsay should be permissible insofar as it corroborates or serves as circumstantial proof of guilt, but not as direct and critical evidence.

Change of venue A request by the defendant to have his or her trial take place in a different location.

Circumstantial evidence Evidence that requires jurors to draw their own conclusions concerning whether the evidence in question should be taken as proof of the defendant's guilt or lack thereof.

Code of Hammurabi The first known written legal code, expressed as an eye for an eye philosophy.

Collective facts doctrine A doctrine that allows witnesses to offer an opinion where recitation of factual perceptions would not convey to the jury what the witness heard or observed.

Common authority Ability to give consent to search by persons who have mutual use of the property and generally have joint access or control for most purposes.

Common knowledge Facts generally known by informed individuals within the jurisdiction of the trial court.

Common law Judge-made law.

Competency The presence of particular characteristics, and the absence of particular disabilities that render the witness legally qualified to testify in court.

Competent evidence Evidence that is in a form the jury is permitted to hear or see; evidence not gathered illegally.

Compulsory process clause A clause within the Sixth Amendment that says a person may be compelled or forced to serve as a witness.

Conclusive presumption A presumption that cannot be challenged by either the prosecution or the defense.

Confrontation clause A clause in the Sixth Amendment that specifies that in all criminal prosecutions the accused shall be confronted with the witnesses against him.

Consent This defense is raised when the victim gives consent to suffer what would otherwise be considered a legal harm.

Constitution A document that creates a government.

Constructive possession Possession of property without physical contact.

Corroborative Evidence Evidence in support of another witness's testimony.

Credibility The believability of the witness.

Cumulative evidence Evidence that repeats what is already known.

Curtilage An area to which extends the intimate activity associated with the sanctity of one's home and the privacies of life.

Custodial interrogation The questioning of a suspect while he or she is in police custody.

Custody The level of police control in which a suspect either believes he or she is not free to leave or actually is not free to leave.

D

Daubert test A two-tailed test used to determine whether the field of the expert witness has reached the level of "scientific knowledge."

Deadly force Use of force substantial enough to cause the death of the suspect.

Declarant Anyone who makes a statement.

Declarations Sworn statements.

Defendant's privilege The Fifth Amendment privilege against self-incrimination; i.e., the defendant has the right not to answer any questions or testify at trial.

Defense attorneys Lawyers who represent their client as effectively as possible while acting within the rules of the court.

Demonstrative evidence Evidence intended to demonstrate a certain point.

Depositions Sworn testimony given prior to trial.

Derivative use immunity A type of immunity in which the state cannot use any evidence derived from the immunized testimony against the witness.

Direct evidence Evidence that proves a fact without the need for the jurors to presume anything from it.

Directed verdict A judge in a criminal case may direct the jury to return a "not guilty" verdict if he or she feels that the prosecution has not proven their case, but a trial judge may not direct a verdict of "guilty" because that would deprive the defendant of a trial by jury.

Discrediting The prosecution's or the defense's challenging of a witness's credibility.

Diversity of citizenship A situation in which the opposing parties in a case are from different states.

Documentary evidence Documents and writings used as evidence.

Dual sovereignty doctrine The idea that a person may be legally tried in both state and federal court for the same offense.

Due process A provision that governments must follow certain procedures designed to protect individual rights before depriving them of their liberty or property.

Duplicate A counterpart produced by the same impression as the original, or from the same matrix, or by means of photography, including enlargements and miniatures, or by mechanical or electronic rerecording, or by chemical reproduction, or by other equivalent technique that accurately reproduces the original.

Duress Duress may be raised as a defense when the defendant was forced to commit the crime in question.

E

Effects Personal items; any tangible piece of property that a person possesses.

Election A method of selecting judges.

En banc Situation in which appeals court justices sit as a group consisting of every judge on the court, in order to clear up any conflicting decisions between two panels of justices involving the same legal issue.

Enhancement device Any device used to enhance one of the five senses, such as binoculars, drug dogs, satellite photography, or thermal imaging.

Equal Protection Rules barring legislatures from making unequal, arbitrary distinctions between "suspect classifications of people." Which is generally taken to mean distinctions that are without reason or based on race, gender, or other suspect classification.

Evanescent evidence Evidence that is likely to disappear if time is taken to obtain a search warrant.

Evidence law A set of rules that govern how trials are conducted.

Excited utterances Statement relating to a startling event or condition, while the declarant was under the stress or excitement caused by the event.

Exclusionary rule A judicially-created remedy for violations of the Fourth Amendment.

Excuse defenses When a defendant admits what he did was wrong but argues that under the circumstances he is not responsible.

Execution Indication that a document was written or adopted by the signer.

Execution of public duties An agent of the state, such as a police officer or soldier, is permitted to use reasonable force in the lawful execution of his or her duties.

Exigencies Circumstances that make it impossible for an officer to obtain a warrant before entering a premises or arresting a suspect.

Exigent circumstances Emergencies in which the police are not required to obtain a warrant, such as hot pursuit, danger to officers, danger to third parties, possible escape, or possible destruction of evidence.

Ex post facto laws Legislation making prior conduct criminal.

F

Fair examination rule A rule ensuring that witnesses at either a trial or grand jury hearing can be compelled to answer questions once they have waived their Fifth Amendment privilege and begin to testify.

Federal court of appeals (circuit courts) Courts with jurisdiction over appeals from several federal administrative agencies, patent claims, and decisions of the Claims Court and the Court of International Trade.

Freedom of Information Act Act granting the public access to most, but not all, government documents.

Frisk Refers to a police pat down of the outer layer of a suspect's clothing to look for weapons.

Frye test A test to determine if expert testimony is based on scientific knowledge that is generally accepted and reliable in the relevant field.

Fundamental rights The freedoms essential to the concept of ordered liberty; rights without which neither liberty nor justice would exist.

G

General jurisdiction The authority of a court to hear a variety of cases; the court is not limited to one type of case.

Geographic jurisdiction The authority of courts to hear cases that arise within specified boundaries, such as a city, county, state, or country.

Good faith exception An exception to the exclusionary rule. If an officer is supplied with information by another person that turns out to be incorrect, the officer is not guilty of an illegal search and evidence obtained may be used at trial. An example might be an incorrect address on a search warrant.

H

Habeas corpus A method of appeal whereby an inmate will protest his incarceration and the right of the state or government to imprison him.

Hearsay An out of court statement, made by a speaker other than the in-court witness, offered in evidence to prove the truth of the matter asserted.

Hierarchical jurisdiction The division of responsibilities and functions among the various courts.

Holder of the privilege The person who has the right to keep certain information from being revealed.

Hostile witness A witness who is either *hostile in fact* (he or she is resistant or uncooperative) or *hostile in law* (he or she identifies with an adverse party).

Hot pursuit An emergency that permits dispensing with the 4th Ammendment warrant regulations.

House Any structure a person can occupy on a temporary or long term basis, including hotel rooms, garages, sheds, and so on.

I

Immunity A guarantee that any information obtained from the defendant will not be used against him or her at trial.

Impeachment The formal term for attacking a witness's credibility.

In camera A private hearing, often held in the judge's chambers.

Incorporation The process by which most provisions of the Bill or Rights have been extended to the states by way of the Fourteenth Amendment.

Indisputable fact A fact that speaks for itself and requires virtually no interpretation or debate as to its truthfulness.

Individual rights The rights possessed by an individual that protect him or her from others or the government.

Inevitable discovery exception Permits the use at trial of evidence illegally obtained by the police if they can demonstrate that they would have discovered the evidence anyway by legal means.

Inference A logical deduction or conclusion from an established fact.

Insanity A legal term that describes mental illness. To be found insane, defendants must prove that they have a mental illness and that they were unaware of either the consequences of their actions or that they did not know right from wrong.

Inscribed chattels Marks of affiliation that include logos, badges, crests, and so on.

Intentional nonliteral statement A statement made intentionally but with a literal meaning that is opposite of the content of the statement.

Intoxication Voluntary intoxication is not a valid excuse defense. Involuntary intoxication may be used as a defense if the defendant can prove that he or she was unaware of being drugged.

Inventory A list of items taken by police during a search.

J

Judge A referee responsible for enforcing court rules, instructing the jury on the law, ruling on the admissibility of evidence, and determining the law.

Judicial notice A procedure that courts use to determine the facts of a case without having to follow the normal rules of evidence.

Judicial notice of adjudicative facts Matters of general knowledge not otherwise connected to statutes, constitutions, administrative rules, or other sources of law.

Judicial notice of law A court's acceptance of what is written in statutes, constitutional provisions, and court cases.

Judicial notice of legislative facts Facts that courts rely on when interpreting statutes, constitutional provisions, and the like.

Judicial review The power of a court to review laws made by the legislature, or rulings of lower courts, and determine whether the laws or court decision are constitutional.

Judiciary Act of 1789 The act that established Supreme Court membership at six justices and that created 3 federal circuit courts and 13 district courts, one in each state.

Jurisdiction The legal authority of a court to hear a case.

Justification Appropriate reason to believe a criminal act will take place or has taken place.

Justification defense When the defendant admits to the offense but stated that what he did was not criminal. Examples might be self-defense, defense of others or property, consent, or the execution of public duties.

K

Knock and announce The requirement that police officers knock on a suspect's door and announce their presence before breaking in.

L

Lay opinion Evidence given by a witness who has not been presented as and is not qualified to be an expert.

Leading question A question that suggests to the witness the answer that the examining party desires.

Legally operative conduct Words that affect the legal relationship of the parties, especially words in a contract.

Legislation Rules enacted by the legislature.

Limited jurisdiction Authority of a court to hear only a particular type of case, such as traffic court, juvenile court, or probate court.

Lineups A method of witness identification in which a suspect is made to stand beside several people of generally the same size, coloring, race, and body type while the witness tries to identify the perpetrator.

M

Magistrates Lower-level judges who conduct preliminary proceedings in cases before the district court and who issue warrants.

Marital communications privilege Protects confidential marital communications from disclosure.

Marital testimony privilege The regret of one spouse to refuse to testify against the other.

Material evidence Evidence that significantly affects the matter at issue in a case.

Mens rea Criminal intent.

Merit system or Missouri plan A method of selecting judges.

Minimalist theory Entitles the defendant to be present and cross-examine witnesses who testify but does not stop the prosecutor from offering testimonial accounts of what others said or from freely using prior statements by those who do testify.

Miranda warnings Warnings police must give when taking a suspect into custody that inform the suspect of his or her constitutional rights.

Mistake of fact Excuses criminal liability when it negates a material element of the crime. The mistake must be both reasonable and honest.

Mistake of law Ignorance of the law is an excuse if the defendant undertakes reasonable efforts to learn the law, but is still unaware that he has violated some obscure, unusual law.

Modus operandi Method of operation; the specific way that the crime was committed.

Motive The reason that a crime was committed.

N

News reporter source privilege The right of news reporters to refuse to reveal their sources of information.

Nonsearch Occurs when the police look for evidence but their actions cannot be considered a search within the meaning of the Fourth Amendment.

Nonstop Occurs when a person is confronted by police but is still free to leave.

O

Open field Any unoccupied or undeveloped real property outside the curtilage of a home.

Opinion evidence Evidence of what the witness thinks, believes, or infers in regard to facts in dispute, as distinguished from his or her personal knowledge of the facts themselves.

Original The writing itself or recording itself or any counterpart intended to have the same effect by a person executing or issuing it.

Original jurisdiction The power of the court to hear a case initially and the place where the trial takes place.

P

Papers Diaries, business records, and similar documents.

Particularity requirement Fourth Amendment requirement that a warrant must particularly describe the place to be searched and the persons or things to be seized.

Past recollection recorded A written document that becomes a substitute for the witnesses testimony.

Perjury Lying while under oath.

Person Describes individual people, whether citizens or not.

Personal jurisdiction The authority of a court over a person.

Photographic arrays A method of witness identification in which several photographs, including one of the suspect, are shown to a witness so he or she can identify the perpetrator.

Plain view Doctrine that an officer is legally in an area where contraband is immediately apparent and is discovered inadvertently, the contraband may be seized without a warrant.

Precedent Decisions of another court or judge that the judge trying a case will rely on as justification in forming his or her decision.

Present memory revived Allowing a witness to refresh his or her memory by reviewing certain documents.

Present sense impression Statement made regarding action observed. Must be contemporaneous to the action.

Presumption A procedural device that not only permits an inference of the presumed fact but also shifts to the opposing party the burden of producing evidence to disprove the presumed fact.

Presumption against suicide The presumption that a dead person did not die by his or her own hand.

Presumptions of fact Presumptions of fact deal with facts, issues, and circumstances as they arise.

Presumption of innocence The legal requirement that all defendants are presumed innocent until proven guilty.

Presumption of law A presumption in which the law requires that an inference or deduction be drawn.

Presumption of sanity The presumption that every person tried in a criminal case is of sound mind—until evidence to the contrary is presented.

Prima facie Latin for on its face, referring to a lawsuit or criminal prosecution in which the prosecution's evidence is sufficient to prove the case unless there is substantial contradictory evidence presented at trial.

Privilege A right held by a person who was a party to a confidential relationship, the sanctity of which the law values above even the search for truth.

Privileged communication Certain communications that are protected from being revealed in court.

Probable cause Occurs when the facts and circumstances within the officers' knowledge and of which they have reasonably trustworthy information are sufficient to warrant a prudent man in believing that the suspect had committed or was committing an offense; indicates a greater probablity than not that a crime has occurred.

Procedural rights theory Holds that the state should gather and present as much live testimony as possible.

Production theory Holds that the confrontation clause requires the prosecutor to produce the "speaker" at trial whenever possible.

Profiles Compilations of common characteristics shared by certain types of offenders.

Proof beyond a reasonable doubt This standard is used in criminal trials and means that the facts asserted are highly probable. A difficult burden to meet.

Proof by a preponderance of the evidence This standard is used in civil trials and means that the facts asserted are more probably true than false. An easy burden to meet.

Proof by clear and convincing evidence This standard is used in some civil and criminal trials and means that the facts asserted are quite likely true. This burden lies somewhere between "preponderance of the evidence" and reasonable doubt.

Prosecutors Attorneys responsible for prosecuting cases on behalf of the state.

Public defenders Attorneys hired by the state to work for defendants who cannot afford to hire their own lawyer.

Q

Qualified immunity A defense for conduct that, while unconstitutional, prevents the police from being held liable.

R

Rational basis A method of determining whether a state may abridge someone's fundamental rights; a lesser standard of proof is required than with strict scrutiny, and the courts generally find in favor of the state.

Real evidence Any tangible item that can be perceived with the five senses holds that hearsay is permissable as long as it is reliable.

Real/physical evidence Consists of actual tangible items that can be displayed. Things that are discernable by the senses without the use of witnesses.

Reasonable expectation of privacy What a citizen may reasonably expect to be able to keep private.The person's activity needs to be one that society can construe as reasonable.

Reasonable suspicion In general, below probable cause but above a hunch.

Reasonableness clause Fourth Amendment clause that proscribes against unreasonable searches and seizures.

Rebuttable presumption Presumption for which the party against whom it operates may introduce evidence to disprove the presumption.

Rehabilitation The act of introducing evidence or calling additional witnesses to reinstate the credibility of a witness who has been impeached.

Relevancy Logical relationship between evidence and a fact in issue or to be established.

Relevant evidence Evidence that pertains to the matter at hand, that has some bearing on the trial.

Reliability Theory Holds that hearsay is permissible as long as it is reliable.

Reputation What people think about someone.

Retained counsel Attorney selected and paid by the defendant.

Rule of four The idea that in order for the Supreme Court to accept a case, four or more justices must vote to accept it.

S

Search An action by government actors where the expectation of privacy is violated. A uniformed police officer acting in his or her official capacity is an example of a government actor.

Search incident to arrest Search of an arrestee and his or her grabbing area (grabbing area is the area in which a person could grab or lunge for a weapon) following arrest.

Secondary evidence Any evidence of the contents of a writing other than the original.

Seizure (1) The taking of evidence or property; (2) the taking of a person as in an arrest, or investigative stops in which a reasonable person would believe that he or she is not free to leave.

Selective incorporation The process of how some, but not all, of the Bill of Rights were made applicable to the states through the due process clause of the Fourteenth Amendment.

Self-defense This defense may be raised when the defendant has used force to repel and imminent, unprovoked attack that would have caused them serious injury. Self-defense may also apply to the defense of others or of property.

Self-incrimination clause Part of the Fifth Amendment that says "no person shall be compelled in any criminal case to be a witness against himself."

Showup A method of identification in which the suspect is brought before the witness, alone, so the witness can be asked whether the person was the perpetrator.

Silver platter doctrine This happened after the exclusionary rule was created but not yet applied to the states. State officers would sometimes illegally obtain evidence and give it to the federal officers. The federal officers would then be able to use this evidence in court because they had not personally violated any evidence rules.

Spousal privilege Privilege granted to a spouse to not give adverse testimony against a marital partner.

Standing Being the victim of a Fourth Amendment violation. To have standing a person must be directly involved, not a friend, relative, or spouse of the "victim."

Stare decisis Latin for "let the decision stand."

Statement A verbal assertion or a nonverbal act intended to be an assertion.

Stationhouse detentions Detentions used for the purposes of obtaining fingerprints, ordering lineups, administering polygraph examinations, or securing other types of evidence.

Statute A law enacted by the legislature.

Stipulations Agreements between opposing attorneys about some important fact.

Strict Scrutiny A method of determining whether a state may abridge someone's fundamental rights; generally found in favor of the individual.

Subject matter jurisdiction Authority conferred on a court to hear a particular type of case.

Subpoena A court document requiring the presence of a particular witness.

Subpoena duces tecum An official court document requiring that a witness bring certain documents or material to court.

Substantive objections Objections based on particular rules of evidence.

Supreme court The court of "last resort" for all cases arising in the federal system, as well as all cases in state courts that involve a federal constitutional issue.

Suspect classifications Classifications based on race or gender.

Syndrome A pattern of behavior or mental attitude exhibited by a particular person.

T

Tacit judicial notice Form of judicial notice in which the judge does not provide any statement to the court that judicial notice is being taken regarding a certain fact.

Terry stop Situation in which reasonable suspicion of criminal activity gives police officers the authority to stop and frisk people.

Testimonial evidence What a witness says.

Testimonial privilege Privilege invoked when a witness is either shielded or barred from testifying.

Testimony Oral or verbal description of a witness's present recollection of some past event or set of facts.

Total incorporation Applying the entire Bill of Rights to the states.

Total incorporation plus Applying the entire Bill of Rights as well as other nonspecified rights, such as the right to privacy, to the state.

Transactional immunity Extending immunity to matters discussed far beyond the scope of the questions asked.

Trial de novo An appeal for a new trial in the court of original jurisdiction, requested by the losing party of a case.

U

Ultimate issue rule A rule that prohibited experts from expressing opinions on final issues of which the judge or jury was charged with deciding.

Uniform Judicial Notice of Foreign Law Act An act requiring that every court in a specific state give notice of the common law or statutes of every other jurisdiction in the United States.

United states district courts Courts that have original jurisdiction over both civil and criminal cases involving federal statutes.

Use and derivative use immunity Use and derivative use immunity bars the use of a witness' testimony against him or her in the future.

Use immunity Immunity in which anything the witness says on the stand cannot be used against him or her in a criminal proceeding.

V

Venue The same as geographic jurisdiction.

Voir dire A questioning process used with either jurors or expert witnesses.

W

Warrant clause A Fourth Amendment clause that requires no warrants shall be issued but on probable cause, supported by oath or affirmation, and particularly describing the place to be searched and the persons or things to be seized.

Witness A person who has knowledge about the facts of a case.

Witness exclusion Keeping witnesses from hearing the testimony of other witnesses prior to their turn on the witness stand.

Witness privilege A witness's ability to invoke his or her right against self-incrimination.

Witness sequestration A process that keeps witnesses separated while they are outside the courtroom.

Writing Every means of recording on any tangible thing in any form of communication or representation.

Writ of Certiorari An order issued by the Supreme Court to a lower court to send the record of a case up to the Supreme Court. ✦

Index